Evangelical Affirmations

Evangelical Affirmations

Edited by *Larry C. Towne*

KENNETH S. KANTZER & CARL F. H. HENRY

EVANGELICAL AFFIRMATIONS
Copyright © 1990 by Trinity Evangelical Divinity School

Academie Books is an imprint of Zondervan Publishing House, 1415 Lake Drive, S.E., Grand Rapids, Michigan 49506.

ISBN 0-310-59531-2

Printed in the United States of America

90 91 92 93 94 / AM / 10 9 8 7 6 5 4 3 2 1

CONTENTS

ACKNOWLEDGMENTS 11

PREFACE 13

FOREWORD 17
Carl F. H. Henry
Visiting Professor of Biblical & Systematic Theology,
Trinity Evangelical Divinity School; Former Editor,
Christianity Today

CHAPTER ONE — AFFIRMATIONS
The Evangelical Affirmations 27

CHAPTER TWO — ADDRESS
Keynote Address...41
Charles Colson
Chairman of the Board, Prison Fellowship Ministries

CHAPTER THREE — THE EVANGELICALS

Who are the Evangelicals? 69
Carl F. H. Henry
    Visiting Professor of Biblical & Systematic
    Theology, Trinity Evangelical Divinity School;
    Former Editor, *Christianity Today*

Response to Carl F. H. Henry 95
Nathan O. Hatch
    Acting Dean, College of Arts and Letters,
    University of Notre Dame, Notre Dame, Indiana

Questions for Discussion 103

CHAPTER FOUR — SALVATION

**Evangelicals and the Way of Salvation: New
Challenges to the Gospel — Universalism, and
Justification by Faith** 107
James I. Packer
    Professor of Systematic Theology, Regent College,
    Vancouver, British Columbia, Canada

Response to James I. Packer 137
John Ankerberg
    Host & Moderator "The John Ankerberg Show,"
    Chattanooga, Tennessee
John Weldon
    Senior Researcher of "The John Ankerberg Show."

Questions for Discussion 149

CHAPTER FIVE — BIBLICAL AUTHORITY

**Word and World: Biblical Authority and
the Quandary of Modernity** 153
David F. Wells
Professor of Systematic Theology, Gordon Conwell
Theological Seminary, South Hamilton,
Massachusetts

Response to David F. Wells 177
Robert Sloan
Assistant Professor, Department of Religion, Baylor
University, Waco, Texas

Questions for Discussion 191

CHAPTER SIX — PERSONAL ETHICS

Christian Personal Ethics 195
Kenneth S. Kantzer
Director of the Ph.D. Program, Trinity Evangelical
Divinity School; Chancellor, Trinity College;
Former Editor, *Christianity Today*

Response to Kenneth S. Kantzer 241
Ralph D. Winter
General Director, U.S. Center for World Mission,
Pasadena, California

Questions for Discussion 253

CHAPTER SEVEN — SOCIAL ETHICS

Evangelicals and Social Ethics 257
Harold O. J. Brown
   Professor of Biblical and Systematic Theology,
   Franklin Forman Chair of Christian Ethics and
   Theology, Trinity Evangelical Divinity School

Response to Harold O. J. Brown 285
Myron S. Augsburger
   President, Christian College Coalition, Washington, D.C

Questions for Discussion 295

CHAPTER EIGHT — BLACK EVANGELICAL THEOLOGY

Reflections on the Scope and Function of a Black Evangelical Black Theology 299
William H. Bentley
   Chairman, Commission on Theology, National Black
   Evangelical Association; National President, United
   Pentecostal Council of the Assemblies of God
Ruth Lewis Bentley
   Learning Skills Specialist, Counselling Center,
   University of Illinois at Chicago

Response to William H. Bentley 335
Reverend H. O. Espinoza
   President, PROMESA, San Antonio, Texas

Questions for Discussion 343

CHAPTER NINE — THE CHURCH

Evangelicals, Ecumenism and the Church 347
  Donald A. Carson
    Professor of New Testament, Trinity Evangelical
    Divinity School

Response to Donald A. Carson 387
  Joseph M. Stowell
    President, Moody Bible Institute, Chicago, Illinois

Questions for Discussion 397

CHAPTER TEN — MODERN SCIENCE

Evangelicals and Modern Science 401
  Robert C. Newman
    Professor of New Testament, Biblical Theological
    Seminary, Hatfield, PA

First Response to Robert C. Newman 423
  Pattle P. T. Pun
    Professor of Biology, Wheaton College, Wheaton,
    Illinois

Second Response to Robert C. Newman 439
  Wayne Frair
    Professor of Biology, The Kings College, Briarcliff
    Manor, New York

Questions for Discussion 453

CHAPTER ELEVEN — RELIGIOUS LIBERTY

Tribes People, Idiots or Citizens?
Evangelicals, Religious Liberty and
a Public Philosophy for the Public Square 457
Os Guinness
Executive Director of Williamsburg Charter
Foundation, Washington, D.C.

Response to Os Guinness 499
David P. Scaer
Professor of Theology, Concordia Seminary, Fort
Wayne, Indiana

Questions for Discussion 509

CHAPTER TWELVE — AFTERWORD

Afterword: Where Do We Go From Here? 513
Kenneth S. Kantzer
Director of the Ph.D. Program, Trinity Evangelical
Divinity School; Chancellor, Trinity College;
Former Editor, *Christianity Today*

APPENDIX

Conference Personnel 527

ACKNOWLEDGMENTS

In addition to the presenters of the major papers and their respondents, many other individuals contributed significantly to the production of this volume. Dr. Kenneth Meyer, President of Trinity Evangelical Divinity School, gave it his continuous, enthusiastic support and guidance. Dean Walter Kaiser lent his wisdom at point after point and contributed directly to the process by which study papers became a book. Dr. John White of Geneva College, likewise, gave the work his full support and guidance throughout the consultation. Especially valuable was his responsible chairmanship of the plenary sessions in which the participants responded to the work of the writing committee. Dr. Billy Melvin, General Director of the National Association of Evangelicals, early on gave enthusiastic support to the entire project.

Not least worthy of special mention is the behind-the-scenes work of many who kept the wheels moving in the internal production of the manuscript. Lois Armstrong, secretary to the Dean, monitored the flow of manuscripts from beginning to end. Mary Morris, secretary to the Director of the Ph.D. Program at Trinity, typed the seemingly endless revisions of the Evangelical Affirmations through the various stages of its production. Staff members from the Trinity faculty secretarial pool assisted her. Wayne Kijanowski, Debbi Hjelle, and Paul Haroutunian shared in the labor of page layout. Eric Bolger and David Johnson assisted in the formation of "Questions for Discussion." And finally, Dr. Gleason Archer, Anne McIlhaney and Sheila West proofed the various editions of the manuscript. Evangelical Affirmations was a team project, and we are grateful to each one who had a part in its production.

11

PREFACE

In May, 1989, The National Association of Evangelicals and Trinity Evangelical Divinity School co-sponsored a consultation on Evangelical Affirmations. To this consultation they invited representative leaders from among evangelical scholars, pastors and outstanding lay leaders. The four-day gathering saw over six hundred fifty registered participants representing a broad range of denominations and theological viewpoints within the stream of evangelical Christianity.

The purpose of this working consultation of theologically concerned leaders was to unite evangelicals in their commitment to the great biblical truths of our faith by calling the church to vigorous evangelism and discipleship, responsible social action, and sacrificial service to a needy world.

The event focused on the crucial issues facing evangelicals today. Participants met in a series of ten plenary sessions in each of which one or more distinguished scholars presented a paper followed immediately by a respondent. Participants then met in a sequence of round-table discussions with a chairman and a recorder who reported the action of the discussion group and any suggestions the group directed to the writing committee. Early in the conference the writing committee presented a rough draft of affirmations to the participants. As a result of directions growing out of the round-table discussions, the rough draft was completely rewritten several times. A final draft was presented to the participants in a plenary session at the end of the consultation. After numerous changes approved by the participants, the body voted overwhelmingly to approve the document subject to final wording by the writing committee. Over two thousand additional pages of suggestions were received by the writing committee. These were all carefully read; and, insofar as there was agreement among them, the writing committee revised and edited the final draft to represent the views of the conference participants.

Although the writing committee must take final responsibility for these *Evangelical Affirmations*, their content and form represent, in an unusual way, the real convictions and work of the delegates.

Of course, this is not a perfect document. It was done too hastily, and we are imperfect people. Let us pray that it will prove to be a useful document that our Lord can use in a humble way. The final document, together with all the main presentations and the responses to them, as well as the names of the round-table leaders, the theologians who sat with them, supporting pastors, administrators and lay leaders are listed in the appendix of this publication.

These affirmations do not represent requirements for membership in the church or for ordination to the Christian ministry. They are not intended to be a confession of faith for any body of Christians — least of all for the participants working together at this consultation. They would never have agreed that this document is appropriate for either purpose. It certainly was never intended to set forth a short creed for the church or to be a short confession of faith. Many of the participants do not think short creeds are desirable or useful and would still less have agreed as to what the content of a creed should be.

We intend this, rather, to be a confession of what it means to be an evangelical. In a day when this term is used loosely to cover a broad variety of belief and unbelief, we trust that a clear statement of those common convictions that constitute our evangelical heritage will prove useful to the church. Now let us pray that God will take our humble effort and use these evangelical affirmations to clarify what we stand for and lead us to a better understanding of the truth of Scripture and bring great glory to our God though the furtherance of the Gospel.

Unlike the document *Evangelical Affirmations,* the individual presentations including both the main papers and those of the respondents, in each case represent the position of each individual thinker and are not necessarily to be considered as the view of the participants. Since each author wrote as an evangelical, however, their papers present an evangelical viewpoint and, on all essential points, reflect generally the viewpoint of the consultation set forth in the *Evangelical Affirmations* approved by the participants.

FOREWORD

Carl F. H. Henry

The term "evangelical" has taken on conflicting nuances in the twentieth century. Wittingly or unwittingly, evangelical constituencies no less than their critics have contributed to this confusion and misunderstanding. Nothing could be more timely therefore than to define what is primary and what is secondary in personifying an evangelical Christian.

At the beginning of our century the term "evangelical Christianity" represented supernatural miraculous theism as taught by the Old and New Testaments. It affirmed the triune God known in his self-revelation both in nature and history, and in human reason and conscience, and known as well in the authoritative, inspired and fully trustworthy Scriptures. To be an evangelical was to enunciate among life's control-beliefs the singularly unique incarnation of God in Jesus Christ; his virgin birth, sinless life, substitutionary death and bodily resurrection; his Saviorhood of penitent sinners, and his end-time return to vindicate good and subjugate evil. Evangelical orthodoxy, in a word, exulted in the once-for-all Hebrew-Christian revelation of the Living God supremely manifest in the crucified and risen and returning Redeemer.

Protestant Modernism challenged the very heart of evangelical orthodoxy, namely its insistence on miraculous revelation and redemption. Modernism championed instead scientific empirical method as the supreme way of identifying truth. Since scientific observation and verification in principle exclude once-

17

Carl F .H. Henry

for-all events, Modernism declared evangelical Christianity to be prescientific, unscientific, and therefore outmoded. Given this context, those who considered themselves paragons of modern thought wanted to distance themselves as much as possible from evangelicalism. Modernism presumed to do the Christian religion a great service by reprobating evangelicalism. It took over evangelically-founded and evangelically-funded schools and agencies, and replaced biblically-orthodox professors with its own proponents.

The fact is, however, that Modernism itself rested on an unstable philosophical compromise and soon found itself challenged by religious humanism on the left and by neo-orthodoxy as well as evangelical orthodoxy on the right. Especially in America, evangelical orthodoxy experienced a remarkable resurgence that began in the early 1940s. Noteworthy contributory developments to this change were the formation of the National Association of Evangelicals in 1942, the reemergence of mass evangelism under the leadership of Billy Graham, who promoted spiritual renewal in mainline Protestant denominations, the formation in 1947 of Fuller Theological Seminary in California as a center of evangelical orthodoxy, and the founding in 1956 of *Christianity Today* magazine as an interdenominational voice of evangelical scholarship. From many lands and different denominations, *Christianity Today* enlisted competent conservative scholars as theological and literary contributors. In 1966, it sponsored the World Congress on Evangelicalism in Berlin. Through Key '73, it gave domestic stimulus for nationwide evangelistic outreach.

In 1976, the cover story of *Newsweek* titled "The Year of the Evangelical" attested the cresting influence of the evangelical movement. *Newsweek* reported that 50 million Americans professed to be "born again." Theologically conservative churches, it noted, enjoyed noteworthy spiritual growth and channeled unprecedented numbers of students into America's evangelical colleges and divinity schools.

The term "evangelical," which nearly a half century earlier an intellectual elite viewed with disdain, now became so popular at grassroots that quite diverse groups—Catholic, Anglican, Protestant, Pentecostal, charismatic, and so on—found it useful and desirable.

A remarkable aspect of the evangelical resurgence was the emergence of national and even international religious radio and television programs. A major stimulus in establishing the National Association of Evangelicals had been the fact that during the 1930s modernist dominated ecumenical churches preempted free public service time for religious broadcasting. Ecumenical leaders not only excluded evangelical churches from public media benefits but also opposed the sale of network time to evangelicals. The commercial value of Sunday network radio time soared because of evangelical eagerness to purchase it. Approval by the Federal Communications Commission of the network sale of such time to religious groups, in time, opened a vast new window of evangelical access to the masses. Evangelists in turn brought the newest technology to their network programming of religion.

National Religious Broadcasters' annual convention of conservative radio and televangelist celebrities as a media event

Carl F.H. Henry

surpassed gatherings of the parent National Association of Evangelicals. Because of the commitment of televangelists to traditional values and to conservative political agendas, N.R.B. conventions attracted leading public figures, including even presidents.

By an ironic turn of events, the very electronic visibility that had given prominence and public support to religious personalities suddenly become as much of a liability for the evangelical movement as it had been an asset. Financial and/or sexual transgressions by a small number of religious televangelists thrust a gloom of suspicion over the entire evangelical enterprise. The secular city, and not least of all the secular media, now perceived evangelical Christianity in terms of Elmer Gantry manipulation and exploitation. Financial contributions declined for some enterprises aggressively engaged in evangelism, world relief, and other evangelical activities. But for long entrenched works whose ministries were beyond criticism, the main body of support remained in place. Now, however, all organizations that appealed for public funds faced the need to make annual audits available to their constituencies, an already established policy of most reputable ministries.

Nevertheless, in less than a single decade, the public perception of evangelical Christianity had suffered a costly change. Its respectable reputation as a constructive national spiritual movement fell into open caricature and ridicule encouraged by the misdeeds of a small but prominent group of mostly Pentecostal and charismatic televangelists who, worse yet, emphasized that workings of the Holy Spirit can render one virtually immune to temptation. Interestingly enough, almost from its beginnings the

National Association of Evangelicals had pursued membership
by Pentecostal churches more energetically than by evangelical
churches in ecumenically-affiliated denominations. Inroads of a
deteriorating social morality left their mark on many strands of
evangelical engagement as the quest for secular self fulfillment,
materialistic greed and sexual hedonism permeated the culture.
Even while some entrepreneurial evangelicals heralded the inevi-
tability of an evangelical awakening, other leaders raised questions about the normative nature and identity of evangelicals.

To be sure, the evangelical movement retained considerable
momentum. Even if they increasingly outpaced the "mainline
churches"—which are now frequently called "old line"—American evangelical churches as a whole nevertheless exhibited less
initiative and less of the joy of God's good news than did Christians in the third-world countries like Korea, Nigeria and Kenya.

The energies of American evangelicals were being siphoned
into somewhat competing activities. About the same time that
Newsweek heralded "The Year of the Evangelical," they plum-
meted, for example, into internal disagreement over the reliability
of the Bible. This debate concerning scriptural truthfulness soon
deteriorated into a sad conflict over true and so-called false
evangelicals.

Evangelical campuses were rocked by charges that only a
handful of institutions any longer aggressively defended scriptural inerrancy. Reconciled to pluralistic theology, ecumenical
seminaries, by contrast, seemed little dismayed that their epistemological foundations lay in shambles. Church historians and sociologists sought to identify normative evangelical positions by
observing historical phenomena, rather than by appealing to

Carl F.H. Henry

Scriptural teaching, as if the theological "ought" could be established by analysis of the empirical "is."

At about the same time, the evangelical enterprise was parrying also the relationships of evangelicalism and social action, an issue raised to prominence but not resolved by the Lausanne Conference on Evangelism. Church historians left little doubt that the many humanitarian movements of the West originated through the evangelical theology of the Cross, that is, in a divinely engendered compassionate response to the needy and afflicted. The question remained, however, whether social action is evangelism, and whether concern for the whole man and for social justice is integral to evangelism.

There were other evangelical concerns. The mainline evangelical movement, no less than the ecumenical movement, had assumed for several decades that American fundamentalism was terminally ill. Numerous large churches, Sunday schools and numerous day-schools notwithstanding, fundamentalists were committed to double separation—separation from world culture and separation from crusade evangelism, the latter in reaction to Billy Graham's cooperation with ecumenically-affiliated churches. But Jerry Falwell's leadership of the Moral Majority managed, nonetheless, to pull much of fundamentalism out of its social isolation. This was achieved by widespread political protest against federal intrusion into the area of religious values such as prohibiting of public prayer in public schools, for example, and government funding and legalization of abortion.

Moral Majority shaped no evangelical overall public philosophy but concentrated rather on a constellation of single issues. For a time, the movement was perceived as seeking to legislate

Christian values on a pluralistic society. But its enlistment of conservative Catholics, Jews, Mormons and others soon established a heightened political morality and not theology to be its objective while it placed ethical concerns firmly on the national agenda. Moral Majority achieved none of the legislative specifics it endorsed. It therefore raised new questions over whether politically active fundamentalists were now expecting too much from politics in an era when secular humanism has ensnared Western society and is itself deteriorating into raw paganism. Yet the absence of an evangelical public philosophy is evident and paves the way, as some see it, for Protestant-Catholic political cobelligerency.

These prefatory comments are intended to be but a gateway to the major papers presented at the 1989 Evangelical Affirmations conference. Those of us who first spoke of the need for such dialogue and declaration amid the present confusion and misperceptions of evangelicalism hardly expected to be involved as platform participants. We sincerely hope that the papers and the responses will help fellow Christians, and will help others as well, to identify what is essential and inessential to an evangelical spiritual testimony in our era of woeful cognitive and ethical confusion.

1

AFFIRMATIONS

THE EVANGELICAL AFFIRMATIONS

Evangelical Christianity is engaged in a broad conflict on many fronts. Internally, it is struggling over moral improprieties, doctrinal lapses, and problems of self-identity. Externally, it is carrying on a lingering battle with liberal Christianity and seeking to plug leaks in its doctrinal structure that still come from that source. Moreover, new pressures are rising from the occult and from various syncretistic movements combining elements of paganism, Islam, Buddhism or other historic religions with Christianity. In Western Europe and North America (and increasingly in other parts of the world as well), modern secularism has become a major foe of evangelical Christianity.

Each of these religious movements presents its own conception of reality, and all differ from evangelical faith in doctrines that lie at the very core of biblical Christianity.

Modern secularism sees the world without God; or if it formally acknowledges the existence of some ill-defined "god," it squeezes God and all religion to the periphery of life. Either way, a theoretical atheism or a practical, functioning atheism views the universe as controlled merely by natural or human forces. Logically, the exclusion of God from the universe rules out the very possibility of miracle in any biblical sense and yields a world view without incarnation, resurrection and judgment. Unfortunately it is possible to give lip allegiance to theistic or even Christian beliefs while choosing to live practically as though God does not exist.

27

By contrast, historic Christianity has always affirmed that God lives and acts in this world. Evangelical faith insists on the reality of divine action in creation, providence, revelation and redemption. History is not a mindless process, but the unfolding events through which the triune God works out his purposes in the universe. The God and Father of our Lord Jesus Christ, and the God of the Bible is the sovereign Lord who controls the destiny of the nations and guides the intimate details of personal life. The hairs of our head are numbered, and God sees every sparrow that falls.

Both the existence and the nature of God, therefore, are fundamental questions. For atheism, whether it be theoretical or practical, the issue is settled negatively in advance: the supernatural intervening God who worked miracles, revealed himself in Jesus Christ and the Bible, and is now active in and important to our daily lives, is impossible.

World religions and modern occultic concepts of reality introduce a strange and exotic dimension to this spiritual warfare. New manifestations of spiritism, Satanism, demonology, the New Age movement, various syncretistic cults, and other developments have set a much larger and more complicated agenda for evangelical witness.

Conflicts have sometimes escalated into cataclysmic confrontations between belief and unbelief and between good and evil. Such confrontations have increased in intensity due to a resurgent evangelicalism, now variously estimated to number between 30 million adherents (Christianity Today poll) and 66 million adherents (Gallup's poll) in the United States and 500 million worldwide (according to David B. Barrett).

Neither evangelicalism nor its conflicts, both internal and external conflicts, are new in the history of Christianity. Evangelical faith has deep roots in the history of mainstream churches. It did not suddenly rise from eighteenth- and nineteenth-century revivals. It can be traced back through the Reformation and the ancient church to find its base in New Testament Christianity.

Recently, however, some have declared that several evangelical doctrines are theologically innovative and do not represent the central traditions of the Christian church. Other observers have asked if the evangelical movement has become so fragmented theologically that it no longer has a coherent self-identity. In another vein, the moral failure of a number of prominent evangelicals has been all too apparent. We are shamed by our inconsistencies in living out the ethical values we profess, and we recognize the need to confess our sins before God.

In the last decade of the twentieth century, a number of these troubling issues have come into sharper focus. We realize that our own house is not entirely in order. Many of our worst problems we have brought on ourselves. Not only on the outside, but even within our own ranks, some confusion exists as to exactly who are evangelicals.

Evangelical Affirmations seeks to clarify the character of the evangelical movement and to affirm certain truths critical to the advancement of the church of Christ. As we do so, we sadly confess that our own sinful failures have often discredited our proclamation of those great biblical truths. For our sinful lapses into sexual misconduct, neglect of the poor, lack of accountability on the part of our leaders, and self-seeking divisiveness, we repent before God and our neighbors.

The following affirmations do not constitute a complete doctrinal statement or a comprehensive confession of faith. Rather, they represent evangelical truths that specially need to be asserted and clarified in our day. We address these affirmations primarily to our fellow evangelicals who, though confessing their personal commitment to these doctrines, have sometimes raised questions as to their importance and as to how essential they are to an authentic evangelical faith. Only secondarily have we addressed these affirmations to non-evangelicals. In this latter case we are concerned to clarify differences between evangelicals and non-evangelicals within the Christian churches. We also wish to remove some of the caricatures of evangelicalism the general public often holds and to state what evangelicals really believe on issues growing out of the interaction of evangelicals with modern culture.

1. Jesus Christ and the Gospel

We affirm the good news that the Son of God became man to offer himself for sinners and to give them everlasting life.

We affirm that Jesus Christ is fully God and fully man with two distinct natures united in one person. The incarnation, substitutionary death and bodily resurrection of Jesus Christ are essential to the gospel. Through these events a gracious God has acted in time and history to reach out to humanity and save all who believe in him.

Without Christ and the biblical gospel, sinful humanity is without salvation and is left to create its own "gospels". These "gospels" take various forms and many are set forth by so-called "Christian" sects that omit the heart of the biblical gospel. Any "gospel" without the Christ of the Bible cannot be the saving gospel, and leaves sinners estranged from God and under his wrath.

We affirm that the people of God are commanded to witness to the world concerning God's offer of redemption in Christ. The gospel, working by the Holy Spirit, is powerful to transform the lives of individuals lost in sin; provides believers with meaning for life on this earth; empowers the church to accomplish Christ's work in the world; serves as a leavening influence in society; and sustains the faithful in hope for the life to come.

2. Creation and Fall

We affirm that the triune God created heaven and earth, and made human beings, both male and female, in his own image. In his providence God upholds all things and reveals himself through creation and history.

Because of Adam's fall, all became sinners and stand under God's righteous judgment. Human rebellion against God shows itself today in many ways: such as in atheistic denials of God's existence; in functional atheism that concedes God's existence but denies his relevance to personal conduct; in oppression of the poor and helpless; in occult concepts of reality; in the abuse of earth's resources; and in theories of an accidental naturalistic evolutionary origin of the universe and human life; and in many other ways.

As a result of the fall of the race into sin, human beings must be born again to new life in Christ. They can be pardoned and redeemed by faith in Christ alone.

3. God as Source and Ground of Truth

We affirm that God the Creator is the source of truth and the ground of the unity of all truth. By revelation God makes known the truth concerning himself, the world, human sin and redemption. God's revelation addresses the whole person—intellect, will, and emotion. The Holy Spirit accompanies his Word in convicting, instructing, nurturing, and empowering his people so they learn to live in fellowship with God and other persons in accordance with scriptural directives.

We reject irrationalistic theologies and philosophies that compromise or deny objective truth. We also reject rationalistic alternatives based on autonomous human reason.

We recognize that as finite and sinful creatures we do not have complete knowledge of God, and that "now we know in part." We rejoice, nonetheless, that God reveals himself in creation and the Bible.

We encourage Christian churches and Christian schools to develop and implement disciplined instruction that relates the mind of Christ to all knowledge, that emphasizes the compatibility of scientific inquiry with biblical teachings about nature, and that challenges believers to understand and apply a Christian view of the world to all of life.

4. Holy Scripture

We affirm the complete truthfulness and the full and final authority of the Old and New Testament Scriptures as the Word of God written. The appropriate response to it is humble assent and obedience.

The Word of God becomes effective by the power of the Holy Spirit working in and through it. Through the Scriptures the Holy Spirit creates faith and provides a sufficient doctrinal and moral guide for the church. Just as God's self-giving love to us in the gospel provides the supreme motive for the Christian life, so the teaching of Holy Scripture informs us of what are truly acts of love.

Attempts to limit the truthfulness of inspired Scripture to "faith and practice," viewed as less than the whole of Scripture, or worse, to assert that it errs in such matters as history or the world of nature, depart not only from the Bible's representation of its own veracity, but also from the central tradition of the Christian churches.

The meaning of Scripture must neither be divorced from its words nor dictated by reader response. The inspired author's intention is essential to our understanding of the text.

No Scripture must be interpreted in isolation from other passages of Scripture. All Scripture is true and profitable, but Scripture must be interpreted by Scripture. The truth of any single passage must be understood in light of the truth of all passages of Scripture. Our Lord has been pleased to give us the whole corpus of Scripture to instruct and guide his church.

5. The Church

We affirm that the church is a worshiping and witnessing community of Christians who profess faith in Christ and submit to his authority. Christ is building his church where his Word is preached and his name confessed. He sustains his church by the power of the Holy Spirit.

We affirm that the church is to provide for corporate worship on the part of believers, the instruction of the faithful in the Word of God and its application, and the fellowship, comfort, exhortation, rebuke, and sharing in the needs of the entire body of Christ. In a day of lax doctrine and even more lax discipline, we specially affirm that Scripture requires the defense of sound doctrine, the practice of church discipline, and a call for renewal.

We affirm the mission of the church to be, primarily, that of evangelism of the lost through witness to the gospel by life and by word; and secondarily, to be salt and light to the whole world as we seek to alleviate the burdens and injustices of a suffering world. Though some are specially called to one ministry or another, no believer is exonerated from the duty of bearing witness to the gospel or of providing help to those in need.

We distance ourselves from any movement that seeks to establish a world church on the premise of a religious pluralism that denies normative Christian doctrines. Rather we encourage efforts that help believers and faithful churches move toward fellowship and unity with one another in the name of Christ, the Lord of the church.

6. Doctrine and Practice

We affirm the critical need to conjoin faith and practice. To profess conversion without a genuine change of heart and life violates biblical teaching and substitutes dead orthodoxy for a living faith. Christian leaders , responsibility to serve as spiritual role models and moral examples. Any disjunction between faith and practice generates hypocrisy.

We send forth an urgent call for the practice of holiness and righteousness. Justification by faith must issue in sanctification. By the power of the indwelling Holy Spirit, we are to deny such characteristics of a selfish nature as immorality, evil desire, and covetousness, to walk in righteousness and integrity, and to practice justice and love at all times. Purity of doctrine must be accompanied by purity of life.

7. Human Rights and Righteousness

We affirm that God commands us to seek justice in human affairs whether in the church or in society. In accord with the biblical call for righteousness, God's people should model justice in social relationships and should protest, confront, and strive to alleviate injustice. We must respond to the plight of the destitute, hungry, and homeless; of victims of political oppression and gender or race discrimination, including apartheid; and of all others deprived of rightful protection under the law. We confess our own persistent sin of racism, which ignores the divine image in humankind.

We affirm the integrity of marriage, the permanence of the wife-husband relationship, the importance of the family for the care and nourishment of children, and the primary responsibility of parents for the instruction of their children.

We affirm that evangelicals living in democratic societies should be active in public affairs. We advocate a public philosophy that advances just government and protects the rights of all. In cooperation with like-minded persons, we should support and promote legislation reflecting consistent moral values. We condemn abortion-on-demand as a monstrous evil, deplore drug and alcohol abuse, and lament sexual hedonism, pornography, homosexual practices, and child abuse. We encourage evangelicals to exercise responsible stewardship of their own personal wealth and the conservation of the earth's

8. Religious Liberty

We affirm the duty of state and society to provide religious liberty as a basic human right. We deplore any oppression to maintain or elicit religious commitments. We hold that civil government should not arbitrate spiritual differences, and that neither church nor mosque nor temple nor synagogue should use political power to enforce its own sectarian doctrines or practices. We do not consider laws to protect individual rights, such as the right to life or the freedom of anyone to confess his or her faith openly in society, to be a sectarian position.

9. Second Coming and Judgment

We affirm that Christ will return in power and glory to bring full and eternal salvation to his people and to judge the world. This prospect of the Lord's return to vindicate his holiness and subjugate all evil should accelerate our witness and mission in the world.

We affirm that only through the work of Christ can any person be saved and be resurrected to live with God forever. Unbelievers will be separated eternally from God. Concern for evangelism should not be compromised by any illusion that all will be finally saved (universalism).

We affirm the preaching of ultimate hope in and through Christ. In an age of anxiety and despair, the blessed hope of God's ultimate victory is not only a warning of divine judgment, but a wonderful hope that gives light and meaning to the human heart.

Conclusion: Evangelical Identity

Evangelicals believe, first of all, the gospel as it is set forth in the Bible. The word evangelical is derived from the biblical term *euangelion* meaning "good news." It is the Good News that God became man in Jesus Christ to live and die and rise again from the dead in order to save us from our sin and all its consequences. The Savior's benefits and his salvation are bestowed upon us freely and graciously and are received through personal faith in Christ. They are not conditioned on our merit or personal goodness but are based wholly on the mercy of God.

Evangelicals are also to be identified by what is sometimes called the material or content principle of evangelicalism. They hold to all of the most basic doctrines of the Bible: for example, the triuneness of God the Father, God the Son, and God the Holy Spirit; the pre-existence, incarnation, full deity and humanity of Christ united in one person; his sinless life, his authoritative teaching; his substitutionary atonement; his bodily resurrection from the dead, his second coming to judge the living and the dead; the necessity of holy living; the imperative of witnessing to others about the gospel; the necessity of a life of service to God and human kind; and the hope in a life to come. These doctrines emerge from the Bible and are summarized in the Apostles' Creed and the historic confessions of evangelical churches.

Evangelicals have a third distinguishing mark. In accordance with the teaching of their Lord they believe the Bible to be the final and authoritative source of all doctrine. This is often called the formative or forming principle of evangelicalism. Evangelicals hold the Bible to be God's Word and, therefore, completely true and trustworthy (and this is what we mean by the words *infallible* and *inerrant*). It is the authority by which they seek to guide their thoughts and their lives.

These then are the three distinguishing marks of all evangelicals. Without constant fidelity to all three marks, evangelicals will be unable to meet the demands of the future and interact effectively with the internal and external challenges noted in these affirmations.

Evangelical churches also hold various distinctive doctrines that are important to them; but nonetheless, they share this common evangelical faith.

We offer these Affirmations to God, to Christians everywhere, and to our world. In sincere repentance and sorrow, we remind ourselves of our own sins and failures; and we pray that God would renew us in confessing Christ as our Lord and Savior in all that we say and do.

Soli Deo Gloria

The consultation on Evangelical Affirmations co-sponsored by the National Association of Evangelicals and Trinity Evangelical Divinity School, May 14 to 17, 1989.

2
ADDRESS

KEYNOTE ADDRESS

Charles Colson

Thank you very much and good evening. What a pleasure it is for me to be part of this awesome gathering of theologians and church leaders, who have come from all around America to be here for this week.

Whenever I see a meeting like this, with all the distinguished names from the evangelical world, I'm reminded of one of my favorite stories, a true story of a few years back—a couple of decades ago.

Two of the best-known figures in the evangelical world, Harold Ockenga and Donald Barnhouse, went on a preaching tour across the country. Every day they preached in different cities, in different churches, for 30 days. Every day they would rotate. One night Harold Ockenga would speak first and Donald Barnhouse would speak next. The next night Donald Barnhouse would preach first and Ockenga would follow. They were great preachers.

Ockenga, at every single appearance, would preach a different sermon. Barnhouse, for 30 days, preached exactly the same message. Ockenga, who was a fine scholar, listened throughout that 30 days to the same sermon that Barnhouse preached day after day. When they got to the final stop, which was in Richmond, Virginia, at a Presbyterian church, it was packed out—much as this church is tonight with a wonderful crowd.

This was to be their final night. Ockenga, who had a great mind, had succeeded in memorizing Barnhouse's sermon verbatim. Yes, you guessed it! Ockenga went first! He gave Barnhouse's message verbatim and flawlessly. All the while he was preaching, he kept looking over at Barnhouse, who was sitting there stoically, absolutely impassive, not an expression on his face.

When Barnhouse, being the great preacher that he was, got up to give his message, he gave another sermon and gave it absolutely brilliantly. As they were walking out of the church, Barnhouse said not a word to Ockenga. Ockenga could contain himself no longer. As they were getting to the door of the church to leave, Ockenga looked over and said, "Donald, they seemed to like your sermon here tonight." Barnhouse said, "Not nearly so much as they did when I preached it here three months ago."

That's why I asked for the privilege of speaking first this evening.

I am indeed honored to open this gathering. Let me express my gratitude first of all to my beloved friend, Dr. Carl Henry, to Dr. Kenneth Kantzer, to this church, and to this congregation. How important it is that we come together as Christians to reaffirm that which we believe, in an era in which the Christian, the evangelical Christian, has been so tragically stereotyped and caricatured.

Make no mistake about it, we have been. I've just been in six countries in Europe, and judging by the press conferences in every country, it's very easy for me to tell you exactly who the best-known religious figures in America are today. Mercifully, Billy Graham remains number one. But close on his heels are Jim and Tammy Bakker, then Jimmy Swaggart, and then Oral Roberts. And after that, it's anybody's field.

The cynicism is wide and deep around the world toward evangelicalism today. At the very time when a clarion call to the gospel must be issued to the world, the world has put evangelicalism into its mold—and tragically has done so abetted by our own mistakes. I am so grateful for these men who have had the vision for this conference. I pray that these succeeding days will be days in which the Spirit will come upon them as they restate the historic confession upon which we as Christians must take our stand.

My thanks as well to Pastor Bill Hybels. The work of this church is clearly one of the great outpourings of God's Spirit in our day. We are certainly honored and thrilled that you would have us here in your church, my friend. Thank you.

"Hold fast to the Word," said Paul in the text that we have just heard. "For I delivered to you as of first importance what I also received, that Christ died for our sins, was buried and was raised on the third day according to the Scriptures." That's the essence of the message that according to the Scriptures, and in Luke's words, "turned the world upside down," a doctrine that by the power of God was able to make the multitudes of sons and daughters of Adam's race wise unto salvation. That message 2,000 years ago was the heart of the gospel. That message 2,000 years later, today, is still the heart of the gospel.

I was in India a few years ago. I had an opportunity to speak in Bombay at a luncheon meeting of 250 government and business leaders at a hotel dining room one noon. I was told to be very careful and be very sensitive about what I said because at the time there were laws, as there are laws today, against proselytizing in India. So I decided (because I knew it would not be a Christian meeting, but largely composed of Hindus and some Muslims) that I would simply share my faith in Christ from my own personal experience.

Charles Colson

I spoke of how 16 years ago this summer, on a hot summer's evening, I went to my friend's house, and he shared with me what it meant to know Jesus Christ. That night in a flood of tears I surrendered my life to Christ. I did that in the first 15 minutes of my talk; and then in the second 15 minutes I talked about the historic evidence for the truth of the fact that God sent His Son to die on a cross for our sins, that he was crucified, buried, and bodily resurrected.

I offered evidence from my own personal experience and my own studies of the resurrection of Jesus Christ to prove its validity. I have discovered in Asian cultures what a powerful message that is! At the end of the meeting, people were coming up to me and asking me questions. One man, a large rotund man with a jolly grin on his face, said, "Mr. Colson, I want to tell you what a wonderful message that was and how much I enjoyed it." He then introduced himself, gave me his name, and told me that he was the chairman of the All-Islamic Congress of India and also the editor of the *Islamic Times*.

He said to me with a great smile on his face, "It's wonderful to have you come here and talk about Jesus the way you do because you and I really believe the same thing."

Now I have to tell you that the first thing that went through my mind was, "I'm in a foreign country. Here is a very powerful and influential man, one of the leading Muslims in India. He's being very gracious and very friendly to me. Should I say to him what I am really thinking, or should I be equally gracious?" He was smiling with this wonderful expression on his face, all very genuine, communicating, "Welcome to India. Isn't it wonderful that you can come and we believe the same thing?" I decided I wasn't there to win a popularity contest, so I looked at him square in the eye and I said, "No sir, I'm sorry. We really do not believe the same thing." He looked as if I had just punched him in the stomach and knocked the wind out of him.

I continued, "We don't believe the same thing. I believe that Jesus Christ was bodily raised from the dead, and I believe it can be proven."

He said, "I know you do. I had never heard that case made before today. I had never fully understood what you Christians believe. You've made a very powerful and very persuasive case."

I replied, "Why don't you talk more about this to some of these Christian men right over here?"

He answered, "I think I'd like to do that." As I walked out of the room that day I saw the man sitting closeted with a group of Christians. I don't know what happened to him afterward. But I discovered one very important thing that day — never, ever should we back away from the truth of the central fact of the Christian faith, that is, that our Lord was raised bodily from the dead and appeared to his apostles. They saw him in the flesh. They knew that they had seen Christ risen. He is risen and he lives! And that's the pivot point of history. That's where the finite and the infinite intersect. That was when God invaded planet earth to provide redemption for all mankind. That was when the Creator of heaven and earth, through the cross and the resurrection (the central fact of human history), revealed himself in person.

Here is what I want you to be sure to take away from this conference and to understand. Make no mistake about it. The apostles were not talking symbolically. Modern critics, as you know, have said that we don't really believe that the apostles were talking literally or meant precisely what they said about the resurrection. Modern critics claim we don't know that they said the things they actually said in the Scriptures.

That's nonsense. The Hebrew tradition was so powerful and strong that no one would ever write anything down unless they had an actual eyewitness account, with two or three witnesses to corroborate the facts. Don't you wish the media did the same thing today?

No, we know they said those things. Were they talking in symbols, as many critics have said? No! No, they were talking as eyewitnesses. "We did not follow cleverly devised tales when we made known to you the power and coming of our Lord Jesus Christ, but we were eyewitnesses of his majesty," Peter said. "That which we have seen and heard, declare we unto you," the Apostle John said. Paul made it very clear that they had seen the risen Christ, that the resurrection, the bodily resurrection of Jesus, is a fact.

Could they have been mistaken? Could they have been lying?

Let me tell you as one who was inside the White House in 1972. The 12 most powerful men in America gathered around the President of the United States and began the great scandal known as Watergate.

One day, one of the men involved (John Dean) walked into the office of the President of the United States and said, "Mr. President, there is a cancer on your presidency." And for the first time, on March 21, 1973, he laid out for us everything he knew about the Watergate scandal. He let us know for the first time that the President of the United States could be involved in a criminal conspiracy. In less than two weeks (by his own account), he went to the prosecutors to bargain for immunity. As he wrote later in his memoirs, it was not to save the Constitution but to save his own skin.

I was among the most powerful men who surrounded the President of the United States. I could press a button and have an airplane waiting for me at Andrews Air Force Base to take me anywhere in the world. I could have aides coming in and out of my office saluting all day long. I could call up government officials and congressmen and tell them what to do. (They didn't do it, but I called them anyway.)

In spite of all that enormous power, the Watergate cover-up conspiracy only lasted two weeks. When John Dean went to the prosecutors to bargain for immunity, for all practical purposes Mr. Nixon's presidency was doomed. After that, every other aide went out to save his own skin. Imagine, the 12 most powerful men in the United States sitting around the desk of the President of the United States could not keep a lie together for more than three weeks.

You're going to tell me that 11 apostles lied for 40 years? They were beaten, persecuted, thrown into jail. All except one lost their lives, dying a martyr's death. Yet they never once renounced the fact they had seen Jesus raised from the dead. That's humanly impossible—unless, in fact, they had seen Jesus. Otherwise, there would have been a John Dean in their midst who turned government evidence. The Apostle Peter had already done that once, no, three times.

The fact of the matter is, my friends, that men will give their lives for something they believe to be true. Muslim terrorists do it with terrifying frequency. But a man will never give his life for

Charles Colson

something he knows to be false. The apostles, who were first-hand witnesses, knew what they had seen, and they never would have given their lives if they had not believed what they had seen to be true.

Even David Hume, one of the great intellects of the Enlightenment, an agnostic Scottish philosopher, the great critic and skeptic of Christianity, said that it is humanly impossible for 11 men, over an extended period of time, to maintain a lie without one of them cracking. It's humanly impossible. The only thing Hume thought was more impossible was for a man to be raised from the dead.

If you don't believe in the supernatural, then you obviously can't believe in the resurrection of Jesus. But if you believe that God is at work in the world, then the evidence is overwhelming that Jesus was bodily raised, and on that *fact* our faith must rest. If it is not true, go look for another place to worship.

I was in Japan. They have a Buddhist sect called the Perfect Liberty Church. It reminds me of some churches that I've been to in America. You can do anything you want—play golf, dance, meditate—whatever you do, it's worshipping God. It's the fastest-growing sect of Buddhists in Japan today. Look into it if the resurrection did not take place.

Christianity is uniquely a historical event. What we need to understand about our faith is that it is not based on wise writings or philosophies or books written in so-called prophetic trances. It is not based on ideologies, which come and go. It is based on the facts of history, real events. God called out his chosen people, and promised in a covenant to deliver them to the place that he had chosen for them. When his people rebelled, he brought his only

Son to die on the cross for forgiveness of their sins. And then he raised him again from the dead. That's what Christianity is: history. The Bible is a recitation of historical events. God's dealings with man. The one true God.

Paul Johnson is one of the great historians of modern times. He's the man who wrote *The History of Christianity,* and more recently, *The History of the Jews.* He's a British historian. I had the pleasure of meeting and visiting with him when I was in London recently. He's also written a magnificent and insightful book, perhaps the most powerful history of the 20th century, entitled *Modern Times.*

Paul Johnson gave a speech in Dallas over a year ago. It is one of the most remarkable documents I've read. Speaking purely as a historian, he says, "Christianity is a historical religion or it is nothing. It does not deal in myths or metaphors or symbols or in states-of-being in cycles. It deals in facts and the evidence supports the facts."

Western civilization was built on the premise that men and women understand that there is a source of truth. It is the God who is, the God who reigns, the God who is the Author of history. It was not until the 20th century that modern skeptics and theologians began to quarrel over the historical accuracy of the recounting of God's dealing with man found in Holy Scripture. Modern critics began to assail the dating of documents to make them less than contemporaneous. And Christians, defensively, then began to argue only on the basis of experience. Christ is true because by our personal experience we know him to be true. Other German scholars even went so far as to question whether Jesus ever in fact existed as a man, let alone as God. By the 1920s Christians were

49

on the defensive. The low-water mark was reached as higher criticism seemed to demolish the historical accuracy of the Judeo-Christian account.

But as Johnson points out in his speech, there has been a dramatic change in the past 70 years. Archaeological discoveries in the 1920s were able to validate Biblical history, including the discovery of Ur from which Abraham came. Other sources (mainly Egyptian) confirmed the dates of Solomon's reign. As Johnson says, the books of Samuel, Kings, and Chronicles are today regarded as the finest, most accurate, and most dependable history available.

Then came the discovery of the Dead Sea Scrolls, with the entire text of Isaiah, in the dry sands of Egypt. One by one over the past 70 years, the archaeological discoveries have begun to put the so-called modern critics on the defensive. Our archaeological illumination continues. Biblical revelation is being validated day by day as more and more discoveries are encountered. Today there are nearly 80 papyrus fragments dating back to the 2nd through the 4th centuries — nearly contemporaneous with the time of Christ. Some can be dated back as far as 50-60 A.D., and the gospel of John can be dated no later than 90-100 A.D.

Now stop and think about how silly this is. You go on campuses across America today and you will find people who will ridicule you. That happens to me all the time when I go on secular campuses or when I go on interview programs. They will ridicule me and say, "You don't really believe the Bible to be true. I mean, after all, the history, the scholarship is not there to support it."

Friends, there are 80 papyruses that have been dated back to the second through the fourth centuries. Written, first-hand accounts about Jesus! On those same secular campuses, no one questions the existence of Aristotle or anything that Aristotle wrote. And yet the oldest dated manuscript we have of Aristotle is from 1100 A.D., 1,400 years after his death! No secular scholar would question Aristotle, but they all question Jesus. Why? Because we Christians simply haven't taken our stand.

Hold fast to the truth and let the world know what we believe is historically validated.

Johnson, in the conclusion of his speech, says something truly wonderful: "It is not now the men of faith; it is the skeptics, who have reason to fear the course of further discovery." Don't shrink from it. Scripture is revealed propositional truth. God, the Author of all, is the ultimate truth, made evident in his Word and in the person of Jesus Christ.

Now, what you have to understand is that in today's environment it would be difficult to make a statement more radical than that. God is the original source of truth. The Word is true. There is an absolute! Dare you really say that in today's culture? The prevailing ethos is the reason that we are in as much trouble as we are in American society today. The real ethos is relativism; that is, there is no truth. Truth is only what you find it to be. There are no absolute rights and no absolute wrongs.

Alan Bloom exposed this fallacy in his brilliant book, *The Closing of the American Mind.* In the opening chapter of that book he writes, "There is one thing a professor can be absolutely certain of. Almost every student entering the university believes, or says he believes, that truth is relative."

Let me give you an illustration of how far this thinking has gone in academia. Not too long ago at Harvard University there was a conference of educators and students. They came together from all over the United States. The discussion was the curriculum being taught in American universities. President Frank Rhodes of Cornell stood up in the midst of the meeting and he said, "I think perhaps it is time that we gave real and sustained attention to students' intellectual and moral well-being." Suddenly there were gasps, catcalls, boos, and hisses. People began to shout and say he ought to sit down.

One student stood up and said, "Who's going to do the moral instructing?" Another yelled, "Whose morality are we going to follow?" With that there was a thunderous applause and President Rhodes sat down, silenced. No one even thought to answer. Any generation before this (almost instinctively and automatically) would have answered Biblical revelation, natural law, or at the least the 2,300 years of accumulated wisdom of Western civilization.

The problem is that we've lost the capacity in this relativistic society to argue ethics or values. In a relativistic society they can't exist. As a political science professor at Bryn Mawr recently said, "The moral standards which we increasingly do not practice, the intellectual leaders of our day cannot even talk about."

That's why just a year ago at Stanford University the students marched across the campus shouting, "Hey, hey, ho, ho, Western civilization has got to go!" I mean, go where? They were protesting a great books curriculum because they were being forced to read the great books of Western civilization. Their objection was that these books were written principally by white males. As one commentator said, observing what the Stanford students did, "It's just a shame that Plato was not a lesbian Comanche."

The tragedy is that the Stanford faculty decided that it really was discriminatory to read the great books of Western civilization because they were written by white males. So they changed the curriculum, revising history.

Here is where this trend becomes a problem for us. Not only is the decay of society taking place all around us because there are no recognized absolute truths, but those of us who step forward and proclaim that something is true are automatically labeled as bigots. You have to be. If tolerance is the supreme virtue, you become a bigot the moment you say that there is truth.

Let me tell you what happens to a society when relativism takes the sort of grip that it has upon American culture today. First, there is never a way to settle a moral debate. All moral debates become interminable. You can't say murder is wrong. All you can say is, "I prefer not to murder." You can't say it's wrong.

There was a poll in the *Los Angeles Times* recently concerning abortion. People were asked whether abortion was murder or not. To my astonishment, 57% of the American people said that abortion is murder. Only 35% disagreed. It was even considered murder by 1/3 of the women who have had an abortion and by 1/4 of the people who generally favor it.

The American public realizes that to take the life of an unborn child, consciously and deliberately, is murder. But the same poll asked whether they agreed or disagreed with this statement: "I personally feel that abortion is morally wrong, but I also feel that whether or not to have an abortion is a decision that has to be made by every woman for herself." Seventy four percent agreed! The same people! Can they really understand what they're saying? "I think it's murder, but I think you ought to be able to go ahead and murder if you want to because I'm not going to impose my views on you"! No wonder this society is in trouble! That's what relativism has done to us. You can't settle any moral argument because there is no standard by which it can be settled. Ultimately this logic leads to the total dissolution of a society. The fact of the matter is, brothers and sisters, that, if a person has no transcendent standard above himself, he will always do what is in his or her own self-interest. Grasping ego and selfish desire become the only yardstick by which a society's behavior can be measured.

I love the wonderful story told of Samuel Johnson's reaction when informed that a guest in his home arrogantly maintained that all morality is a sham. Johnson said, "Why sir, if he really believes that there is no distinction between virtue and vice, be sure to count the spoons before hc leaves."

A society depends upon the elements of character for its very existence: duty, valor, honor, justice. These virtues simply cannot exist if the only measure of value in life is grasping ego or self-interest.

I read another poll recently in *Rolling Stone* magazine that shocked me. Forty percent of the so-called baby-boom genera-tion—the leadership of America over these next several dec-ades—when asked whether there was any cause for which they would fight for their country, said no. The social contract is eventually torn asunder when the only value system in a society is self. That's what happens in a relativistic value system. And the societal horrors that flow from this are simply endless. If we no longer believe that God is truth and the basic premise of life, it not only gives us a distorted view of God; it gives us a distorted view of ourselves.

That's why people can't understand what happened up in Central Park recently. It's a horrible story. Young men randomly and brutally assaulted, beat, raped, and mutilated a 28-year-old woman who was out jogging. Everyone has tried to come up with a plausible explanation for this tragedy because it defies explanation. These young lads were not out of the ghetto. They were from fine homes. These young lads were doing well in school. These young lads were from an apartment house that had a doorman out front.

What was the explanation? It's something our society has totally lost sight of because we have taken God and the truth of God out of society. The answer is that we are desperately wicked and depraved. Sin! Sin! Man's sin is the answer.

I was recently in a country (which best remains unnamed) visiting its prisons. There were 100 inmates in the prison in which I preached. The prison psychiatrist came out after I preached and gave those of us who were visiting the prison a briefing. She said 72% of the men in that prison are classified as psychiatric cases. They are mentally unbalanced. I went up to her afterward and said, "72% of the people? Is this a mental hospital?" She said, "No, no — it's because of the crimes that they have committed." I said, "What do you mean, because of the crime?" She said, "Well, when anyone in our country commits a crime as heinous as rape and murder or any violent act, we automatically classify them as a mental case."

You see why? Because people are basically good! We've lost sight of the basic Christian truth that man is a sinner in need of the grace of God. Therefore, if a man commits a terrible crime, we should give him therapy, not punishment. That's precisely what they did in this prison.

55

Charles Colson

Two days after I preached there, a beautiful young corrections officer, 26 years old, blonde hair, an attractive woman — came up to me and said, "Mr. Colson, that was the most marvelous message today. Thank you for bringing the gospel into this prison. These inmates don't hear it very often." She said, "I'm a Christian and I witness to them every chance I get." Two days later, that same correctional officer was required to take one of the inmates downtown to see a violent movie. Neither she nor the inmate ever came back. A few days later they found her mutilated body in a ditch a mile from the prison.

Why? Because we believe a distorted picture of man as basically good, and that's not true! But that's what happens in secular society today. If you take God out, you get a wrong view of man. Instead of punishing people and treating them as the sinners that they are, in need of redemption, we treat them as sick people in need of therapy and cures. So we take them to movies. That's what is happening in society.

The greatest tragedy of all is what relativism does to the church. Robert Bellah, the sociologist, conducted a poll recently of 200 average, middle-class Americans, to try to find out what American values currently are. He found out that 81% of Americans believe that an individual should arrive at his or her own religious belief independently of any church or synagogue. He quoted one young woman by the name of Sheila who said, "I believe in God. . . but I can't remember the last time I went to church. My faith however has carried me a long way." It's Sheilaism. Just my own little voice. Do-it-yourself God kits. Make up your own God. Worship as you wish.

In a relativistic society, the church is no longer looked upon as the repository of truth. It is looked upon as simply a place where people come to feel good — for personal fulfillment. The reason the New Age movement is sweeping America; the reason that 25% of the American people say they believe in reincarnation; the reason they listen seriously to Shirley MacLaine and go off on mountain tops and talk about harmonic convergence; the reason they go into these ridiculous things is because they no longer see the church as the one place where there is a repository of truth.

They simply see religion as "being" —finding something that will make you feel good. Believe me, friends, you can do a number of things that will make you feel much better than the news of Jesus Christ, which convicts you of your sin, that is, before it becomes the good news of redemption. And that's the tragedy of a relativistic society.

What's the challenge? The challenge for us today, Christians, is to hold fast to the truth, to know and believe that there is a God who lives, who has spoken, and who reigns in his heaven today. A God who sent his Son, who was bodily raised from the dead. And that's a fact of history. What we believe in is not philosophy or ideology or myth. We believe in the facts of God, who has revealed himself. We need to take our stand on doctrine and hold fast to that truth as a beacon of light and truth in a world that is in disarray. We need to offer a compelling apologetic to a world that's collapsing around us. The world desperately needs this. No society has ever been able to survive that eliminated a transcendent standard of truth by which people could live, one which provided harmony, concord, and justice, as Cicero put it, even in pre-Christian times.

Charles Colson

That's why we are here tonight. That's why this conference is gathered here, that we might reaffirm our orthodoxy, the classic doctrines of our faith rooted in objective truth, truth revealed by God and confessed by the saints down through the centuries from Athanasius to Augustine, from Aquinas to Calvin to today. Several thousand of you gathered in this church tonight perhaps are saying, "That's all well and good for the theologians and scholars, but what's that got to do with me as a layperson?"

It's fascinating to me that church people never question the need for conversion, for faith, for commitment, or sacrifice, or Bible study, or prayer, or holy living, but they always wonder about doctrine. Why is doctrine so important? Doctrine is important because as Christians we believe in the historic validation of our faith and of the truth that is handed down to us through the centuries, originating with those who were eyewitnesses to the truth. Doctrine is crucially important. It's important because all knowledge of God comes from him for the purpose of his glory and the salvation of those to whom it is savingly committed. John says in his gospel, "Eternal life is found in the knowledge of God."

First, the knowledge of God is essential to our own salvation. How can you worship a God whom you know nothing about? There is no proper loving of God without a proper knowledge of God. It's the fuel that fires our devotion.

Second, Christianity is a missionary religion. We are told by our Leader to go and make disciples, "teaching them to obey all that I have commanded you." If we're going to get the message out, we had better get that message right.

Third, how can we possibly present an apologetic to the world today if we do not understand the truth of the timeless

58

message of the gospel? Not that we interpret it in today's light, but that we understand the essence of that truth so that we are able to present an essential apologetic to a world adrift.

This is no small concern. This is no idle matter. This is not just the business of theologians and church scholars and people who write books. This is the business of every single Christian layperson, because when we fail to stand on solid doctrine, we undercut individuals, we undercut denominations, we undercut our witness to the world.

Some years ago, a Christian leader (whose name I will not mention tonight), and I were in a Bible study together. He was out speaking at prayer breakfasts. I had just discovered the difference between Arminianism and Calvinism. I had just read about Jacob Arminius and something of his work. I was excited. I came to the Bible study one day and said, "This is really interesting, have you ever thought about whether you are an Arminian or a Calvinist on this view of Scripture?"

This fellow looked at me and he said, "Don't get into those discussions." I said, "Why not? I'm fascinated. I'm really interested. I really want to study about this." "No," he said, "That's not what matters. What matters is that we love Jesus and follow Him and live the way He teaches us to live." Later, that man left his wife, literally left the church, and now says he's trying to struggle to go on with the Lord. But his witness has been destroyed.

Doctrine gives us the foundation of what we believe, and if we haven't the minds to seek it, we haven't the heart to worship it.

Ignoring doctrine can undermine denominations. Ronald Nash writes about one denomination where people were not

59

concerned with doctrine and curiously neglected it. The laypeople talked about holy living and prayer and Christian experience, but meanwhile the professors in the seminaries were moving farther and farther away from the classic doctrines of that denomination until the entire denomination was lost. Why? Because its teaching centers were no longer teaching solid, orthodox Christian doctrine.

I was in Sri Lanka some years ago. When I landed at the airport, I was met by an Anglican priest. He was the head of our ministry, Prison Fellowship, in Sri Lanka. We were on our way into the city when I asked a question I ask everywhere I go, "Desmond, how is the church doing here in this country?" He said, "Not well; we're doing very badly. The Muslims are just killing us."

He said, "They're going from village to village taking the statement of Bishop Jenkins in England that the resurrection was nothing but a conjuring trick with bones. They are saying to all the Christians, 'You see, that's what we've always told you. You can be a Muslim and still believe in Jesus. Look at what the Anglican Bishop in England is saying.'" Christians were being swept away by the Muslims in village after village because some woolly-headed bishop in England had made an absurd statement about the resurrection of Jesus Christ. Abandon doctrine and you undercut the witness of the church.

Look at the ideologies today that have crept into the Christian church. All through Latin and South America liberation theology is exploding, yet it is nothing but an ideology in gospel language. People have lost their traditional stand on doctrine. So the church has been corrupted. Both the right and the left have made exactly the same mistake.

I would warn you, however, that when you take your stand on historic, classical doctrine, be prepared for one thing. People who have stereotyped evangelical Christians will say, "Oh, you're one of those backward Bible thumpers, aren't you?"

I was at a banquet a few years ago where I was receiving an award. I happened to be sitting next to one of the mainline church people. We were talking all through dinner about books we've read. About two-thirds of the way through the evening, this man turned to me and said, "Mr. Colson, you've read Bonhoeffer and you've read this and you've read that—all these works that we've talked about tonight. You seem like a very educated and intelligent person. You're certainly not a fundamentalist, are you?"

I said, "How do you define 'fundamentalist?' The five fundamentals of the faith? The virgin birth, the resurrection of Jesus Christ, the deity of Christ, the fact that he's coming again, and the authority of the Scripture?"

He said, "Yes, my view is much more modern than that. You don't believe all that, do you?"

I looked at him square in the eye and I said, "Well, of course! Don't you?"

Don't back away. Don't be defensive. What virtue is there to something being modern? Does that mean it's enlightened?

A great systematic theologian, one of Princeton University's greatest theologians, Charles Hodge, once said, as if to describe a great virtue, that during his many years at Princeton, the institution had never brought forth a single original thought. He was ridiculed at the time. But what he was saying was we stand on the great historic confessions of faith. Our communion is not sitting with the people who are only at the table today. It is sitting with the saints down through the ages back to the apostles. We believe in the historic confession of Christian truth, and we are not afraid to say that we aren't modern in that sense. Don't be intimidated. Don't be put out.

I love what Joseph Sobran, the columnist, said, "It can be exalting to belong to a church that is five hundred years behind the times and sublimely indifferent to fashion; it is mortifying to belong to a church that is five minutes behind the times, huffing and puffing to catch up." Wonderful.

It is no overstatement for me to stand here tonight at the outset of this conference and to tell you that we must adhere to Scripture and the classical confessions of faith; to truth; to what we might broadly call orthodoxy; to what C.S. Lewis called "the central core of what we believe"; to "mere Christianity"; if we are to present Christian truth today to a dissolute culture.

Secularism can only advance as orthodoxy retreats. That's why this conference, which reaffirms the historic evangelical statement of belief and truth, is so absolutely vital.

What happens when we take our stand on doctrine? Nothing is more revolutionary.

When I first became a Christian, I started to read the Scriptures. Now people say to me, "Isn't it a wonderful ministry you're in, Chuck Colson—34 countries around the world, 500 prisons across America, 30,000 volunteers? Isn't that wonderful?" A stewardess on the airplane flying from Denver today stopped to talk to me. "What a wonderful ministry it is that you have." They all say, "Isn't it wonderful that you're doing all that good?" Do good. You're looked upon as a do-gooder.

No! That's not why I do what I do. I don't do what I do because I think I can reform the prison system. I don't do what I do because it's my way of making contrition for what happened during Watergate. I don't do what I do out of any set of human motives at all.

I do what I do because I read this Book. I read the classic doctrines of the faith. I believe them to be true. I read that my God cares about justice. Because he calls me to take a stand and to do his work, I am compelled by the living Word of the living God to obediently go and do what I do in the prisons. Not because I'm a do-gooder, but out of gratitude to God!

I read Dr. Henry's books. I studied at his feet every chance I had. I came to see the truth. I thought I'd been something of a scholar in college. No. Nothing compared to understanding what God's truth means. One day I took a set of tapes out by R. C. Sproul on the holiness of God. I played them on my VCR. Before those tapes were over, I found myself down on my knees before the majesty of a holy God, in awe that he would call any one of us to be his own. When we really understand the truth of Scripture, it drives us to our knees and it compels us to live in obedience to Christ.

That's what's at the heart of the Right-to-Life campaign today. I've been talking to people all across America who have been arrested. They have been in prison because they have taken a stand — not out of convenience, not because they're comfortable doing it, not because they are trying to grandstand; but because they believe the Word of God to be true. They believe that human dignity is rooted in the fact that man is created in the image of God and that as Christians we must take our stand on that truth.

Charles Colson

Two centuries ago that conviction caused a man by the name of William Wilberforce to stand on the floor of the House of Commons as a member of Parliament and denounce the most barbaric practice of man in his time, the slave trade. Black bodies were put in the holds of ships in Africa and taken to the Western hemisphere. He stood alone against what was then the primary source of revenue to the British government, the slave trade. Why? A do-gooder? No. A social conscience? No. He'd been converted by the preaching of John Wesley. He had fallen on his knees and surrendered his life to Christ. He had written a magnificent book about Christian living. It had 26 words in the title. It has been reprinted today under the title of *Real Christianity*. The actual title was *Real Christianity as Practised and Preached in the Scriptures as Contrasted With That Practised and Preached in the Churches of England Today*. Wonderful.

We could use a book like that in America today. Moved by that book and by the desire for holiness, he stood as one man against the slave trade. The battle raged for 20 years, until eventually England declared the slave trade illegal. Six days before Wilberforce died, slavery was abolished in Europe. Why? Because one man took his stand upon God's truth and believed the Scriptures to be real.

That's what changes the world, and that's what the Christian church needs today — to take our stand on the holy Word of God; to believe God's truth; not to be dismayed or detoured by ideologies of the day; but to stand on the truth and to be motivated by it to follow God accordingly.

It is significant that we gather tonight, isn't it? On this day, Pentecost, the Christian Church celebrates that momentous event when the Holy Spirit came upon 120 believers huddled together in an upper room in Jerusalem. And beginning from Jerusalem, a company of Christ's disciples plunged themselves into a world blinded by its own self-imposed darkness. They embarked on a mission given to them by the One who had claimed all authority in heaven and on earth. Under the power of the Holy Spirit, they made disciples by teaching the truth to those entrusted to them by the One who is truth. And Christ, as he promised, was with them. On the rock of the apostles' confession and proclamation that "Jesus is the Christ, the Son of the living God," the church was built and the gates of hell crumbled before it.

Is it too much to dare to pray that that Spirit might fall afresh on us and on the church today? Think what that might mean if we were called and responded to a new commitment to the truth of the doctrine of God's Word. Yes, Holy Spirit, come. Come, Holy Spirit. Give us that courage.

If you are rooted in the Word of God, having taken up the whole armor of God that he has provided, you will stand strong and tall in this evil day. Martin Luther captured it, the solid hope of all believers when he wrote in 1529:

> That Word above all earthly powers,
>   no thanks to them abideth;
> The Spirit and the gifts are ours,
>   through Him who with us sideth;
> Let goods and kindred go,
>   this mortal life also;
> The body they may kill:
>   God's truth abideth still;
> His kingdom is forever.

Charles Colson

Don't you see? We stand under God's authority. It was because of Luther's great conviction that God is truth that he was able to witness to that truth. He had the courage to boldly and disdainfully cast aside even the threat to his own life. My brothers and sisters, a generation that does not share that conviction will never share that courage. And so I call upon you, if you would serve the living God in your generation, amidst the terrors and dangers that threaten on every hand—hold fast to the truth! Hold fast to the truth, that God may be all in all. Amen.

3

THE
EVANGELICALS

WHO ARE
THE EVANGELICALS

Carl F. H. Henry

A missionary home on furlough was asked recently what had changed most during his five-year absence from America. When he left, he replied, the general public used the term "evangelical" with respect; when he returned, it was used with derision. The term "evangelical" had become a symbol for confrontational politics; worse yet, it was linked to religious exploitation and manipulation akin to Sinclair Lewis' *Elmer Gantry*.

Little more than a dozen years ago, *Newsweek* magazine in a 1976 cover story heralded "The Year of the Evangelical". "The religious phenomenon of the '70s," reported *Newsweek*, was "the emergence of evangelical Christianity into a position of respect and power." But in a decade or so, the evangelical movement has squandered much of its moral and spiritual initiative, and secular society has placed a large question mark over its motives, its goals, and even its integrity.

Although a few fraudulent ministers and scandalous tele-vangelists have lent undeserved credence to this graceless calumny and defamation of evangelical religion, we should never forget that secular modernity routinely doubts the intellectual legitimacy of even the most elemental historic Christian beliefs and has little regard for its moral principles. The largely humanistic media treat any and all religion merely as a private concern, an optional commitment, and view biblical theism in particular as cognitively outmoded.

Carl F.H. Henry

What specially offends the secular mind is not lust for money, or luxurious lifestyle, or pursuit of sexual gratification. To these evils, contemporary society is no less vulnerable than are televangelists and the rest of us. Secular modernity is in fact the very lifeline of cultural hedonism and other temptations that have embarrassingly ensnared elements of the evangelical movement.

But when religious spokesmen publicly inveigh against such vices and seek sacrificial gifts for holy causes while they privately transgress what they preach, one can hardly blame secular society for its condemnation of hypocrisy. Had they been morally alert, evangelical leaders would have led the way in calling spiritual renegades to account, instead of forfeiting to the secular media the opportunity (more importantly, the duty) of judging religious spokesmen by the lofty ethical standards that biblical theism addresses to the pagan West. Moral criticism is a necessary part of what it means for all of us—church and world, including the media—to square our lives with the scriptural plumbline by which all humanity will one day be finally judged.

Yet deep down, secular modernity is playing games with us. What it is really saying about evangelical lust and greed is "welcome to the club", and not "back to the Bible!" What really offends the secular mentality about evangelical religion is our belief that God has public importance. What disturbs the media about periodic Washington-for-Jesus rallies, for example—to which the press generally devotes no more space than to a hundred reactionary atheists demonstrating nearby—is the evangelical conviction that personal repentance and spiritual renewal actually impact on a nation's historical destinies. What seems to the media ridiculous about Pat Robertson's over-publicized effort to redirect a hurricane by prayer are the theistic beliefs that God preserves and controls the world of nature and that prayer affects the external course of events. Televangelistic improprieties and charismatic or pentecostal nuances aside, what is most at stake in the current caricature of evangelicals is a philosophical struggle that pits modern naturalism against biblical supernaturalism and ranges in colossal conflict the theistic and materialistic views of man and the cosmos.

Whatever may be one's academic stature, political role, corporate leadership, cultural achievement or contribution to societal well-being, the secular media are prone to catalogue as cultic survivors from a now antiquated past all who dare to be evangelical Christians. An unbelieving press subtly tends to caricature Bible-believing church-goers as a group, and our secular neighbors more and more secretly revel in this amusing satire. In the midst of an unprecedented information explosion, much of the secular media deploys its technological genius and resources in a manner that obscures the factual realities of the Judeo-Christian heritage. Television as a public entertainment enterprise even stoops at times to handle religion simply for its amusement value.

The deeper question arises whether in these circumstances we can any longer effectively mass-communicate the Gospel of Christ to an entertainment-hungry society that would prefer to throw aggressive Christians to the lions. Do hard core naturalists any longer comprehend the Gospel in the terminology most televangelists currently use? What does the contemporary mind understand by the testimony that "I was saved in June, 1933" and that "you too need to be saved"? Are we like Jesus now speaking

Carl F.H. Henry

in parables, not to religionists but to professional secularists for whom spiritual truth remains impenetrable while the ordinary people readily grasp it? Are the media masters too culturally biased to get it right? Ask today's scribes who evangelicals are, and some will prattle about bizarre born-againers, fundamentalist ignoramuses and snake-handlers.

Dare we put sole blame upon the media for their confusion? Expository preaching and doctrinal teaching have been at low ebb in a generation that has pitched evangelism at an experiential high. Many professing evangelicals themselves seem somewhat unsure of their religious identity. The transition to "political evangelism" now preoccupies some who long prioritized preaching the Gospel to the spiritual rebels of our age. The term "evangelical" has become a synonym for the conservative right's confrontational politics, even if much of the evangelical mainstream has a considerably broader agenda. Televangelism improprieties rendered the term even more ambiguous; while specially embarrassing to the fast-growing Pentecostal wing, they nonetheless cut deeply into marginal support for evangelical enterprises in general and adverse publicity slowed evangelistic penetration by biblically-oriented churches.

For all that, the theologically conservative churches continue to grow. A recent Gallup report numbers evangelicals at more than 66 million, and George Gallup, Jr. himself has become one of them.

Yet confusion persists over precisely what "being an evangelical" means. In the face of external and internal stresses, some people wonder whether the movement ought to abandon the term "evangelical," gently administering euthanasia to it just as some worldlings now dispose of their unwanted aging. Shall we doom the descriptive "evangelicalism" to the same transitory fate that earlier overtook the term "fundamentalism" ?

Or shall we join Jerry Falwell's projection of a revitalized fundamentalism in *The Fundamentalist Phenomenon* (Doubleday, 1981), and concede his claim that the fundamentalists have now permanently hijacked the evangelical jumbo-jet? In *The Bible in the Balance* (Zondervan, 1979), Harold Lindsell opts for the term "fundamentalist" on the ground that self-styled progressive neoevangelicals have so debased the term "evangelical" that "it has lost its usefulness" (ibid., pp. 319 f.). Or shall we follow Edward John Carnell's lead when he deplored and disowned fundamentalism as cultic and wrote instead of *The Case for Orthodox Christianity* (Westminster, 1959)? Shall we rally instead to those who now stress a doctrinally definitive "Reformed" Christianity and who reject diversity as subtly leading to an uncritically diluted evangelicalism and to theological pluralism? Yet George Marsden links the prestige of the Reformers instead to Fuller Theological Seminary's modified evangelicalism when in *Reforming Fundamentalism* (Eerdmans, 1987) he discusses a critical view of Scripture and ecumenical openness.

Shall we designate ourselves as Pentecostalists who trace their distinctiveness to the Azusa Street Revival (1906-09), and whose emphasis on tongues and healing marks the fastest-growing segment of North American and South American Christianity? Or instead fly the banner of denominationally-transcending charismatics who emphasize the present availability of the apostolic gifts? Shall we instead affirm a more specifically "Wesleyan" identity that traces evangelical roots, as does David L. McKenna, to a Wesleyan Holiness heritage ("Evangelicalism: An Alternative Perspective", *The Asbury Herald*, Spring, 1988, pp. 8-10)? Shall we rally rather to what Richard John Neuhaus calls the "Catholic moment in America", one that proposes to transcend the sporadic and theonomous nature of much evangelical political involvement through a Catholic shaping of public philosophy that outflanks both the liberal Protestant left and the Catholic left (*The Catholic Moment. The Paradox of the Church in the Postmodern World*, Harper & Row, 1987)?

Or shall we follow many American black Christians who prefer the simple unpretentious expression "Bible believers"? Shall we opt for the label "Jesus-people", or has that term now also acquired associations that render it only problematically serviceable? Shall we ignore the disdain of secular humanists and unprotestingly bear the full reproach of being "Christers" or "Gospelizers" or "Jesus-freaks"? Or shall we return to the term "Christian", by which Jesus' followers were first designated in Antioch (Acts 11:26), or is that descriptive now too blurred by Christendom's competing ecumenical branches and obscured by cults like Christian Science? Shall we bow to the ecumenical plea for a unity and mission "apostolic, catholic, and evangelical" yet which postpones a further definition or redefinition of all three terms? Shall we dissolve the term "evangelical" into a "history of religions" framework, abandon the distinction of true/false religion, and accommodate the secular humanist bias that all religions are functionally useful yet that none has cognitive authority to tell us how the real world is truly structured?

Or do we face a *kairos*, a providential moment in the historical course of Christianity, one that challenges contemporary Christian multiformity and offers us an opportunity for clearer self-identification? Can we rise above the pervasive secular confusion about religious realities, wrench ourselves free of a lust for statistical bigness, and clarify the propriety or impropriety of unsure designations like Anglican evangelical, Catholic evangelical, charismatic evangelical, pentecostal evangelical, fundamentalist evangelical or evangelical fundamentalist, neo-evangelical, neo-orthodox evangelical, or even liberal evangelical? "What's in a name?" asks Shakespeare. "That which we call a rose," he adds, "by any other name would smell as sweet." In an age of revisionary empiricism that resists finalities, can we make clear that there is more to the name "evangelical" than meets the senses?

The term "evangelical" has its roots deep in the bedrock of the Greek New Testament. *Euangellion* means "good tidings" or Gospel. The evangel is the momentous biblically-attested good news that God justifies sinners who for spiritual and moral salvation rely on the substitutionary person and work of Jesus Christ.

The good news or evangel is not, simply as such, the dramatic death of Jesus of Nazareth the veritable Son of God. What good news marks the ghastly crucifixion of the godly Nazarene whose holy life all who knew him intimately affirmed, and in whom not even Pilate could find fault? Nor is the incarnation per se good news, nor the sinless life of Jesus per se, nor the Lord's return per se in final judgment of men and nations, nor the truthfulness of the Bible per se. For humanity in the grip of sin, all such realities are terrifying.

Carl F.H. Henry

The good news is the scripturally anticipated-and-fulfilled promise that God's sinless Messiah died in the place of otherwise doomed sinners, and moreover, that the crucified Redeemer arose bodily from the dead to resurrection life as helmsman of the eternal moral and spiritual world.

Some pulpiteers may experientially dilute the good news into the personal realization of self-fulfillment, or into the promise of a repentance-conditioned new birth, or into the prospect of an inner fullness of the Holy Spirit, or into a capacity to speak in strange tongues or to work miracles, or into a prospect of material enhancement or physical well-being. But in 1 Corinthians 15:3 ff. the Apostle Paul headlines the good news not in terms of effusive inner experience, but in terms of divinely revealed truths and redemptive acts. Without these core beliefs, evangelicalism emasculates the evangel and is not worth the space it takes to print its six syllables, or the time it takes to utter them.

The evangel, Paul affirms, is "that Christ died for our sins according to the Scriptures, and that he was buried, and that he rose again the third day according to the Scriptures, and was seen." Paul is talking primarily not about your religious experience or my religious experience, but about revelatory truths and historical events—the bedrock on which human salvation rests for its very possibility, and without which there is no prospect of salvation for sinners. He does not confuse the good news with an unscratchable tickle in one's heart, with an incomparably delightful tingle. The good news has nothing to do with internal effervescence, nor is it a matter of speaking in exotic languages or of doing miracles. It is not a matter of our doing at all, for our works even at their best are too tawdry to survive divine scrutiny. Scripture applauds not your works or mine, but rather Jesus Christ's saving work in our stead, and inspired Scripture itself as the truthful and trustworthy source of this good news.

It is on the miracle of Jesus Christ, on his atoning death and resurrection, that Paul focuses; it is the Word of God he emphasizes, not human tongues and world wisdom. Apart from Christ's substitutionary death and bodily resurrection we are all doomed; apart from the scripturally-attested evangel we are condemned all the more that in human flesh God himself came, that in our human nature Jesus lived a sinless life. Apart from that good news, what solace is borne by assurance that Christ will return in cataclysmic judgment on men and nations? To be sure, the divine incarnation and sinlessness of Jesus, and the Lord's final righteous judgment all become joyous affirmations through the grand tidings that the God-man died for the sins of the penitent and, as the revelatory Scriptures foretell and attest, that he lives even now as our risen Redeemer.

In less than two dozen Greek words the Apostle Paul epitomizes this incomparable good news. Remarkably, more than a fourth of that total word-count he devotes to the fact that Scripture vouchsafes this good news; twice, in fact, he declares the evangel to be "according to the Scriptures". The good news is scripturally-identified, scripturally-based, scripturally-validated; inspired Scripture is its verifying principle. Without authoritatively true Scripture the good news might be garbled a hundred ways, as indeed it now often inexcusably is by those who stray from scriptural revelation.

Some reference is needed to concessive scholars who contend that by *kata tas graphas* Paul means to indicate not the unqualified reliability of Scripture, but rather the general trustworthiness of the biblical witness. This distinction has the aura of a 20th century novelty. For one thing, in 2 Corinthians 4:13 Paul uses a somewhat similar construction (*kata to gegrammenon*), literally "according to the thing having been written", an expression that points to the very specifics of the writings and not merely to their testimony in general. The perfect passive tense implies that divine inspiration is a fixed quality of the text itself, not merely a matter of the reader's conceptual inferences. This is the point also of 2 Timothy 3:16, where the writer stresses that Scripture—whether every part or the whole—is divinely inspired and profitable. One may recall also numerous references that equate the phrase "Scripture says" with what "God says", the presupposition being that Scripture as a textual phenomenon is plenarily inspired. For that reason Paul elsewhere argues even from the very minutiae of Scripture: "The Scripture does not say 'and to seeds'...but to...seed" (Gal. 3:16).

It is unjustifiable therefore to broaden the definition of evangelical identity in a way that excludes a specific view of Scripture. The reduction of evangelical authenticity to the affirmation of a "minimal gospel" (salvation solely on the ground of Christ's substitutionary work appropriated by faith) therefore obscures the inviolable truth of Scripture, which the Apostle Paul affirms. Evangelicals as a body of believers have stood traditionally not for a truncated definition of the good news, but provide an overwhelming precedent for the view that a consistent and complete statement of the Gospel embraces also the truthfulness of the Scripture.

The Protestant Reformers summarized the enduring good news in two maxims: *sola scriptura* and *sola fide*—Scripture alone and faith alone! The Reformers promoted evangelical trust in Christ's redemptive work over against both a pagan reliance on the adequacy of human works and against an ecclesiastical reliance on the efficacy of sacraments, and they contrasted the truthfulness of God's Word with both world-*gnosis* and ecclesial tradition. Any attack upon either the revelatory character of Scripture or the salvific significance of Christ they deplored as a dilution and defamation of the good news.

The biblically-accredited good news, the evangel of the atoning death and bodily resurrection of the crucified Jesus, obliges us above all else to be heralds of the evangel, or, if you wish, "evangelicals". Just as the Apostle Paul relayed the evangel to the Corinthians, so we who are its modern beneficiaries are to "pass it on" to our generation. In a society skeptical of absolute truth and distrustful of words, the Evangelical Theological Society clearly focused the evangelical epistemic affirmation: "The Bible alone, and the Bible in its entirety, is the Word of God written, and therefore inerrant in the autographs."

Yet something remains to be said for a more positive statement that focuses on the truthfulness and trustworthiness of Scripture consonant with its diverse genres, rather than defensively on inerrancy. The problem with the term inerrancy is not simply that its very prefix conveys a negative meaning, but that it too readily accommodates a shift of emphasis from the comprehensive truth of Scripture to the defense of isolated components supposedly on empirical grounds. In consequence, a deductive derivation of inspiration and inerrancy from the living God as the primary theological axiom is replaced by an inductive approach to Scripture. The inerrancy of Scripture—and not its divine authority and inspiration—then is declared the first and most important statement to be made about Scripture.

The positive regard for Scripture as God's Word is found in the Old Testament prophets and in Jesus' teaching and that of the apostles; they considered Scripture wholly reliable and dependable.

But in our age of Orwellian "double-speak", concessive critics often affirm the divine authority and inspiration of Scripture while they speak simultaneously of scriptural error. It is no tribute to theological lucidity or integrity when religious double-talk requires orthodox believers to reinforce the self-evident meaning of the truthfulness of Scripture by appending the clarification that truth means "truth without any admixture of error."

As destructive higher criticism gained ground, some evangelicals reoriented their presentation of the truthfulness of Scripture from its traditional theological foundations to the empirical vindication of specific textual phenomena. The integrity of Scripture as God's Word was earlier deduced from God's authoritative self-revelation and from the divine inspiration of the canonical writings. But the case for the Bible's truthfulness was now shifted to a defense of critically-disputed passages, a defense that appealed to the same historical methodology that critics invoked in a venture that conservatives themselves characterized as a vindication of inerrancy.

To be sure, some churchmen championed the case for inerrancy by stressing Jesus' high regard for Scripture, thereby connecting the debate over the Bible not only with empirical compatibility, but also with christological considerations. But others appealed mainly to historical precedent, notably the teaching of the church fathers, and/or the Protestant Reformers, and/or the consensus of contemporary evangelical scholarship. If we examine such considerations, we must recognize frankly that despite the importance of tradition, what evangelicals affirm in any generation is not per se definitive of what they ought to believe. Church tradition is not a self-sufficient norm, and sociological statistics do not decisively establish the standard of doctrine. The appeal to majority approval can always be manipulated to reflect changing winds of doctrine, or can be reconnected with the opinions of elitists holding contrary views, but regarded as having superior wisdom.

Yet, for all that, the appeal to tradition is not by any means worthless and, in fact, is significantly impressive in acclaiming the truthfulness and trustworthiness of Scripture.

Nowhere does a biblical prophet or apostle as much as hint that scriptural teaching is untrue. The entire biblical heritage concurs with the stance of Jesus, who regarded Scripture as inviolable (John 10:35) and attributed error to those who disregard its teaching (Matt. 22:29). The early church was not embarrassed by Jesus' insistence that "not a letter, not a stroke" (N.E.B.) of God's scripturally-given law would remain unfulfilled (Matt. 5:18). The Christian apostles view Scripture as "God-breathed" (2 Tim. 3:16) and as divinely-imparted wisdom (2 Pet. 3:15). Frederick C. Grant acknowledges that the New Testament everywhere "takes for granted that what is written in Scripture is trustworthy, infallible and inerrant. No New Testament writer would ever dream of questioning a statement contained in the Old

Testament...." (*Introduction to New Testament Thought,* New York, Abingdon-Cokesbury Press, 1950, p. 75).

The church fathers nowhere attribute error to inspired Scripture, whether Old Testament or New; the truthfulness of the sacred writings is regarded as implicit in their divine authority and inspiration. Irenaeus explicitly declares that, as inspired, the biblical writers were "incapable of false statement" (*Against Heresies,* iii.16).

The medieval theological greats unhesitatingly affirm the inerrancy of inspired Scripture. Augustine writes: "Only those books of Scripture which are called canonical have I learned to hold in such honor as to believe their authors have not erred in any way in writing them" (*Epistolas,* XXXII, i [Pt. 33.277]). Thomas Aquinas declares: "...It is plain that nothing false can ever underlie the literal sense of Holy Scripture" ("The Nature of Sacred Doctrine", *Summa Theologica,* Article 10).

The Roman Catholic Church has historically affirmed that Scripture is inerrant. *The New Catholic Encyclopedia* (ed. Catholic University of America, New York, McGraw Hill, 1967) avers that "the inerrancy of Scripture has been the constant teaching of the Fathers, the theologians, and recent Popes in their encyclicals on Biblical studies" (Vol. II, p. 384). The Protestant Reformers maintain a commitment to the uncompromising truthfulness of Scripture. Luther commends Augustine's axiom "that only Holy Scripture is to be considered inerrant" (Weimar Ausgabe, 24:i, 347). M. Reu, in his classic study *Luther and the Scriptures* (Columbus, Ohio, Wartburg Press,1944) confirms that this is in fact Luther's view also. Calvin's stance is that of biblical inerrancy, as James Packer affirms ("Calvin and the Scriptures", in John

Warwick Montgomery, *God's Inerrant Word,* Minneapolis, Bethany Fellowship, 1974), and as even James Barr concedes *(Fundamentalism,* London, SCM Press, 1977, pp. 137 f.), and Emil Brunner also *(Revelation and Reason,* Philadelphia, Westminster Press, 1946, p. 275)—even if now and then Calvin inconsistently applies this principle.

The notion that the doctrine of inerrancy is a recent modern artifice—and more expressly that American fundamentalists invented it during the last half of the 19th century—is therefore discredited by the facts. The comprehensive truthfulness of Scripture is the historic Christian view. Frances Turretin insisted in his *Institutio Theologiae Elencticae* (1674) that the "words" of the divinely inspired biblical writings were "kept free from error". Rationalistic efforts to weaken the doctrine of inspiration were resisted from the late 16th century onward. Christian Pesch avers that "the very first softening of the doctrine of inspiration proceeded from the professors in the Academy of Saumur among whom [John] Cameron [1578-1625] introduces a difference between the Word of God and the books which contain it. He teaches that the substance is inspired but not the words....Nevertheless the students of Cameron did not apply this distinction but rather stated that God is the author of the whole Scripture but all things including details which are contained in it were written by men moved by the Holy Spirit and were stated by God to men" *(De Inspiratione Sacrae Scripturae,* Freiberg: Herder, 1906, pp. 250 f.). In the latter quarter of the 17th century, it was the Remonstrant church historian Jean LeClerc (1657-1736) who argued against the inerrancy and inspiration of some parts of the Bible. But before LeClerc affirmed mistakes in Scripture, even critical scholars—

Carl F.H. Henry

whether Protestant or Catholic—were extremely reluctant to suggest the possibility that the inspired Bible contains errors.

During the latter part of the 17th century, English churchmen characterized the Bible as "infallible truth". The founder of Methodism, John Wesley (1703-91), wrote of the Scriptures: "Every part thereof is worthy of God; and all together are one entire body wherein is no defect, no excess" (*The Works of John Wesley*, Grand Rapids, Zondervan, 1949, pp. 402 f.). The theologian who first told the English-speaking world that one can be a Christian while repudiating the verbal inerrancy of Scripture, Stephen Neill affirms, was the Cambridge divinity professor Herbert Marsh (1757-1839) who, as Bishop of Peterborough, "had an intense dislike of Evangelicals, and was determined to have none in his diocese, if he could possibly prevent it," and in fact, "none were licensed to serve" (*The Interpretation of the New Testament,* London, Oxford University Press, 1964, pp. 4 f.). Insistence on biblical inerrancy is found from the 1820s onward. Edward Bickersteth (1825-1906) declared the Bible "altogether true...without any admixture of error." Britain's Inter-Varsity Fellowship, founded in 1927, championed "the infallibility of Holy Scripture as originally given."

But the enthronement of higher criticism in the universities and the fascination it increasingly held for influential ecclesiastical leaders led to a diminished emphasis on biblical authority and encouraged an attitude of empirical openness. In David Bebbington's words: "A deductive approach to biblical inspiration, the belief that since the Bible is the Word of God and cannot err, the Bible is inerrant...has been a current in [British] Evangelicalism since the 1820s, but it never became unanimous and was weak in the early twentieth century. Its greater popularity in the post-war period has been associated primarily with the esteem of the Reformed wing of Evangelicalism...and it has been treated with reserve by others." As critical views of the Bible gained force, British proponents of scriptural inerrancy championed it less and less openly, and strict adherence to biblical teachings increasingly gave way among so-called "liberal evangelicals". (*Evangelicalism in Modern Britain: A History from the 1730s to the 1980s.* Winchester, Mass: Unwin Hyman, 1989.)

In America, by contrast, many influential 20th century evangelical theologians maintained biblical inerrancy, among them A. A. Hodge, B. B. Warfield, J. Gresham Machen, J. Oliver Buswell, Jr., William Childs Robinson, Roger Nicole, Kenneth S. Kantzer, Millard Erickson, Allan Coppedge, and also James Packer who had earlier championed the view in England. The inerrancy of the biblical autographs was affirmed by the Evangelical Theological Society and was reaffirmed by the International Council for Biblical Inerrancy. The view is reflected in the doctrinal statement of the National Association of Evangelicals as well as by all the major fundamentalist movements, and remains the commitment of the vast majority of American evangelicals. The term "infallibility" used in the National Association of Evangelicals' statement was not projected as a disavowal of inerrancy.

In summary, the comprehensive truthfulness of Scripture is the view of Jesus of Nazareth and of the Bible itself; the church fathers and medieval theologians affirm it; the Roman Catholic Church and the Protestant Reformers maintain it; and it remains normative for evangelical believers in our own time as well.

Carl F.H. Henry

At the same time, such conservative commendation of Scripture on the ground of apostolic and church tradition readily accommodates the notion that the doctrine of the truthfulness of Scripture is not intrinsic to Scripture. Even the appeal to Scripture's self-testimony, however important, gains a certain defensive cast if Scripture is not antecedently deduced from God in his authoritative disclosure and his consequent divine purpose and provision of Scripture as a revelatory instrument.

Some evangelicals focused readily on textual phenomena without reference to interpretative presuppositions, and hence engaged in conflict with radical critics by adopting a methodology to which such critics had already attached a naturalistic bias. In such debate, as Nigel M. de S. Cameron remarks, neither side lent importance to the fact that Scripture finds its necessary presupposition in the supernatural conveyance of rational truths to chosen prophets and apostles, and the consequent accurate inscription of that truth in human language (*Biblical Higher Criticism and the Defense of Infallibilism in 19th Century Britain,* Lewiston, N.Y., The Edwin Mellen Press, 1987). Destructive criticism meanwhile concealed its anti-supernatural or anti-miraculous bias. Insisting that the supposed inspiration of Scripture supplies no basis for treating Scripture differently from any other literature, and claiming to be philosophically neutral, it professed to derive its verdicts solely from the textual phenomena. In this way, *Religionsgeschichte* presuppositions subtly displaced divine inspiration as the overarching canopy within which the textual teaching was approached.

The normative theological view is that the Bible is revelatory because divine inspiration is a predicate of the text, and not merely because the Bible is a pious record of anterior divine self-disclosure or of anterior historical redemptive acts, or merely because it reflects a devout prophetic consciousness, and far less merely because of venerable church tradition. But the critically-altered approach to Scripture reflects a rationalistically trans-formed view of the supernatural and of the world, one whose presuppositions readily control the methodology. The probability or improbability of a miraculous event that somehow breaches "ordinary history" is not independent of the interpreter's cognitive approach to the data. The critical interpretations of the text depend for their validity upon a pejoratively qualified metaphysics, one that favors explanation by natural causes and is skeptical of the miraculous. The verdict on the reliability of the Bible is not unrelated to a prior judgment about the existence, nature and activity of a supernatural self-revealing God.

To be sure, biblical redemptive history does not differ from ordinary history in respect to its historicity, and the criteria for establishing historical factuality do not require a special evaluative canon. One might be tempted to say that what distinguishes revelatory redemptive acts from ordinary history is that redemptive acts are supernatural. But the limits of empirical historical method are such that it cannot in any case establish whether any act is supernatural. All historical acts—redemptive and non-redemptive—might in some sense be supernatural, but historical method is incompetent in any case to decide the matter. But if a historian is skeptical about the supernatural, he will be skeptical as well about the historicity of acts that are overtly declared to be supernatural.

Carl F.H. Henry

Historical method can provide initial help in interpreting the text, unless it is ventured on a conception that judges outcomes in advance and superimposes a preliminary bias that precludes hearing the text. If the interpreter channels the text's revelatory claims through reductionistic categories, he strips the text of its very capacity to speak a transcendent Word of God.

In defending scriptural inerrancy without stressing the limits of critical methodology, "mediating" evangelicals obscured the theological supports of the truthfulness of God's inscripturated disclosure of his nature and purposes, and they unwittingly yielded the initiative to negative critics who viewed textual phenomena through *Religionsgeschichte* premises. A precedent was thereby established that would later serve the subversion of the supernatural through a merging of form-criticism with existential philosophy, and through the acceptance of the historicist perspective based on Martin Heidegger's rejection of a creator-God for a supposedly "neutralist" attitude toward God's existence.

Many exegetes first yielded ground to the assault on scriptural reliability simply on the basis of historical criticism. Neo-orthodox scholars deflected this attack on the costly ground that historical argumentation was wholly irrelevant to the content of faith. Other mediating conservatives defended Scripture by appealing to extra-theological factors, such as evangelical consensus, yet allied themselves with anti-inerrantists who despite their forfeiture of the unbroken truthfulness of Scripture still claimed evangelical credentials because they retained most of the core beliefs. Still other conservative scholars, caught up in the debate over textual phenomena, all but abandoned or reinterpreted theological warrants, such as the teaching of the apostles or of Jesus of Nazareth, and apologetics replaced dogmatics as a forefront interest. Instead of affirming the integrity of Scripture as the comprehensive Word of God, their disclaimer of biblical error became the primary statement about Scripture. This reflected a defensive posture in which evangelical epistemology yielded and responded to the initiative of those who questioned the Bible's reliability.

The insistence that Scripture is inerrant is no doubt appropriate to an embattled and beleaguered church, one that seeks to stave off retreat by resisting aggressive higher criticism. But thereby it condemns itself to the task of apologetics as its main activity, and moves from admittedly flawed texts to unavailable autographs rather than from divinely-given originals to dependent copies; it leaves revealed theology and its implications too far in the background and, worse yet, encourages a recasting of dogmatics itself along empirico-inductive lines. As the ensuing apologetic debate proceeded, evangelical countermoves dwarfed the basic connection of the supernatural with the revelatory status of Scripture. Defense of scriptural inerrancy has an unfruitful prospect if interpretation leaves unchallenged the organic unity of all history grasped only in terms of anti-miraculous relationships. For contemporary history—and a particular view of contemporary history at that—then becomes determinative for all past possibility. The temptation arises to continue to speak of Scripture as the Word of God while avoiding the unabashed affirmation that Scripture *is* God's Word; thus a distinction is made between revelation and the Bible that prizes revelation while it accommodates an errant Bible.

Carl F.H. Henry

To be an evangelical is therefore not simply to champion biblical inerrancy rather than papal infallibility or empirical finality. It is to have a theistic mega-view that yields a distinctive role for the Bible as the literary corpus in which the self-revealing God of Judeo-Christian theology expounds his nature and plan for humanity and the nations. An abstracted emphasis on inerrancy readily sacrifices an awareness that two competing world views underlie the conflict over the Bible. Its attempt to rescue particular disputed passages may even unwittingly obscure a necessary challenge to anti-supernaturalist presuppositions that already implicitly assure critical victory by correlating literary analysis with disbelief in the miraculous. An anti-supernatural bias inevitably involves a secular misperception of inspiration and accommodates a devaluation of the text.

The tenuous nature of empirical argument concerning the text is graphically indicated by the growing skepticism of biblical scholars over what was perhaps the most deeply entrenched critical dogma of this century, namely the documentary hypothesis. The theory assumes that behind the Bible there exists an earlier more reliable text which the biblical writers revise by incorporating myths and legends that promote Hebrew-Christian religion. Despite its critical acclaim for several generations, many scholars now greet that theory with great skepticism, and others firmly disavow it. What was long held to be incontrovertible textual evidence, is acknowledged at last to have been only a speculative reconstruction rooted in arbitrary assumptions. Yet even so-called mediating evangelical scholars approached Scripture under the documentary theory's influence as if its permanent victory was assured. Critical assumptions were made decisive for the nature of the text and for the status of miracles, and adverse inferences were drawn from Genesis through the Gospels.

Thomas Kuhn's *The Structure of Scientific Revolutions* (Chicago, University of Chicago Press, 2nd ed., 1970) has familiarized our generation with the importance of paradigm shifts in the history of science. These shifts, involving the acceptance of once incongruous principles and axioms, provide strikingly different ways of accounting for observed data and constitute major turning-times in the history of thought. Kuhn likens such "transfer of allegiance from paradigm to paradigm" to "a conversion experience that cannot be forced." The naturalist sees the Bible through conceptual lenses adjusted only to impersonal processes and quantum events. This presuppositional framework adjusts all probabilities to its own premises, and espouses non-supernatural explanations. The interpreter greets any incompatible phenomena with assurance that "given enough time" all the data will prove to be congruent with his controlling assumptions.

The credibility of Christianity's claim for scriptural authority does not rest on the acceptability of biblical teaching to champions of contemporary empirical observation. Evangelical confidence in the truthfulness of the Bible derives not from empirically-limited observation but from Scripture's theologically-given status as God's supernaturally inspired Word, and its consequent status as the rule of faith and practice by which the living Christ through the Spirit exercises headship over the regenerate church.

For evangelical thought, a verdict on Scripture is a verdict on the nature of Christian revelation. Debate over this or that disputed text will inevitably occur when an empirically-oriented culture deals with supra-empirical phenomena or historical phenomena that cannot be reduplicated for laboratory observation, or empirical evaluations that are by nature incomplete and revisable. To be intimidating, problems must carry sufficient weight to threaten an entire system, that is, must comprise a menace to the undergirding postulates of Christian theism. The evangelical asks whether there is greater probability that Scripture is wrong or that a particular interpretation is wrong. Evangelical theology affirms the fallibility of all biblical expositors or critics—popes and theologians included—and reserves inerrancy for the divinely inspired scriptural autographs.

Among non-evangelicals the object of religious knowledge is more obscure, and religious language is necessarily more ambiguous and imprecise, than for evangelicals. The reason for these differences lies in the evangelical insistence that God has revealed himself intelligibly and can be rationally known, and moreover, that divine disclosure in sentences—to put it more technically, in propositional revelation—means that true information about God is available. Much as evangelicals insist on the incomprehensibility of God—that is, that God is knowable only in his self-revelation, and that our finite knowledge even on the basis of that revelation is not exhaustive—they do not glory in divine mystery but in God as revealed in his scriptural disclosure. To be sure, intellectual apprehension is not per se salvific, for personal faith is a gift of the Spirit, but faith is the whole self's appropriation of knowledge, for the Spirit uses truth as a means of persuasion.

Evangelical theologians consider theology an intellectual enterprise and shun claims that God can only be imagined or felt, or spoken of only in symbolic, metaphorical and figurative images. God's revelation is unfolded in the universally-sharable truths of inspired Scripture; and Scripture, not religious experience, remains the trustworthy source of valid information about God and his will. The Bible identifies God's redemptive acts and also states the divine interpretation and significance of those acts.

What the canon of Scripture teaches therefore conveys the comprehensive revelatory message, and christological truth—Jesus crucified for sinners and risen as Lord—is the dramatic focal center to which all the core beliefs are integral. The biblically-embedded gospel of Jesus' atoning death and bodily resurrection crowns the theological doctrines that divinely inspired Scripture authorizes. The *kerygma*, or apostolic preaching, was not confined to an agenda of selective doctrines specially useful for polemical purposes. Important as is Jesus' virgin birth, apostolic preaching did not make an obsession of it; important as is the inerrancy of Scripture, apostolic preaching proclaimed Scripture more than inerrancy. The apostles did not isolate certain fundamentals, but rather proclaimed the whole counsel of God (Acts 20:27).

Any abridgement of the complete canonical context threatens to put the redemptive message at risk. Not even a five-fold doctrinal test—or, if you prefer, a ten-fold test—will do. The core is Christ's salvific death for penitent sinners and the crucified Christ's resurrection from death; the context is God's complete counsel, the entire biblical disclosure. What do we hope to gain if we protest the critical dilution of biblical authority and then distill the essence of the whole into some five-fold fundamentalist test or ten-fold evangelical affirmation over and above the *evangel*, so

Carl F.H. Henry

that the *evangel* as such becomes in effect merely one plank among many, or if we elaborate some supposedly relevant modern credal confession that deliberately veils scriptural authority? In forging contemporary confessions of faith, the temptation is always present, and seldom resisted, selectively to disengage the Christian community from unwelcome doctrines and to applaud preferred aspects of Scripture that through such detachment from the whole become tendential.

Christianity is unapologetically a supernaturally-grounded religion. It gains nothing through a process of chipping and chopping that presumes to make it more acceptable by emphasizing only what least offends a naturalistic mindset.

Evangelicals, in summary, are spiritually regenerated sinners who worship the supernatural self-revealing God as the sovereign source, support and judge of all creaturely life. They affirm that on the ground of the substitutionary life and work of Jesus Christ, the holy Lord mercifully delivers the penitent from spiritual death and its dire consequences, and restores them to fellowship and service. This God does, moreover, in accord with the inspired Scriptures that comprise his authoritative Word and Truth and constitute the rule of faith and doctrine by which the risen Christ through the Holy Spirit governs the regenerate church. Evangelicals are a people of the Bible and of the risen Redeemer; historically speaking, consistent evangelicals have never been cognitively constrained either to demean the Saviour or to demean the Book in order to be wholly faithful to one or both.

RESPONSE TO CARL F. H. HENRY

Nathan O. Hatch

It is an honor to be at this conference and a double one to have the opportunity to interact with a paper of Dr. Carl F.H. Henry. Over the last half-century, no evangelical voice has been more articulate, insightful, and wise in calling theologically conservative protestants in America to carry out their responsibilities in the modern world. His defense of theological orthodoxy, his call to responsible involvement, and his leadership in bringing together evangelicals of varying ecclesiastical persuasion all attest to his powerful vision that evangelicals engage the modern naturalistic world with the claims of historic, supernatural Christianity. Mr. Henry, all of us stand deeply in your debt for a lifetime of faithful service to the Kingdom.

In his paper to us, "Who Are the Evangelicals", Mr. Henry reiterates several themes that have characterized his writing over the years. First, he depicts the terrain of the 20th century to which the Church is called as a fundamental philosophical struggle that pits modern naturalism against biblical supernaturalism, theism versus a materialistic view of the cosmos. Secondly, Mr. Henry struggles to portray the motley array of theologically conservative Christians and Churches in America as an identifiable "evangelical" movement. The question of definition which he asks, "What's in a name?" underscores Mr. Henry's long concern to challenge the rampant pluralism of evangelicals and to bind them more into a common movement, one that can better defend supernatural Christianity before a secular world.

95

Nathan O. Hatch

A third theme in this paper that resonates with Mr. Henry's long-established concerns is an effort to clarify theological boundaries. What does it mean to be evangelical or to use his phrase to be "consistent evangelicals?" As he has done for the last decade, Mr. Henry takes what might be called a moderate view of inerrancy: defending its importance as a staple of evangelical identity, but critiquing those for whom the disclaimer of biblical error becomes the primary statement about Scripture. This defensive posture, he suggests, can sacrifice an awareness that two competing world views underlie conflicts over the Bible. Henry calls for proclaiming the whole counsel of God rather than remaining fixed upon certain fundamentals.

I heartily agree with each of these points, as would most people here assembled. Mr. Henry's definition of "evangelical," focusing on the work of Christ and the trustworthiness of Scripture, is straightforward and, I think, uncontroversial. But it is also frustrating in at least one respect. It is a definition that has a timeless and abstract quality. His brief biblical statement of evangelical identity could be applied to Christians anywhere in the world today or to any epoch in the history of the Church. By all means we need this kind of definition; but it also does little to orient us as evangelicals living in a specific place and time: American evangelicals facing particular problems and opportunities at the close of the 20th century. "If we knew where we were and whither we were tending," Abraham Lincoln said, "we would know better what to do and how to do it." My comments today address the structure of evangelical life today, the specific challenges that will face those who defend the name of Christ and the authority of Scripture.

Response

I see at least three great challenges that face American evangelicals in the coming years: 1) the reality of rampant pluralism; 2) a need to recover a higher view of the Church; and 3) a need to nurture first-order Christian scholarship. Let me briefly state why I think these are pressing challenges for American evangelicals on the eve of the 21st century.

1. The Reality of Rampant Pluralism.

I am not as sanguine as Mr. Henry in speaking about the evangelical movement. In truth, there is no such thing as evangelicalism. The vitality of conservative Protestantism in America, since the very early 19th century, has been directly related to its entrepreneurial quality, its populist and decentralized structure, and its penchant for splitting, forming, and reforming. Fundamentalism, The Holiness Movement, and Pentecostalism, the most immediate heirs of most of us in this room, were generic names that easily mask the pluralism and decentralization of these movements. All were extremely diverse coalitions dominated by scores of self-appointed and independent-minded religious leaders.

The emergence of "card carrying evangelicals" after World War II under the banner of Billy Graham, Wheaton College, *Christianity Today*, the NEA, organizations such as Campus Crusade and Young Life and seminaries such as Gordon-Conwell, Trinity, and Fuller led to certain concerted efforts among theologically conservative protestants and a certain deference to recognized leaders such as Billy Graham, Harold Ockenga, and I might add, the two conveners of this conference, Kenneth S. Kantzer and Carl F.H. Henry. This has been an era characterized by evangelical congresses, conferences, caucuses, councils, and

Nathan O. Hatch

consultations. Yet unhappily that age is now coming to an end and the next generation simply does not have the same kind of recognized leaders. Nor will it have the Billy Graham Organization, which has provided the financial and organizational glue to make much common activity possible.

I would suggest that in the coming years centrifugal forces will continue to accelerate and leadership will be parceled out by powerful figures, self-appointed, many with media orientation. No one can predict the rise to authority of a James Dobson, a Chuck Swindoll, a John MacArthur, a D. James Kennedy, or a Bill Hybels. The evangelical world is extremely dynamic, but there are few church structures to which many of its adherents or leaders are subject. The evangelical world is decentralized, competitive, and driven by those who can build large and successful organizations. It is this instability that I think is problematic for theological integrity.

2. The Need to Recover a Higher View of the Church

That leads me to the second challenge facing us: to recover a higher view of the Church as an institution. The instability and volatility that I suggest faces evangelicals is compounded by how little most evangelists value the traditions that develop in any institutional expression of the Christian Church. In a world increasingly rootless, evangelicals need to draw sustenance from the Church and its traditions. So much of evangelical life is freshly minted new congregations, new publications, new seminaries. Few of us stand in a religious tradition which provides ballast and long-term orientation.

Never has this problem been more acute. Jonathan Edwards knew he was Reformed and a part of The Standing Order of New England; and he wrestled within that tradition to clarify and preserve evangelical distinctives. John Wesley, for all his insistence upon evangelical reform, cherished the institutional Church and worked within its structures. Too many of us evangelicals today divest ourselves of being Presbyterian or Baptist, or Disciples, or Lutheran, or Methodist. We fall into reinventing the Church every time a new vision seems workable, or anytime strong disagreement disturbs a congregation.

The decline of denominational identity is a trend affecting all Americans. It does open new opportunities for evangelicals, but it also leaves us more subject to the whim of the moment, more cut off from the riches of given traditions and less capable of expressing Christianity in its intellectual depth as powerful and profound.

3. The Need to Nurture First-order Christian Scholarship.

This leads me to the third challenge: that of nurturing first-order Christian scholarship. In recent years the United States has become more secular and more religious at the same time. The crucial point to note is the contrasting sectors of society in which these trends are taking place. Religion is abounding in the realm of popular culture and in ways that concentrate on breadth of audience rather than depth of insight. In the realm of high culture–in the best universities, in the arts, in literary circles–the juggernaut of secularism rolls on, pressing religious belief into territory that is smaller and of less consequence.

Nathan O. Hatch

For at least two reasons, evangelicals are not prepared to face this challenge to win the right to be heard by 20th century intellectuals.

1) First, the decentralized structure of the evangelical world inhibits the expensive and painstakingly-slow task of Christian thinking. There simply is no evangelical college or seminary today (amidst the scores that exist) that begins to provide faculty with the time for thought and writing provided at any good research university. We simply are not competing on an equal field.

2) The very structures of the evangelical world that have developed since World War II inhibit evangelicals from writing in ways that would be taken seriously by non-evangelicals. Evangelicals have developed their own publishing houses, their own journals, their own media outlets, their own associations. The very success of these evangelical ventures make it all too easy for evangelical scholars to write only with their own theological works in view. Instead of engaging those who hold naturalistic assumptions, we too easily spend our energies in intramural debate discussing issues which are incomprehensible to those outside the evangelical camp.

Since I am a historian, let me draw a lesson from the past. In the nineteenth century, evangelicals were every bit as committed to a vital and living faith in Christ as we are now. But they were also committed to biblical visions of social reform and intellectual discourse. Shortly after World War I, however, evangelicals by and large abandoned both social activism and their participation in the intellectual life of the nation in what has since come to be called "The Great Reversal." In the last generation evangelicals have heeded the prophetic words of Carl Henry's 1947 book *The Uneasy Conscience of Modern Fundamentalism* and have taken significant steps forward in reclaiming that lost vision of social service. Evangelicals are committed in the strongest possible terms to translate their faith into down-to-earth service to other human beings.

This morning I want to leave you with the challenge to reclaim the lost vision of Christian intellectual life just as we have reclaimed the lost vision of Christian social service. It is once again time to broaden our vision back to our original biblical calling, to give our minds, as well as our hearts and souls, in unstinting service to Christ. I think in some ways evangelicals today are less inclined and less capable of speaking beyond our own borders than they were 40 years ago. The very success of evangelical institutions conspires to make us more rather than less insular.

For many years now the best evangelical minds have conceded scholarly inquiry to intellectuals with naturalist assumptions, but now might be an especially propitious time to turn this trend around. In some ways the larger scholarly community seems to be questioning its assumptions, and the small but vital cadre of evangelical scholars which has developed in the last forty years may be positioned to offer an alternative voice in the academic world. Should evangelicals and their institutions begin to support scholarship seriously, to proclaim God's sovereignty in the life of the mind as well as the life of the heart, evangelical scholars might be able to put together a communal effort which would begin to reclaim strategic enclaves within an intellectual terrain that remains dominantly secular.

QUESTIONS
FOR DISCUSSION

1. In what ways have evangelicals of recent years hurt their own cause? What can be done differently in the near future?

2. Is a positive image for evangelicalism in the secular media possible today? Why or why not? How important is it for evangelicals to maintain a positive image?

3. How can evangelicals best clarify who they are and what they believe for the secular media?

4. What distinguishes evangelicals from non-evangelicals? Are some of these distinguishing elements more important than others?

5. Does a "complete statement of the Gospel embrace the truthfulness of Scripture"? What is the relationship between the Gospel and the authority of Scripture?

4

SALVATION

EVANGELICALS AND THE WAY OF SALVATION

New Challenges to the Gospel: Universalism, and Justification by Faith

J. I. Packer

I

Whether in this land of pitchers, plates, diamonds and strikes I can make a point by talking of English cricket I do not know. But I am going to try.

Half-way through the afternoon of Monday, July 20, 1981, in Leeds, Yorkshire, England was in trouble. It was the fourth day of the third of six five-day test matches against Australia. The first had been lost, the second drawn, and this, the third, now seemed doomed. The seventh player in England's second inning had just been dismissed with the score at 135; this was still 92 runs behind Australia's first inning total of 401, and only three more Englishmen remained to bat, while Australia had an entire second inning still to come. In cricket the batsmen (whom you may call strikers if you prefer) operate in pairs, and as the new man walked to the wicket, his partner, Ian Botham, who had so far scored 23, went to meet him. The following dialogue then took place, in the idiom that you might call sportsman's swagger. Botham: "You don't fancy hanging around on this wicket for a day and a half, do you?" New batsman: "No way." Botham: "Right; come on, let's give it some humpty." Which they did, hitting the ball all over the field to such good effect that, incredibly, England's score rose to 356, with Botham making 149, before the last man was out. Australia

J. I. Packer

was then dismissed for less than the 129 runs needed to win, and an apparently inevitable defeat had been turned into a famous victory, vividly illustrating the truth that attack is the best form of defence. [1]

I tell you that story so as to tune you in to the fact that, as I see it, the subject area that I have been given requires that, like Botham, I too give it a bit of humpty, and attack. Truths that seem to me vital are threatened, and to reaffirm them effectively I shall have to hit out — not only at non-evangelicals, but at some of my evangelical brothers too. I have no wish to hurt anyone's feelings, but I must take a risk on that, for my judgment is that on matters so grave only forthright statement can be appropriate or adequate. So prepare for strong words.

II

First, I would like to make clear where I come from. I speak out of a heritage that is several centuries old, namely the theological approach that is rooted in the two tenets once singled out by Melanchthon as the foundation-principles of the Reformation. The first foundation-principle is the formal one, namely the authority of the Scriptures, or, more fully, their sufficiency for all questions of faith, life, and action of the authoritative, God-breathed, self-interpreting biblical canon, which the Holy Spirit opens our minds and enlightens our hearts to understand. The second foundation-principle, the substantial one, is justification by faith only, or more fully, our entire and final acceptance by God, here and now, on Christ's account, through the faith that in self-despair and a sense of guilt, shame, weakness, and spiritual hunger looks to Jesus Christ in conscious trust to worship and serve him as our sin-bearing Savior. I shall shortly focus attention on the second of these principles, but I see need at the outset to state my methodology in a clear and sharp-edged way, for I think it is a lack of clarity here that produces the erosions of belief elsewhere on which I have to comment.

I begin, then, by affirming, with Reformed theology generally, that acceptance of all that Scripture teaches, and a refusal either to add to it or subtract from it in our thinking about God, and the absolutizing of it as our interpretative framework for understanding everything else, is categorically necessary, for two reasons.

The first reason is that the fallen human mind, biased and warped as it is, more or less, by the universal anti-God syndrome called sin, fails to form and own and retain within itself true notions about the Creator drawn from general revelation, whether in the order and course of the world, our own created makeup, or the workings of natural conscience. God's general revelation of himself, though genuinely given to all, is correctly received by none. Scripture makes this point by speaking of our human minds as *darkened* and *blinded*, and of our hearts as *hardened*.[2]

The second reason is that regenerate believers, to whom the Spirit interprets the Scriptures, are nonetheless still prone to lapse intellectually into the world's ways of thinking, just as sometimes they lapse morally into the world's ways of behaving, and so they need constant critical correction and redirection by the Word of God.

The reality of spiritual darkness in all minds was recognized by none of the subjectivist theologians of the Enlightenment and the Romantic movement, whatever spot on the spectrum that links rationalism and mysticism each occupied; and nowadays it is hard to get even evangelicals to take it seriously. But the Bible acting as judge and guide is a cognitive necessity for benighted sinners like ourselves, and evangelicals no less than others must learn to suspect themselves when they find themselves embracing innovations and modifications of view that reflect in a direct way the secular culture around them. To fall victim to secular philosophy and ideology has been a characteristic Protestant vice for three centuries, and it is one from which evangelicals are by no means free. To be an avowed Bible-believer is no guarantee that one's interpretation of the Bible will always be right, or that secularist distortions will never invade one's mind to discolor one's thoughts. We affirm this, pontifically enough, with regard to (for instance) Jehovah's Witnesses; we need humbly to remember that we face the same danger also.

How then may we avoid subjectivist eccentricity in our own biblical interpretation? The first necessity is precision in handling texts. The canon that God in his wisdom gave us is a miscellany of occasional writings, each anchored in a particular socio-cultural milieu and grammatical-historical exegesis. To discover what each passage meant as a message about God written on his behalf to a particular envisaged readership, must be our first step. But then, in order to determine what meaning God has for us in this historical material, we must go on to an *a posteriori* theological analysis and application according to the analogy of Scripture. By theological analysis, I mean seeing what truths about God and his world the passage teaches, or assumes, or illustrates. By theological application, I mean reflecting on how these truths impact our lives today. When I say that this analysis and application must be *a posteriori,* I mean that nothing must be read into texts that cannot be read out of them. When I say that it must be faithful, I mean that nothing taught by any text may be disregarded or left unapplied. When I speak of the analogy of Scripture, I am referring to the traditional procedures of letting one part of Scripture throw light on another that deals with the same subject, and of maintaining internal theological coherence by interpreting ambiguous passages in harmony with unambiguous ones, and of allowing things that define themselves as primary and central to provide a frame of reference and a perspective for looking at those that are secondary and peripheral.[3] By observing these principles we may with the help of God's Spirit rise via the teaching of each author in his own situation to perceive the teaching of God himself as it bears on us in our situation. But if we allow ourselves, as so many do, to discount specific teachings of Scripture as being out of line with the Bible's main thrust, or to think it possible that God's penmen did not always manage to express what they intended to say, or to suppose that while God kept them right on major matters he left them free to go wrong on details, we may expect, I think — and here, *pace* Jack Rogers and Donald McKim, I have nearly five centuries of responsible evangelical opinion with me — to be constantly going astray on matters of importance.[4] The instances of relativistic and impressionistic slippage that we shall discuss now might well be cases in point.

III

Evangelicals have always seen the question of salvation as one of supreme importance, and their witness to the way of salvation as the most precious gift they bring to the rest of the church.

J. I. Packer

This conviction rests not on the memory of the conversion of Paul or Augustine or Luther or Wesley or Whitefield or any other evangelical hero, but on the emphasis with which the Bible itself highlights salvation as its central theme. The Scriptures — or perhaps I should say, preachers like Christ, Peter, Paul, Isaiah, and Ezekiel, as recorded in the Scriptures — clearly regard ordinary human beings as lost, and accordingly call on them to repent, turn or return to God, come to Christ, put faith in him, and so find the pardon, peace, and newness of life that they need. The main concepts that the New Testament uses to delineate this salvation are reconciliation, redemption, and propitiation, all won for us by the sacrificial death of Christ; forgiveness, remission of sins, justification, adoption; regeneration or renovation (that is, new birth); the indwelling of the Holy Spirit as God's seal of ownership within us; sanctification; and glorification. By contrast the chief notions that are used to describe the condition of those who do not believe in Jesus Christ, whether they have heard the gospel or not, are spiritual deadness, darkness of mind, delusion with regard to God, gods, and supernatural powers generally, moral delinquency bringing guilt and shame, and a destiny of certain distress. Paul speaks of "the day of God's wrath, when his righteous judgment will be revealed, and God will give to each person according to what he has done. To those who by persistence in doing good seek glory, honor and immortality, he will give eternal life. But for those who are self-seeking, and who reject the truth and follow evil, there will be wrath and anger" (Rom. 2:5-8). Thus, those who are not Christ's are perishing, and need to be saved. Historic evangelicalism, with some differences, I grant, of nuance in exposition and of evangelistic practice, but with great solidarity of substance, as the literature from Luther on attests, has constantly affirmed these things. Modern evangelicalism will stand revealed as a degenerate plant if it does not just as constantly do the same.

There are, however, strong tendencies at work today that press evangelicals to revise these views. I shall deal with four such tendencies, which in *ad hominem* form may be stated as follows:

1. The question of salvation is less *urgent* than evangelicals have thought. This contention raises the issue of universalism, and the destiny of those who never heard the gospel.

2. The question of salvation is less *agonizing* than evangelicals have thought. This contention raises the issue of conditional immortality, and the annihilation of unbelievers following the last judgment.

3. Justification by faith is a less *central* doctrine than evangelicals have thought. It is contended that for Paul, its chief expositor, justification was only significant for anti-Jewish polemic, and the heart of his gospel was elsewhere.

4. Faith is a less *substantial* reality than evangelicals thought. Some dissolve away its cognitive substance, treating it simply as an existential commitment to a behavior pattern like that which the gospels ascribe to Jesus, while denying that it assumes or requires any specific beliefs about Jesus' deity, saviorhood, or even (in Tillich's case) historicity. Others dissolve away every element in faith except its cognitive substance, treating it as simply the mind's grateful acknowledgment that Jesus, the incarnate Son of God, died for one's sins. On that view, cheap grace as denounced by Bonhoeffer is gospel truth after all; easy-believism is the true way of salvation, just as the Western religious world on

the fringe of the churches wishes to think, and antinomianism really is the true Christian life.

We will review these proposed revisions of historic evangelical soteriology in order, though spending most time on the first (the big one!).

IV

The basis of the first revision, whereby the urgency of the question of salvation is destroyed, is the belief that some form of universalism is true. By universalism I mean, not Christianity's claim to be a faith for all mankind as distinct from a tribal or ethnic religion, but belief that, as the late C. H. Dodd somewhere put it, "as every human being lies under God's judgment, so every human being is ultimately destined, in God's mercy, to eternal life." This is *apokatastasis* (restoration) according to Origen, the doctrine of the guaranteed future salvation of all mankind, including Judas, the thieving hypocrite of whom Jesus himself said: "Woe to that man who betrays the Son of Man! It would be better for him if he had not been born" (Mt. 26:24). Universalists, however, must respectfully decline to endorse Jesus' judgment here, at least in its obvious meaning, since they themselves expect Judas to be saved.

Universalism, which was condemned in the fifth century and quiescent till the nineteenth, is currently popular, and on the march, among both Protestants and Roman Catholics. Its motivations are complex. A last-century story pinpoints two of them. The question was asked: what is the difference between Unitarians and Universalists? The answer given was: The Unitarians believe that God is too good to damn anyone; the Universalists believe that man is too good for God to damn. Today, only the most thoughtless sentimentalist could maintain that man is too good for God to damn, for all the facts about human nature that the twentieth century can claim to have uncovered highlight our moral flaws. Many, however, press with zeal the momentous claim that only a doctrine of universal salvation does justice to the reality of God's love for mankind, and of Christ's victory won on the cross, and of the praiseworthiness of God who has providentially permitted so much inhumanity of man to man, so much unfruitful suffering, and so much waste of good, in the course of world history.[5] Other motivations towards universalism operate too. The monist or panentheist conception of God's relation to the world makes it necessary that the eschatological consummation whereby, as Paul puts it, God "heads up" all things in Christ (Eph. 1:10), with every knee bowing at the name of Jesus and God himself becoming "all in all" (1 Cor. 15:28) should involve every rational being relating harmoniously to the God of love in responsive loving rapport. This is the characteristic view of process theology, the fag-end of Anglo-Saxon liberalism, which, though uncertain whether the consummation can ever actually happen (because its God is so far from being omnipotent and sovereign over his world), is quite certain that the responsive love of every rational soul to God is part of the definition of it. Without universal reconciliation to God the consummation would not be a consummation: that is the argument. So among the theologians it is the supposed demands of eschatology, as well as of Christology, soteriology, theodicy, and doxology, that prompt universalist opinion.

It is not only at the level of reflective theology that motivations to universalism have emerged in our day. Pastoral motiva-

J. I. Packer

tions operate too. H. O. J. Brown identifies as a "motive to universalism a sense of the futility and failure of the Christian enterprise. It is not on the mission field that universalism is strongest, despite its obvious emotional appeal to those with unconverted loved ones. Nor is it in North America, where evangelism and renewal are prominent if not dominant features of the Christian scene. It is in Europe, among the theologians, preachers, and people especially of the state-supported churches, who observe that most of Western Europe ignores Christ and has no higher value than hedonistic self-fulfillment. Because they are not winning others to Christ, but are being ignored, some people like to say, 'It doesn't really matter; everybody will be saved in the end' — a confession of failure, a sort of baptizing of our own powerlessness."[6] And this rationalizing reaction (as I believe it to be) to gross evangelistic and pastoral failure will, as Brown notes, itself operate as a cause of further failure in the future, because "if one thinks this way, there is scant motive to seek to bring people to conversion or renewal." If all are, as the title of a 19th century tract put it, "Doomed to be Saved", then the heat is off so far as evangelism is concerned, and it will be proper to give other ways of loving your neighbor a permanent priority over evangelizing him. It is no accident, I think, that universalism and Christian socialism have long walked hand in hand, nor that the theological thought of the World Council of Churches, which has in effect redefined mission as the necessary quest for socio-politico-economic *shalom,* with church-planting evangelism as an additional option if circumstances, time, and energy allow it to be fitted in, has a pronouncedly universalistic cast.

Evangelicals and the Way of Salvation

No evangelical, I think, need hesitate to admit that in his heart of hearts he would like universalism to be true. Who can take pleasure in the thought of people being eternally lost? If you want to see folk damned, there is something wrong with you! Universalism is thus a comfortable doctrine in a way that alternatives are not. But wishful thinking, based on a craving for comfort and a reluctance to believe that some of God's truth might be tragic, is no sure index of reality. Yesterday's evangelicals felt the attraction of universalism, I am sure, just as poignantly as we do, but they denounced the doctrine as morally weakening and spiritually deadening. They equated it with the world's first falsehood, the devil's declaration in Eden, "you will not surely die." They saw it as the modern version of the first piece of armor that the devil puts on Mansoul in Bunyan's *Holy War,* namely "the hope of doing well at the last what life soever you have lived." And they preached and prayed as they believed — especially, it seems, prayed. Evangelicals know that the power behind the eighteenth century revivals and the great nineteenth century missionary movement was prayer, and that the prayer was made out of hearts agonizing over the prospect of all who leave this world without Christ being lost. Was such prayer misconceived? uninstructed? foolish? wrong-headed? An evangelical who values his heritage must ponder that question, recognizing that if universalism is true, all that missionary passion and praying was founded on a monstrous mistake. Could so much evangelical piety have been so far astray?

But universalism, like all other matters of doctrine, is ultimately a biblical question, and the evangelical way to assess it is by reference, not to our heritage, but to the Bible. So I shall now attempt a biblical response to the universalist thesis.

117

J. I. Packer

The universalist task is to circumvent the seemingly solid New Testament witness to the fate of the unbelievers, who are declared to be under sin, law, wrath and death (so says Romans 3:9, 19, 1:18, 5:17), alienated from God and without hope (so says Ephesians 2:12), facing exclusion from God's presence as punishment for their non-subjection to as much of the law and the gospel as they knew (Rom. 1:18-2:16). Jesus himself is strong on the horrific consequences of rejecting him: as W. G. T. Shedd said a century ago, "Jesus Christ is the person who is responsible for the doctrine of eternal perdition."[7] Granted that Jesus' references to weeping and grinding teeth, outer darkness, worm and fire, gehenna, and the great gulf fixed, are imagery, the imagery clearly stands for a terrible retribution. Nor, be it said, do Bible writers find a moral problem in catastrophic retribution; instead, they see such retribution as solving the moral problem of evil being allowed to run loose in God's good world, because retribution vindicates God's righteousness as judge of all the earth (see Rev. 19:1-5). How can universalism be affirmed on a biblical basis, we ask, in the face of all this?

Here the ways divide. Roman Catholic universalists refuse to believe that any human beings fail to receive grace that moves them to seek God inwardly here and now, or that any form of religion in this world fails to bring its faithful adherents the salvation that Christians know through Christ. Serious attempts to find biblical support for such speculations are, however, lacking. Protestant universalists, however, usually follow a different route, arguing that those who leave this world in unbelief do indeed go to hell, but in due course come out of it, having been brought to their senses, and so to a positive response to Christ, through the harrowing torment they have tasted. Hell thus does for unbelievers what Rome thinks purgatory does for believers — that is, it fits them for heaven. So Protestant universalism appears as a doctrine of salvation out of what the New Testament calls "eternal destruction", "eternal punishment", and "perdition", through some kind of post-mortem encounter with Christ and his offer of mercy (a "second chance" for some, a "first chance" for others). This view is a speculation that differs from other "second-chance" speculations by its categorical confidence that the post-mortem invitation to turn to Christ will succeed in every single case. Debating responses leap to mind: if as a Calvinist one posits God's sovereign ability to call all men effectually to himself after death, the question arises as to why in that case he does not do it here, while if as an Arminian one thinks it beyond God's power to bring all men to faith here, the question arises as to how in that case he will be able to do it there. But is there biblical warrant for universalist speculation? There does not appear to be. Exegetical arguments fail, for no text certainly and unambiguously asserts universal final salvation, and those that verbally admit of such a construction are more naturally taken in a more restricted sense, as the standard commentaries do in fact take them.[8] And there are Bible-based counter-arguments, some of which I shall now briefly deploy, casting them into question form.

(1) Does not universalism deny the sufficiency of Scripture? What warrant have we for embracing any speculation that lacks explicit biblical support, and basing our attitudes and actions directly upon it?

(2) Does not universalism ignore something that Scripture stresses, namely the unqualified decisiveness of this life's deci-

sions for our eternal destiny? What point is Jesus making when he warns the unbelieving Jews that they will die in their sins (Jn. 8:21), and speaks of the great gulf fixed between two sorts of people, the godly and the ungodly, after death (Lk. 16:26), and declares that speaking against the Holy Spirit will not be forgiven either here or hereafter (Mt. 12:32)? What point is Paul making when he declares that spiritually one reaps what one sows, either eternal life or destruction (Gal. 6:7f.), and that at Christ's judgment seat each person will "receive what is due him for the things done while in the body, whether good or bad" (2 Cor. 5:10)? Heb. 2:1f., 3:8-4:11, 6:4-8, 10:26-31, 12:15-17, 25, and Rev. 20:6, 10, 14f., 27, 21:8, 14f., would also come into the argument at this juncture.

(3) Does not universalism imply that the preaching of Christ and the apostles, who warned people to flee from the judgment of hell-fire by repentance here and now, is either inept or immoral? If the preachers did not themselves know that all were finally to be saved, their preaching was inept (and so today's universalists are wiser than Christ); if they knew it but concealed it, so as to bluff people into the kingdom by using the fear motive, their preaching was immoral (and so today's universalist preachers can be more righteous than Christ). Is either alternative acceptable? "We must preach hell," wrote Nels Ferré, "as having a school and a door in it."[9] But why did not Jesus preach hell that way? The question presses; and if no satisfactory answer to it can be found, can universalism be right?

(4) Is not universalism rejected by each Christian's own conscience? Charity and wishful thinking may make us want to affirm a universalism that embraces everyone else, but would we

be able to envisage our own spiritual pilgrimage in the terms in which we would then be envisaging theirs? Surely there is no answer to the dictum of James Denney: "I dare not say to myself that if I forfeit the opportunity this life affords I shall ever have another; and therefore I dare not say so to another man."[10] To hand others a lifebelt to which I could not entrust myself is neither compassionate nor humble, but at best thoughtless and at worst cynical. But is not this where universalism would lead me?

But if, under pressure from such questions, we stop our ears to the universalist siren song, how shall we then rebut the claim that in this world of sin and pain, where it seems that in every Christian era most people die without knowing the Gospel and most who hear it are unmoved by it, universalist belief is needed to do justice to the biblical themes of God's love, Christ's victory at Calvary, and divine competence in world-management? Is there any viable theodicy — any way, that is, of showing God to be gloriously in the right, and thus worthy of our praise — other than that of process theology, which sees God as intending universal salvation but does not know if he can bring it off, or of universalism, which rests its theodicy on the certainty that he can and will? Yes, there is a further option in theodicy; it is the option that evangelical theology has historically embraced, and that direct biblical exegesis without extrapolation and speculation actually establishes. It can be set out like this.

(1) The sin that God mysteriously chooses to permit and humans madly choose to commit so offends God, and so robs them of value in his sight, that retribution for the impenitent becomes the natural reaction whereby he expresses his holy nature. This self-vindicating judicial righteousness is glorious, and calls for praise.

J. I. Packer

(2) Mysteriously again, God chooses to extend mercy to the penitent — mercy at which general revelation hints, and which the gospel shows to be based on costly blood atonement and defined in generous promises of justification, regeneration, and glorification. This marvelous mercy is glorious, and calls for praise.

(3) Mysteriously once more, God maintains in all developed human beings the power of self-determining moral choice, and respects their choices, while yet, paradoxically, all who choose to trust God's mercy find themselves constrained to say that it was not their own intelligence or will-power, but the illuminating and drawing action of God himself that brought them to faith. Both aspects of this situation are glorious, and call for praise.

(4) Mysteriously, too, God sanctifies all believers' sufferings, through their faith-experience of the power of the risen Christ, as a means of furthering that character conformity to Christ that is their destiny. This also is glorious, and calls for praise.

(5) Mysteriously yet once more, God sends his people to publish the gospel throughout the human community, promising that as they plead with people to trust God through Christ and plead with God to touch people through grace, others will enter that new life that is being proclaimed. Here, again, is a glorious fact that calls for praise.

My use of "mysteriously" is meant as a reminder that in each of these purposes and works of God there is much that is beyond us to grasp, and moreover that many of our questions about them are left unanswered by the Word of God. But my contention here is that despite this ignorance we have in the awareness, which my five points encompass, that all who are saved are saved by grace through faith, while all who perish do so through the fault of their own choice and impenitence, a magnificent theodicy that for time and eternity must prompt undying praise.

One final point. A British lay theologian, Sir Norman Anderson, poses an often-asked question as follows: "Might it not be true of the follower of some other religion that the God of all mercy had worked in his heart by his Spirit, bringing him in some measure to realize his sin and need for forgiveness, and enabling him, in his twilight as it were, to throw himself on God's mercy?"[11] The answer surely is: yes, it might be true, as it seems to have been true for some non-Israelites in Old Testament times: think of Melchizedek, Job, Naaman, Cyrus, Nebuchadnezzar, the sailors in Jonah's boat, and the Ninevites to whom he preached, for starters. In heaven, any such penitents will learn that they were saved by Christ's death and their hearts were renewed by the Holy Spirit, and they will worship God accordingly. Christians since the second century have voiced the hope that there are such people, and we may properly voice the same hope today. But — and this is the point to consider — we have no warrant from Scripture to expect that God will act thus in any single case where the Gospel is not yet known. To cherish this hope, therefore, is not to diminish in the slightest our urgent and never-ending missionary obligation, any more than it is to embrace universalism as a basis for personal and communal living. Living by the Bible means assuming that no one will be saved apart from faith in Christ, and acting accordingly.

V

Now we turn to the second proposed revision of historic evangelical soteriology, the view that the question of salvation is less agonizing than we thought because after judgment day the unsaved will not exist. This is universalism in reverse: like universalism, it envisages a final state in which all are saved; unlike universalism, it anticipates, not post-mortem conversion, but annihilation and non-being for those who leave this world in unbelief. The exponents of this view, which for our purposes may be called either annihilationism or conditionalism,[12] are all Protestants or cultists.[13] Having been condemned at the fifth Lateran Council in 1513, it is not an option for Roman Catholics. Among the Protestants are some distinguished evangelicals,[14] including recently my fellow Anglicans John Stott[15] and Philip Edgcumbe Hughes,[16] and I think it is currently gaining more evangelical adherents.[17] But the question, whether an opinion is true, is not resolved by asking who holds it.

Conditionalism is never advocated as expressing the obvious meaning of Scripture, for this it does not do. Its advocates back into it, rather, in horrified recoil from the thought of billions in endless torment — a thought to which the memory of Hitler's holocaust, and the modern statistical mind-set, no doubt add vividness. The arguments for conditionalism, however, are far from convincing. They boil down to four, which I state as Bible-believing conditionalists state them.

First, it is said that the New Testament terms for the fate of the lost — destruction and death, corruption and punishment, the worm and the fire — might mean annihilation. So they might, but this possible meaning is not the natural meaning. In all the contexts cited, the natural meaning of the phrases in which these words appear is ruin and distress, not entry upon non-existence. Conditionalism can be read into these passages, but not read out of them. And in all Bible study it is the natural meaning that should be sought.

Second, it is said that everlasting punishment is not required by God's justice, and would in fact be needless cruelty. But, leaving aside the question of how the conditionalists can know this, I would point out that this argument, if it proves anything, proves too much: for if it is needlessly cruel, and not required by justice, for God to keep the lost in being after judgment, no reason can be given why it is not needlessly cruel for him to keep the lost in the conscious misery of the intermediate state (on which see Jesus' story of Dives, Lk. 16:23 ff.), and then to raise them bodily in what Jesus calls "the resurrection of judgment" (NIV, they "rise to be condemned"; Jn. 5:28). What God sought to do, on conditionalist principles, is annihilate unbelievers at death — but Scripture shows that he does not do this. So the conditionalist argument, which ought to clear God of the suspicion of needless cruelty, actually puts him under it.

Third, it is said that the harmony of the new heaven and earth will be marred if somewhere the lost continue to exist in impenitence and distress. But again it must be asked how the conditionalists know this. The argument is pure speculation.

Fourth, it is said that the joy of heaven will be marred by knowledge that some continue under punitive suffering. But this cannot be said of God, as if the expressing of his holiness in retribution hurts him more than it hurts the offenders; and since in heaven Christians will be like God in character, there is no reason to think that their joy will be impaired in this way either.

What troubles me most here, I confess, is the assumption of superior sensitivity by the conditionalists. Their assumption

J. I. Packer

appears in the adjectives (awful, dreadful, terrible, fearful, intolerable, etc.) that they apply to the concept of eternal punishment, as if to suggest that holders of the historic view have never thought about the meaning of what they have been saying. John Stott records his belief "that the ultimate annihilation of the wicked should be accepted as a legitimate, biblically founded alternative to their eternal conscious torment."[18] Respectfully, I disagree, for the biblical arguments are to my mind flimsy special pleading[19] and the feelings that make people want conditionalism to be true seem to me to reflect, not superior spiritual sensitivity, but secular sentimentalism which assumes that in heaven our feelings about others will be as at present, and our joy in the manifesting of God's justice will be no greater than it is now. It is certainly agonizing now to live with the thought of people going to an eternal hell, but it is not right to reduce the agony by evading the facts; and in heaven, we may be sure, the agony will be a thing of the past.

VI

The third and fourth of the proposed revisions concern the central tenet of the Reformation and of the older forms of evangelicalism, namely the doctrine of justification by grace through faith on the ground of Christ's vicarious obedience to death. This doctrine has been somewhat in eclipse in recent years. For liberal and radical Protestantism, which denies the realities of judgment and atonement, the assertion of justification in the evangelical sense has been an impossibility; and conservative evangelicalism has in recent years tended to stop short at proclaiming present forgiveness of sins and a personal relationship with Jesus, as modern Roman Catholicism also does, and to neglect the larger implications about the believer's relationship with God that the doctrine of justification carries. Recently the Anglican-Roman Catholic International Commission was given the topic of justification by faith to explore; they extended their terms of reference unilaterally and came up with a report titled *Salvation and the Church,* in which the key issues of the Reformation debate, namely the formal cause of justification and the content of Christian assurance, were ignored entirely; and few noticed the omission.[20] As for the proposed revisions at which we shall now briefly look, it can be said at once that acceptance of them would virtually guarantee that justification by faith, as the Reformers understood it, would never be back on the Christian map again. So I make no apology for arguing polemically against them.

First question, then: Should we agree with Wrede, and Albert Schweitzer, and many exegetes and theologians since their time, that Paul's doctrine of justification was no more than a controversial device developed for use against Jews and Judaizers, and so need not greatly concern us? No, for at least these reasons:

(1) Paul's letter to the Romans is by design a full-dress statement of his gospel, and the doctrine of justification is its backbone.

(2) In all the places where Paul writes in the first person singular of the convictions that made him the man and the missionary that he was, he couches his testimony in terms of justification by faith (Gal. 2:15-21; 2 Cor. 5:16-21; Phil. 3:4-14; cf. 1 Tim. 1:12-16). The terms in which a man gives his testimony indicate what is nearest his heart.

J. I. Packer

(3) Present justification, God's declaration that the believer is in the right with him, is for Paul God's basic act of blessing, which both saves from the past by remitting guilt and assures for the future by its guarantee of continuing acceptance. For justification is the judgment of the last day brought forward, a final, irrevocable verdict bringing peace and hope to sinners who previously had neither. The centrality of final judgment in Paul's view of life is plain, and justification is part of that central reality.

(4) Paul's total account of salvation has justification in and through Christ as its central reference point. It is in terms of justification that Paul explains grace (Rom. 3:24, 4:4 f.); the reconciling, redemptive, and revelatory significance of Christ's death (2 Cor. 5:18 f.; Rom. 3:24, 5:5-11; Gal. 3:13); the covenant relationship (Gal. 3:15 ff.); faith (Rom. 4:23 ff., 10:8 ff.); adoption and the gift of the Spirit (Gal. 4:6-8); and Christian assurance (Rom. 5:1-11, 8:1-39) — to look no further. Justification is thus seen to be at the heart of Paul's soteriology.

(5) The question that Paul deployed his doctrine of justification to answer in debate with Jews and Judaizers, namely, "Who are the true children of Abraham?", was for him central to the gospel. For God's salvation is for Abraham's seed, and the mediatorial significance of Christ is that in union with him Jewish and Gentile believers become Abraham's seed for salvation (Gal. 3:6-29).[21]

The threefold claim, drawn mainly from Paul, that justification is a status, given now, and that the formal cause of its being given is the righteousness of Christ, and that the result of its being given is that sinners know themselves to be permanently right with God in a way that daily stumbling into sin cannot affect, revolutionized spiritual life in the sixteenth century, turning Christianity at a stroke from an affair of apprehensive aspiration into a joyful experience of assurance. That experience cannot survive, however, if its doctrinal foundation gets obscured or sidelined. Luther is said to have predicted that after his death the devil would counter-attack with this sidelining as his objective, and that appears to be something that he is still doing today. Surely Scripture requires us to restore the often neglected emphasis on a coming personal judgment for each of us at the hands of a holy God, and against that background to reinstate the precious truth of justification[22] — the wonderful exchange, as Luther called it, whereby Christ took our sin on himself and set righteousness upon us in its place. (Never forget that penal substitutionary atonement and the righteous justification of sinners are the two sides of a single coin, the two elements in the one saving transaction whereby God rescues us from hell.) It would be ruinously enfeebling for us to be allured away at any stage from a central emphasis on justification by faith.[23]

So we move to the fourth revisionary suggestion, which we shall consider in the form in which it is made by an evangelical school of thought which, ironically, has done more than most over the past half-century to keep the doctrine of justification by faith at the center.[24] The suggestion is that saving faith is an assent to the truth about the atonement, and a formalized receiving of Jesus as Savior, without any necessity of turning from sin to become his disciple and, in the relational sense, follower; and that to ask for more than this as a response to the gospel is a legalistic lapse into justification by works, and an unwarranted restriction of God's free grace. To this suggestion I make a threefold response.

J. I. Packer

(1) Faith must be defined, just as it must be exercised, in terms of its object. But the Christ who is the object of saving faith is the Christ of the New Testament, he who is prophet and king no less than he is priest; and more particularly it is the Christ of the gospels, who constantly called for a life of active discipleship as the means of benefiting from his ministry, who is our only basis of salvation. Surely it is undeniable that God has joined faith and repentance, in the sense of change of life, as the two facets of response to Christ, and has made it clear that turning to Christ means turning from sin and letting ungodliness go. Surely it is undeniable that in the New Testament true faith is not only knowing facts about Jesus, but coming to him in personal trust to worship, love, and serve him. Surely it is undeniable that if we put asunder these things that God has joined together, our Christianity will be seriously distorted.

(2) There is an evident confusion here between faith as a psychological act, that is, something that you do (in this case, "closing with Christ" as the Puritans used to put it), and faith as a meritorious work, that is, a means of earning God's favor and inducing his acceptance. When it is argued that to call for active commitment to discipleship as a response to the gospel is to teach works-righteousness, the confusion is clear. The truth is that every act of faith, psychologically regarded, is a matter of doing something (knowing, receiving, and trusting are as much acts in the psychological sense as is resolving to obey); yet no act of faith ever presents itself to its doer as other than a means of receiving undeserved mercy in some shape or form. This is as true of a trustful commitment to follow Christ as it is of a trustful resting on the Savior's promise of pardon. There is no need to restrict faith to

130

passive reliance without active devotion in order to keep works-righteousness and legalism out of the picture.

(3) The pastoral effect of this teaching, if taken seriously, can only be to produce what the Puritans called "gospel hypocrites" — persons who have been told, or who have told themselves, that they are Christians, eternally secure in Christ, because they believe that he died for them, when their hearts are unchanged and they have no inward commitment to Christ at all. I know what I am talking about, for I was just such a gospel hypocrite for two years in my teens before God mercifully made me aware of my unconverted state. If I seem harshly critical when I categorize this proposed redefinition of faith as a barren intellectual formalism, you must remember that I was once myself burned by teaching of this type, and a burned child dreads the fire.

VII

"Stand at the crossroads and look; ask for the ancient paths, ask where the good way is, and walk in it, and you will find rest for your souls" (Jer. 6:16). The only recommendation to which my survey leads me is that in relation to all the proposed revisions of evangelical faith that we have discussed, we should take these words to heart.

J. I. Packer

Some sources for the paper *"Evangelicals and the Way of Salvation"* by J. I. Packer.

1. On universalism:
   John Hick, *Evil and the God of Love*
   J. A. T. Robinson, *In the End God*
   M. Rissi, *The Future of the World*
   D. P. Walker, *The Decline of Hell*
   J. H. Leckie, *The World to Come and Final Destiny*
   H. H. Farmer, *The World and God*
   J. Baillie, *And the Life Everlasting*
   G. Rowell, *Hell and the Victorians*
   G. C. Berkouwer, *The Return of Christ*
   N. Ferre, *The Christian Understanding of God*
   Articles in *Themelios* 4:2, Jan. 1979
2. On conditionalism:
   J. W. Wenham, *The Goodness of God*
   John Stott, *Essentials* (with David Edwards)
   Philip E. Hughes, *The True Image*
   O. C. Quick, *Doctrines of the Creed*
   L. E. Froom, *The Conditionalist Faith of Our Fathers*
   S. H. Travis, *Christian Hope and the Future*
   A. A. Hoekema, *The Four Major Cults*
3. On justification:
   Tom Wright in *The Great Acquittal* (ed., G. Reid)
   H. N. Ridderbos, *Paul: An Outline of His Theology*
   J. Buchanan, *The Doctrine of Justification*
   H. Kung, *Justification*
   A. E. McGrath, *Iustitia Dei: A History of the Christia Doctrine of Justification* (Vol. 2)

Evangelicals and the Way of Salvation

ARCIC II report: "Salvation and the Church": text and responses in *Evangel* 5:2, Summer 1987; responses also by A. E. McGrath in *Themelios* 13:2, Jan. 1988, and *Latimer Studies* 26 (1987), *ARCIC II and Justification*.

C. F. Allison, *The Rise of Moralism*
4. On saving faith:
J. MacArthur, *The Gospel According to Jesus*
Z. Hodges, *The Gospel Under Siege*
Dictionary articles on "universalism", "annihilation", "conditionalism", "justification", "faith".

[1] Ian Botham, *The Incredible Test* (London: Pelham Books, 1981), p. 65.
[2] See Rom. 1:21; Eph. 4:18.
[3] The idea of the analogy of Scripture assumes that the extent of the biblical canon is fixed and known. In the contemporary context this assumption, which many Protestant liberals query and which Roman Catholics claim presupposes the infallibility of the canonizing church, requires exposition and defense, which is not possible here. Materials which in my judgment make possible a convincing defense of the 66-book Protestant canon as fixed and certain in its God-givenness are contained in Roger Beckwith, *The Old Testament Canon of the New Testament Church* (London: SPCK and Grand Rapids: Eerdmans 1985); F. F. Bruce, *The Canon of Scripture* (Downers Grove: InterVarsity Press, 1988); Bruce Metzger, *The Canon of the New Testament* (Oxford: Clarendon Press, 1987); H. N. Ridderbos, *The Authority of the New Testament Scriptures* (Philadelphia: Presbyterian and Reformed Publishing Co. 1963; 2nd rev. ed., *Redemptive History and the New Testament Scriptures*, 1988); Karl Barth, *Church Dogmatics* I.ii. (Edinburgh: T. & T. Clark, 1956), chapter 3, pp. 457-740; G. C. Berkouwer, *Holy Scripture* (Grand Rapids: Eerdmans, 1975), chapter 3, pp. 67-104; A. B. du Toit, *The Canon of the New Testament*. In *Guide to the New Testament*, Vol. 1, ed., A. B. du Toit (Pretoria: N. G. Kerkboekhandel Transvaal, 1979); David G. Dunbar, "The Biblical Canon," in *Hermeneutics, Authority, and Canon,* ed. D. A. Carson and John D. Woodbridge (Grand Rapids: Zondervan, 1986), pp. 295-360.

J. I. Packer

[4]In the *Authority and Interpretation of the Bible* (San Francisco: Harper and Row, 1979), Rogers and McKim maintain that authentic, healthy Christian theology has always recognized, implicitly if not explicitly, that God so accommodated himself to the humanity of the Bible writers as to produce for us a Bible that, while functioning as a safe guide for faith and life, contains various sorts of mistakes on matters of factual detail. This thesis in historical theology with its implications for healthy bibliology today and tomorrow is effectively countered by John D. Woodbridge in *Biblical Authority: A Critique of the Rogers-McKim Proposal* (Grand Rapids: Zondervan, 1982).

[5]For the thesis that divine love points to universalism, see J. A. T. Robinson, *In the End God* (London: James Clarke, 1950; 2nd edition, London: Fontana, 1968) and Nels Ferré, *The Christian Understanding of God* (London: SCM Press, 1952), pp. 219ff. For the idea that the victory of Christ on the cross and in the resurrection entails universalism, see G. C. Berkouwer's critique, *The Triumph of Grace in the Theology of Karl Barth* (Grand Rapids: Eerdmans and London: Paternoster Press, 1956). pp. 262-96, 361-68. For the view that theodicy requires us to posit universalism, see John Hick, *Evil and the God of Love* (London: Fontana, 1968), and Nels Ferre, *Evil and the Christian Faith* (New York: Harper, 1947). There are useful brief reviews of universalist thinking in Stephen H. Travis, *Christian Hope and the Future* (Downers Grove: InterVarsity Press, 1980), pp. 124ff, and in *Themelios* 4.2, Jan. 1979, articles by R.J. Bauckham, N.T.Wright, E.A. Blum, and B.J. Nicholls.

[6]H.O.J. Brown, "Will Everyone be Saved?," *Pastoral Renewal*, June 1987, p. 13.

[7]W.G.T. Shedd, *Dogmatic Theology* (Edinburgh: T. & T. Clark, 1889), II.680.

[8]The texts in question are Jn. 12:32; Acts 3:21; Rom. 5:18f, 11:32; 1 Cor. 15:22-28; 2 Cor. 5:19; Eph. 1:10; Col. 1:20ff; Phil. 2:9-11; Heb. 2:9; Tit. 2:11; 1 Tim. 2:4; 1 Jn. 2:2, 2 Pet. 3:9. In Hasting's *Dictionary of Christ and the Gospels* (Edinburgh: T. & T. Clark, 1908), II.785, Robert Mackintosh, himself a wishful universalist, observed: "The question (sc., of universalism) is generally argued as one of New Testament interpretation. The present writer does not think that hopeful. He sees no ground for challenging the old doctrine on exegetical lines." Nothing that has been offered during the past eighty years seems to invalidate that verdict.

[9]Ferre, *The Christian Understanding of God*, p. 241.

[10]James Denney, *Studies in Theology* (London: Hodder and Stoughton, 1902), p. 244.

[11]Sir Norman Anderson, *Christianity and World Religions* (Leicester and Downers Grove, Inter-Varsity Press, 1984), p. 148f.

[12]Annihilationism is the version of this view that assumes the natural immortality of created human beings, conditionalism the version that denies it. Since no creature has life at any level, or existence in any form, for a single moment apart from God's active upholding, this is a verbal distinction that corresponds to no theological difference. Only within a deistic frame of reference would the distinction mean anything.

134

[13]Jehovah's Witnesses, Seventh-day Adventists, and Herbert W. Armstrong's World-Wide Church of God are committed to conditionalism.

[14]"In conservative circles there is a seeming reluctance to espouse publicly a doctrine of hell, and where it is held there is a seeming tendency towards a doctrine of hell as annihilation... Our interest here is with conditional immortality, which appears to be gaining acceptance in evangelical orthodox circles" (Peter Toon, *Heaven and Hell,* Nashville: Thomas Nelson, 1986, pp. 174,176). In *The Conditionalist Faith of our Fathers* (Washington, D.C.: Review and Herald, 1966) Leroy Edwin Froom, a Seventh-day Adventist, highlighted the conditionalism of Basil F.C.Atkinson, an able lay theologian of Cambridge, England (II.881-88), who seems to have influenced many gifted evangelical students to embrace this view. H.E. Guilleband, author of *The Righteous Judge: A Study of the Biblical Doctrine of Everlasting Punishment* (Taunton: Goodman, [1964]), a careful conditionalist statement, was close to Atkinson, Atkinson's own conditionalism, already explicit in his *Pocket Commentary on Genesis,* was later spelt out in *Life and Immortality: An Examination of the Meaning of Life and Death as they are Revealed in the Scriptures* (Taunton: E. Goodman, n.d.).

[15]David Edwards and John Stott, *Essentials* (London: Hodder and Stoughton and Downers Grove: InterVarsity Press, 1988), pp. 312-20.

[16]Philip Edgcumbe Hughes, *The True Image: The Origin and Destiny of Man in Christ* (Grand Rapids: Eerdmans, 1989), pp. 398-407.

[17]Among recent evangelical writers of distinction who incline more or less explicitly towards conditionalism are Edward William Fudge, *The Fire That Consumes,* with (dissenting) preface by F.F. Bruce (Houston: Providential Press, 1982); John W.Wenham, *The Goodness of God* (Leicester and Downers Grove: Inter-Varsity Press, 1974), chapter 2, pp. 27-41; Stephen H. Travis, who declares: "If pressed, I must myself opt for" conditional immortality (*I Believe in the Second Coming of Jesus,* Grand Rapids: Eerdmans, 1982, p . 198).

[18]Stott, op . cit ., p. 320.

[19]For detailed argument confirming this verdict, see Robert A. Morey, *Death and the Afterlife* (Minneapolis: Bethany House, 1984), chapter 8, pp. 199-222.

[20]Among those who did notice it, and comment on it, were Alister McGrath (*ARCIC II and Justification: an Evangelical Anglican Assessment of Salvation and the Church,* Oxford: Latimer House, 1987; "Justification: the New Ecumenical Debate," in *Themelios,* 13.2, Jan.-Feb. 1988, pp. 43-48); Christopher J.L. Bennett, "Justification and ARCIC II," in *The Banner of Truth,* 297, June 1988, pp. 6-11, 32; and, with profound pastoral insight matching theological acumen, Christopher Fitzsimons Allison, "The Pastoral and Political Implications of Trent on Justification: A Response to the A.R.C.I.C. Agreed Statement *Salvation and the Church,*" in *Churchman* 103.1, 1989, p. 15-31; reprinted from *St. Luke's*

J. I. Packer

Journal of Theology (Sewanee), XXXI.3, 1988. Bishop Allison's *The Rise of Moralism: The Proclamation of the Gospel from Hooker to Baxter* (Wilton: Morehouse-Barlow, 1986) is the authoritative account of Anglican responses to the Tridentine teaching on justification in the sixteenth and seventeenth centuries. See also McGrath, *Iustitia Dei: A History of the Christian Doctrine of Justification* (Cambridge: Cambridge University Press, 1986), II. 1-134.

[21]For development of this point, see the brilliant chapter by Tom Wright, "Justification: the Biblical Basis and its Relevance for Contemporary Evangelicalism," in *The Great Acquittal: Justification by Faith and Current Christian Thought*, ed. Gavin Reid (London: Fount Paperbacks, 1980), pp. 13-37.

[22]Alister McGrath's otherwise admirable exposition, *Justification by Faith: What it Means for Us Today* (Grand Rapids: Zondervan, 1988), fails us here: amazingly, it makes no mention whatever of judgment to come.

[23]I develop some of these points in my introduction to James Buchanan's, *The Doctrine of Justification* (London: Banner of Truth, 1961) and my chapter, "Justification in Protestant Theology," in J.I. Packer and others, *Here We Stand: Justification by Faith Today* (London: Hodder and Stoughton, 1986), pp. 84-102.

[24]See John MacArthur, Jr., *The Gospel According to Jesus* (Grand Rapids: Zondervan and Panorama City: Word of Grace, 1988), citing and interacting with relevant works by Zane Hodges, Charles Ryrie, Lewis Sperry Chafer, and G. Michael Cocoris. Darrell L. Bock wrote a judicious review of the interaction in *Bibliotheca Sacra*, Jan.March, 1989, pp.21-40. The debate continues.

RESPONSE TO JAMES I. PACKER

John Ankerberg with John Weldon

I. Introduction

It is my pleasure to be among the distinguished participants of this vital conference seeking to reaffirm scriptural truths to God's people and "to contend earnestly for the faith once for all delivered to the saints" (Jude 3).

I sincerely appreciate what Dr. Packer has said and his evident concern for biblical truth and God's glory. May I commend each of you as well for your participation in this Evangelical Affirmations Congress.

In Matthew 25:45 our Lord and Savior Jesus Christ clearly taught, "Then they will go away to eternal punishment, but the righteous to eternal life." Surprisingly, more and more Christians are disagreeing with our Lord concerning his teaching on eternal punishment.

In this paper, our response to this trend will be to reaffirm with Dr. Packer the traditional view of the church concerning the eternal, conscious punishment of the wicked. In addition, we will show that the new challenges today to the gospel almost all embrace universal views and deny eternal punishment. Finally, as respected Christian scholars and educated laymen increasingly reject the doctrine of hell and teach others that conditional immortality, annihilationism or various forms of universalism are true or legitimate options of Christian belief, we will prove that such scholars, whether they know it or not, are embracing the same doctrine endorsed and taught today by the devil and his demons.

In considering the different errant views, perhaps a brief definition of terms will be helpful.

Universalism is the teaching that all men (and sometimes, even the devil and all demons) will eventually be saved. *Annihilationism* assumes the immortality of the soul but teaches that God will forever annihilate all who are not saved; their immortality will be taken from them in judgment. *Conditional immortality* assumes the soul of man is not immortal, and therefore those not saved are simply never resurrected to eternal life. Nothing is taken from them or added to them; they just cease to exist.[1]

For nineteen centuries the church has done all in its power to post warning signs along life's way concerning the consequences of a sinful life and the rejection of God's salvation. Our Lord himself taught—"But I will show you whom you should fear: Fear him who, after the killing of the body, has power to throw you into hell. Yes, I tell you, fear him" (Luke 12:5).

But in the last one hundred years—and increasingly today—and as an evangelist I weep as I say this—even in the evangelical church, the warning signs are being taken down by some of the very ones who should be fervently posting them.

Dr. Packer has said elsewhere that universalism "has in this century quietly become part of the orthodoxy of many Christian thinkers and groups."[2]

D. B. Eller asserts, it is clear that "universalism, in a variety of forms, continues to have appeal for contemporary faith, in both liberal and conservative circles."[3]

Stephen Travis observes, "In recent years very few theologians have expounded and defended [the] traditional approach" of eternal hell.[4]

In his paper, Dr. Packer has refuted the proposed revisions of historic evangelical soteriology, particularly universalism, and also expressed concern that the church reaffirm its commitment to the doctrine of justification.

In our own field dealing with the new challenges to the gospel, we have found that the doctrine of justification by faith has been replaced and the doctrine of eternal punishment vehemently rejected. At this point in history, the situation is sufficiently critical that blunt words are needed in addressing the church. In light of the research we have done in defending the faith face-to-face with those challenging the gospel, the following affirmations summarize what we are convinced needs to be said.

II. Affirmations

Affirmation 1: Jesus Christ is the principal figure responsible for the doctrine of eternal punishment. The denial of eternal punishment is tantamount to a denial of the deity of our Lord and Savior. If Jesus Christ was misinformed or in error on this vital issue, he cannot possibly be God incarnate as he claimed, nor could we trust him in other areas, such as his promises concerning our salvation (Titus 1:2).

Affirmation 2: Rejection of hell is a denial of biblical authority which opens the door to additional revisionist and syncretistic tendencies in other areas. To reject scriptural truth at one point is to be able to reject scriptural truth at any point and thereby to substitute human speculation for divine revelation.

139

Recent evangelical infection with universalism, annihilationism and conditional immortality is to the point.

Affirmation 3: The problem is not a scriptural issue but an emotional issue, contaminated by secularist and humanistic thinking. Nearly 2,000 years of church history confirm Dr. Packer's contention that exegetical arguments fail to discredit the doctrine of eternal punishment. Indeed, given the difficulty of this doctrine, only its scriptural *clarity* can account for its near universal acceptance by Christians over the centuries. Likewise, we must not allow our emotions to dictate truth. The issue is not what we feel or think but what God has revealed in his Word. For example:

> "Just as our emotional aversion to the pain and suffering we see in this life does not alter the fact that they exist, neither does our aversion to any future punishment in the eternal state alter the fact that it will exist."5

Affirmation 4: To reject eternal punishment and accept other ways of salvation is to affirm that the cross was unnecessary.

Affirmation 5: To affirm universalism is a denial of the church's mission to preach the gospel and warn men to escape God's wrath and eternal punishment (2 Corinthians 5:11; Luke 3:7, 9, 17, 18).

Affirmation 6: The doctrine of eternal punishment is the watershed between evangelical and non-evangelical thought. The doctrine of eternal punishment is interrelated with many other doctrines. It conditions our thinking in many areas of preaching and teaching. When friends, such as John Stott, Philip Edgcombe Hughes, Clark Pinnock, John Wenham, Basil Atkinson and other well-known and reputedly evangelical leaders, reject the traditional view of eternal punishment, the Church suffers serious or even fatal erosion in its doctrinal foundation.[6]

Affirmation 7: Universalism logically repudiates the doctrine of justification by faith. The doctrine of justification affirms that if there is "no faith in Christ, no justification." On the other hand, universalism teaches that the Atonement bestows justification upon all men of all ages whether or not they personally believe. When universalism rejects the authority of Christ and the Bible, offers men a false hope, impugns the doctrine of justification by faith, and hinders missions, its teaching is not merely an issue of "academic freedom" or personal conscience, but an outright refusal to accept the divine authority of Christ's teaching as such.

How important is the doctrine of justification by faith? Dr. Packer has well said that the doctrine of justification by faith is:

> ... theological, declaring a work of amazing grace; anthropological, demonstrating that we cannot save ourselves; Christological, resting on incarnation and atonement; pneumatological, rooted in Spirit-wrought faith-union with Jesus; ecclesiological, determining both the definition and the health of the church; eschatological, proclaiming God's truly final verdict on believers here and now; evangelistic, inviting troubled souls into everlasting peace; pastoral, making our identity as forgiven sinners basic to our fellowship; and liturgical, being decisive for interpreting the sacraments and shaping sacramental services. No other biblical doctrine holds together so much that is precious and enlivening.[7]

Those who hold out the slightest ray of hope for men and women who die outside of Christ, teaching they will be saved or annihilated, dare to do what God and Jesus have not done. Conditional immortalists and universalists dare to speak for God in the most solemn and sobering of all human realities—and in effect speak against God and call him a liar.

In conclusion, when a conditional immortalist text, such as Edward Fudge's *The Fire That Consumes*, is chosen as an alternate selection by the Evangelical Book Club, and when some of our most respected evangelical voices are denying the doctrine of eternal punishment, my fellow colleagues, we are in serious trouble.

III. Development

This discussion is not just an academic exercise among theologians. Almost all groups and organizations which constitute the new challenges to the gospel embrace universal views and deny eternal punishment.

We shall go one step further. In our ministry at The John Ankerberg Television Show, we hear this kind of thinking daily from those espousing liberal theology, those in the cults, the occult, and those in the New Age Movement. After a decade of research, it is abundantly clear that those who embrace the various forms of universalism and reject eternal punishment are unwittingly embracing the same doctrines endorsed and taught by channeled spirit entities. This is what the Bible identifies as "things taught by demons." Proof of this can be seen by examining the authoritative teachings of those today who are vigorously issuing new challenges to the gospel of our Lord Jesus Christ:

1. "Ramtha" is the spirit speaking through medium J. Z. Knight, who has guided Shirley MacLaine. MacLaine has sold at

least seven million books concerning her occult experiences. Ramtha teaches, "God has never judged you or anyone."⁸ "No, there is no Hell and there is no devil."⁹

2. "Seth," the spirit guide who has authored twenty books through medium Jane Roberts, teaches, "He [Jesus] will not come to reward the righteous and send evildoers to eternal doom."¹⁰

3. Dr. Elisabeth Kübler-Ross, world famous psychiatrist and best-selling author of the book, *Death and Dying,* publicly admits she is receiving information from several spirit guides. Thousands of courses based on her philosophy are being taught to doctors, nurses and students in America. Kübler-Ross believes that Jesus' reference to hell "was [only] symbolic language ... that God is *all* love...."¹¹ She teaches, "God is not a punitive, nasty God. [Traditional hell] is not a right interpretation of judgment.... You make your own hell, or your own heaven by the way you live."¹²

4. José Silva, founder of the popular Silva Mind Control Course, teaches people how to invite two "psychic counselors" into their minds on the third day of his course. This course was originally taught to him by two of his own "psychic guides." Now, close to seven million people have graduated from this New Age instruction. Silva teaches, "'the devil' is just plain ignorance ... hell is not a place full of flames but a situation that causes us to hurt...."¹³ He also said: "Rabbi Jesus did not mean to tell us anything about the spiritual kingdom of God that we enter when we die, when we cease to exist on this plane. We believe that after we die, we enter another dimension. Maybe ... the dimension we came from, where we were before."¹⁴

Silva claims, "Jesus never said, 'Being cleansed with my blood will save you,' and He [Jesus] never said, 'If you let me enter into your heart you will be saved.'"[15]

Finally, Silva states:

> Thank God for sending Christ to enlighten us on how to use our inner kingdom (the alpha dimension) . . . [where we can] learn to use our right-brain hemisphere, and become clairvoyant. Thank you, Rabbi Jesus Christ, and forgive us for being almost two thousand years late in understanding your message.[16]

5. Daisaku Ikeda, President of the fastest growing religion in America, Nichiren Shoshu Buddhism, teaches: "The life of the individual cannot be said to exist in any specific place after death. It is, however, part of universal essential life and is awaiting remanifestation in the world of actuality. The remanifestation will not take place in a mystical heaven or hell."[17]

6. Maharishi Mahesh Yogi, founder of Transcendental Meditation, the most popular Westernized form of Advaita Vedanta, with two million graduates, teaches, "Every creature is on the path to perfection. . . . No one should grieve over the death of another."[18] He complains that it is a false religion which "creates fear of punishment and hell and the fear of God in the mind of man."[19]

7. Sun Myung Moon, the Oriental cult leader and spiritist of The Unification Church, teaches: "The ultimate purpose of God's providence of restoration is to save all mankind. Therefore, it is God's intention to abolish Hell completely, after the lapse of the period necessary for the full payment of all indemnity."[20]

8. Mary Baker Eddy, a dabbler in spiritism and founder of Christian Science, believed, "To us, heaven and hell are states of thought, not places. People experience their own heaven or hell right here. . . ."[21]

9. Charles Fillmore, founder of the Unity School of Christianity, which has influenced millions, teaches, "There is no warrant for the belief that God sends man to everlasting punishment. . . . Hell is a figure of speech that represents a corrective state of mind."[22]

10. The Unitarian Universalists teach: "[It is totally] unthinkable for God, as a loving Father, to damn any of his children everlastingly to hell. The Nicene Creed must then be in error."[23] One of their authors has written, "It seems safe to say that no Unitarian Universalist believes in a resurrection of the body, a literal heaven or hell, or any kind of eternal punishment. . . ."[24]

11. Jehovah's Witnesses, who number approximately three million members, maintain:

> Biblical evidence thus makes it plain that those whom God judges as undeserving of life will experience, not eternal torment in a literal fire, but 'everlasting destruction.' They will not be preserved alive anywhere. The fire of Gehenna is therefore but a symbol of the totality and thoroughness of that destruction.[25]

These statements should remind us of the Apostle Paul's words, "The Spirit clearly says that in the later times some will abandon the faith and follow deceiving spirits and things taught by demons" (1 Timothy 4:1). If Christians deny Jesus' teaching on eternal punishment, it should be clear that they are embracing the same doctrines endorsed and taught by demons.

IV. Conclusion

Since our allegiance is to Christ, we should not imply salvation exists apart from his work on the cross or that eternal punishment for the unrepentant is less severe than he warned.

In *Death and the Afterlife*, Dr. Robert Morey cogently refutes the arguments of the leading universalists and answers the so-called arguments of leading conditionalists such as Seventh-day Adventist L. R. Froom, the author of *The Conditionalist Faith of Our Fathers* (which influenced John Wenham), Edward William Fudge, author of *The Fire That Consumes*, and B. F. C. Atkinson who wrote *Life and Immortality*. Concluding his argument, Dr. Morey addresses the church:

> . . . unless fundamental and evangelical colleges and seminaries take a strong stand against neo-liberal professors in their midst who are peddling Barthian Universalism, within a generation or two, these institutions will be denying the Trinity, the vicarious atonement, the inspiration of Scripture, etc.

> History has a nasty habit of repeating itself. Just as the descendants of Kelly and Murray ultimately became humanists and joined with the Unitarians in 1961, the descendants of the neoevangelicals will be Unitarian in theology within a generation or two. Let us hope that evangelicals will remember this sad fact of history and return yet to the orthodoxy of their fathers.

> One last consideration which must be pointed out is that the breakdown of belief in the inspiration of Scripture and the growing peril of Universalism and annihilationism are preparing the way for future descendants of the evangelical church to be swept into the world of the cults and occult.[26]

Response

The truth of hell is that eternal punishment is a vital doctrine. It cannot, it must not, be ignored or abandoned. We must have the courage to preach it from the pulpits, in Bible schools and seminaries, and to a lost world. Vernon Grounds is correct, "It is impossible to exaggerate the seriousness and urgency that the doctrine of hell imparts to life here and now."[27]

Lest we be tempted to ignore this issue, let us remember the Apostle's admonition:

> I solemnly charge you in the presence of God and of Christ Jesus, who is to judge the living and the dead, and by His appearing and His kingdom: preach the word; be ready in season and out of season; reprove, rebuke, exhort, with great patience and instruction. For the time will come when they will not endure sound doctrine; but wanting to have their ears tickled, they will accumulate for themselves teachers in accordance to their own desires; and will turn away their ears from the truth . . . .
>
> (2 Timothy 4:1-4).

[1] Conditionalists variously assert a resurrection prior to annihilation; nevertheless, there is no resurrection to eternal life.

[2] James I. Packer, *Christianity Today*, January 17, 1986.

[3] D. B. Eller, "Universalism" in Walter A. Elwell (ed.), *Evangelical Dictionary of Theology* (Grand Rapids, MI: Baker, 1984), 1130.

[4] Stephen H. Travis, *Christian Hope and the Future* (Downers Grove, IL: InterVarsity, 1980), 118.

[5] Robert A. Morey, *Death and the Afterlife* (Minneapolis, MN: Bethany, 1984), 100.

[6] Clark Pinnock, "Fire Then Nothing," *Christianity Today*, March 20, 1987; John Wenham, *The Goodness of God* (Downers Grove, IL: InterVarsity, 1974), 40, 41; J.I. Packer, preceding article and also personal conversation, May 12, 1987.

Ankerberg and Weldon

[7] James I. Packer, *Here We Stand: Justification by Faith Today* (London: Hodder and Stoughton, 1986), 5.

[8] Ramtha, with Douglas James Mahr, *Voyage to the New World: An Adventure into Unlimitedness* (New York: Fawcett Gold Medal/Ballentine, 1987), 62.

[9] Ibid., 252.

[10] Jane Roberts, *Seth Speaks* (Englewood Cliffs, NJ: Prentice-Hall, 1972), 389 .

[11] Elisabeth Kübler-Ross, Interview, *Mother Earth News*, May-June 1983, 22 .

[12] Elisabeth Kübler-Ross, "Death Does Not Exist, " *Journal of Holistic Health* (San Diego: Association for Holistic Health/Mandala Society, 1977), 65 .

[13] José Silva, *The Mystery of the Keys to the Kingdom* (Laredo, TX: Institute of Psychorientology, Inc., 1984) 70.

[14] José Silva, *The Mystery of the Keys*. 141.

[15] José Silva, *The Mystery of the Keys*. 162 .

[16] José Silva, *I Have a Hunch : The Autobiography of José Silva* (Laredo, TX: Institute of Psychorientology, 1983), vol. I, appendix 10a.

[17] Daisaku Ikeda, *Buddhism: The Living Philosophy* (Tokyo: The East Publications), 31.

[18] Maharishi Mahesh Yogi, *Maharishi Mahesh Yogi on the Bhagavad Gita: A New Translation and Commentary Chapters 1 to 6* (Baltimore, MD: Penguin Books, 1967), 107.

[19] Maharishi Mahesh Yogi, *Transcendental Meditation* (New York: Signet/ New American Library, 1968), 251.

[20] No author (Sun Myung Moon is generally conceded as such), *The Divine Principle* (Washington, D.C.: The Holy Spirit Association for the Unification of World Christianity, 2nd ed., 1973), 190.

[21] No author, *Questions and Answers on Christian Science* (Boston, MA: Christian Science Publications Society, 1974), 6.

[22] Charles Fillmore, *Dynamics for Living* (Lees Summit, MO: Unity Books, 1967), 278-79.

[23] J. Mendelsohn, "Meet the Unitarian Universalists," Nov. 1974 (UUA pamphlet), 14.

[24] W. Argow, "Unitarian Universalism: Some Questions Answered," October 1978 (UUA pamphlet), 8.

[25] Watchtower Bible and Tract Society, *Is This Life All There Is?* (Brooklyn, NY: WTBS, 1974), 115-16.

[26] Robert A. Morey, *Death and the Afterlife* (Minneapolis, MN Bethany, 1984), 220.

[27] Vernon C. Grounds, "The Final State of the Wicked," *Journal of the Evangelical Theological Society*, 24/3, 220.

QUESTIONS
FOR DISCUSSION

1. What influence do the teachings of universalism, annihilationism, and conditionalism have upon one's belief in Christ's death on the cross? Are these influences sufficient to jeopardize an understanding of one's need of Christ as Savior?

2. What natural tendencies of mankind promote the conclusions of universalism, annihilationism, and conditionalism? What biblical teachings are offered to support or challenge these tendencies? Evaluate these teachings as to how clearly they are taught in Scripture.

3. Would a Christian's view of the persons and nature of God differ through accepting the doctrine of universalism, annihilationism, or conditionalism? In what ways? Are these differences supported by Scripture?

4. Can one believe the teachings of universalism, annihilationism, or conditionalism and still be identified as an evangelical? Why or why not?

5

BIBLICAL
AUTHORITY

WORD AND WORLD
Biblical Authority and
The Quandary of Modernity

David F. Wells

Introduction

There is a woodcut from the sixteenth century which shows two preachers facing one another—presumably from pulpits that are not in the same church! — and they are evidently in debate with one another or, at least, the ways in which their messages are being authorized are in antithesis to one another. The one preacher is wagging his finger at the congregation and saying, "Sic dicit Papa"; the other has his finger pointed at the page of Holy Scripture and is saying, "Sic dicit dominus deus!" It is not difficult to deduce from this that the maker of this woodcut was a Protestant!

The simplicity of this statement of Protestant conviction, however, should not lead us to conclude that the Protestant theology of the Word of God, epitomized in the sola Scriptura slogan, has been simply maintained or can be simply maintained. For, in the modern world in particular, both the notion of authority — of any authority — and the idea of a divine disclosure have come under fierce siege. This, however, is really part of a wider social transformation whose full consequences we are yet to see;[1] and these will have profound consequences for how Scripture will function in the years ahead.

David F. Wells

Authority, Power, and Tradition

The ligaments which have held together Western civilization — authority, power, and tradition — have, in their mutual
relations become so stretched and damaged in our time as to raise
the specter that civilization as we have known it could collapse .
What sounded alarmist when uttered by Spengler earlier this
century sounds almost commonplace when described by Solz-
henitzen now. And the reason is that we know that two of these
ligaments are no longer functional.

From at least the time of Plato and Aristotle and coming
down through much of the modern period, authority, power, and
tradition have been sharply distinguished from one another in
their nature though it has been recognized that they may overlap
in their function.

Authority has had to do with *rights* and hence with the
legitimacy of beliefs and actions in society. For centuries this legitimacy has been found in some higher order, or set of laws, from
which human society took its bearings. It is not difficult, however,
to trace the breakdown in the belief in such an order and hence in
the functioning of authority in the West. Modernization, the
technologically driven reordering of our world around economic
goals which require heavy urbanization, has produced drastically
lowered cognitive horizons. For most people, their "world" extends no further than their own personal circumstances and no
higher than the secular and trivial thought that pours out the
television set seven hours a day into the average home. Artists and
novelists in the twentieth century have signalled the breakdown in
meaning with increasing shrillness by first turning away from the
transcendent and looking in society itself for meaning and values

and then, in recent decades, by turning away from our disordered society and looking within human consciousness. This cycle of alienation is now running toward its completion in the deconstructionists who have despaired even of finding the meaning of a novelist's work in relation to that person's inner life. There is no order left for meaning or values, be it above us, or around us, or within us, from which legitimacy can be derived for our beliefs and actions. Authority is gone.

Tradition is the conduit by which values are transmitted from generation to generation. It has been the way in which one generation was inducted by its predecessor into its thinking and wisdom, most importantly as this has had to do with values and meaning and the family has been its main conduit. With the collapse of functioning families and the onslaught of modernization, the role of tradition in our social life has evaporated. Modernity powerfully shifts attention from the past to the future, casting the awful stigma of obsolescence over what is traditional. Tradition can be quaint, even charming, but it is always viewed in our society as something that is also outdated, irrelevant and useless. Thus, of the three original ligaments, only power remains.

The collapse of authority into power[2] and the disappearance of our collective memory, tradition, is evident all around us today.[3] In its crudest form, we hear this in the Nietzschean aphorism that might is right, but in less flat-footed ways we hear it in just about every public discussion about our social life. For if Richard John Neuhaus is correct that the public square has become "naked,"[4] stripped of values, it is because we no longer have an Archimedean point outside of the flat plane of human discourse from which to apply moral meaning and leverage to

155

David F. Wells

what we are doing. There is, in consequence, a constant erosion
in society of any common held morality or sense of duty to which
appeal can be made. There are few shared values which can act as
the arbiters in the clash of self interest which is the brew out of
which social policy emerges. That being the case, the passage of
social life can only be directed through the exercise of power,
whether this is done in subtle or in blatant ways, and only very
rarely will it be directed by those who ask whether something is
right in any sense other than what seems to "make sense" to
private experience, and that is often indistinguishable from base
self-interest. This context, then, is not only providing the environment in which biblical authority has to be thought about but it is
also providing the major impetus for the recasting of traditional
ideas of authority in contemporary theology. It is with the latter
that I wish to begin before moving to the former, the question of
biblical authority.

The Bible as the Instrument of Authority

David Kelsey has observed that "virtually every contemporary Protestant theologian along the entire spectrum of opinion
from the 'neo-evangelicals' through Karl Barth, Emil Brunner, to
Anders Nygren, Rudolf Bultmann, Paul Tillich and Fritz Buri, has
acknowledged that any Christian theology worthy of the name
'Christian' must, in *some* sense of the phrase, be done 'in accord
with Scripture.'"[5] It is also the case, of course, that the contemporary crisis in academic theology has produced some who have
finally decided that the Bible cannot serve as authoritative in *any*
sense. Nevertheless, Kelsey has correctly identified where the
swamp is especially murky.

Text and Meaning

The reason that the Bible has functioned in so many diverse ways in modern theology, supposedly authorizing a multitude of theologies that are jarringly incompatible with one another, is that text and meaning have been disengaged. Theological meaning is, in practice, merely prompted by the biblical text, or suggested by it, or perhaps the text is the locus where it is given or the clue to where it might lie; but so often theological meaning is suspended upon or derived from something outside of the biblical text itself. This meaning swings and floats loose of the text. It is not controlled by the text. And theologies as diverse as those of Barth, Bultmann, and Buri can all in some sense be viewed as being biblica; but, unfortunately, that "sense" is neither the same nor does it provide clear criteria for assessing the propriety of the theological proposals which are offered.

Ronald Thiemann recently noted this hermeneutical quagmire and illustrated the problem by reference to a dreadful parable that occurs in Kafka's *The Trial*.[6] The parable in Kafka is about existence in general but Thiemann applied it to the hermeneutical task. This parable concerns a man who was intent upon entering the practice of law. The door through which he had to pass, however, was always guarded by tyrannical and forbidding doorkeepers who prevented his entrance. The man bribed and cajoled them but to no avail. After many years of waiting the man began to slide toward death. Just before dying, however, he noticed a bright and beautiful light shining beyond the doorway. He asked the doorkeepers what it meant. He was told that the door had been kept open only for him but now that he was dying it was being closed. And so he died a stranger to the realm in which he

David F. Wells

longed to be, but into which he could never enter. So it is in
contemporary hermeneutics. The text is but a doorway beyond
which is a meaning that shimmers as if it were a bright light; but
it is a meaning which is so elusive as always to be beyond our
reach, or so polyvalent as to allow for a diversity of understandings that can never be resolved. And so the exegete always stands
on the outside. The door always closes shut before the bright light
has been understood.

The earlier polemic over whether revelation is personal or
propositional — the neo-orthodox arguing that it could not be the
latter if it were the former and evangelicals arguing that if it were
to be the former it had to be the latter — disappeared with the final
collapse of neo-orthodoxy in America in the 1950s. But the issue,
in fact, has never died; it has simply taken on fresh forms that are
more numerous and inventive than anything that Barth or Brunner
had thought were possible. For once again the biblical text is not
itself the locus of revelation; but it is, rather, the doorway to
something else that it is hoped in some way will yield some direc-
tional meaning for the doing of theology.

This bifurcation between text and meaning was even affirmed, for example, in Barth's theology, although with qualifica-
tions. For him, one did not have the Word of God in one's hands
because one had the Bible in one's hands, as he put it . Rather, the
Word of God, the divine meaning, came to one in conjunction
with the reading or hearing of the text of Scripture. It came from
above and the inspiration of Scripture was to be understood, not
of the biblical documents, but of the person to whom this insight
had come as a result of which the very human words of Scripture
became witnesses to God and his Christ.[7]

For Bultmann, the Scriptures and the "revelation" were similarly disengaged, for the latter came from within. The biblical authors were themselves responding to the existential realities that they knew in their own world. Their world cannot be ours, for world views cannot be put on and taken off like garments. Our world is scientific, theirs pre-scientific; we cannot believe in miracles or in a miraculous Christ; they could. What we do have in common with them, however, is human existence, the same quest for internal authenticity. It is this interest in authenticity, an interest which is internally and existentially formulated and which is heavily influenced by the twentieth century Western outlook which Bultmann then allowed to dominate what the text can say.[8]

In much Gospel criticism today, by contrast, the assumption is that the real meaning is to be found not in the interpreter, not in the text itself, not above it, but *behind* it. For, as Norman Perrin has explained with respect to redactional assumptions,[9] each saying of Jesus had three contexts: the words he actually used in speaking to the listeners who were present; the subsequent history and development of these sayings in the early communities of faith; and the reworking and adaption by the gospel authors of this material in line with their own theological interests. The key, then, to the meaning of the biblical text is not in the words themselves but in a reconstruction of the history *behind* the text, and it is this reconstruction in which religious meaning is to be found and not in the text itself. The text is, at best, a clue to what happened; what happened has to be reconstructed, as far as this is possible, from the fragmentary access that we now have to it and it is this reconstruction that is important.

David F. Wells

Finally, the dominant fascination in the World Council of Churches currently is with a family of theologies which see the meaning to lie chronologically *beyond* the text. The assumptions are Hegelian. Social context — whether this is looked at with a liberationist, feminist, or ethnic interest[10] — provides the evidence of what God is "doing"; for if God always identifies with the poor and always opposes the powerful, then in those events today in which the rich and powerful are overthrown, and the poor are liberated, are to be found the "prophetic witnesses" to God's presence. Thus the Scriptures as well as contemporary experience testify to the revelatory presence of God in society and both are commentaries upon it. The Scriptures by themselves, of course, are only a part of this narrative of revelation, the other part coming from contemporary social experience. And thus what Scripture looks forward to in its eschatology can only be grasped by seeing how God is bringing this to pass in our world today.

The Reformation Tradition

What is truly remarkable about this situation today is how few there are who realize that the hermeneutical wheel has turned full circle. The Protestant Reformation was founded on the conviction that God had disclosed revelatory meaning in and through the words of Scripture and it was for this reason that Luther and Calvin opposed the older system of allegorizing. The Holy Ghost, Luther declared is "the all-simplest writer in heaven or earth" and therefore the words of Scripture can have no more than one "simple" sense. The kind of allegorizing that Origen engaged in, for example, Luther described as nothing but "scum." Why was he so vehement?

160

What was at issue was whether Scripture would be treated as having its own self-contained authority. The debate with Rome was not over the inspiration of Scripture; on that the two sides were agreed. Nor was it really over tradition. It was over the claim of the Catholic Church to have the authority to give to Scripture a meaning which the text itself could not obviously sustain. That is what allegorizing lead to, for it supposed that there was a "deeper" meaning behind or above the text which was only hinted at in the text. And it was what the radical Anabaptists were to do later on by suspending the function of the exterior Word of the text upon the interior "Word" of insight and intuition, the former not being allowed to function until validated by the latter. The principle in each case was the same. By different means the connection between what the language of the text meant and what the text was taken to mean was broken; the linguistic controls of the text were severed, in the one case by a supposed higher meaning behind the text, in another case by the Church and its supposed fuller meaning beyond the text, and in still another by a fuller meaning from within the interpreter. It was against these aberrations that the Reformers argued that unless the Scriptures are seen to be self-interpreting, they cannot be reforming, for private interests can hold captive their meaning. That is exactly what is happening today.

The position developed by Warfield earlier this century, then, is not at all the radical departure that some have claimed it to be. It assumes that words and meaning in Scripture coincide and what secures this is inspiration. Meaning is not to be found above the text, behind it, beyond it, or in the interpreter. Meaning is to be found *in the text*. It is the language of the text which determines what meaning God intends for us to have. Warfield's own way of asserting this was to say that the N.T. authors made their "habitual appeal to the Old Testament text as to God himself speaking." They made an absolute identification between the Scriptures (text) and "the living voice of God" (i.e., meaning).[11] This argument was built on two types of passage: those in which the Scriptures were spoken of as if they were God speaking and those in which God is spoken of as if he were the Scriptures. "God and the Scriptures," he said, "are brought into such conjunction as to show that in point of directness of authority no distinction was made between them."[12] It is this identification of text and meaning, of the language of Scripture with the words of God, that is, as Warfield noted, "the fundamental fact of the case."[13]

In so arguing, Warfield actually placed himself closer to current semantic thinking than is much contemporary hermeneutical practice.[14] Words do not mean. Words have meanings. They have semantic fields, ranges of meaning, and it is the *author* who, knowing the ranges, employs the words in such combinations that the desired meaning is communicated. There is no language which functions in the way that the biblical text is commonly treated. No language allows meaning to float free of the words used. It is not the biblical language that allows this, but it is our contemporary mysticism which demands it.

Unless words and their meaning are rejoined in hermeneutical practice, we can have no access to revelation in anything but a mystical sense. To be sure, language is versatile and the language used in Scripture shows the full range of this versatility; so the access to meaning, and hence to revelation, is an access that is secured through the way in which this language works. This versatility, however, does not in any way detract from the fact that, when text and meaning coincide, they produce an authority which is external and objective. The versatility of the language simply informs the way in which the referential nature and function of that external, authoritative source is to be understood.[15]

In the immediate post-War period among evangelicals, the identification of text and meaning which is accomplished through inspiration was typically described under the language of infallibility. This is language that has primary reference to Scripture's *function* whereas inerrancy, which has for significant parts of the evangelical movement since this time supplanted infallibility, has to do with Scripture's *nature*. Inasmuch as the function of Scripture depends upon its nature as inspired, these terms have, in practice, become synonyms except where the newer hermeneutical spirit has affected evangelical thinking.[16] Infallibility has been stretched by some to allow for a disengagement of meaning from text that simply is not possible when inerrancy is adhered to. While this in-house debate may seem to outsiders a little like "strife over a diphthong" (to use Gibbon's haughty dismissal of the patristic debates as to the definition of Christ's nature), the fact is that very large consequences sometimes turn on small linguistic adjustments. There was, after all, a significant difference between saying that Christ had the same being as did God (*homoousios*) and that he had a being (*homoiousios*) that was only similar to that of God. The language used to safeguard the nature of Scripture is no more a matter of indifference now than was the choice of terms for the early Fathers in regard to Christ. The voices urging the disengagement of text from meaning, both in academia and in the

163

culture are now so loud that only the greatest conceptual bonding between them will be adequate to meet the challenge.

The language we use to describe this bonding obviously has to reflect the nature of the bonding itself, and here the analogy between christology and bibliology is vitally important. The analogy, it seems to me, does not lie primarily in the fact that in both cases there is a human and a divine element. It is, rather, that in both cases, function is dependent upon nature.

In christological discussions in recent years there has been a concerted attempt made by some to get around having to make prior commitments to the exact nature of Jesus' divinity, or to the mode by which he came to be divine.[17] Instead, it is argued that we should begin with his human biography, a biography which in its humanity is not different in principle from any other human biography, and then see if from this some idea of his being can be constructed. The functional is seen to be the access, the only access, to the ontological. The problem with this approach, of course, is that his divinity was often "hidden" within his actions and could not simply be read from them; he came to his own people who had been nurtured on the Scriptures to expect him, and they neither recognized nor accepted him. A christology "from below" may appear to spare us from embarrassing metaphysical commitments, but it also leaves us with a truncated Christ. Not only so, but it also leaves us with a Christ who really could not conquer sin, death, and the devil, as the New Testament declares that Christ did; for this is work that only God in all of his fullness could accomplish. Christ's person and work, the ontological and functional, are inseparably linked. They are like the two foci in an ellipse, distinct but always having to be understood in relation to one another.

So it is with the nature and function of Scripture. Scripture can disclose the character, will, and acts of God and accomplish its purposes of making God's people wise about salvation, because it is God himself who has disclosed these truths by inspiration. To be God's Word in function requires, not simply that we accord it this status as Kelsey thinks, but that it be in actuality God's Word. It can have no assured function of divine disclosure if in its nature it is not divinely inspired. Furthermore, it can have no authority if it is not inspired, for without this inspiration it cannot accord legitimacy to any beliefs or actions. Without a transcendent reference point, legitimacy is simply indistinguishable from personal preference.

Evangelicals have made so much of the importance of authority that it is no small irony that James Hunter has found the generation of younger leaders now in our institutions of higher education succumbing to the habits of privatization that modernity demands. A process of "cognitive bargaining" is now in full spate. Hunter notes, for example, that many younger evangelicals are willing to treat as "symbolic" significant historical material in Scripture, to treat the truth of Scripture as non-cognitive, and to look for special personal "experiences" from its reading. The certainty that derives from divine authority appears to be melting away. Indeed, Hunter charges that at a practical level, neoorthodoxy is making inroads into this generation of evangelicals;[18] they, too, are disengaging text from meaning and deriving the meaning from internal, private intuition. This raises some troubling questions as we think about the future and the ways in which we are going to have to address modernity.

Biblical Authority and Modernity

No one who has had an eye on the book trade in the last two decades, or on the cycle of learned journals during this present era, could have failed to notice that there has been a growing interest in how theology should be "done."[19] It is an interest that has become urgent and intense to such an extent that the perception has emerged that theology in all its shades and stripes has lost its viability as a discipline. So what has brought on this doubt?

The Breakdown of Theology

David Tracy has suggested[20] that the recent history of theology has involved a struggle to accommodate three relationships, the combination of whose claims upon theology has not been possible to satisfy. This triangle is made up first, of the confessional source (Scripture or the teaching of the Church in the case of Roman Catholics), second, of culture and third, of academia. And his argument is that modern theologies can be grouped into families, depending upon which point on the triangle has had to be excluded to accommodate the others.

This breakdown Tracy believes can be mapped out more or less chronologically. From about 1930 to 1950 on the Protestant side neoorthodoxy was dominant and thus the element of confession was to the fore. By the 1960s, the neo-orthodox consensus had collapsed. A culture racked with uncertainty about the Vietnam war and increasingly experiencing in itself the forces of relativism and pluralism now heard the death-of-God theologians projecting their uncertainty into the being of God himself. The culture provided the means of crafting the substance of theology.

What it provided, however, was so destructive that by the end of the 1960s the death-of-God theology was itself dead. Attention now shifted to the third of the three components, that of academia. Can theology find principles of construction which will be recognized as viable within the academic process, given the fact that that process cannot accept external, supernatural revelation?[21] Indeed, Brian Hebblethwaite recently asked whether, given the necessary revelational vacuity in theology, anything but philosophy can remain.

Whether the story is actually as antiseptic as Tracy's account leaves us to believe could be disputed, but he is undoubtedly correct in seeing how the voice of theology has changed from being confessional to being cultural to being philosophical. He is correct, too, in seeing that theology for the most part has given up the struggle to hold in a unified whole the three elements of which he has spoken. And, the truth is, this triangle can only be sustained if one starts with a view of biblical authority such as has been outlined here; and at the very moment when the Bible as the source of confession proceeds to erode, cultural and academic perspectives pour in to fill the vacuum and, singly or together, destroy whatever remnants of revelation are still there.

The revolution in the university, the consequences of which are a fact of academic life today, occurred mainly in the period from 1870 to 1910, as Richard Hofstadter has noted.[22] The Civil War eliminated all but 20% of the colleges that had existed in the first half of the century and in its wake a complete revamping of the system occurred. The major universities moved to emancipate

David F. Wells

themselves from denominational control and from the hold which religious interests had exercised over them. Increasingly, the model of the German university came to be accepted as normative for America. And in this model only two conditions were seen to be necessary for a university education: scholarship and freedom. This represented the final collapse of the older model in which the goals, as Matthew Arnold in England had declared, were to be three: the formation of gentlemanly conduct, moral development, and intellectual enrichment. The first to go had been the gentlemanly conduct; the next was moral formation. At the turn of the century, universities saw themselves as only providing intellectual enrichment and they chose to do so on a constricted, Kantian basis which assumed that God could not be known directly, though he might have to be postulated to exist if we are to understand ourselves as moral beings. Thus freedom came to be understood as emancipation from all external constraints, values, and authorities. To be free was to be alone in one's own universe.

With this freedom, however, has also come a relativity in thought that is destructive to the educational process. Allan Bloom, in his book *The Closing of the American Mind,* notes that students today have lost the capacity for thought and logic and that they no longer believe that this is a deficiency that should be corrected. They intuitively feel that time expended in trying to think clearly, to establish the difference between right and wrong, true and false, would be time invested in a lost cause, since there is nothing in reality that corresponds to these categories.

Carl Henry has also noted that "the most sudden and sweeping upheaval in beliefs and values has taken place this century. No generation in the history of human thought has seen such swift and radical inversion of ideas and ideals as in our time."[23] We have moved from an educational system that was theistically based to one that is humanistically based. The result is the disappearance of a modern mind and its replacement by a modern mood that is transient, relative, shifting, and owes no allegiance to anything except itself. His conclusion is that what is at stake in the crises of learning is the survival both of the university and of society. Unless learning and unless Western society recover a core of common values that is theistically centered, relativism "will doom man to mistake himself and his neighbor for passing shadows in the night, transient oddities with no future but the grave."[24] It is no surprise, therefore, that the canons of academic "integrity" more or less demand as a condition of acceptance into the guild that text and meaning be disengaged. It is permissible to study the text as an ancient document; it is not permissible to employ that text as an external authority, for that surely violates the very conditions without whose presence academic learning supposedly cannot proceed. But what happens in the university is not really different from what happens in a society in whch modernization is a powerful reality. Contemporary sociologists have shown how modernization sunders apart private from public life, the internal from the external. Christian meaning, therefore, is relegated to the interior, to the simple function of providing a sense of personal coherence, of inner meaning, and the connections to the external world are often almost entirely lost. This, too, is a mysticism, for once again text and meaning are largely disengaged.

Tracy was entirely correct to argue that theology is, in its nature, triangular. It has a confessional dimension which it has to relate to both culture and to academia. He was also correct in noting that most contemporary theologies have abandoned the struggle to do this for the claims of each of these elements can only be satisfied at the price of each other. The conception therefore becomes self-destructive. The reason for this is that most contemporary theology has not seen that a confessional base composed only of a mystical meaning cut loose from a biblical norm simply is not able to adjudicate the competing claims that bear down upon it from culture and academia. This kind of mysticism may give the illusion of having a controlling center, but in fact at its center is an emptiness whose functions have to be assumed either by social interests or by the academic culture.

The Agenda

The agenda that Tracy saw is an agenda awaiting fulfillment. The evangelical understanding of Scripture as a disclosure of transcendent truth, communicated in and through the language of Scripture, is not a foolish irrelevance that stands in the way of doing serious theology; it is the *sine qua non* without which serious theology cannot be done at all, for without it there is no way of authorizing any belief. Without it, the authorization is at most on the grounds of personal preference. What makes this alternative seem desirable to contemporary people is that it allows large scope for the reality of pluralism and diversity. Our experience of social diversity, secured and guaranteed under the Constitution, should not, however, spawn in our minds the kind of relativism which inevitably results from grounding truth claims simply on internal preference.[25] In the end, as Bloom has observed, this becomes self-destructive.

What actually stands in the way of doing serious theology, then, are the unexamined assumptions of the twentieth century mind, many of which simply echo the social environment in which we now live. Theologies which are conceived in this environment, and which are not able to rise above it through a meaning divinely given, will simply be voices that bounce from side to side in the echo chamber of modernity. There will be no legitimacy, no authority, to what they say, no matter how long and hard they try to absolutize personal preferential options.

The prospects for creating a new, vital, cogent, and compelling theology which is revelational in its assumptions and content are now extraordinarily bright but also extraordinarily threatened. What is most needed is what the historic Christian view on biblical revelation actually secures and that is the means to authorize and prescribe what is right, not because of horizontal preferences, but because of a vertical and transcendent meaning which has been divinely given and which has the power to relativise all human thought. However, the evangelical capacity to deliver on a confessional source such as this has been deeply undermined by modernity. When biblical inerrancy is privatized, it is stripped of its capacity to address either academia or the culture. Biblical inerrancy may remain privately compelling to evangelicals, and serve as a party rallying cry, but it becomes publicly irrelevant because in the context of modernity it, too, can be reduced to nothing more than private preference.

The question that evangelicals have to face is not whether they will give a ritual consent to inerrancy, but whether they really think that human beings have access to *truth* which, because it is divinely given and secured, is the final measure of what is there,

David F. Wells

whether this is truth that spans both private and public life, and whether it is the same truth for all people in all cultures.

This is the historic Protestant position; it is not always the position on which evangelicals act today. We need, therefore, not only to affirm Scripture's inerrancy, which has to do with its *nature,* but also to act on its infallibility, which has to do with its authoritative and certain *function* in our modern world. We cannot have this function unless Scripture is, by the Holy Spirit's inspiration, God's Word in which text and meaning coincide; it is, however, possible to have a Scripture which is believed to be textually inerrant but which is, regrettably, shorn of its authoritative function of meaning. In the end, this produces a modern orthodoxy which, because of its modernity, is no longer orthodox, but an exercise in futility. "Let the buyer beware — *caveat emptor!*"

---

[1]The exact religious condition of the American people is not easy to read. It is clear that a substantial core of traditional beliefs remains intact and in that sense secularism has made only the most modest progress. On the other hand, those beliefs do not appear to be very functional or determinative and so in that sense America has been secularized. See Richard John Neuhaus, ed., *Unsecular America* (Grand Rapids: Eerdmans Publishing Co., 1986).

[2]The collapse of authority into power has had a profoundly destabilizing effect on society. Specifically, it raises questions about the legitimation of social institutions. On this see, for example, Robert Wuthnow, *The Restructuring of American Religion: Society and Faith Since World War II* (Princeton: Princeton University Press, 1988) 242-50. Indeed, the disappearance of some moral realm from which values can be derived, Anthony Arblaster believes, goes a long way to explaining the disappearance of the Liberal tradition in the West. See his *The Rise and Decline of Western Liberalism* (Oxford: Basil Blackwell, 1984) 334-39.

[3]For a discussion of how the disappearance of the function of tradition has affected one theological tradition, see James Davison Hunter, *Evangelicalism: The Coming Generation* (Chicago: University of Chicago Press, 1987) 157-64.

[4]Richard John Neuhaus, *The Naked Public Square: Religion and Democracy in America* (Grand Rapids: Eerdmans Publishing Co., 1984).

[5]David H. Kelsey, *The Uses of Scripture in Recent Theology* (Philadelphia: Fortress Press: 1975) 1.

[6]Ronald F. Thiemann, *Radiance and Obscurity in Biblical Narratives* (Unpublished paper presented to the Boston Theological Society, March, 1989).

[7]This brief summary scarcely does justice to the intricacies of Barth's view which is developed in his *Church Dogmatics,* trans. G.T. Thomson (5 vols.; Edinburgh: T.and T. Clark, 1936-77) I, parts 1 and 2.

[8]For Bultmann's general views, as opposed to the technicalities of the demythologization program, see especially his *Existence and Faith: Shorter Writings,* trans. Schubert Ogden (New York: Meridian Books, 1960).

[9]Norman Perrin, *What is Redaction Criticism?* (Philadelphia: Fortress Press, 1969).

[10]Examples of this approach are Juan Luis Segundo, *Liberation of Theology,* trans. John Drury (Maryknoll: Orbi Books, 1976); James Cone, *A Black Theology of Liberation* (Philadelphia: Lippincott, 1970); Letty M. Russell, *Human Liberation in a Feminist Perspective: A Theology* (Philadelphia: Westminster Press, 1974).

[11]Benjamin Breckenridge Warfield, *The Inspiration and Authority of the Bible* (Philadelphia: Presbyterian and Reformed Publishing Co., 1970) 299.

[12]Ibid.

[13]Ibid., 348. The position that Warfield developed within a circumscribed biblical focus, Carl Henry has most completely filled out in relation to contemporary thought. See his *God. Revelation and Authority* (5 vols., Waco: Word, 1982-84).

[14]The current thinking that I have in mind is what is seen, for example, in James Barr's *The Semantics of Biblical Language* (Oxford: Oxford University Press, 1961). See also Arthur F. Holmes, "Ordinary Language Analysis and Theological Method," *The Bulletin of the Evangelical Theological Society,* 11 No. 3 (Summer, 1968) 131-38.

[15]For a careful exploration of the role of language in the communication of revelation, see Wayne Grudem, "Scripture's Self- Attestation and the Problem of Formulating a Doctrine of Scripture," *Scripture and Truth.* ed. D.A. Carson and John D. Woodbridge (Grand Rapids: Zondervan, 1983)19-59.

[16]This categorization is not entirely accurate. The newer hermeneutical interests are evident in those works which make a studied preference of infallibility over inerrancy such as G.C. Berkouwer, *Studies in Dogmatics: Holy Scripture,* trans. Jack B. Rogers (Grand Rapids: Eerdmans Publishing Co., 1975); Dewey Beegle, *Scripture, Tradition and Infal-*

David F. Wells

libility (Grand Rapids: Eerdmans Publishing Co.,1983); and Stephen Davis, *The Debate about the Bible* (Philadelphia: Westminster Press, 1977). On the edges of inerrancy are those, however, who argue for a "limited" inerrancy which, in practice looks like a form of (loose) infallibility. See, for example, J. Barton Payne, "Partial Omniscience: Observations on Limited Inerrancy," *The Journal of the Evangelical Theological Society*, 18, no. 1 (Winter, 1975)37- 40; Vern Sheridan Poythress, "Problems for Limited Inerrancy,"*The Journal of the Evangelical Theological Society*, 18, no. 2 (Spring, 1975)93-103; Richard J. Coleman, "Reconsidering 'limited Inerrancy,'" *The Journal of the Evangelical Theological Society*, 17, no. 4 (Fall, 1974) 207-14.

[17]I am here summarizing the conclusions to my own study entitled *The Person of Christ: A Biblical and Historical Analysis* (Westchester: Crossways, 1984) 21-84.

[18]Hunter, 27-8.

[19]Some of the more notable contributions to the discussion on methodology would include: Anton Grabner-Haider, *Theorie der Theologie als Wissenschaft* (München: Kosel-verlag, 1974); Edward Farley, *Ecclesial Reflection: An Anatomy of Theological Method* (Philadelphia: Fortress Press, 1982); Anders Nygren, *Meaning and Method: Prolegomena to a Scientific Philosophy of Religion and a Scientific Theology*, trans. Philip S. Watson (Philadelphia: Fortress Press, 1972); Bernard Lonergan, *Method in Theology* (New York: Herder and Herder, 1972); Gordon Kaufmann, *An Essay in Theological Method* (Missoula: Scholars Press, 1975); George Lindbeck, *The Nature of Doctrine: Religion and Theology in a Postliberal Age* (Philadelphia: Westminster Press, 1984); David Tracy, *Blessed Rage for Order* (New York: Seabury Press, 1970); and Thomas Torrance, *Theological Science* (London: Oxford University Press, 1969). Among the journal articles, see the following: A.A. Glenn, "Criteria for Theological Models," *Scottish Journal of Theology*, 25 (Aug.,1975)296-308; Alfred T. Hennelly, "Theological Method: The Southern Exposure,"*Theological Studies*, 38 (Dec., 1977) 709-35; Robert D. Knudsen, "Analysis of Theological Concepts: A Methodological Sketch," *Westminster Theological Journal*, 40 (Spring, 1978) 229-44; R.P. Scharlemann, "Theological Models and Their Construction," *Journal of Religion*, 53 (Jan. 1973) 65-82; and Don Wiebe, "Explanation and Theological Method," *Zygon*, II (March, 1976) 35-49.

[20]David Tracy, "Whatever Happened to Theology?" *Christianity and Crisis* 35, no. 8 (May 12, 1975) 119-20. These themes, of course, are expanded in his book cited earlier and in this summary I have kept in mind his expansion. See also his "Modes of Theological Argument," *Theology Today*. 33 (Jan. 1977) 387- 95.

[21]See the acute analysis offered of these problems in Van Austin Harvey, *The Historian and the Believer: The Morality of Historical Knowledge and Christian Belief* (New York: Macmillan, 1966). More recently Mark Noll has explored similar terrain,

especially as this has related to American evangelical scholars in the biblical field. See his excellent book *Between Faith and Criticism: Evangelicals, Scholarship, and the Bible in America* (New York: Harper and Row, 1986).

[22]Richard Hofstadter, "The Revolution in Higher Education," *Paths in American Thought.* ed. Arthur M. Schlessinger and Morton White (Boston: Houghton and Mifflin, 1963) 269-90. Among historians there are not substantial differences with regard to the facts of college and university life in America in the second half of last century. There is substantial disagreement, however, over what we should make of those facts, specifically, whether the disappearance of a Christian world view has been a good or a bad thing. On this point see the fine essays by William C. Ringenberg, "The Old-Time College, 1800-1865," *Making Higher Education Christian: The History and Mission of Evangelical Colleges in America,* ed. Joel A. Carpenter and Kenneth Shipps (Grand Rapids: Eerdmans Publishing Co., 1987) 77-97, and the two essays by Mark Noll in the same volume, "The Revolution, the Enlightenment, and Higher Education in the Early Republic" (56- 76) and "The University Arrives in America, 1870-1930: Christian Traditionalism During the Academic Revolution" (98-109).

[23]Carl F. H. Henry, *The Christian Mindset in a Secular Society: Promoting Evangelical Renewal and National Righteousness* (Portland: Multnomah Press, 1978) 81.

[24]Ibid.

[25]Peter Berger has explored this reality with considerable insight, arguing that modern pluralization undercuts plausibility structures in society which in turn spawns pluralism and, hence, relativism as belief becomes increasingly subjective. See, for example, his *A Rumor of Angels: Modern Society and the Rediscovery of the Supernatural* (New York: Doubleday, 1969) 35-60. Cf: James Hunter, "Subjectivization and the New Evangelical Theodicy," *Journal for the Scientific Study of Religion,* 21 (March, 1982) 39.

RESPONSE TO DAVID F. WELLS

Robert Sloan

David Wells' presentation on May 15, 1989, to the Evangelical Affirmations consultation was substantially different from the paper which he now presents for publication in this volume. Nonetheless, in keeping with the intended purpose of this volume, I have chosen, except for this prefatory statement, *not* to revise my paper in light of Dr. Wells' most recent deletions, revisions, and additions. I, of course, run the risk of having my paper appear to the reader who did not attend the conference, as a response to issues that were not raised. However, to the careful reader, I think Dr. Wells' original arguments regarding the nature of biblical authority can be understood from my summary of his views and my responses thereto. It is, I think, especially unfortunate for the larger readership of this volume that Dr. Wells has withdrawn many of the assertions upon which much of my response was based since, according to his original text, the kind of argumentation he used to substantiate both the divinity of Christ and, in a related argument, the inspiration and authority of Scripture "is, of course, a commonplace among traditional theologies." If that is true, then certainly this issue needs wider discussion.

In his revision, Dr. Wells now additionally (and rightly) bemoans the work of the literary deconstructionists who radically separate text from meaning. I had, however, already responded to his (to me) oversimplified treatment of the separation of text and meaning. What follows, then, with very minor changes, is the paper I originally prepared for the conference.

Finally, I should like to emphasize once again my deep gratitude to the sponsors of the consultation on Evangelical Affirmations, recalling warmly what was, overall, a very edifying and stimulating experience.

* * *

Professor Wells' paper is, to summarize it briefly: (1) a lament over the loss of two of the three ligaments of Western civilization, tradition and especially authority, leaving only power; (2) a brief discussion of the terms exousia (authority) and dynamis (power) followed by (a) an argument for the divinity/legitimate authority of Christ, which is paralleled by (b) the inspiration of Scripture; (3) a plea for the engagement/coincidence of text and meaning for the hermeneutical enterprise as a conceptual bonding which is both (a) accomplished by inspiration and secured in the use of the word "inerrancy" and (b) necessary to meet the challenge of providing valid authorizations for theological proposals; and (4) the observation that modern theology, having given up any external authority (such as the Bible) whereby it is capable of speaking to both culture and academia will continue to lack legitimacy so long as it continues to reject the historic Christian view of biblical revelation, which alone can authorize and prescribe what is right for both life and thought.

I'm very appreciative of Professor Wells' paper on at least three accounts. First, I applaud his strong appeal for biblical authority. Secondly, I think he is correct in his desire to relate biblical authority to christology. Thirdly, I think he is correct in pointing to the problem of hermeneutics/interpretation/meaning as integrally related both to the authority of Scripture and the truthfulness/relevance of theological proposals. Having agreed with Professor Wells regarding the importance of these specific thought areas, however, I must admit that I find little to agree with in terms of his actual development of these issues.

To begin with, I think Professor Wells' argument regarding the divinity of Christ is historically faulty. His logic runs like this: (1) since the kingdom is God's kingdom, only God can exercise its rule; (2) God's rule was inaugurated by Christ; (3) therefore, Christ had to be divine. The logic seems impeccable, but I question the restrictive interpretation given assumption (1) above. The fact that it is God's kingdom and that, therefore, the rule of the kingdom is ultimately God's does not, it seems to me, necessarily rule out God's use of various other, nondivine, agencies to accomplish "what only God could do." Certainly Christ is divine. The New Testament affirms it rather strongly and Christians have historically believed it. But I would not myself hang the incarnation on this particular line of reasoning. Certainly long before the coming of Christ the Jews had expected a Messianic reign. That is, at least by the time of Christ the reign of God was in some sense conceived of as a Messianic reign. But there is no evidence that the Jews ever thought of Messiah as God. Why did *they* not make the connection between Messiah and divinity? Messiah was to be God's *agent*. Put simply, to say that one does the work of God, and/or does "what only God could do" does not make one God. The writing of Holy Scripture is something only God can do, but that does not make his agents divine. While there is no doubt that the New Testament authors make a rather extensive identification linguistically between Jesus and Yahweh, the *warrant* for this identification is not, as Professor Wells too generally argues with reference to the "authoritative words" and "miraculous acts" of Jesus, "because the 'age to come' was inaugurated in Christ and by Him. . . ." The more specific New Testament warrant for the Lordship of Christ, where "Lord" is not merely a reverential title but is linked to Old Testament names for God, is the resurrection and exaltation of Jesus to the right hand of God (Acts 2:33-36; Phil. 2:6-11). The exaltation of Christ, of course, culminates the initiation of God's reign in the teaching and miracle ministry of Jesus, but warrants for His divinity are grounded more in the former than the latter. Indeed, prophetic (divinely authoritative) teaching and the doing of miracles are elsewhere attested in Scripture, but nowhere, save in the case of Christ, and that for different reasons, is the agent of such deeds acclaimed as Lord.

Of course, Dr. Wells' point is not primarily to argue for the divinity of Christ but to establish the connection between function and ontology: that is, the divine identity of Christ is the only adequate explanation of his function in the Gospels. But his *way* of establishing the divinity of Christ is somehow also related (I think the connection is fuzzy) to his way of establishing the inspiration of Scripture, for Dr. Wells then proceeds to declare that this relationship between function and essence in Christ has a clear parallel with Scripture. I quite agree that christology and the doctrine of Scripture are integrally related, but I can see no basis for this particular parallel. In the first place, one need not point to the experience of Christ to establish what seems to me to be the rather sound metaphysical principle that says function is related to essence. If that is so, then I see no reason for Professor Wells' argument to begin with the divinity of Christ.

I, myself, would argue that the connection between Christ and the inspiration of Scripture should be thought of in terms of the life (including the death and resurrection) and theology of Jesus as indispensably and correctly interpreted via what I would call the apostolic theology and preserved for us in those occasional pieces which the Church, in the providence of God, has preserved and collected into a canon of Scripture. That is, the authority of the New Testament is inextricably linked up with the truthfulness of Christianity and not Christ's divinity per se, though the latter is to be strongly affirmed. Put another way, since the earliest Christian preaching/theology preceded historically the text(s) of the New Testament, either collectively or individually (i.e., since the documents themselves were produced in environments of Christian confession and theology), then it seems likely that the authority of the New Testament, viewed historically in terms of its emergence in the life of the church(es), is a derivative of the normative apostolic theology/authority of the earliest Christian leaders and is best defended on these grounds.[1]

Professor Wells, on the other hand, seems to argue on two fronts. First, he argues that the Scriptures must be inspired because, parallel to the relationship between function and identity in Christ, there is a parallel between function and identity in Scripture. That is, because it serves "to reveal the character, will, and deeds of God, thus doing only what God himself could do, Scripture must be inspired." But the warrant for this particular parallel between Christ and the Scripture, this parallel of identity and function, is never made clear.

Then, Professor Wells shifts arguments to state that Jesus viewed and used the Old Testament as inspired Scripture, and that it was "plainly his intention that the church would have in its hands

181

the completed account of God's redemptive acts in history, and their interpretation, so that his people would have an objective authority to legitimate and correct belief and practice." I know of no Scriptural warrant to justify Professor Wells' assumption that Christ intended his church to have a completed account (presumably the New Testament) of God's redemptive acts in history. Certainly I am glad that we do, but Professor Wells' assertion in this regard is textually and historically unwarranted.

Professor Wells' next argument seems to be that Christ's commissioning of his apostles was for the express purpose of producing Scripture. Granted, Professor Wells never precisely says that, but that seems to be the clear impression of his words on page 6 when he writes, "Christ therefore (emphasis added) commissioned his apostles as his representatives so that John could boldly assert that they were 'of God' and whoever knew God would recognize this (I John 4:6)." I may have misunderstood Professor Wells here, but I can see no other function for the "therefore" in this sentence, which immediately follows the one quoted earlier regarding our Lord's "intention that the church would have in its hands the completed account of God's completed acts in history. . . . " In fact, Dr. Wells' general argument seems to be that (1) Christ the divine one exercised authority as God; (2) Christ commissioned and authorized his apostles to teach in his name, the clear implication being that this would involve the writing of Scripture; and (3) the Holy Spirit, the Spirit of Christ, "secured and directed this function."

I see several problems here. First of all, the two or three Scriptural warrants given to support the authority of the apostles' writings — especially John 14:26 where the apostles are told that the Holy Spirit will "teach you all things, and bring to your remembrance all that I said to you" and the reference in II Tim. 3:16 to the inspiration of Scripture — are themselves very dubious warrants for the authority of the New Testament. Second, certainly the apostles are authorized by Christ, but (a) the New Testament by and large was not written by the Twelve, nor even mostly — even accepting a wider definition for the term "apostles" and accepting as well all the traditional authorships — by apostles; and (b) to say that Christ authorized his apostles as divine spokesmen is not yet to say that what they write is to be regarded as *Scripture*. I will readily admit, indeed I would strongly argue, that the words of, say, Paul were both thought of by Paul as authoritative and intended by him to be received by his audiences as authoritative. But the authority must be thought of as an apostolic/prophetic authority. That is, the Pauline letters are a substitute for the apostolic presence. As such, of course, they possess the authority of the apostle himself. But to say (1) that they are authoritative, or even to say (2) that their authority was on a par with either Old Testament Scripture or the words of the historical Jesus for both Paul and the original recipients — the latter statement being one which I doubt we can make — is still not yet to say that Paul's writings possess authority as *Scripture*. With the single exception of I Cor. 14:37, every example adduced by Professor Wells to support his notion that the apostles claimed "divine authority for their words and writings" are texts which illustrate the divine authority which they attached to their *preaching*. And the text in I Cor. 14:37 cannot plausibly be expanded much beyond the immediate context of I. Cor. 12-14 and/or at best the context of I Cor. as a whole. At any rate, while the authority of those referred to as "apostle," whether of the Twelve or not, is certainly explicit, their words are nowhere in the New Testament clearly designated as *Scripture* (I Tim. 5:18 and II Peter 3:15,16 notwithstanding).[2]

All of which is certainly not, for my part, to deny the ultimate correctness of that designation in succeeding generations. But it is to say that I find Professor Wells' arguments regarding the divinity of Christ as integral (1) to a "function reveals nature" substantiation of Biblical inspiration, or (2) to establishing a chain of authority passing from God/Christ through the apostles and ultimately to our texts to be (1) logically unnecessary, (2) textually unwarranted at several points, (3) polemically unparalleled in Scripture (i.e., the New Testament doesn't argue that way), and (4) largely unrelated to the "hermeneutical quagmire" that Professor Wells so rightly laments. With this latter point (4) I am assuming that arguments for the inspiration of Scripture should not be separated from the purpose of Scripture — i.e., its theologically unified testimony to the crucified, risen, and exalted Lord Jesus. One should not make an appeal *for* the authority of Scripture without appealing *to* its central message, which means that hermeneutical decisions must be made about its theological unity and core.

In addressing the current "hermeneutical quagmire" Professor Wells observes the fact of the many jarringly contradictory theologies on the modern scene and attributes this fact to the disengagement between text and meaning. I would agree that the disengagement of theology from the biblical text is certainly a significant cause for the current plurality of theologies vying for the name of "Christian," but it is not the only reason for current difficulties. Even those who insist upon deriving theology from the text of Scripture differ in not insignificant ways.[3] I would argue that some people simply have not learned how to read.

But granting the problem of separation between text and "meaning" (Dr. Wells does not, it seems to me, distinguish between what a text "meant" and what a text "means"; the best I can tell, by "meaning" he means something like "the proper theological meaning for us"), I still have a multitude of problems with Professor Wells' analysis of this issue. After lamenting Barth's attempt to derive meaning from "above," Bultmann's attempt to derive meaning from "within," Perrin's attempt to derive theological meaning from "behind" the text, and the World Council of Churches' attempt to locate meaning "chronologically beyond the text," Professor Wells then appeals to B. B. Warfield as arguing that the inspiration of Scripture secures the coincidence of words and meaning. Apart from the fact that it is difficult to see exactly how the fact of inspiration should dictate a particular hermeneutical method, or in what way it does so, if it does, this is not in fact, what Warfield argued. Warfield's point was not to identify text with meaning, but to identify the voice of God and the Scriptures *with regard to their authority.*[4] The fact that "when the Scriptures speak, God speaks" meant for Warfield that the Scriptures speak with the authority of God; but not that, when God speaks in Scripture, a certain hermeneutical model is mandated and thus a more theologically accurate meaning is made possible. To say that the Scriptures and/or the voice of God is utterly authoritative does not mean that we will more easily or more accurately come by the meaning of either. One must still do the hermeneutical/interpretive task. Indeed, it is all very well to say

Robert Sloan

with Professor Wells that meaning is "in" a text, but since text and
meaning (either the original meaning or its ongoing significance)
are not identical, and thus must be separated one from the other,
I see nothing sacred in the preposition "in." Whatever preposition
we use to define the relationship between text and meaning, we
must maintain not only that the text exercises determinative
control over the parameters of meaning which may be derived
from it, but we must realize that the hermeneutical task is always
unavoidable.

Meaning certainly is not only "in" a text, but is also "evoked"
by a text, and I would also argue, can be "behind" a text, and even
(I am thinking here of the parousia) in some sense "chronologically beyond" the text. One must never forget that our texts are
both particular and universal. And while these two functions are
inextricably related — that is, I quite agree that any non-particu-
larist meaning falls under the controls of the particularist — they
must not be confused. Our texts were written for particular people,
addressing particular problems, at particular times in their history
(I am thinking here especially of New Testament epistles). Once,
for example, Colossians was read to the church at Colossae, and
once it was passed on to the Laodiceans (4:16), there is a sense in
which its *particular* meaning and relevance were exhausted. That
is, for example, the instruction to send the letter on to Laodicea
would not have had the same meaning upon a second reading —
once the letter or a copy thereof had been sent to Laodicea — as
it will have had upon a first reading. Indeed, since Colossians was
apparently intended primarily for the church at Colossae, the
meaning of that same phrase, not to say the entirety of the epistle,
cannot have been exactly the same for the Laodiceans as it was for

the Colossians. Almost immediately the text, once it is preserved and re-read, can no longer remain a particularist document — though it does become a document of abiding value, whose particularist meaning (i.e., that which I would tie to such things as authorial intention and original audience and setting) is still both to a greater or lesser extent (depending on all kinds of historical factors) recoverable and determinative of the ongoing and legitimate significance(s) the text will have for subsequent generations of devoted hearers and readers. From the very beginning, the interpretative "leap" from original intention and original audience to "on-going application and relevance" must be made.

Indeed, even the *first* reading of a text — I am thinking here of II Thessalonians — not only involves the normal hermeneutical processes of deciphering what is "in" the text, but must surely involve, for a proper understanding of its meaning, events and realities which are "outside" the text. Surely the Thessalonians' personal knowledge of Paul, their experience of him in Thessalonica, their knowledge of his theology, his voice, his personality, and the things that he had previously written and taught (2:56,15; 3:6-10) affected their hearing of his letter. Certainly their knowledge of Paul and the other above mentioned factors, and indeed *Paul's knowledge of their knowledge of him* are factors that, though no doubt virtually lost to us in terms of our "universal" reading of the text, were not only "outside" the text, *but relevant to the meaning of the text as intended by Paul.*

One last series of observations. Professor Wells ends his paper by saying that we need an external, objective authority to legitimate values and belief. In fact, something of that sort is said throughout the paper. I want to inject, however, that what we "need" is not the issue. The real issue is what do we *have*. The fact that some people, indeed most of us, want various kinds of certainty tells us something about ourselves, but it need not tell us anything about the Scriptures that in fact we have. We simply must no longer argue that, since modern theology is in a mess, flailing about with no objective authority to regulate it, modern man must therefore posit the authority of the Bible as an epistemological way out of the mess. We can offer only what we have, which also means we can neither avoid the question of what legitimates the Bible, nor can we expect the unbelieving world to refuse to ask the question.

Our commitment to the authority of Scripture may be taken as a premise only in so far as we are prepared to accept the Christian *tradition* of Scripture as authoritative. I readily agree that the modern rejection of tradition is to be lamented, but I am nonetheless not prepared to insist upon the uncritical acceptance of any tradition. Martin Luther's rather radical, and correct, reassessment of the canon of Scripture is too recent historically for any of us either to be the slaves of tradition ourselves or to insist upon the authority of the Bible for others simply upon the basis of our tradition. The authority of the Scriptures for us/the modern world must derive, as it seems to me it did from the very beginning, from a pattern and complex of reasons which themselves are subject to the normal canons of inquiry.

I would suggest the following as belonging to a complex of reasons whereby we may argue for the authority of the Scriptures:

1. Though never forgetting the example of Luther and others who dared to challenge the weight of tradition, we may accept (and the modern world ought at least to respect) the

authority of Scripture because we receive it as such in our tradition.

2. The power of the Scriptures in the context of worship both to evoke and to authenticate the experience of the risen Lord attests to their divine origin.

3. Their primitive, historical connection to Christ and/or eye-witness testimony about Christ, argues for the authenticity of the New Testament writings as a true witness to the real Jesus.

4. The theological conformity of the New Testament Scriptures to the theology of Jesus (and his reading of the Old Testament) and the cross/resurrection (kerygmatic) theology of his immediate followers argues for the indispensable function (and thus authority) of the New Testament writings as the correct interpretation of both the Jewish Scriptures and all that God has done through the person of Jesus Christ. We must never forget that early Christian theology preceded the rise of both the individual New Testament documents and their collection within one binding. That is, the correctness and/or use of any given document may well have been decided by its conformity to the apostolic theology, that is, the core of early Christian thought, preaching, and worship.

As Professor Wells himself insists, Christian theology cannot fail to address the academy. But to do so, we cannot presuppose that the academy will accept either our tradition about the authority of Scripture, or our circular appeals to the self-attestation of Scripture. We will have to supply warrants for the Bible in much the same way as we argue for the truthfulness of Christianity: i.e., by the canons of history and reason. In this way, christology/soteriology are related to inspiration, and the doctrine of

Robert Sloan

inspiration — because it relates to a particular and historical body of literature, and because the message of everlasting life contained therein must also be announced to the academy, and because the texts themselves are of a piece with the divine activity that has culminated in the person of Jesus Christ — must itself be subjected to the same kinds of historical scrutiny and, alas, even skepticism, that are applied to the message of salvation itself. The task is not easy, but our mandate is clear. And, though the academy may sneer to hear us say it, we live in the hope of ultimate vindication, for truth is on our side.

[1] I am here assuming what must, in another context, be defended, i.e., that there is a theological center and/or unity which holds together these documents and thus becomes not only a guide to their interpretation, but also an adjudicating norm for competing theological proposals—proposals that in the modern era appeal to many different (e.g., non-cross/ resurrection) construals of Jesus.

[2] One occasionally sees these passages referred to as examples of one portion of the New Testament referring to another portion as "Scripture"; see, e.g., Wayne Grudem, "Scripture's Self-Attestation and the Problem of Formulating a Doctrine of Scripture," in *Scripture and Truth*, ed. D. A. Carson and John D. Woodbridge (Grand Rapids: Zondervan, 1983) 46,48; but the issues involved in each case are manifold and not easily resolved. In the case of I Tim. 5:18 the allusion to the saying contained in Lk. 10:7 (assuming Luke's Gospel as the literary source for the saying) could well represent, taking the *kai* as epexegetic, the standard Christian interpretation (learned from Jesus) of Deut. 25:4, so that the reference to "Scripture" in I Tim. 5:18 is a reference to Deut. 25:4 and not Lk. 10:7. In the case of II Peter 3:15,16 the reference to "the rest of the Scriptures," an expression which seemingly includes the letters of Paul, may, but need not, be so understood. See Charles Bigg, *Epistles of St. Jude and St. Peter* (Edinburgh: T & T Clark, 1902) 301f.

[3] Roman Catholics, Jehovah's Witnesses, Presbyterians, and Baptists all affirm the authority of Scripture, but that fact has not prevented their extremely divergent ways of reading Scripture.

[4] B. B. Warfield, *The Inspiration and Authority of the Bible* (Philadelphia: Presbyterian and Reformed Publishing Co., 1970) 299.

QUESTIONS
FOR DISCUSSION

1. What is the difference between power and authority and why is this important?

2. What is the connection between divine authority from God and the prophetic and apostolic authority of the Bible?

3. What does Kafka's parable illustrate with regard to biblical interpretation?

4. How might B. B. Warfield's view of text and meaning "take on fresh currency" in the light of the problem illustrated by Kafka's parable?

5. Modern biblical interpreters say that the meaning of the text is found in the text, above the text, behind the text, beyond the text, or in the interpreter. Define the differences between the various loci of meaning. Where do you think meaning is found? Why? How does your answer affect your study of the Bible?

6. Distinguish between the infallibility of the Bible as that term is used by some modern thinkers and the inerrancy of the Bible as evangelicals understand that term. Why have evangelicals insisted on the inerrancy as well as the infallibility of the Bible?

7. How is the evangelical view of text and meaning (i.e. biblical authority) important to the modern church?

6

PERSONAL
ETHICS

CHRISTIAN PERSONAL ETHICS [1]

Kenneth S. Kantzer

What most Americans want, so poll after poll reveals, and therefore, what they are motivated to seek, is first, good health and second, a good secure job.[2] There is nothing inherently wrong with either of these goals. If we are honest, most of us would readily confess we should like to have good health and a good secure job with a dependable income. Yet all of us know that not everybody is going to enjoy either good health or a secure job. Anyone who makes this his ultimate goal in life is headed for frustration and discouragement.

One of the most observable facts of life, moreover, is that those who make personal happiness their goal do not find it.[3] The happiest people are those who do not seek happiness but, rather, are unhappy with the world as it is, and so choose to become change agents in the world to make the world a better place to live.[4]

Nowhere in the Bible is the Biblical way of life presented in sharper contrast with the way of life typical of most Americans than in the second chapter of Paul's epistle to the Philippians: "Have this mind in you which was also in Christ Jesus, who being in the form of God did not consider this a matter of grasping things for himself but instead chose to forego his divine prerogatives and give himself in service to others."[5]

This profound Biblical truth, characteristically enough, is embedded in a solid theological lesson about the deity of Christ,

Kenneth S. Kantzer

the purpose of the incarnation, the atonement and the plan of God for humankind.[6] This is no accident. Biblical ethics is based, solidly and irremovably, on Christian theology. To destroy one is to destroy the other.[7]

This is the major lesson to be learned from the late nineteenth century movement we call "Liberalism." Its fundamental error lay in its rejection of supernatural Biblical doctrine. Liberalism was so enamored of Christian ethics that it sought to retain Biblical ethics intact without its foundation in Christian doctrine.[8] Needless to say, it didn't work. The malaise of institutions dominated by this radical perversion of Biblical Christianity proved devastating even when it was not fatal.[9]

We must begin our discussion of Biblical personal ethics, therefore, by establishing it firmly on its proper foundation of Biblical doctrine. This task has not been made easier by the vast neglect of personal ethics among Biblical scholars of the last generation.[10] For the most part, their quite justifiable concern for social ethics took them out into the world where they rarely found it necessary to tap back into the Biblical roots. Literally, their ethical agenda as theologians was set by the social and political movements of the culture around them.[11] The realm of personal ethics was largely left in the hands of fundamentalist and evangelical scholars. And for the past two generations now, evangelical scholars have, all too often, not done their homework in serious exegesis of the Biblical material relating to the personal Christian life.[12] For the most part the energy of conservative scholars has been consumed by apologetics and foundational theology,[13] and they have relegated personal ethics to popular expositions which concentrate on exhortation rather than on solid Biblical exegesis.[14]

Even so, I hesitate to fault them. They were endeavoring, with limited resources, to stand in the gap. Yet in the final analysis, sound doctrine without its necessary complement of personal ethics, is as unbiblical as its Liberal alternative of ethics without doctrine.[15]

To itemize all the Biblical doctrines that form the foundation of Christian ethics would necessitate a complete systematic theology. We dare only mention, and outline in briefest fashion, some of the most crucial doctrines undergirding a truly Biblical ethics.[16]

In each case, I have tried to formulate the statement so that Martin Luther, John Calvin, John Wesley and Menno Simons could have signed it with full approval.[17]

Some Doctrinal Foundations of Biblical Ethics

1. The God of the Bible is a holy, loving, sovereign, personal being. He is our Lord. As our Lord, he demands and has a right to demand of us, our gratitude, love, worship, and the ultimate commitment of our soul.[18] In fact, if he were not holy, loving and sovereign, it would be morally wrong for us to make such a commitment to him.[19]

2. God created man and woman in his own image[20] with a physical earthly body and an immaterial immortal soul[21] — a being of infinite value.[22] He created Adam and Eve free, capable of choosing between right and wrong;[23] and he holds all human beings ultimately responsible for their choices.[24]

The human conscience represents a part of the original endowment of human kind. It involves a code of what is right and wrong and a self-judging function (often referred to as the conscience "prick,") to indicate whether or not we have acted according to our own standard. The human conscience is not the immediate work of the Holy Spirit, but a psychological device that is an inherent part of our nature as a moral being made in the image of God.[25]

Sin warped the conscience code and almost destroyed it.[26] But all normal human beings know that some things are right and wrong and are never able completely to erase the code God intended them to have.[27] The code is structured by our earliest training, usually from our parents. It becomes our own as we appropriate it for ourselves; and, ideally, it should be instructed according to the Word of God.[28]

The conscience prick can be dulled or sharpened. There is, in reality, no such thing as too sharp or too keen a conscience. The "overly conscientious" person is not the person who obeys his conscience too faithfully, but rather, the person with a misinformed conscience code so that he thinks he ought to do things that, as a matter of fact, he really ought not to do.[29] Or it is a conscience without forgiveness when we go wrong. A conscience at peace is only attained when we accept by faith God's full and free forgiveness and rest in it. There is no true peace of soul unless we have found this freedom from guilt within our own conscience.[30]

Needless to say, though the voice of conscience is not necessarily the voice of the Holy Spirit, it may become the vehicle for the Holy Spirit by which he convicts of sin, exhorts to good, warns of evil, drives us to repentance and faith, and comforts the soul.[31]

3. Man chose to rebel against God and fell into sin. Most sin is due to pride and selfishness, but all sin is rebellion against God or, in Biblical terminology, unbelief. Sin is unbelief in the sense that it always represents a lack of commitment of oneself to God's lordship. It is always some form of idolatry in its broadest sense — namely a choosing to please ourselves rather than a committing of ourselves to God or a committing of ourselves to anything or anyone other than God.

The fall of our first parents brought moral depravity upon the whole human race.[32] It is total in the sense that it pervades the entire human personality — intellect, will and emotions. No aspect of the human psyche remains pure and uncorrupted by the fall.[33] Accordingly, humankind is now incapable of achieving its own ultimate good. Left to himself, man is morally helpless.[34] Moreover, his depravity has so corrupted his moral sense that he often prefers the bad and does not like what is good. His natural inclinations, therefore, are no reliable guide to what is really right or wrong or what is good or bad for him.[35]

4. Out of love for fallen man, God chose to become incarnate in the God-man, Jesus Christ, who by his life and death made adequate provision for all man's moral needs. He bore on himself the penalty that man deserves and brings to man God's full and free forgiveness on the simple condition of faith or repentance and personal commitment to Christ.[36] Our Lord then sent the Holy Spirit into the world and into his church to apply these benefits to those who turn in trust to him.[37] If, therefore, man does not achieve his highest good, it is not at all because Christ's provision is insufficient. On the contrary it is because of his own wickedness and unwillingness to turn to the Savior for forgiveness and victory over sin.[38]

Kenneth S. Kantzer

[I have specially tried to word this paragraph so that any good Wesleyan as well as good Calvinist will find my language acceptable even if not entirely in accord with his preference.][39]
5. The Bible is the only infallible rule of faith and practice. Its first purpose is to lead us to know Jesus Christ as our divine Lord and Savior, and thus to find salvation from sin.[40] Its second purpose is to provide instruction for the Christian life of the believer who acknowledges Jesus Christ as Lord and Savior.[41] The Bible must not be conceived of, however, as a divine rule book in which God places us under his thumb and commands us to do his bidding. What we call the "law" of God is much better understood in most cases as the Torah or instruction of God for the living of our Christian life. It provides a divine "pre-interpretation" of all that is best for mankind.[42]

The Bible, of course, is not organized as a code of rules, but rather traces the history of God's special dealings with the entire human race and, particularly, with his people of both the older and the newer Testament.[43] There we can find his instructions, spelled out in the concrete historical situations of life.[44] In securing the instruction of Scripture, however, we must always be careful, on whatever topic we are seeking to understand God's guidance, that we have all the teaching of Scripture and not just partial aspects of it.[45] The Bible provides the broadest possible moral axioms, general principles, sub-principles, sub-sub-principles and many specific applications–all of which together represent our necessary and adequate instruction for the living of life on planet earth and the development of Christian character.[46]

6. The crux of Christian Biblical ethics is love applied. In Scripture, love is set forth both as a norm or standard for what is

truly love, and as a motivation — that is, the love for God and men that motivates the believer to do the act which is the act of love. As a norm, love is primarily intellectual. As motivation, it is primarily emotional and voluntary. These functions of the soul, however, cannot be separated. All are intertwined and simultaneously involved in any moral act.[47]

Our Lord sums up the whole of the teaching of the Scripture in the two-fold law of love: "You shall love the Lord your God with all your heart, and with all your soul, and with all your mind. This is the great and foremost commandment. The second is like it, 'You shall love your neighbor as yourself.' On these two commandments depend the whole Law and the Prophets."[48]

In Scripture, therefore, love is a sacrificial desire to give oneself to another, and to bring good to the other; and a true Biblical love is always an instructed love.[49]

In the course of church history, this Christian ethic, based on instructed love, has suffered from constant twisting and warping in almost every possible direction. It would be impossible within the limits of this paper even merely to enumerate the devious ways in which humans have sought out alternatives to the Biblical ethics. We dare list only some of the most common of these perversions or misinterpretations of Christ's love ethics.[50] Some of these alternatives, it should be noted, are fatal to the good life. That is, they so severely warp the basic love ethic of the Bible that they have really moved outside the realm of what can rightly be called "Christian."[51] Others are essentially Christian in their outlook on life, but fail to incorporate the power and beauty of the simple Biblical pattern of a love ethic that combines norm and motivation.[52]

Kenneth S. Kantzer

Misinterpretations of Christ's Love Ethics

1. Pietism: With a long history in the Christian church, pietism becomes the special danger of those who take the Christian religion seriously. Its essence is to make religious practices or one's own Christian experience the central focus. In the Bible, the focus of the life of faith is always upon God, his Christ, our love for the triune God, and in a secondary sense, our neighbor defined as anyone in need.[53]

Of course, it is important to have a right experience and to engage in the right practices. But when our focus is turned aside to our own experience with Christ, or to our faith, or worse yet to our religious practices, we have just to that extent lost the driving force of the Christian gospel. It is not our experience that saves us. Strictly speaking, it is not even faith in Christ that saves us; it is Christ and Christ alone who saves us.[54]

2. Deweyism: John Dewey was the most influential educator the United States has ever produced. He taught that man is essentially good or neutral and, therefore, it is appropriate to give a child what he wishes so as to avoid psychoses. This is contrary to our experience and certainly to the teaching of Scripture. The child is not neutral or good, but shares with the human race a bent toward evil. It is easier for a child to be selfish than for it to be unselfish. It is easier for a child in a tight scrape to lie than to tell the truth. And while it is true that discipline may create psychoses, lawlessness and selfishness must also be guarded against.[55]

Even worse was a second error taught by Dewey: the goal of human development and of all education is conformity or adjustment to the society around us. Dewey believed that this is the way to teach democracy.[56] The same philosophy lies behind the widely read and widely followed book by Dale Carnegie, *How to Win Friends and Influence People.*[57]

In actuality a Christian in ordinary human society ought to have tension. His ultimate goal is not relief from tension, but Christlikeness. Jesus Christ experienced many tensions in his earthly human existence, and sometimes this is necessary for us likewise. Christians need to be prepared to function effectively in a society that is evil. This preparation comes best neither by fitting into the society around us, nor by following our own inclinations and desires. Christ didn't. We need, rather, to learn self discipline and how, on occasion, to resist or even confront those around us and then to forgive and forget.[58]

3. Legalism: The term legalism can be used in two quite different ways. In the book of Galatians the Apostle Paul refers to a doctrine of salvation by obedience to law. The term is often used to describe this fatal denial of the gospel. I am using it here to describe a way of living the Christian life by rigorous obedience to rules.[59]

But rules divorced from love lead to hardness and to an inability to live up to the very rules one recognizes with one's mind. Christian ethics or Biblical ethics is neither anti-nomianism which does away with all law or legalism which conceives of the Christian life as obedience to a set of rules.[60]

As we noted earlier, Biblical love is both norm and motivation. It is theoretically possible to follow rigorously a norm of love — the rules or instruction of the whole Bible — but to do so completely without motivating love. The love of Christ urges us on to a successful Christian life and to the daily living of a life of instructed discerning love. The Levite, travelling along the road to Jericho, knew the Old Testament. As a Levite, it is reasonable to assume that he knew in detail the laws of the Old Testament including the law of love embedded in it. His trouble was not that he lacked the Biblical norm of love. Indeed, he prided himself on his Torah. His lack was the actual experience of love in his heart for the wounded Jew lying along the road. Scripture instructs us as to what true love is. But the motivation to do those things that represent enlightened love should not be the motivation of legal obedience but the motivation of experiential love towards a personal God and towards personal human beings for whom we actually do have true love.[61]

4. Antinomianism: Antinomianism is often supported by a misunderstood quotation from Augustine: "Love God and do as you please". The idea is that, if we love God then we should do exactly what we wish to do and we shall automatically do right.[62]

If we were both omniscient and possessed of a permanent character of complete love, this would be an excellent rule to follow in all cases. But it is never a completely adequate rule for finite, sinful human beings. Our love is never perfect. We often find ourselves loving the wrong things. Moreover, God never intended us to live our lives wholly apart from his instruction. Even Adam lived in the light of his immediate and perfect communion with God. And so we need instruction to enable us to know what really is the act of love.

The basic truth in Antinomianism, of course, is that we do not succeed in the Christian life merely by doing right acts. God could have secured perfect obedience to all his laws simply by creating us as automata who, by nature, could not do otherwise. God preferred to create free persons who would develop a moral character of discerning love. The Bible's happy medium between legalism and antinomianism is instructed holy love.[63]

5. Mysticism or Direct Immediate Revelation: Certainly the Holy Spirit has promised to guide us. God may, if he chooses, provide this guidance through miraculous special revelation on a continuous basis. But he has never promised to do so; and, therefore, we may not claim this from him. He has, however, promised to guide us through Scripture. Therefore, we must know what the Scripture teaches, and we must know the whole of that which it teaches about every ethical matter we face. The better we know the Scripture and the more rigorously we apply it to the details of life, the greater can be our degree of sanctification.[64]

6. Pharisaism: By Pharisaism I mean the selection of particular applications of love and choosing to live one's life on the basis of them. The Pharisees of Christ's day, of course, were also legalists, who trusted in their good works for salvation. Here I refer to their practice of evaluating the quality of life by certain favorite virtues. Christ rebuked them on both grounds. In the Sermon on the Mount he rebukes the Pharisees for following their own ethical traditions. He objects to these traditions just because they circumvent the Biblical ethics, that is, the divine instruction that we ought to follow.[65]

When we today select particular applications of love or particular virtues that we specially prize, we almost invariably choose those in which we ourselves do best. When we judge ourselves on this basis, we naturally find that we do well on our favorite virtues, and thus fall into pride and self-righteousness. By contrast, we judge all others as not doing so well on our favorite rules. No doubt if we chose their favorite rules, they would do better; but on our rules they do not do so well. As a result, our attitude towards others becomes condescending and judgmental and our own spiritual pride increases.[66]

But the worst effect of this situation comes from weighing our own life solely on the basis of our favorite virtues. We thus cannot come to grips with the whole of Biblical teaching. Sin is unrecognized, and unrecognized sin remains unconfessed and unconfessed sin remains unforgiven sin and, therefore, sin that is never overcome.[67] By contrast, God's way of taking care of sin involves the following steps: First, self searching and self judgment (I Cor. 11:31 f.); Second, confession of sin (I John 1:9); Third, repentance from sin (II Cor. 7:8-11); Fourth, restitution where this is possible (Matthew 6); And, finally, fifth, belief in God's promise of forgiveness with a resultant reinstatement into God's fellowship and favor and service (Psalm 51).[68]

Note that God's forgiveness depends upon our honest judging of the sins in our own lives. God does not forgive Pharisees for they do not recognize their soul's sin and, therefore, do not apply to him for forgiveness. God forgives the publican because he sees his need and turns to God.[69]

7. Conventional Morality: Pressure from the group of which we are a part more often than not determines our conduct. We follow the crowd. The great danger from determining what we do by the crowd around us is that we do not live in a Christian world. Hence, when Christians get away from the protection of their Christian home or of their local church club, they need to live by principle and not by pressure. Or, perhaps, it is more accurate to say their love needs to be guided by instruction from Scripture.[70]

It is especially easy for us to fall into the lordship of man instead of the sole lordship of Christ because, when we were children, we were commanded, even commanded by Scripture, to obey our parents.

This is proper.[71] So long as our ideas of right and wrong are determined by our parents, however, we remain ethically immature. It is, therefore, the duty of parents and those who instruct the young to lead them on to maturity. This necessitates instructing children in what is right and wrong according to Holy Scripture *and* gradually weaning them so they do not permanently either decide what is right or wrong on the basis of a parent's "say-so" or do what is right merely out of love for parents. This weaning process must begin very early, for if the child's faith has not become independent of his parents by the time he leaves his parental home, he will find he has no faith adequate for life.[72]

No human being, even the best of parents, is good enough or safe enough for the mature Christian to trust as the ultimate guide for his life. He must find his guidance personally from God not man. No one but God has the right to bind a Christian's conscience.[73]

Yet the Christian does not live out his life in isolation with God. He has been bonded by God into a community of love — the church. The Holy Spirit works upon each believer through his participation in this body. Guidance is to be sought in mutual dependence upon each other. The body life of the church is an important source of our daily strength as Christians and is a primary instrument of God's guidance. Yet the ultimate standard by which all other sources of truth and strength are to be tested is the Word of the living God, and it alone can bind our conscience

Kenneth S. Kantzer

It is true that the Apostle says we are to obey our government "for conscience sake" (Rom. 13:5). But that is only because and to the degree that God has bidden us obey our governments.[74] The only infallible guide by which to set our conscience is the teaching of the whole of Scripture. It becomes the instrument by which the Holy Spirit communicates to us the will of our Lord for our lives.

This does not mean that we never modify our actions to suit others. Oftentimes we compromise our actions to fit the prejudices, even the very thoroughly mistaken prejudices, of those around us. It is right that we should do so. But we are never to compromise our principles. We are never to decide what is right and wrong on the basis of the lordship of any but the one true holy loving sovereign God who has revealed himself in Holy Scripture.[75]

8. The Imitation of Christ: This motivation for ethics can be traced back through Thomas á Kempis to the early church. It received great impetus from the famous novel by Charles Sheldon entitled *In His Steps*.[76] Moreover, according to the New Testament, we are commanded to be like Christ. This is the ultimate goal of the Christian life.[77] Yet the Scriptural command to be like Christ is to be like him in loving and sacrificial service to others. It does not mean that our daily life is to be lived out in conscious imitation of the things that he did. Rather all our action, like all of his, is to be motivated by pure love to God and to our fellow human beings.[78] The Christian life is not a life of imitation. At root, rather, it is a genuine personal life, our own life, but a life lived, like Christ's, in loving service for others.[79]

Of course, we would always be better off if, as a matter of fact, we did follow Christ. Yet our lot falls in different places; and

208

what we are to do is not the thing that was necessarily the loving act in first-century Palestine, but the loving act as we face our world today. Even so, the pattern of Christ still stands as the only perfect life that we have seen on planet earth and, therefore, is our best guide as to what a human life should be like when it is actually lived out in a wicked world.[80]

9. Self-esteem: In recent years, particularly, self-esteem has been held up as a major goal in the Christian life and as a major motivation for living the Christian life.[81] Of course, there is a significant piece of truth in this. We are not encouraged by Scripture to think that we are worth nothing, but just the reverse. We are of infinite value in God's sight. Moreover, we are to be appropriately concerned (not anxious) about our own situation.[82] As Christians we are to seek to grow in our own character. On the other hand, we find our true worth not in concentrating upon building up our own self-esteem but in living out a useful life in ministry for others and in the service of God. Our value, as we perceive it, comes indirectly out of a conscious commitment, not to ourselves, but to others.[83]

All of these perversions of Christian ethics represent a denial of the freedom of the Christian man. The believer, committed to Christ, is bound in his conscience to no man and no society. He is bound only to the Lord himself. It is the Lordship of Christ that we wish at all times to keep pre-eminent in the Christian life. What the Lordship of Christ requires is love to God and love to neighbor, properly instructed by the Holy Scripture as the Spirit of God applies it to our hearts and minds.[84]

The Christian life *begins* with the new birth. The new birth itself provides a new governing disposition that makes the sinner capable of loving God and in loving God also to love his fellow human beings.[85]

It is *structured* by love — love in Scripture providing both norm and motivation. As motivation, human love stems from a relationship of gratitude to the Creator who is the ultimate source of my being[86] and has become, through Christ's incarnation and atonement, my redeemer and deliverer from sin.[87] Thus, love is the response of a grateful heart to God for all that he is and has done in our behalf.

The Christian life *grows* as a struggle against sin with absolute and final victory never complete in this life, although a measure of victory is always present even during our lifetime here below if we are truly a son or daughter of God. That is, justification is on condition of faith alone; but there is no such thing as a justified sinner standing alone, justified but without any sanctification.[88]

Christian growth is *nourished* by what might be called spirituality or our relationship to God. The Christian life flows out of this relationship to God. It is from this relationship that the Christian receives his power to live ethically. God is the source of our spiritual life, our sanctification, our guidance and our blessing.[89]

The Christian life is *instructed* by the Word of God that provides us needed warnings, awareness of resources for motivation and guidance so as to enable us to live useful and productive lives in the service of God and of man.[90] The Christian life is experienced by our worship of God, in deeds of loving kindness to those around us and in our witness by life and by word to the community beyond us. No Christian is free from responsibility to share the gospel with others. His own calling may take him to special areas of service only indirectly related to evangelism. But he can never free himself altogether from the great commission to preach the gospel and to instruct his fellow believers in the church.[91] His contact with the world brings him into social outreach, but I shall leave this in the capable hands of my friends, Bill and Ruth Bentley and Jo Brown.[92]

The Christian life *grows and matures* in community. The primary communities for the nourishment of believers are the family and the church. Believers disciple each other, instruct, and encourage and warn fellow believers in the faith so that together they may grow into Christlikeness.[93]

Finally, the *goal* of the Christian life is goodness. It is not the doing of right things, for God then could have created automata that would always have done perfectly, exactly what was according to his will. Rather, the goal God has set for each believer is the production of a kind of person who will always choose to do what is right. It is not the doing of the right, however, but the perfect moral character or the Christlikeness of character that represents the goal.

Perhaps this is as good a point as any to digress for a moment on the matter of psychological counselling. Half a century ago, evangelicals looked upon psychological counselling as an unbiblical alternative to pastoral ministry. Frequently today, psychological counselling is regarded as a spiritual ministry — at best, a complement to pastoral ministry and, sometimes, a substitute for it. Indeed, it is hard to draw a clear line between spiritual counselling and psychological counselling. Most Christian psychologists soon find themselves functioning as spiritual counsellors and as instructors in the Word of God, either directly, or at times, indirectly and even subconsciously.[94]

The difference between the two is the goal of each. The psychological counsellor seeks to enable a person to function effectively as a human being — that is, to see things realistically as they are and not to create illusions. The patient needs to be able to make decisions on the basis of what the real world is like, and this often means he must get rid of excessive guilt or false guilt. The goal of the psychological counsellor is to enable his patient to function "normally" as a "well" person in society.[95]

By contrast, Christian *or* "spiritual" counselling is concerned about our relationship to God and morality, about how we can make decisions about right and wrong, what are the resources for making these decisions and what is the goal of the Christian life. On the basis of this division, we can get help from a psychological counsellor who may not even be a Christian. Spiritual counselling we generally seek from someone we trust as a mature Christian — that is, one who knows the Bible, knows Christ, knows what the Christian resources are, and has proved that he is able to put them into practice in his own life.[96]

Of course, the two areas and the two goals become thoroughly intertwined. Each tends to do in part the work of the other. The temptation of the psychologist is to become a spiritual advisor and the temptation of the spiritual advisor is to become a psychologist. This is unfortunate because each is trained to do very different things.

Common Objections to Christian Ethics

1. Asceticism: The charge is that Christianity is too other-worldly and repudiates the healthy, robust normal life that is

appropriate for modern living. This objection usually comes as a reaction against a warped view of Christianity. Actually, in its basic ethic Christianity is almost the antithesis of asceticism. Asceticism is interested in the self. It seeks to repress certain aspects of the life of the individual, namely, his desires (whatever they may be) in order to foster and strengthen an inner self. Asceticism represents a denial of one part of the human whole in order to build up another part of it.[97]

Christianity, by contrast, does not focus on the self at all. It does not ask, "How can I build up my own inner self," but rather, it asks, "How can I be of greatest service to God and to my fellow human beings." Biblical Christianity may actually require us to forego certain pleasures and joys of this life. But it doesn't deny them for selfish reasons to build up one's own inner soul. Rather, it sets them aside only when they obstruct our progress towards the overall goal to serve God and our fellow human beings. The Christian life is always other centered rather than self centered.

As a matter of fact, Christianity is not opposed to enjoyment or to the proper use and care of the human body or to the nourishment of the soul. God made us as whole human beings and created in us an aesthetic nature that needs to be nourished by music and art. He gave us physical bodies that we are commanded in Scripture to take care of and to use appropriately. A Christian does not deny that these things are good or desirable or hold an appropriate place in the Christian life. In order to gain certain other goals, the Christian may forego them for a time. Yet he does so knowing that God will not let him ultimately suffer loss.[98]

When the divine Son of God completed his ministry to save humanity, his heavenly Father restored to him the glory that was his before the foundations of the world. So it is with every believer. God will never permit his child, ultimately, to suffer loss in view of a ministry and service to God and fellow human beings.[99]

2. The second objection is that Christian Biblical ethics is a defeatist ethics. It sets up a very lofty ethical goal, but considers human kind so depraved as to be incapable of achieving any ultimate good. This debased view of man actually weakens us, so it is said. Nothing succeeds like success and nothing helps man more than confidence in himself and in his own ability to succeed.

By contrast, our Christian faith holds that self-confidence is false confidence. Man can be psychologically helped by grit and determination, but these are not adequate. In God the Christian possesses a help to enable him to do what he can't do in himself. The Christian is ultimately optimistic; and this encourages him even while he is realistic about his own powers. So, Martin Luther declares, "God and I are a majority." By depending on the Holy Spirit, the Christian gets a true success confidence. But it is success confidence, not self-confidence. Like the greater ferocity of the pack of wolves as opposed to the cowardice of the lone wolf, so the Christian gains confidence and moral strength as he works hand in hand with God to battle against sin and the rampant evil in the world.[100]

3. Christian ethics, so it is also alleged, are too idealistic. That is, Christian ethics require us to act in love and to turn the other cheek. Law is built on the opposite of this. It is based on justice, not on love and forgiveness. Society would be destroyed if we took Christian ethics seriously.

But this forgets that many Biblical principles are impossible or impractical for the natural man, but not for the supernatural, Spirit filled man or woman to whom God gives the resources and the strength to live according to these extraordinary demands.[101]
We must remember, also, the role of the civil government.[102] Maintaining justice is not a private, but a public duty. A private individual does not take personal vengeance into his own hands, but ought to forgive and forgive and forgive again. Yet in a just society the apparent disadvantage of a Christian will often be set aright by the just law that requires each man to receive his due. We may not force a person to pay his bills. But we can take the issue to the church if the debtor is a believer; and if he refuses to respond to this, then we may treat him as an unbeliever. In short, we must distinguish personal ethics from social and political ethics.[103]

A careful application of hermeneutical principles quickly solves many problems. We must analyze Christian teaching to discover what it really means in its context. The Bible often speaks in hyperbole and is not intended to be taken literally or woodenly. Many Biblical commands, superficially silly, when understood in their context are not so, but form a coherent whole with other Biblical instructions. Each troublesome passage must be carefully examined and interpreted in the light of the whole of Biblical teaching.[104]

4. A fourth objection against Christian ethics is that they depend on the supernatural. This is the frequent objection of many contemporary thinkers. Sometimes, as with Lenin, the father of Russian communism, this only means that Christians depend on God, and since there is no God, this is a false dependence. Religion tells people who get in trouble to pray. They would be

Kenneth S. Kantzer

more effective were they to depend on themselves — for example, join a labor union. Of course, the real issue is whether or not there is a God who can hear and answer prayer.[105]

Sometimes, however, the objection runs deeper: dependence on the supernatural makes men weaker. The evidence, however, is on the other side. It is worthy of note that Roepke, the Swiss economist, wishes to revive Christian ethics in order to preserve the Western economic system. The objection is valid only if reliance on the supernatural makes us morally lethargic. But the Christian knows he is responsible for acting and will be judged by God accordingly. The non-supernaturalist may legitimately hold: "This is my own business, to do or not to do as I wish." Accordingly, suicide in pagan Roman times was considered the personal affair of the individual. The Christian, however, knows that nothing is entirely his own business. He must face the sovereign Judge of the universe who holds him to account and will one day punish him for wrong doing. By the mere fact that he does believe in the supernatural, therefore, the Christian has an added incentive, and a very powerful incentive, to lead him to do what is right.[106]

5. Christian ethics are often alleged to be contradictory. For example, "An eye for an eye and a tooth for a tooth" flatly contradicts the personal love ethics of the Bible. But, in one case we have a law that applies to civil government, and in the other case we have a law for the individual. Each case of contradiction must be examined in context on its own merit.[107]

6. Christian ethics, it is said, originated in an ancient and alien culture and were intended for an agricultural society. Hence they are not applicable to us today. What, for example, do

216

Christian ethics tell us about slum clearance? Or about atomic warfare? The Christian recognizes that the Bible does not deal directly with every moral issue that arises in modern industrial society. Yet the Bible never provided a complete code covering all situations in the ancient world to which it first came. Biblical ethics is not an ethics of codified law, but a love ethics. The Bible does not give us precise directions for every conceivable situation. But it does give us principles and many life applications to guide us. And so long as human nature remains the same and we continue to act it out in our lives in a rational world, these Biblical applications are relevant to guide us to an instructed life of love to all.[108]

7. Finally, it is alleged that Christian ethics are divisive and undemocratic. All absolutes, so the charge goes, but especially absolute religions, lead necessarily to intolerant and undemocratic social relationships.

The piece of truth in this charge is that some truths are important. The fallacy in this objection is the assumption that Christian ethics lead to divisive and undemocratic attitudes. Christian ethics is in actuality a love ethics. It must be conceded that some Christians have failed to see this or, at least, have failed to practice it. Bible believing Christians do believe in truth — absolute truth. And it is their earnest prayer and heart's desire that all men should accept Christianity as true and act on it. Yet they have universally repudiated the use of force to support their faith. Religious convictions are of such a sort that only if they are offered freely from the heart are they of any value. Hence the Christian rejects force and is limited to moral persuasion to lead another to become Christian. On the contrary, Christian theology

217

gives the only truly rational ground for democracy. Its stress upon the worth of the individual and the value of human personality makes democracy worthwhile. And the doctrine of human depravity explains why it is better not to trust our God-given rights to another. The best human being to protect anyone's rights is that person himself. Christian doctrine recognizes this, and democracy puts it into practice. [109]

Moreover, we must never confuse toleration and indifference. The Christian can never be indifferent to a single issue upon which the welfare of a soul hangs. For example, he is not indifferent to rejection of Christ. He wishes to do all he can to persuade others to turn to Christ. Yet he may very well be, and indeed ought to be tolerant. He is willing to die for the freedom of any person to deny Christianity, but he will also die for the privilege of witnessing to anyone why that person ought to become a Christian.[110]

It is also important to distinguish between a disciplined membership in a voluntary association, working for a specific goal such as a church, and toleration for the rights of others in an involuntary society such as the national government. Even in the Old Testament, alien residents who were not a part of the Jewish community of faith were to be treated fairly and honestly and allowed their independence. The Christian believes in the purity of the church and in its right to control its own affairs including its right, as a voluntary society, to discipline its membership. The Christian also believes with even greater commitment in the freedom of religion including the right to propagate one's faith in the larger involuntary society.

Many ethical issues deeply troubling our world we have not even touched on in this paper. The family, divorce and remarriage, the right of a woman to abort an unwanted fetus, the alleged right to sexual preference, embryo implantation, all sorts of sexual issues, euthanasia, and genetic engineering are but a few from an almost infinitely long list that could be adduced. Evangelicals are deeply troubled over these issues — some because they are not sure where the right answer lies; others because of the devastating consequences that flow to human society by the flagrant violation of what they believe to be God's holy instruction given to us for our good.[111]

It is my sincere hope and earnest prayer that what we have covered will provide a framework to help all of us to see the direction in which we ought to go. The key to every ethical dilemma must be found in our personal relation to God through Jesus, our divine Lord and Savior. All else flows from this. Because Jesus Christ is divine, he has full right to govern our lives. Because he is our Lord, we ought to receive gladly the instruction he has given to us for our good. And because he is both Creator God and our Savior, we love him, worship him, obey him, and commit our lives wholly to him.[112]

A great and, in truth, a very surprising danger is the threat to both the doctrine and the way of life in our churches caused by their very success in the last few years. Generally speaking, evangelical churches are growing. Our evangelical seminaries are overflowing, and even our colleges, in spite of the tremendous additional financial burden they lay on the parents of our youth, are now showing increased enrollment. Certainly the evangelical churches in other parts of the world are growing — in Africa, South and Central America, China, Korea and east India.[113]

But this very growth creates, even in our soundly evangelical churches, the threat of a new Constantinian lapse in faith and in life. When large numbers of people are brought into the church faster than they can be assimilated, inevitably they bring their worldly thinking and worldly standards of life in with them. And this can prove disastrous. As D. L. Moody once said: "A ship belongs in the sea, but woe betide the ship when the sea comes into it." So the church belongs in this world, but the result is spiritual disaster when the world enters the church. Of course, in one sense, we want the world to come into the church. That is only to say that we believe in evangelism.[114]

The tragedy is that in America, we have not been able in any adequate manner to transmit our doctrine and way of life to our children.[115] Far less are we capable of instructing and assimilating those who are entering the church in such large numbers. From what we learn from abroad, Christians in other areas where the church is growing with even far greater rapidity than here are experiencing the same problem.[116]

In summary our God has called us to live and witness in a civilization whose intellectual leadership is, at best, quite indifferent to the cause of the gospel and, at worst, stands in open opposition to an evangelical faith and an evangelical way of life. If we do not already find ourselves in a post-Christian era, the intellectual leadership of our world, evidenced in our government, in our great universities and in the great cultural centers of our day, is rapidly moving in that direction.

Meanwhile God calls us, his believing people, to stand in the gap. He calls us to be faithful. And we must obediently respond by witnessing, through life and word, to our Lord Jesus Christ, and to his gospel and to the way of life appropriate for the faithful people of God.

Long ago, the prophet Jeremiah warned the people of his wayward and unbelieving generation: "This is what the LORD Almighty, the God of Israel, says: . . . obey me and I will be your God and you will be my people. Walk in all the ways I command you, that it may go well with you. But they did not listen or pay attention; instead they followed the stubborn inclination of their evil hearts. They went backward and not forward" (Jer. 7:21-24).[117]

To our witness let us add earnest prayer to God for a mighty outpouring of his gracious Spirit in our day, so that our generation may not "refuse to listen or pay attention"; but, rather, may hear and heed the Word of the living God for our day.

[1] This topic was assigned, and I interpreted it to exclude social ethics as well as basic philosophical presuppositions of Christian ethics. Of course, treatment of personal ethics that avoids social ethics altogether is impossible; and by seeking to keep the topics separated, no doubt I have biased the discussion too much in the direction of an individualistic ethics. A truly Christian personal ethics cannot be individualistic. Man was not intended to live alone.

[2] So poll after poll in *Good Housekeeping* and similar family magazines .

[3] This is often referred to as the fundamental paradox of any hedonistic ethical system. See the classical text on ethics by John S. MacKenzie, *Manual of Ethics* (4th ed. New York: Noble and Noble, c. 1925), pp. 67-71.

[4] Lenin, speaking for Communism, declared: "The point is not to understand the world but to change it." After all, communism is a Christian heresy.

Kenneth S. Kantzer

[5]Phil. 2:5-11; my own translation based on the analysis of this text in C. F. D. Moule, "Further Reflections on Philippians 2:5-11" in *Apostolic History and the Gospel* , ed. F. F. Bruce, W. W. Gasque and R. P. Martin (Grand Rapids: Eerdmans, 1970). The point is not that the Christian life is a life lived in imitation of Jesus Christ, the perfect example, but that, like God, we too are to live lives of self giving sacrifice for others.

[6]Christian ethics is based on the principle that love is mightier than fear or a desire for personal gain. We love God, and therefore seek to serve him and our fellow humans because he first loved us and gave himself for us (I John 4).

[7] To deny the deity of Christ or his substitutionary atonement is necessarily to eliminate the supreme motive for the Christian provided in the gospel. In the Old Testament God promised to do whatever was necessary to save man (Gen. 3:16 & 17 expanded further by the sacrificial system). In the New Testament fulfillment, God in Christ has done all that is necessary to save us. Our response in both the Old and New Testaments is by faith to accept his love and then, in turn, to love him and to serve him.

[8]No single work has brought this into such sharp focus as J. G. Machen, *Christianity and Liberalism* (New York: The Macmillan Co., 1923).

[9]It took two centuries for Liberalism to penetrate the church sufficiently for this result to become evident. All along its beautiful ethics has floated on false capital — the theological truth of Biblical Christianity and the ethical system in the Bible that is based on that theology. In our generation the religious moral bankruptcy of Liberalism is now patent.

[10]In the older systematics, personal as well as social ethics were often discussed under the heading of the Ten Commandments. In the latter half of this century, social ethics has flourished but personal ethics has been neglected. Probably the most influential American writer on this subject was Reinhold Niebuhr. See his *Moral Man and Immoral Society* (New York: Scribner's Sons, 1932): and *Nature and Destiny of Man* (2 vols. New York: Scribner's Sons, 1945). The two most helpful works on personal ethics written from a consistently evangelical position were those by Carl F. H. Henry, *Christian Personal Ethics* (Grand Rapids: Wm. B. Eerdmans, 1957) and Robertson McQuilkin, *An Introduction to Biblical Ethics* (Tyndale House: Wheaton, Illinois, 1989).

[11]For example, the ethical agenda of Liberal Christian scholars could scarcely be distinguished from that of the extreme left wing of the major political parties or the secular humanists.

[12]Since the First World War, evangelical scholarship in America has either been pushed out or withdrawn from the center of serious scholarship. The effect of this on all areas of theology is all too apparent. Fortunately this tendency has begun to reverse itself in the last quarter of the century. Westminster Seminary was, undoubtedly, the most notable exception to the trend.

[13]Among the most notable evangelical authors of post World War II period were VanTil, Clark, Buswell, Chafer, Stonehouse, Ramm, Henry and Carnell. All published primary works in apologetics and foundational theology. Only two (Buswell and Chafer) wrote systematic theologies although a number of popular summaries of doctrine appeared. In the Biblical area Archer, Harrison and Guthrie produced excellent defences of conservative positions on introduction problems. The working principle of evangelical theologians seemed to be: Why present an agenda for Christian ethics to those who have rejected the foundational theology on which any valid ethics must be built? However, Cornelius VanTil prepared an unpublished text for his class in Christian theistic ethics; and Carl Henry published two major volumes in the area of ethics — *Christian Personal Ethics* and *The Uneasy Conscience of Modern Fundamentalism* (Grand Rapids: William B. Eerdmans. 1947).

[14]Fundamentalists and evangelicals, in fact, produced quite a flood of ethical material, but almost all on a very popular level. Carl F. H. Henry's early volume, *The Uneasy Conscience* was the first lonely voice raised by a recent evangelical in a serious scholarly defense of social ethics and much the same can be said for his *Christian Personal Ethics*.

[15]All evangelical theologians have insisted upon the interdependence and absolute necessity of both theology and ethics for any view that purports to be remotely Biblical. There is, almost, only a relative logical priority for the theological foundation. Any complete systematics must include ethics. A concentration on theory rather than practice created the impression, both within and without evangelicalism, that Christianity, as understood by evangelicals, was primarily a matter of right ideas (orthodoxy) and not right living (orthopraxis). Nothing could be farther from the Biblical revelation.

[16]To discuss Christian personal ethics without the theological foundation would, however well meant, warp Biblical ethics beyond recognition. A full-orbed Biblical theology is the necessary foundation for Biblical ethics.

[17]This is possible, of course, because, though each of these thinkers stands as a symbol of a major division of historical Christianity, they are, in spite of their differences, all evangelicals. And it is this evangelical faith that unites them that also serves as the foundation for their ethics — however differently they may have worked it out.

[18]This is the point of Romans one: even from the natural revelation, we ought to have recognized God as deity and as our infinitely powerful creator — the one to whom we are ultimately responsible . Our sin lies in our unwillingness to recognize him for who he is. And this failure to recognize the sovereign, holy, creator God leads irresistibly to the moral chaos that characterizes man without God.

[19]The point is often made and never more powerfully than by Paul Tillich: An ultimate commitment to anyone or anything that is not ultimate is idolatry. See his *Dynamics of Faith* (ed. Ruth N. Anshen. New York: Harper, 1956).

Kenneth S. Kantzer

[20]The essential meaning of the Genesis passage is that both man and woman — and both in the same sense and in the same degree — are created like God and, thus, unique among beings whose home is planet earth. To find this image in the maleness and femaleness of the human species, as Karl Barth does is to go beyond what is clearly stated, although the point that every member of the human race is mutually interdependent is certainly implied by the passage. *Church Dogmatics* 3:1:41.2 (G. W. Bromiley and T. F. Torrance, eds. Edinburgh: T & T Clark, 1958), 192-198. The social likeness of humankind to the triune God and the economic likeness of man as the under lord of the planet may also be implied. Man is given the right to establish order and govern the resources of the planet including other forms of life. The New Testament teaching on the image does not reflect a new and different image but a re-creation of the original image destroyed in the fall. Yet the image was not totally effaced because of sin. Murder is wrong because man is created in the image of God, thus bearing unique value. And it is wrong to murder any human because all still bear the traces and, therefore, the value of this divine image.

[21]Humanity is both of the earth, physical, and like God, spirit. We know so little of what matter is essentially and of what spirit is (except that it is not material), that it is even more difficult to understand the unity of the two in a human soul — an embodied spirit. Of course, we know our bodies reflect light, have weight, can be measured, and otherwise are accessible to the five senses. Here we come face to face with vast areas of ignorance on our part. Yet Scripture is unequivocally clear that we have a body and an immaterial part joined mysteriously in each member of our race.

[22]The infinite value of each human person is conveyed not only by the unique God-likeness of man and woman as created but is most unambiguously set forth in the value of the human soul to God — a value so great that it led to his incarnation and his redemption of human kind at infinite cost.

[23]That Adam and Eve were created free with the power to choose between good and evil is not only implied in the Genesis account but is the only alternative to a complete determinism that makes God ultimately responsible for evil.

[24]The freedom of fallen man has proved to be a highly controversial matter in Christian theology. Luther and the Reformers, of course, held that sinful man is bound by his sin and, therefore, not free. Many recent followers of the Reformers have made the distinction between psychological freedom and moral ability (See A. H. Strong, *Systematic Theology* [3 vols. Valley Forge, Pa: The Judson Press, 1907], 509-510). Psychological freedom refers to the capacity of the mind to make choices; moral freedom refers to the moral ability of man to make right choices. Man is free to choose to fly to Arcturus, psychologically speaking; but he lacks the ability really to get himself there. According to this analysis humans are not psychologically determined, but their freedom is not accompanied by a moral ability to do the good.

[25]The conscience is a part of our "natural" make up — natural in a two-fold sense. It is natural in that it is part of the created order and, therefore, reflects the truth. It is also natural in the secondary sense of what is normal to fallen man. Note Calvin's double use of "natural" in the *Institutes*. (John Calvin, *Institutes of the Christian Religion* Ed. John T. McNeill. Trans. Ford Lewis Battles. 2 vols. [Philadelphia: The Westminster Press, 1960] II. i. 11 and the note on I. ii. 2). The Holy Spirit may use the conscience, but the work of the Spirit must be distinguished from the function of the conscience.

[26]The conscience code is not an infallible guide to right and wrong. It was destroyed as an adequate guide for life by the fall of man into sin and his rebellion against God and the good; but it has never been effaced.

[27]Romans 2:14f. describes the fallen conscience of man as still valid to show man that he is a sinner when the Holy Spirit opens his mind to read the conscience code rightly and guides the conscience prick to honesty.

[28]The building of the conscience code (each person's list of rights and wrongs) and the strengthening of the prick (conscience proper) do not begin with each person from scratch. We inherit a code, and the prick is innate. Yet both are educable. The code is ideally to be set according to the Word of God. The prick is to be nourished by careful obedience and dependence on the Holy Spirit's power.

[29]The code can also be developed in a wrong way: by all cultural influences that shape our education, the most important of which influences in early years are usually our parents. We then judge our own conduct according to this fallible and ever-changing standard of our personal code. Much of what is often called "false guilt" is the result of our judging ourselves as having done wrong because our conscience code has reversed its categories and indicates an action to be wrong when it is really right.

[30]Sometimes we fail to repent of our wrong and do not receive God's forgiveness. True repentance receives and accepts by faith God's full and free forgiveness. Then alone can we rightly and with a clear conscience forgive ourselves. It is possible to obtain relief from a guilty conscience either by twisting our code so we no longer hold a thing to be wrong or by dulling and hardening our consciences so that we are no longer bothered by our wrong conduct. These are wrong ways of dealing with a bad conscience. The right way is to create a code that is set according to the standard of Scripture and then to repent where we have violated it, ask for God's forgiveness for Christ's sake and accept his forgiveness. This is the right and Biblical way to true peace of soul. The wrong way usually merely pushes our violation of the code into our sub-conscious where it smolders and, all too often, eventually works its way up into our consciousness in all sorts of strange, and seemingly irrational activity.

[31]True conviction of sin (See John 16:8-11) occurs when the Holy Spirit brings vividly into our consciousness our violation of a code although sometimes the code may actually

225

Kenneth S. Kantzer

remain in the unconscious (John 8:9). The Spirit also exhorts us to find the good and do it, warns against acting contrary to what our conscience condemns (II Cor. 4:2), urges us to repent and believe so as to take care of problems of conscience (Heb. 9:14), and comforts us when we have really done right (and especially when this has brought us into trouble [Acts 24:10]). A splendid book discussing the Christian conscience from a thoroughly evangelical viewpoint is that by O. Hallesby, *Conscience* (Trans. C. J. Carsen, 4th ed. Minneapolis: Augsburg, 1944).

[32]Strict Calvinists teach that Adam's sin brought depravity and guilt to all the race by his one act. They base this primarily on Romans 5:12. Some, like the Federalists, hold that all humans were represented in Adam; and when he fell, they fell because they were all represented in Adam as their head. Others teach that all men were really present in Adam and actively and directly participated in his act. See Heinrich Heppe, *Reformed Dogmatics Set out and Illustrated from the Sources* (Rev. and ed. Ernst Bizer, Trans: G. T. Thomson. London: George Allen and Unwin, 1950), especially pages 330 - 336. Wesleyans usually teach that all men have followed Adam's bad example, and this has brought depravity and guilt upon all. Wesley, himself, and, perhaps, also Calvin (See John Murray, *The Imputation of Adam's Sin* [Grand Rapids: William B. Eerdmans, 1959]) hold that man inherited Adam's depravity then acted accordingly to become guilty. It is my own view that the original Reformers (Luther and Calvin) held none of these explanations as to *how* Adam's sin brought depravity and guilt on the race. What all evangelicals agree on is that all men have become sinners (depraved and guilty), either in part or wholly, as a result of Adam's sin.

[33]Total depravity has frequently become identified in popular speech to mean that every act of man is wholly evil. This is not the teaching of the Bible. As Augustine argued long ago, every evil is really dependent on a good and is always a perversion of a good. Likewise humans are not totally bad in the sense of the worst possible. Rather some are worse than others. Evangelicals agree that the whole human person is pervaded by sin (although they do not always designate these aspects by the terms intellect, emotions and will).

[34]Man is totally unable on his own, apart from the gracious moving of the Holy Spirit, to initiate action that will eventually lead to salvation. If God simply does nothing, man will remain lost. That does not necessarily mean that every act of man is evil. Some are good, at least in a relative sense, although Augustine argues (followed by the Reformers) that every act of man, however good, is also tinged with some aspect of selfishness and thus is never wholly pure but always in part sinful.

[35]See the discussion above on the fallen conscience.

[36]This is the gospel (See, for example, I Cor. 15:3 & 4 and Galatians 2:16 *et passim*).

[37]This is the application of the gospel — the subjective side of redemption made possible by the work of Christ, the objective side of redemption. The Holy Spirit works in the human heart to create conviction of sin, true repentance, saving faith, the new life in Christ, sanctification (or regeneration in the vocabulary of the Reformers), and ultimately perfection in Christ and glorification.

[38]Man is saved *because* of the work of Christ and *if* he believes; he is lost because he is a sinner and because he has rejected God and his grace (Rom. 1 & 2).

[39]Evangelicalism is not the whole of Christianity nor even all of what many who are evangelical hold to be important aspects of Christianity. It is the central core of Biblical Christianity, and it is this central core that represents the common element in traditional Lutheranism, the Reformed churches, Anglicanism (including Wesleyans), Anabaptist Christianity (the Menno Simons branch), and Pentecostal Christianity. Evangelicals focus on the Gospel and what is essential to the integrity of the Gospel. No true Calvinist considers Wesleyan theology a *consistent* system of theology and vice versa. Yet a Calvinist may consider that Wesley adheres faithfully to the gospel and to those doctrines that are essential to its integrity even though they are convinced that he holds other positions quite inconsistent with the integrity of the gospel. Wesleyans, perforce, would return the compliment. In this statement, I have not tried to form a doctrine that would be acceptable to Wesleyans and Calvinists so much as I have tried to form what I believe is Biblical teaching (which both Calvinists and Wesleyans believe) in such a way that both could agree to the statement even though each might prefer a slightly different wording. Whether or not I have succeeded is for convinced Wesleyans and convinced Calvinists to say.

[40]II Timothy 3:14 and 15: That this is the first purpose of the Scripture, most evangelicals, following both Luther and Calvin, agree.

[41]I have omitted the second purpose of the law according to the enumeration of Luther and followed by Calvin. Calvin, picking up on a suggestion from Melancthon, calls this second instructional purpose the third and most important use of the law (*Institutes*, II,viiff. and IV,xx. 15). Luther did not list it. He was dreadfully fearful that this use of the law might lead the Christian back into legalism. Of course, he was right. It is an ever present danger to one who uses the Scripture in this role. Yet not to use the law as a guide for a Christian presents its own danger — antinomianism. A proper use of the law, viewed not as a way to earn salvation but as a way to please God, to serve him effectively and to lead a useful life in service to others, is surely the role envisaged for it by Scripture itself (Psalm 19, 119, II Tim. 3:16 and 17 and many other passages scattered throughout the Bible). Luther himself constantly appeals to the Bible in this role in his treatises and in his commentaries. He sees the Bible as a book of instruction for the Christian in living out his life on earth, but it must be used properly and never as a way to make ourselves right with God. His warning against legalism needs to be taken to heart by all who recognize this (second or

Kenneth S. Kantzer

third) use of the law of God. Many evangelicals who hold clearly to the gospel of grace alone through faith alone for justification, slip into a legalistic use of the Bible for sanctification and the living of the Christian life. See the invaluable discussion of Luther's view in Julius Koestlin, *The Theology of Luther in its Historical Development and Inner Harmony* (Trans. Charles E. Hay. 2 vols. Philadelphia: Lutheran Publication Society, 1897), II, 495-502.

⁴²The Hebrew word "Torah" basically means instruction and carries quite a different connotation from our ordinary use of "law" in English. Torah is not so much a law to which obedience is required with the threat of a penalty for failure to obey, but it is the instruction of a loving father who knows what is best and does not want his child to miss out on the best. It is still true, of course, that it is the instruction of our *heavenly Father*; and there are penalties and disciplines for failure to abide by his instruction. To see Torah merely as law, however, is to miss its primary thrust and thus to jeopardize the delight in the "law" of God characteristic of the Psalmist in the Old Testament and of the delight and reverence for the "law" found in the New Testament — in Paul, for example, as seen in Romans 2 and elsewhere. Paul also has another view of the law which "kills." To understand Paul's theology this complex aspect of the law must be kept clear.

⁴³The Biblical revelation as history (and the gospel as history) represents a significant and valuable way to interpret the Bible. See Hans Frei, *The Eclipse of Biblical Narrative* (New Haven: Yale University Press, 1974). To interpret the gospel as history need not demand an acceptance of all the implications Hans Frei draws from this methodology.

⁴⁴The use of Biblical narratives in drawing out doctrine (or ethics) requires a delicately nuanced hermeneutic. Broadly speaking, an act spelled out in the Biblical text may illustrate a universal good, a universal bad, a right act (or bad act) for the specific instance portrayed, or the significance of the act for our knowledge of right and wrong may be left completely unindicated by the Biblical text. Only context enables us to interpret it rightly and apply it for ourselves. We know on the basis of the Bible's own claims for itself, that all the Bible is profitable for our instruction; but what precisely any particular Biblical narrative conveys to us as its instruction only a careful analysis of each passage in its immediate context and in the context of the whole Bible will enable us to see.

⁴⁵Most heresies have rested on the teaching of single verses interpreted apart from the broader teaching of the whole of Scripture. We do not really have Biblical teaching on any point of doctrine or ethics until we have the whole of what the Bible says on that point. Nowhere is this more clearly illustrated than in the Biblical teaching as to the grounds for divorce. Some passages could be interpreted to mean there are no legitimate grounds for divorce (e.g. Luke 16:18). Matthew teaches that marital unfaithfulness is an exception (Matthew 5:32). I Corinthians 7 may well add another exception. Only when we pull together all relevant passages of Scripture and see how each part fits in with all other parts, do we have the full guidance of God on this matter.

[46]The Reformation principle of the perspicuity and adequacy of Scripture must be carefully stated in Reformation terms or it will be seen to be obviously false. Every believer by the illumination and discerning work of the Holy Spirit, as he is obedient to God and lays himself open to public and private instruction in the Word, can understand Scripture so that he can receive the gospel, be saved and find all he really needs to live now. The point is, the believer needs to know for himself what Scripture says. He must not ultimately allow other human authorities to determine the will of God for him no matter how dependent he may be on their instruction (and we are all dependent on the instruction of the church) and how grateful he is to others and to the church for their guidance and instruction in the faith.

[47]In the great commandment cited by our Lord (see below), the focus is on the norm as standard. Here is how we know what is, as a matter of fact, good and right. In the great love chapter of the Apostle Paul (I Corinthians 13) the focus is on love as motivation. Both are necessary and thoroughly intertwined in our experience. The Levite on the road to Jericho had the former, but not the latter. He knew his Old Testament very well. What he lacked was love in his heart for the injured Jew to motivate him to do what he knew to be right. Soren Kierkegaard has a beautiful passage on this parable in his *For Self-Examination* (Trans. Walter Lowrie, London: Oxford Press, 1941), 64-66.

[48]Matthew 22:37-40.

[49]Love is essentially other directed and, therefore, is different from esteem. Because of the common elements in love and esteem — the recognition of high value and the caring concern both include — many argue that we should love ourselves. The Scripture, too, recognizes this similarity in its command to love others as we love ourselves. The other-directedness of Biblical love, however, distinguishes it from self-esteem.

[50]A Biblical love ethic as we have outlined it involves a standard based ultimately on a God of infinite holiness and infinite love who has given himself utterly to each human so that each one owes his or her all to God. It also means that the highest motive of man is an ultimate commitment of love to this God of holy-love. Although the Bible does not deny that humans are powerfully motivated by desire for power or sex or possessions or fear and, indeed, with proper bounds, ought to be, it still holds that love is a more powerful and better motive than any of these. But, if it is an ultimate commitment, it must be a holy love to a God of holy love.

[51]An example is the "situation ethics" of Joseph Fletcher (*Situation Ethics: the New Morality* [Philadelphia: Westminster Press, 1966]) which purports to be an ethics of pure love, but leaves human-kind with no objective standard of what is truly love.

[52]An example is the love ethic that sees love merely as a standard of loving acts — the kind against which Soren Kierkegaard fought so desperately. Another Christian perversion would be an ethic that sees love as wholly directed towards God and loving acts for fellow humans as motivated only by love for God. The motivation to mission work is often

Kenneth S. Kantzer

wrongly parodied as such. The missionary doesn't love those to whom he or she is bringing the gospel, but does love God. Such missionary work is not very successful because even the most ignorant savage knows when he is loved for himself and when he is just a pawn — being used by others. I have known such missionaries; but, needless to say, they are not the typical missionary and never make a good missionary.

[53]The important distinction needing to be made is that between piety and pietism. Most of the so-called "pietists" I have met are in themselves pious and, according to their own light, they exalt piety and repudiate pietism. The sinful human heart of all of us, including the best Christians, tends inevitably to slip into pietism — our focus shifts to our piety rather than to the God towards whom we experience a divinely approved piety. The charge of pietism is often the derogatory put-down by non-pious folk against those who are pious — and, unfortunately, there is usually a trace of pietism in the most pious to suggest that the charge may have some validity.

[54]Real pietism, as opposed to genuine piety, represents in some ways the antipodes of a Biblical love ethic. The highest motivation is not love to another, but a regard for self and the build-up of one's own pious relationship with God.

[55]For Dewey's religious philosophy and, in particular, his ethics, see John Dewey and James Tufts, *Ethics* (Rev. ed. New York: H. Holt, c 1932). Also see the thoughtful criticism of his views in J. O. Buswell, *The Philosophies of F. R. Tennant and John Dewey* (New York: Philosophical Library, 1950).

[56]See his *Democracy and Education: An Introduction to the Philosophy of Education* (New York: The Macmillan Co., 1916).

[57]New York: Simon and Schuster, 1936. Carnegies's popular influence has been immense — including his penetration of evangelical thought and evangelical ministry.

[58]Carnegie tells us the way to get ahead — even how to get ahead in the cause of Christ. While Carnegie accepts many important Christian principles, his philosophy of life is, at root, quite opposed to the Christian ethic that requires humans to be consumed by a love that is even willing to confront and to suffer the consequences of a pure love. Any truly Christian ethics must be prepared to suffer ultimate defeat in this world (so, in reality, it is not quite ultimate) in loving one's enemies.

[59]The practical and worldly ethics of Ben Franklin represents such a legalism. Virtue is attained by obedience to rules, and we grow morally by vigorous devotion to the rules of right and wrong. See Benjamin Franklin, *Autobiography and Selections from His Other Writing* (Ed. Herbert W. Schneider, New York: Liberal Arts Press, 1952).

[60]These, of course, are the true antipodes — each straying from a Biblical ethics in an opposite direction. Within the evangelical framework, Lutheranism has always had to guard itself from slipping into antinomianism; Calvinism (and Puritanism), from slipping into legalism. Original Lutherans and original Calvinists (and their faithful followers in

each case) avoided both extremes, but each has continually had to guard against its own special "slippery slope."

[61]The ostensible point of our Lord's teaching was to answer the question: "Who is my neighbor?" The good Samaritan models that answer — anyone in need. For a Samaritan, a Jew in need is my neighbor (and by analogy, for a Jew, even a Samaritan). The Levite also illustrates the necessity for love as motivation, As a fellow Jew, the Levite knew the injured Jew was his neighbor; but he lacked the necessary love.

[62]"Love God and do what you will?" — Aurelius Augustine, *Homilies on the First Epistle of John* (Vol. VII in *A Select Library of the Nicean and Post-Nicean Fathers* [Ed. Philip Schaff, Grand Rapids: Wm. B. Eerdmans, 1956], vii, 8). But this must be understood in the context in which Augustine placed it.

[63]For an interesting and valuable discussion of the role of law in the Christian life, see *Interpretation,* Vol. XLIII, No. 3 (July, 1989).

[64]The Bible, it is important to remember, is not a ledger of codified laws. It is a book of life. It contains universal laws, but more frequently it provides applications of the universal law of love worked out in individual lives or group experiences living in a particular context. These must be interpreted in the light of the cultural setting in which they are found and applied to the cultural setting in which we are functioning. Faithfulness to the Bible does not always involve our doing just what the Bible requires in its own setting but rather the taking of what it says and applying it honestly and faithfully to our own situation today. It doesn't always tell us in so many words what we are to do now, but it tells us, with divine infallibility, what we need to know in order to be faithful to God in our day.

In addition, we dare not settle on any one passage of the Bible as the whole of divine instruction on any one topic. The Bible includes very broad principles, sub-principles and sub-sub-principles and their applications. If we are to follow the divine guidance offered to us in the inerrant rule of faith and practice, we need to be guided by the whole of Scripture. This is why we are not to search the Bible desperately when we are in trouble, but to grow in Christian understanding and character as we daily and continuously study the whole of Scripture throughout the whole of our lives. Only in this way does the whole of divine revealed wisdom become available for our daily guidance and Christian growth.

[65]Many Christians who repudiate Pharisaism in the first sense, practice a kind of Pharisaism in the second sense. Christian schools, for example, may inadvertently teach a kind of Pharisaism by setting up prohibitions demanded of all students. The solution, of course, is not to discard all rules, but to teach that these are at best house rules or family rules, appropriate as samples of Christian love and specially suited to the close living conditions of a resident school. The worst alternative would be to teach that *not* doing certain things represents the most important and central core of a truly Christian life.

Kenneth S. Kantzer

[66]The selection of "favorite rules" varies greatly in Christendom and in evangelical circles. The practice of using alcoholic beverages, for example, varies greatly from Lutheran evangelicals to Southern Baptists. For many years northern evangelicals in the U.S. would engage in mixed bathing but often outlawed smoking. Southern evangelicals reversed these favorites; they would smoke but not tolerate mixed bathing.

[67]This was the fatal error of the Pharisees of the New Testament. Unfortunately it represents a tendency inherent in all Christians. To reconstruct our standard by which we judge ourselves is a constant temptation for it frees us from any sense of guilt and discomfort — but with the disastrous results noted.

[68]The fifth and final step of faith is the acceptance of our acceptance; and without this, there is no peace of mind or soul.

[69]Thus we find the sternest rebukes of our Lord against spiritual pride. It also explains the corresponding exhortations to humility. We must be humble enough to admit we are wrong when we really are wrong. The willingness humbly to admit our wrong is the first and necessary step to righting a wrong. And, in one sense, it is the first step in coming to the gospel.

[70]This is the danger of overprotecting a child. The duty of a parent is to shelter a child and protect it from danger. But it is also the duty of a parent to prepare a child so that at the appropriate time it will be able to live in the world apart from the parents constant protection. This weaning process is a necessary and crucial part of parental rearing. The hot-house analogy is valid only because in the long run that is the way to produce the sturdiest plants. Yet part of our hot-house start is to prepare the plant for transplanting. The child, too, must be transplanted if it is eventually to take its place in the world as a strong witness for Christ. It needs to be prepared for transplanting.

[71]Humans, by creation, are social beings. We are commanded to obey our parents, but also all those in authority. The Christian life is not inconsiderate of the wishes or demands of others. The Christian preeminently is to sacrifice for others — to go the extra mile. Nevertheless, the final standard for the Christian is not peer pressure, but what is right according to the standard revealed by God. We must obey God rather than man.

[72]The conflict between parental obedience and child independence is as old as our first parents, and a proper balance between these polarities is the greatest problem a conscientious parent faces. It is probably the most important decision parents make in their child rearing. Unfortunately the balance is never the same — even for two children in the same family.

[73]Parental spiritual and moral nourishment of the young is commanded in Scripture and is a very necessary role in parenting. But equally necessary and equally a part of this parenting is to rear a child so he becomes independent of the parent and dependent upon God. Ultimate dependence on God alone is the key to freedom from slavery to all human lords.

[74]Much has been made of the difference between the Lutheran so-called unqualified obedience to governmental authority and the Calvinistic or Reformed insistence upon the right to disobey and even engage in armed resistance to government. I do not find this radical difference between the two major reformers. When Luther's view is based not on a few statements taken out of context and drawn rather from the perspective of his entire corpus of relative teaching on this point, the differences reduce to near zero. Both Luther and Calvin argued that obedience to government should be complete except when the government insists that we act contrary to God's word. Otherwise, both insisted that the private Christian is to obey his government. On the other hand, rulers who have been placed in authority have a duty to confront evil and will be judged by God if they fail in this duty. They alone have the right in certain restricted situations to engage in armed rebellion against "higher" authorities.

[75]Evangelicals have always made a sharp distinction between compromising principle and compromising action. We are never to determine right and wrong from the pressures of others. Our principles are ultimately to be drawn only from the word of God. Although our fellow humans may instruct us, and we should learn from them gratefully, yet our actions are constantly determined in the light of the wishes or even prejudices of those around us. The one is determined on the sole Lordship of God. The other is determined by our loving sacrificial concern for others. The problem arises when to obey God requires that we hurt others. In such a case, we must obey God and trust that God, who knows best, sometimes knows that humans grow best through their hurts.

[76]Charles M. Sheldon, In His Steps: What Would Jesus Do? (New York: Grosset and Dunlap, 1935).

[77]Phil. 2:5 ff. and elsewhere. The Scripture repeatedly exhorts us to be holy even as God is holy. The Apostle Paul even calls us to be imitators of himself. Our ultimate goal is to be conformed to the image of Christ (Rom. 8:29).

[78]So the great commandment in Matt. 23:35-42. Unfortunately such a pure love is not attained in this life. As Augustine points out, our love for God is always impure — at best, tainted by love of self.

[79]In spite of the clear Scriptural insistence that our ultimate goal is to be like Christ, Scripture is surprisingly reticent about calling us to do as Christ did. Even the Phil. 2 passage does not so much call us to do specific things that Christ did, but like him, to do all we do, not out of a spirit of grabbing for ourselves all we can get, but out of a spirit of self-sacrificial love for others — like Christ.

[80]In short, we are always to act in sacrificial love, but true sacrificial love is different for each person.

[81]See especially Robert Schuller, Self Esteem (Waco, TX: Word, 1982).

Kenneth S. Kantzer

[82]Scripture, particularly the teaching of our Lord, is full of such teaching: "What shall it profit a man if he gains the whole world but loses his own soul?" — Mark 8:30; He who does not "provide for his own . . . is worse than an infidel" — I Tim. 5:8.

[83]The Scriptural statements supporting self esteem must be balanced by the far greater emphasis on living for others. The apostle wrote: "Those things that were gain for me I counted as loss" (Phil. 3:7). Scripture recognizes our infinite worth to God and encourages us to act accordingly. Yet the direct exhortations of Scripture are almost exclusively, to deny ourselves (i.e. be unselfish) and to give ourselves sacrificially to the service of God and our fellow humans.

[84]This does not mean that the Christian life is one of isolation from society and especially that it is freedom from dependence upon fellow believers and the church. Our instruction in the Scripture comes necessarily through the church, and we grow as we mutually depend on one another. Christian growth is not growth in isolation but growth together with other Christians in mutual dependence upon each other. This is the danger in the otherwise beautiful and moving story of the Christian life set forth in Bunyan's *Pilgrim's Progress*.

[85]New birth is a figurative term and is not always used by evangelicals to mean the same thing. In the vocabulary of the older Calvinists (See Calvin, *Institutes*, III/2 f.) regeneration meant rejuvenation and was roughly equivalent to sanctification. Regeneration began with the first movement of the Spirit to enable an unbeliever to believe and continued throughout life. In many contemporary evangelicals, new birth refers to the moment of true faith in Christ when a person first becomes a child of God.

[86]Rom. 1:18-21 teaches that the natural revelation manifested the Creator God to whom we owe everything and who, therefore, deserves our gratitude and is to be given the appropriate glory.

[87]"The love of Christ constrains us . . . ." — II Cor. 5:14 & 15.

[88]Christian growth represents a difficult topic over which evangelicals are far from agreement. They agree that we are justified on condition of a right kind of faith and not on condition of our good works. Faith itself is an act of the whole soul to place one's trust for forgiveness of sin and everlasting life in the divine-human Christ and his finished work on our behalf. Evangelicals are also agreed that true and saving faith will result in good works, but it is the faith not the good works that represents the condition for the gift of our salvation. Evangelicals are not agreed on whether one can have true faith without accepting the Lordship of Jesus Christ over one's life, the most appropriate ways to nourish the Christian life, whether sanctification comes as a crisis or a process, the degree of sanctification attained in this life, and whether and under what conditions spiritual life can be lost completely. The phrase "faith alone" has given rise to much misunderstanding and needs to be carefully guarded. When stated properly, however, it is thoroughly Biblical and touches the very heart of the gospel.

234

[89]It is very important for the understanding of Christian personal ethics that Christianity he perceived not just as a system of truth including ethics. Christianity does not provide merely an ethical system or even a divine revelation of the do's and don'ts of the Christian life. Christianity is also subjectively an appropriation of the divine truth made possible, not just deistically through the truth, but by the Spirit of God working immediately on the human soul. He works to enable us to believe, and enter into mutual personal fellowship with God, and He transforms the weak and sinful human heart to enable it to do good and to be "metamorphosed" (Rom. 12:1 & 2) finally into the perfect character of Christ.

[90]Christians are instructed through many channels; principally through the church. The Bible is the final and only infallible standard by which we determine the Christian life.

[91]Such a division of labor is recognized clearly in the New Testament. Some are called to be evangelists and are given the gift of evangelism. Others are called to be "helpers" and are given the gift of being a "people helper" (See Gary Collins, *How to be a People Helper* [Santa Ana, Calif.: Vision House, 1956]). Yet the universal command to be witnesses and to proclaim the gospel falls alike on every Christian. No Christian should feel guilty merely because he has not lead so many to Christ as the great evangelists, but every Christian ought to feel guilty if he does not, in appropriate ways, bear witness by life *and by word* to the good news of the gospel. The Protestant Reformation stressed and evangelicals have supported the high values of all legitimate vocations. So also ministry is not a duty for some professionals but the privilege and duty of every believer.

[92]See below, pages 299ff. and 257ff.

[93]The Bible knows no such thing as a Christian who is nourished and grows in isolation. Christians are members of a body, and each part is indispensable to every other part and to the whole (I Cor. 12:12-31).

[94]The problem of this overlap of duties becomes serious when the pastor finds counselling more to his liking and allows his spiritual (and sometimes psychological) counselling to encroach upon his pastoral and administrative and preaching duties. His special training and his special expertise usually lie in these latter areas. The problem becomes particularly pernicious when he moves into psychological counselling for which he was never professionally prepared. A similar danger, *mutatis mutandus* attends the professional counsellor.

[95]C. S. Lewis has a helpful section on this distinction in his *Mere Christianity* (New York: MacMillan, 1957) pp. 89-73.

[96]The overlap between the two disciplines and the integral way in which each penetrates the other make the choice between a non-Christian psychological counsellor and a mature Christian spiritual counsellor much more difficult. This emphasizes the need for mature committed Christians to enter the field of psychological counselling. Ideally such a counsellor ought to be available in every community.

Kenneth S. Kantzer

[97]Asceticism is the opposite of hedonism but it is still egoistic. It misses completely the motivating center of Christian ethics.

[98]A much abused Scripture verse is I Tim. 4:8 in the King James Version. "Bodily exercise profits little." The little profit is by contrast with the eternal advancement of the soul. Yet it does profit. Actually Biblical Christianity sets high value on the body. We are not to be slaves to our body's needs, and the body is not our highest value, yet the body was created by God; we are to care for our bodies; they are so valuable that Christ died to redeem our bodies as well as our souls. The first Psalm stresses the happiness of the person who is in a right relationship with God. The Bible recognizes that happiness is largely a by-product of the person who does not set happiness as the ultimate good. But there is no least hint in the Bible that happiness is wrong. Nor is pleasure wrong, though pleasures of the world are often wrong because they do not really bring true and lasting pleasure but moral and spiritual disaster.

[99]Phil. 2:5 ff. puts this in right perspective. Christ did not sacrifice himself to gain his glorious reward. He sacrificed himself for others; but the Father glorified him for what he had done. So it is with each obedient child of God.

[100]The analogy is not altogether happy, but it illustrates that the Christian is realistic. He knows that what he can't do in his own strength, he can do with the resources God places at his disposal and as part of the larger body — the supernatural body of Christ's church — and this strengthens him.

[101]This is explicitly taught in many passages of Scripture: We are without strength, but God . . . . Rom. 5:6-8; David knew his own weakness, but his confidence was in the arm of Jehovah (I Samuel 17); *et passim.*

[102]Romans 13 provides the necessary counterbalance to a Christian's failure to insist on his own rights. The task of government is to protect the innocent from those who would selfishly prey on others. It is important to note that Romans 13 follows immediately the conclusion to chapter 12 that repudiates all personal vengeance.

[103]The Christian is not to take the law into his own hands. Anarchy is not the solution for injustice. The Christian is to work with others for justice in his land. Wrongs against others and against himself, he will seek to redress not by personal vengeance but through public law and public justice. The Christian is not *always* to yield to abuse. He is to turn the other cheek when insulted, but he may also take the injury caused by a fellow believer to the church or a body of other Christians for arbitration and justice. Likewise, if his brother refuses to do this, he may then appeal to the public courts to secure his rights just as he may normally do this with unbelievers. Yet the Christian is slow to respond in kind and should be willing to suffer without instant retaliation.

[104]For example, if we are compelled to go one mile, go two (Matt. 5:41). This onerous duty is cited to illustrate that we should support our government willingly and not shirk our

236

duty. To turn the other cheek warns us against personal vengeance — not that it is *always* the right thing to do when we are harmed. On the other hand, the admonition to forgive seventy times seven means that we are always to forgive and never set a limit to it — so long as we believe there has been sincere repentance for the wrong.

[105]Christian ethics openly and frankly presumes the existence of a personal active God immanent in the universe as well as transcendent.

[106]See Roepke *Two Essays*, edited with an introduction by Johannes Overbeck (Lanham, MD: University Press of America, 1987).

[107]In the Sermon on the Mount, our Lord refers to several Old Testament verses and warns against the application his opponents were making of them. These verses were intended as civil rules for the conduct of society, and some Jewish leaders were interpreting them as guides for personal conduct. Many actions right for a society are wrong for the individual. The right to condemn property for the public domain and capital punishment are merely two examples.

[108]The question as to whether personal and political ethics are to be judged by the same standard is legitimate. Emil Brunner *Justice and the Social Order* (Trans. Mary Hottinger, New York: Harper, 1945) argues that the individual is to be guided by love but the state by justice. One is uncalculating and self-giving; the other is calculating and gives just what is due. If the two perspectives are to be brought together in holy love, it can only be as we view justice as love for the whole of being. Society gives to all and to all equally; all the good that each can take — but this carries us beyond the bounds of this paper.

[109] A Christian can, of course, live a life of love, faithful to God and to his fellow creatures, in almost any kind of government. The Bible does not command democracy. And no democracy is prefect. In fact, a truly democratic government can well be most oppressive — as, for instance, the near pure democracy of free Athenians who put Socrates to death. Even democracy can be no better than the moral quality of the citizens who make up that democracy. The strong monarchy of Frederick the Great or Peter the Great or the limited monarchy of Queen Elizabeth I, was far better than the democracy of Robespierre and the First Republic. Yet human nature being what it is, democracy is, to put it awkwardly, the least bad of all bad forms of human government.

[110]Christian emphasis on evangelism is usually misunderstood by non-Christians. If it is truly Christian evangelism, it is motivated not by a desire for power or control over another, but by love for the other with whom the Christian wishes to share the best thing in life.

[111]The current issue of abortion is an excellent example. Evangelicals are unanimous in their condemnation of free abortions as a violation of the sixth commandment. They are disagreed as to the possibility of exceptions — some would have none, others would allow abortions to safeguard serious risk to the life of the mother, others would add rape and some

Kenneth S. Kantzer

would even go farther. Again they are disagreed as to when abortions should by permitted by law. Some would insist that no abortions should be permitted and all should be prohibited by law and punished. Others point out that not everything that is right should be translated into law and its violation punished. Accordingly some evangelicals think all abortions are wrong but abortions to save a mother's life should not incur legal punishment or penalties. Similarly many evangelicals argue that in some cases abortions that are wrong, should still not be punished. My own view is that abortion is wrong except to save a mother from serious risk to her life, but we should not force a raped woman to bear her child on the grounds that we do not force anyone to sacrifice for the good of another. There is no clear-cut evangelical consensus on some of these points.

[112]A short paper on Christian personal ethics cannot hope to cover any aspect of the subject thoroughly. I have chosen to concentrate on those points on which Scripture lays most stress *and*, at the same time, are most frequently overlooked, I have also tried to draw clear distinctions between evangelical views of personal ethics and those views commonly accepted by our society or by non-evangelicals.

[113]While the nominal Christian church in America has remained static for the last generation, evangelical churches have certainly grown, as Gallop reminds us in his frequent polls. How thoroughly has this growth penetrated into the lives and morals of evangelical Christians? The evidence seems to be that evangelical churches are growing larger in numbers, but its Christianity is becoming thinner and thinner. Something of the same is true in other parts of the world. In the last decade or two, Christianity appears to be growing slightly over the planet as a whole. Evangelical faith, however, certainly seems to be growing significantly faster than the church as a whole — especially in Central and South America, in Africa south of the equator, and in the East Indies, Korea, and in China. See David B. Barrett, *World Christian Encyclopedia* (Oxford: OUP, 1982).

[114]In one sense this lowering of the spiritual quality of a church by the addition of newly converted members is inevitable and even desirable. The New Testament does not contemplate long periods of delay while new members are held in probation without being admitted to the church. The three thousand saved on Pentecost were immediately admitted to full status as believers. The principle of believers only but all believers is thoroughly Biblical. Yet if a church is growing as it ought, this presents an immense problem of spiritual instruction and growth. If the church neglects this spiritual instruction or is incapable of providing the spiritual growth, the end result is disaster. Two New Testament principles are specially important for the protection of the church: (1) No novice should be given an office or role of leadership (I Tim. 3:6) and (2) the church must exercise discipline — including the removal of membership from voluntarily inactive members and especially those who have lapsed morally (I Cor. 5:2). Unfortunately few American churches today

practice any form of church discipline, and almost none makes any requirement for remaining in the church beyond the mere wish to do so.

[115]In the U.S. the problem is a combination of the first amendment and the exclusive public support for public schools. All evangelicals stand solidly for adherence to the first amendment although, as with the general populace (and our Supreme Court), some interpret it more broadly than others. They are all committed to religious freedom not only for themselves but for others. They are also committed in principle to the constitutional amendment that prohibits giving support for any particular religious viewpoint. On the matter of government support for private education, they are quite divided. Some prefer no support for schools with a religious orientation. Others object to direct support but would prefer the government to assist the student and allow each one to choose the school he preferred whether public, private, secular, Roman Catholic or Protestant. The latter would follow the lines of the old G.I. education bill in effect after World War II. The dilemma facing evangelicals in the education of their children is simple. Free public schools consume most of the time and energy of growing children. Quality private schools, where religious instruction is possible, are so expensive that only the rich can afford them. The result is that Protestant children by and large attend public schools and thus are deprived of quality religious education. And from a Christian point of view, effective moral education must include religious and doctrinal content.

[116]Sunday schools are declining and with the trend towards long weekend vacation and open Sundays, the churches are simply not educating their adult converts. Christian education of its constituency is, perhaps, the most serious problem facing the evangelical church today. It is a problem not unique to the U.S. or North America. Particularly in Africa south of the Sahara, where converts number in the millions, the church simply does not have the resources to educate its rapidly growing constituency.

[117]Jeremiah 7:21-24. The warning of Jeremiah needs to be sounded loudly and clearly in our day. The increased numbers that on the surface sound so good may yet come back to haunt us. In spiritual matters depth is to be preferred over breadth. Most American churches opt for breadth and refuse to face the consequences of their increasing lack of depth.

RESPONSE TO KENNETH S. KANTZER

Ralph D. Winter

First of all, I want to thank the men who proposed this consultation. I have long had a keen appreciation for Ken Kantzer, not only because of my personal contacts with him, serving on the same board of a mission project during one period, but also vicariously, due to my younger brother's ecstatic reports of his teaching ability at Wheaton years ago.

In the case of Carl Henry, I have an even closer sense of appreciation since I myself was a student of his, more years ago than either of us cares to recall. He and his wife have been favorite people of mine for at least 40 years.

To the point here, twenty years after those classes under him, Helga Henry's translation from the German of Paulus Scharpf's *History of Evangelism* brought about for me a giant leap forward in my personal understanding of what might be called the evangelical phenomenon. This was at the time of the Berlin 1966 Congress on World Evangelism — another conference which Carl Henry had spurred into existence. The Scharpf book was one of the three official volumes published by the conference.

Then, secondly, I want to make clear what I have understood I am to do in my response. It appears to me that we are here presenting papers and responses and talking to ourselves, but that we hope to generate a statement which will then be directed to the general public, including both evangelicals and the on-looking world.

241

Ralph D. Winter

Thus, what I will be saying is "in-house." I am talking to myself and to you who regard yourselves in the evangelical stream.

Finally, it is obvious that neither Ken nor I can even list much less tackle the veritable onslaught of ethical issues with which our contemporary world confronts us day by day. I have been reading the magnificent, 300 page book by Gordon-Conwell's John Jefferson Davis, called simply *Evangelical Ethics,* and it makes clear that no generation in human history has been faced with so many crucial questions that cry out for serious theological consideration.

Unlike Professor Sloan this morning, I do not have extensive revisions to make of the material we have just heard. But I am glad I was not the presenter. Had I been, I am sure I would have felt similarly responsible to try to cover the basics, as Ken has done so well.

On the other hand, I am not at all sure I would have come up with the same list of distortions or perversions, as he calls them, namely, Pietism, Deweyism, Legalism, Antinomianism, Mysticism or Direct Immediate Revelation, Pharisaism, Conventional Morality, Imitation of Christ, and Self-Esteem.

He does not imply that these are all equally dangerous, of course. And they overlap to some extent. But, I would like to draw your attention to one theme running through several of them. Dr. Kantzer at certain points — no doubt in attempting to ward off a worse evil — introduces what itself can be terribly dangerous, namely the idea that we must above all be free. After concluding his comments on each of the nine perversions, he adds, "All of these perversions of Christian ethics represent the denial of the freedom of the Christian man. The believer, committed to Christ, is bound in his conscience to no man and no society."

(In other parts of his paper he refers to "instructed love", by which he evidently means "Bible informed, but self-instructed love." He speaks of people needing to be weaned from parents as soon as possible. He states that "the key to every ethical dilemma is our personal relation to Jesus Christ.")

I am quite surprised to see that kind of a summary statement. It refers to a certain undeniable truth in one sense, yet if you look back at the nine "perversions," you find that at least five of them are not so much caused by the denial of Christian freedom of conscience, as they are considerably the result of one or another form of the unrestrained heart.

I come to this subject with a certain amount of overseas perspective, as has been indicated in the introduction. My wife and I and our four children lived for ten years within a tribal society, where there exists, as in most of the non-Western world, a life-long authority pattern in the family. On return to the States I have again and again been bothered by the very gradual — and yet by now drastic — breakdown of the Christian family precisely at the very point of Christian freedom of conscience. People in traditional societies who observe the way things are going in the USA look at things very differently from the average American. To the outsider, Americans have gone stark raving mad in their pursuit of individual freedom. (I recall with chagrin how naively in my youth I accepted that famous line from the Declaration of Independence — "life, liberty, and the pursuit of happiness." What a poison for any nation to drink!) At any rate, millions of overseas Christians, drawing on the wisdom of their still-intact traditional societies, would, if they were aware of its true extent, say that our cultural religion of individualism has eaten its way into the very bone marrow of the evangelical cultural stream, because the result in the eyes of these overseas observers is shockingly clear: They see in this distinctively American type of personal freedom something that tears up families, dishonors parents, abandons children and old people, makes fidelity optional, and ultimately breaks apart the parents themselves. And most of this ghastly cancer in our social tradition is recent, historically speaking. Back when Dr. Henry wrote *The Uneasy Conscience of Modern Fundamentalism,* very little of this family breakdown could have weighed on our consciences.

Had the whole transition come quickly, it could have been considered the gravest collapse of morality in Christian history.

Back then not one marriage in 50 broke up, where both parents regularly attended church (whether they were evangelicals or not). Now, our wonderfully elastic evangelical ethics have allowed our country to approach the world's record — and make no mistake, the U.S. now has the world record in divorce rate — in this gruesome reality of the breakdown of the family. Chuck Colson last night could have told us that by comparison with Germany we have twenty times as many people behind bars, and are still needing billions of dollars for more prisons. This is a social problem, but more specifically it is a family problem, and ultimately it falls into the category of personal ethics as all social ethics must.

The point here is, I don't believe all this is the lack of freedom! I don't believe the plummeting ethics in Evangelical circles — either in this area of the family or in the area of evangelical reversion to alcohol — is the result of a denial of Christian freedom.

Much of this breakdown is traced between three different periods in the last 40 years in Hunter's book on evangelicalism; but it has happened with a certain insidious gradualness, and we have not been brought up suddenly to face it.

Thus, it would seem, when we try to be objective about our ideas of personal ethics, we need the help of evangelicals in other cultures. Living overseas can give remarkable insight. On specifically this subject of what has happened to the family, let me give you a glimpse from Singapore. That wonderful little country is the only English speaking country in the world that uses chopsticks. It is young as a nation, cutting loose from Asia, but not entirely satisfied with the West either. It is fascinating to view the U.S.A. from there. It is teeming with global-level evangelical offices. Just as Wheaton is the evangelical Vatican City of the U.S., so Singapore is rapidly becoming the global-level evangelical Geneva. It comes to mind because I happen to have been there three times in a recent four-month period. In two of those visits new world-level organizations were born, serving the global evangelical movement.

I certainly did not take a 20-hour flight (each way) from Los Angeles to read their Sunday paper, but I did happen to be reading their Sunday paper; and I found myself immediately immersed in their own internal debate about their "national identity." It is clear that, for them, their identity is not a simple choice between, on the one hand, their traditional societies, with their outdated religions, and on the other hand, what I would describe as the boiling Western world with its raw chaos and great variety of costly open sores.

Ralph D. Winter

One result is that the bright, up-beat Singaporean, whether Christian or non-Christian, is alarmed by American ethical trends. Let me try you out. The front-page article I saw was about the dangers of Western society and specifically as those dangers were mirrored in the recent Oscar Award ceremony. How did the Singaporeans look at that jolly evening of fun and games? I could not believe what I read. The paper described how the Americans receiving these awards effusively and compulsively thanked everyone for their success . . . their director, their supporting actor, their dog, etc. So, what is the problem? Wasn't that nice of those award winners? Almost Asian courtesy! Not quite.

The paper pointed out something else — in good English but with a horror you could almost feel between the lines. What did they feel was wrong with this ceremony, reflecting danger for a new nation influenced by the Western world? I would have never thought of it. They watched the lengthy program, apparently with eyes getting wider every minute, listening to all these American heroes so generously grateful to others. . . . Their problem? No one, not a single award winner, ever mentioned his or her parents. This was the deadly problem for them.

In the same article — on the front page — they comment on the evils of U.S. school books. No, they are not worried about the absence of Creation. They are worried about what Evangelicals might call the distortion of Creation, if we could just see it. The paper describes the textbooks. It tells about the Dick and Jane stories. It does not look for subtleties evangelicals may rightly worry about. The Singapore paper points out what for us is a phenomenal blind spot — the blatant reality that in those stories are dogs, dolls, automobiles, other children . . . but, you guessed it, no parents. They are staggered. They have a terrible fear. We should also.

Not long ago *Christianity Today* ran an article that complained that we are too worried about the family. The article made out that everyone's "First Family" is the church, not the natural family. Our government seems to agree that real parents don't have the right to know what is happening to their underage daughters.

Well, one fear I have for a meeting like this is that our evangelical movement, with all its merits, having achieved the unthinkable in terms of a glowing, growing world evangelical movement, would not think to draw on the wisdom resident in these diverse societies. Just in this century, mission-field evangelicals have gone from 10% of the world total to 70%. The so-called mission world is teeming with second, and third, and fourth generation evangelicals by now who could mightily contribute to our understanding here of *what is* or *what is not* an evangelical, and, *what the Biblical family might look like.*

So, I would challenge the promoters of this conference to look forward to the amazing contributions that would come — especially in the area of personal ethics — from overseas as people from other lands (mature, sacrificial and sensible people) could help us do something more than pool our own little monocultural perspective.

Otherwise, tragic things will happen. God did not intend for us to close our ears to our brethren overseas. Let me illustrate: I remember seeing a film just recently, produced by Americans, called "The Charm." Filmed in Nairobi, it told effectively how many Christians still carry charms hidden in their clothing and

Ralph D. Winter

bedding and makes clear that they should not do this. But it also seems to teach that young people who come to Christ must have enough guts to turn their parents down and say, "Look, get behind me. I'm going to be a Christian." Now, the amazing thing is that this goes over very well with Americans. In the promotion and backing of the film everyone says, "Oh, you must translate this in Swahili so it can benefit the people in Kenya and East Africa and other places where Swahili is spoken."

But, you know, I honestly believe that the people over there, the Christians overseas, are really going to be appalled by this movie. They are going to be appalled at the absence of any reference to Satan in relation to these charms. That's not even in the picture. You're not dealing with Satanic forces? Oh, yes you are! And, secondly, they will be jolted by the idea of young people just telling their parents to "shove off and let me make this decision." However they look at it, they will not look at it the way we do. We made it — we made the script, we went over there, we produced it; yet it is as un-African as you can possible imagine.

There's something else that bothers me. This is not a criticism at all of what has been said here at the conference. Our topic is the evangelical personal ethics. The assumption that surrounds that innocent topic at our conference this year is the idea that we need to define and defend personal ethics just as we need to define and defend biblical authority. Because if we don't, what is going to happen? Well frankly, I remember the first time I looked at a capital-city newspaper in Guatemala, and noticed throughout the newspaper, three or four places every day, want ads offering jobs specifically to evangelicals. I thought, "Isn't that interesting!" Some of these ads were placed by North American

248

companies which had discovered for themselves, or people in Guatemala had told them, "Hire the evangelicals." Why was this? Because the evangelicals had been taught personal ethics? Or that the Bible is true? I don't think so. The work of God in Guatemala — which is one of the most spectacular things in Latin America — is basically the impact of the Word of God and the Spirit of God, apart from any kind of formal scholarship or training. Now, none of us is especially taken by the scholasticism that followed the Reformation, but we may easily forget that it was another revolution called the "Evangelical Awakening" that made common the concept of the "evangelical experience" beyond all the rationale of all the reformers. It was that thing that happened to John Wesley. Yet some of our rationale here at this conference could just as easily describe Wesley before as after Aldersgate. I was just reading this morning in the Bible itself that Paul, writing to the Thessalonians, said: "Our gospel did not come to you in word only, but also in power and in the Holy Spirit and with full conviction." Now apart from that evangelical reality — which is demonstrated not merely "affirmed" — I do not believe that any in the world would believe the Bible. I do not believe any description of ethics will produce personal ethics. It is something else. It happens. Paul goes on, " . . . just as you know what kind of men we proved to be." They proved to be something. They were not simply bringing credentials on paper; they proved to *be* something. Jesus was believed not because people knew his credentials, but because of the authority with which he spoke. The Bible speaks with authority.

I remember how Charles Fuller (when I was a kid in high school, we used to go down to the Long Beach Auditorium on

Ralph D. Winter

Sunday afternoons) said, "Don't defend the Bible. It's a tiger; let it out!" Thus, I do not deny the truth of what has been said here; I just think this other factor should be added. Throughout the world, the actual, lived-out impact of the Bible is what authenticates it. The actual creation of demonstrated personal ethics, apart from any philosophical apparatus, is what gives credibility to the Christian movement.

The communist official interviewing a young women in a commune in China comes to this tell-tale question: "Are you a Christian?" She looks at him and says, "Yes!" He is astonished because he cannot promote her in her job if she says "yes" to that question. She must know that. Why would she say "yes" to that question? Does she not want the job? What is wrong with this woman? And yet he talks with her for a few minutes and realizes that they need this type of person at the higher levels. And across China they say that Christians are like the jeweled-bearings in the communist movement. Even the communists need a few people they can trust! And so this woman actually gets a promotion. Later this man gets very, very sick. No one can do anything. He finally asks for this woman and her friends to come and pray for him. He is healed. He becomes a Christian. The power of God is what creates and authenticates personal ethics.

Thus, I would hope that we could affirm the fact that whatever we're doing around the world, whether people can read or not, if it is the Word of God that is being preached in the power of the Holy Spirit, that those people who are willing and able to respond to such a Gospel, will in fact discover, personally, the kind of faith of which Luther and Calvin spoke, and we will be able to see the manifestation of that new ethical reality, just as the

250

evangelical awakening of the 18th century widely demonstrated. If we affirm this, then we may not have to be explaining quite so many things. When people get to the place where they insist on explanations, maybe it means that they are already trying to duck out from under the requirements of the living God! In that case no amount of reading of statements of ethics will create the missing reality.

QUESTIONS
FOR DISCUSSION

1. What are the main differences between personal ethics and social ethics? In what ways do they overlap?

2. Why is a solid foundation in biblical doctrine crucial for a discussion of personal ethics? What can happen to ethics if this foundation is not laid?

3. How does each of the six crucial doctrines mentioned in the article affect Christian personal ethics?

4. If, as Kantzer states, the Christian conscience is ultimately to be bound only by God, in what sense is the Christian bound to recognize the legitimate authority of others — especially of his parents and of his government?

5. How does sin affect the human intellect? How does it affect the human conscience? How does the Holy Spirit use human conscience? Why do people have different standards of morals?

6. Discuss this definition of love: Love is a sacrificial desire to give oneself to another. Do you agree that love is the key to the application of biblical ethics? Why or why not?

7. Of the ten perversions or misinterpretations of biblical personal ethics, which has affected your church or Christian community most? What positive steps can be taken to guard against this and other departures from true ethics?

8. In light of the seven common objections to biblical ethics, what steps can Christians take to ensure that their witness in the world is positive?

7
SOCIAL ETHICS

EVANGELICALS AND SOCIAL ETHICS

Harold O. J. Brown

*For it is God which worketh in you
both to will and to do of his good pleasure.*
— Philippians 2:13

Introduction: Faith and Life

Theology is traditionally divided into dogmatic and moral theology, or dogmatics and ethics; the Germans say *Glaubenslehre* and *Sittenlehre*: what to believe and how to behave. The concept of ethics involves knowing the good, but it involves more than merely *knowing* the good; it involves the exercise of the will to choose, and then to carry out that which has been chosen. Ethical theory is worthless without ethical practice. Between the knowledge of facts, principles, and theories on the one hand and acts on the other come *decisions:* decisions must be made to choose a general approach or theory of ethics by which one will be guided, to settle upon the principles that are to be followed, and to determine the facts, or to sort out the relevant facts from the available evidence. We often refer to these distinctions as first principles, middle principles, and applications. After the determination of principles and the establishment of facts, the will is once again involved in the decision to apply one's professed principles to the facts. The challenge of ethics may be put succinctly: *To Will and to Do.*[1] Ethics involves knowledge, will, and action. It involves human responsibility; all these imply the question of the freedom or bondage of man's will.

257

Harold O. J. Brown

"Faith," in "the Christian faith," involves much more than merely assent to a system of dogmas. It involves *obedience.* The old hymn, *"Trust and obey* . . . for there's no other way," states it quite well. There have always been those who would reduce the Christian religion to a system of morality without dogmatic requirements, but these are at best liberals, not Christians. As J. Gresham Machen said in his classic little book, *Christianity and Liberalism,* this is another religion. But we dare not reduce Christianity to a set of articles of faith or dogma without obedience. Can Jesus be Saviour and yet not Lord? Those who think so need not trouble themselves about principles of Christian ethics.[2] I am reminded of the criticism that I received from a Swiss teenager when discussing principles of Christian conduct. She said, "You say that because you are a Calvinist. We are Zwinglians and do not have to have any rules." That is a drastic misinterpretation of Zwingli, who believed very strongly that Christian principles should influence not only individuals and the church but all of society.[3]

Why "Evangelicals and Ethics"? —
Who Are These "Evangelicals"?

Do evangelicals have a distinctive posture with regard to ethics? Should they have such? Let me answer this rhetorical question flatly from the outset: No, they do not; and yes, they should. Evangelical ethics should *not* be distinctive *vis-à-vis* biblical Christian ethics, but it should and must be distinctive *vis-à-vis* the world. Accepting for the moment the contention that evangelicals must be concerned about obedience to Christ, i.e. about *conduct,* is it our duty to be concerned about *social ethics?*

Is there such a thing as ethical responsibility for the Christian community? Few would have trouble answering this question in the affirmative. But does Christian ethical responsibility also extend to attempting to shape the laws of the larger community, of secular society? Again, not to leave the assembly too long in uncertainty, let me answer in a word: Yes.

Because the label "evangelical" has a history, and often a disputed history with variant readings, we must spend a bit of time in defining our terms. The name says that we want to be identified with the Gospel, with the Good News that salvation is a gracious gift, freely offered through faith in the finished work of Christ. In a fundamental sense, it is impossible to be a Christian without being evangelical (by which we do *not* mean without belonging to a party claiming the label "evangelical"). It is also impossible to be a consistent evangelical and be indifferent to ethics. Unfortunately, it is very easy to be an inconsistent evangelical.

Evangelicals are not indifferent to ethics in practice. Indeed, in the realm of individual behavior, many evangelicals are characterized by a zeal for personal morality bordering on legalism. But evangelicalism has been weak in developing a distinctive and coherent pattern of ethics, particularly in the social realm. As long as the surrounding culture was Catholic, Protestantism could take most of its ethical principles straight from the Catholic tradition. When evangelicalism developed as a movement within Protestantism, Protestant doctrine was turning liberal, but Protestant ethics were not. Evangelicalism did not need to show a distinctive profile in the area of ethics. It could simply try to be faithful to the Protestant heritage.

Harold O. J. Brown

The conflict between evangelicals and other contenders for the name "Christian" has been chiefly in the area of doctrine, not morals — at least until the last generation or so. We have fought our doctrinal battles, content to stand with the liberals in the moral area, for little divided us there, or so it seemed. In fact, since the Western world was nominally Christian, not only was it not necessary for evangelicals to "profile" themselves *vis-à-vis* other Christians, it was hardly necessary for them do do so *vis-à-vis* bourgeois society.

This historic fact has resulted in a stunted growth of evangelicalism in the area of ethics, a fact which is coming to trouble us more and more as the world system is ever more clearly revealing that it "lies in the power of the evil one" (I John 5:19) and is bent on exterminating Christianity, or at least to reducing it to impotence.

A Brief Historical Reflection: How Did We Get Here?

The first to use the word "evangelical" to designate a specific party or theological persuasion within Christendom was Martin Luther. Luther wanted the Reformation which he set into motion to bring the good news of justification by faith apart from the works of the Law back to the people. He sought to liberate them from bondage to human traditions and regulations and from the necessity to have recourse to a host of human intermediaries — the clergy and the saints.

In the sixteenth century the "evangelical" movement was identified by contrast with Roman Catholicism. In dispute was the way of salvation. In terms of fundamental stands on ethics, there were no significant differences between Catholics on the one hand

and Lutheran and Reformed Protestants on the other. As they turned away from expressing religious faith largely in terms of sacramental and devotional life, Luther, Calvin, and the other leaders of the Reformation made vigorous if not uniformly successful efforts to foster consistent Christian living. What was new was the shift of emphasis to action, but not the principles, for they were little different from those of traditional Catholicism. But Luther and his successors, despite their efforts to reform the moral life of the people, were so preoccupied with doctrinal controversy that their work produced more polemics than practical piety. After five centuries, something similar has happened in our own day. The need to make a stand on doctrinal issues has drawn too much attention away from ethical questions. Unfortunately in our day — unlike Luther in his — we now confront fundamental ethical errors in ethical *principle* as well as practice, which threaten to swamp our evangelical ark despite all we can do to insure doctrinal correctness on inerrancy and all related matters.

Following the Protestant Reformation, a century and a half of bitter theological polemics, culminating in the Thirty Years' War, gave impetus to "syncretistic" (ecumenical) impulses that sought to find a common ground in practical morality and to minimize dogmatic disputes. (In our own day, we are in danger of finding a "syncretistic" ecumenical unity by leaving practical morality out of the picture altogether. In fact, if we want ecumenism today, we must not only be prepared to coexist with doctrinal differences, not to say with gross doctrinal errors, but also with perverse deformations of bibilical Christian ethics, such as the approval of abortion, of homosexual conduct, and of other practices that the church had hitherto condemned.)

Harold O. J. Brown

In the sixteenth century the Reformed, especially, but not only Calvin, operating on the assumption that society was Christian, used church and civil discipline in an effort to create a pattern of community life and responsibility consistent with Scripture. It foundered on the resistance of major sectors of the population, combined with the extravagant expectations of its advocates. Menno Simons and other "radical" Reformers tried a different approach, summoning individuals and families out of the compromising patterns of society and the established churches to a serious life of consistent discipleship, but their movement remained limited to small, often isolated clusters of followers. Their efforts went largely unrecognized in the confessional conflicts between Roman Catholics, Lutherans, and Zwinglians.

In the nineteenth century, evangelicals on the Continent were no longer so concerned to set themselves off from Roman Catholics, but rather from liberal Protestants. At issue were questions of fundamental doctrines, particularly those of inspiration and authority—but not questions of ethics. On ethics there was still no disagreement. At about the same time, in England "evangelical" meant "opposed to the High Church" — to its traditionalism and sacramentalism, but not to its ethics.

The Twentieth Century Divide

In our own late twentieth century, the situation has changed in two respects. First, among evangelicals the concept of what makes one an "evangelical" has shifted away from right doctrine, but not over to ethics. Instead, without disregarding doctrine, it has concentrated on what we might call personal, existential commitment ("Have you accepted Christ as your personal Saviour?"). This leads to a lessened interest in ethics in general and in social ethics in particular, especially because social ethics seems to have become the province of Protestant liberals. Second, evangelicals must come to terms with the fact that their ethics no longer reflect that of the general culture, but are in opposition to it. This means that we can no longer swim with the ethical tide but must swim against it.

Only in our own era, and especially since World War II, has there been such a marked difference about ethical principles between conservative evangelicals and the others who claim the Christian name.

Unfortunately, evangelicals have been slow to recognize the degree and the rapidity with which the ethical ground has shifted under their feet. There have been two great moral/ethical transformations in the United States since World War II: the civil rights movement and abortion on demand. In the civil rights movement, where evangelicals should have been active, they were slow, while the general society led the way to a positive transformation. Evangelicals let secular society lead them in the right direction. In the abortion situation, as well as with the infanticide and euthanasia that are coming in its wake, evangelicals have been, incredibly, even slower to react. Can it be because the media do not support them on this one? Initially, they let secular society lead them, this time in a dreadfully wrong direction. Prior to World War II, there would have been no doubt among Christians of any tradition that deliberate abortion is a homicidal act. In 1973, however, when the Supreme Court handed down its decision in Roe v. Wade, many evangelicals were so befuddled by their habitual need to oppose whatever the Roman Catholics seemed to support, as well as by

Harold O. J. Brown

the traditional tendency of American evangelicals to regard the political doctrine of a "wall of separation between church and state" as virtually divinely inspired, that they failed to denounce the decision, and in a few cases actually applauded it. Finally, most evangelicals have taken a stand on this issue, but hardly in time to be considered as spiritual guides in a disoriented society.

Evangelicals are so used to having to articulate the doctrinal distinctives of their faith while not needing to distinguish their morals much from those of the better aspects of bourgeois society that they have been tardy and negligent in articulating and defending distinctive ethical standards consistent with their evangelical faith. Until World War II, evangelicals were in a position to accept general Christian ethics more or less as they found them, and limit their controversy to *Glaubenslehre* — dogmatic theology. As a consequence evangelicals as a group are encountering difficulties today in defining and defending ethical principles that are consistent with their doctrinal positions, which latter are, by contrast, comparatively better articulated, more fully defended, and generally consistent with one another. The sluggishness of so many evangelicals in the civil rights struggle and the long delays and compromises of many others on the prolife issue reflect a general evangelical insecurity in the ethical area. This is also making itself felt with regard to sexual ethics, where many of us, although still giving lip service to biblical standards of peemarital abstinence, marital fidelity, and the condemnation of homosexual acts, are in some danger of being swept along with the current of social degeneracy.

Until recently, evangelicals stood out from among the mass of "generic" Christians by virtue of emphasizing faith over

264

against works, ceremonies, and structures — in other words, by majoring in doctrine rather than in ethics. The great temptation is to delude ourselves into thinking that right doctrine, orthodoxy, could be enough, either that there is no need for "orthopraxy," or no need to worry about it, as it will come (super)naturally.

As far as their perception by the public is concerned, evangelicals today often want to be distinguished from "fundamentalists" and to have no truck with what is deemed "fundamentalistic legalism." This desire to avoid a "fundamentalistic" image — a desire made even more burning by the insistence of the media on calling the Ayatollah Khomeini and other fiends "fundamentalists" — has hobbled evangelicals in their efforts to keep pace with ethical challenges. They have tended to let the "fundamentalists" bear the brunt of moral conflicts in which they are too discreet or too delicate to engage themselves. In our twentieth century, then, the term "evangelical" identifies its wearers first *theologically* or doctrinally, with regard to soteriology and bibliology; secondarily, at least among evangelicals themselves, if not among the general public, it identifies them morally, suggesting a distinction from the legalism and separatistic attitudes of a certain kind of *fundamentalism*, not from Roman Catholicism or High Church sacramentalism. (Because the "evangelical" distinction is defined over against liberalism first and fundamentalism secondly, we hear of Catholic evangelicals — not a contradiction in terms — but never, or hardly ever, of "fundamentalist evangelicals," a term which ought to be a tautology but is widely regarded as an oxymoron.)

Harold O. J. Brown

Faith Instead of Morals?

Because of the absolute need to stress true doctrine, especially over against the pernicious errors of biblical fallibility and of universal salvation, which are destructive of both the life of faith and of the moral life, evangelicals still tend to identify themselves only, or at least primarily, in terms of doctrine. While this identification is fundamental (if that word be permitted us in the context of this conference!), it cannot be sufficient and exclusive. (One of the unintended side-effects of the evangelical/fundamentalist distinction has been a dangerous tendency for "evangelicals" to conform to the world, leaving it to the "fundamentalists" to conform to Scripture.) An additional embarrassment to evangelicals lies in the fact that, because ethics governs conduct, and conduct can also be regulated by laws, which are formulated as part of politics, an interest in ethics, both personal and social, brings one into contact with secular laws and with politics, both of which appear somewhat dangerous to the heavenward-bound evangelical.

It would be catastrophic for us as evangelicals to emphasize faith to the exclusion of morals, or doctrine to the exclusion of ethics. Unfortunately, this is what sometimes seems to have been happening. The only justification for even appearing to let evangelicalism mean so much doctrinally and so little ethically and morally is the fact that until just recently, the major assault of liberalism against historic Christian orthodoxy lay in the area of doctrine. Doctrine was attacked, so doctrine was defended — morals were not under attack, and morals were left undefended. Thus evangelicals, like the Catholics in the old joke, may be said to have faith but no morals, leaving it to the Unitarians to have

266

morals with no faith. (Actually, most evangelicals have rather presentable morals, but often they cannot tell you exactly why.)

To sum up: doctrines were disputed, but ethics was not. Until after World War II, the ethical teachings of liberal Protestants as well as of the far less visible liberals among the Roman Catholics — did not differ in any essentials from those of the conservative evangelicals. Consequently, there appeared to be no need to defend the frontier in ethics as there was in theology in general, especially in the areas of the doctrines of inspiration, the deity of Christ, the Trinity, and the Atonement, as well as other important doctrines.

In fact, up until World War II Western Christian societies in general promoted the moral standards of Judaeo-Christian ethics. When individuals were converted to a personal faith in Christ, they needed exhortation and instruction only in the area of doctrine that Christians believe. As far as practice — their ethics — was concerned, they needed only to be encouraged and helped to adhere to the standards of society as a whole, to which the whole culture was at least paying lip service.

La traison des clercs

From World War II onwards, at the latest, however, the general culture of the nominally Christian world has been turning ever more massively away from Judaeo-Christian, biblical ethics, a disastrous development that has been approved if not pioneered by liberal clergy — *la traison des clercs*. We must beware of the temptation as biblical Protestants to follow them in this deflection from the right path. We will not long be able to hold biblical doctrines if we drift far from biblical ethics.

The liberals' turning away has two aspects in the area of personal ethics. First, one begins to say, "Chacun à son goût, — loosely translated, "It depends on your taste." Of course, we all want to have *good taste,* but we don't take "taste" as seriously as we did God's Law. We no longer feel that the moral life is essentially one with the life of faith. In the area of social ethics, liberals do not say, "Chacun à son goût." Some social-ethical tasks are taken with the utmost seriousness. But the tendency is to want to take things out of the hands of the individual and of the faith community and to put them into the hands of the provider state and its welfare system. This second phenomenon affects evangelicals too—not that the tasks have been repudiated, but rather that the tasks that Christian ethics hitherto assigned to the individual Christian, the family, and the community of faith are usurped, or taken over by default, by the secular commonwealth. This sometimes happens because Christians fail to perform them; sometimes it is done in order to prevent Christians from performing them.

In the so-called socialist, i.e. Communist, countries, Christian communities are rigidly prohibited from engaging in works of social welfare, because the government knows that the social ministry of the church has been one of its attractions from the dawn of Christianity and is determined that the people shall be beholden to the State alone. In the Western democracies, the welfare state has accomplished much the same thing by substitution rather than suppression. Christian social ethics appear unnecessary when, "All good things come of thee, O State."

Liberals have been calling on the state to do many of the things that really are tasks committed by the Lord to the family or the church; evangelicals have been ignoring the expansion of the state, or pretending to think that it will not affect them. Both practices allow the state to expand its scope at the expense of the church and of other intermediate communities, with the state becoming the *de facto* censor (in the Ciceronian sense), prescribing the principles of moral conduct to the public.

The Social Component of Christian Ethics

In the early days of Christianity, the social component of Christian ethics was exhibited almost exclusively within the Christian community, just as Paul seems to require in Galatians 5:10. After the Emperor Constantine, the church became more and more contiguous with society as a whole. What the Christian community held to be right, society did, and what society did, it did for Christian reasons. But society in those centuries was not yet the state. Now, with the rise of the pluralistic provider state, the situation has changed dramatically. The state hampers, rather than promotes, Christian personal ethics, and supplants Christian social ethics. New converts as well as children growing up in believers' families are frequently launched into very stormy ethical seas with no other guidance than the residual moral teachings of the general culture. Under such circumstances, many Christians will sooner or later be swamped and go down, never to surface again. An evangelical proclamation that does not supply ethical standards and provide encouragement to behave ethically has fulfilled only part of its mission. This partial fulfillment can hardly endure by itself, unless the second component of the Great Commission is also performed.

Harold O. J. Brown

Trust and Obey

That conduct is a vital concern for Christians is evident from the teachings of Jesus himself, which contain more morality than dogma, at least at first reading. The Sermon on the Mount illustrates this amply. This dual emphasis is very evident in the Great Commission of Matthew 28, which gives us our marching orders as evangelicals. Jesus' parting charge to his disciples makes the unity between faith and morals, between doctrine and ethics quite apparent: *"Make disciples* of all the nations . . . teaching them to observe all that I commanded you, and lo, I am with you always . . . "* (verses 19-20). If verse 20 is an essential part of the Great Commission — and it is — then a substantial part of the evangelical community must be out of commission, because while we are eager to make disciples, we are slow to teach them to observe. It is to this problem of an incomplete fulfillment of the Great Commission that we address ourselves today.

Success and Shortsightedness

Why have modern evangelicals been sluggish in developing and implementing a consistent program of Christian social ethics? Part of the answer lies in the fact that the culture out of which the evangelical movements grew had been Christianized for seven hundred to one thousand years. In the United States, we have been occupied with individual conversion, mass evangelism, church growth, and the charismatic renewal, all of which have been more or less successful; and we have failed to see what is happening to the culture around us. In our century, the falling away of individuals has been noted and counteracted by vigorous evangelistic and discipleship efforts. The full impact of the falling away of whole cultures has not yet been recognized, much less effectively resisted. A culture can become Christian without taking the people with it. This has happened often enough in the past. But a culture may cease to be Christian and effectively turn pagan for quite a while before the Christians to whom the culture once belonged notice what is happening and begin to react to it.

Early Patterns

The first Christians, who lived in a hedonistic, jaded, cynical, pagan culture, were very clearly aware of the fact that their distinctive faith called for distinctive conduct, for distinctive ethics in the individual and in the social realm. It was necessary for pastors and teachers to tell new converts and their children how to live as followers of Christ, for the culture certainly would not tell them. The early history of the church shows that the first generations of Christians heard and heeded the moral side of Jesus' message, the call to repentance and a changed way of life, just as they heard the call to faith in him as Lord and Saviour. Thus the church of the second and third centuries — centuries of persecution, as we all know — was characterized by a great interest in the moral quality of the Christian life. To be redeemed means to be obligated to obey "the Law of Christ."[4]

The early Christians did not sense a conflict between obedience of this kind and the freedom for which Christ has set us free (Gal. 5:1). The concern to keep ethics central is already to be found in the New Testament itself. We are familiar with the example of the Epistle of James, which Luther, in his zeal for justification by faith alone, lampooned as a "right strawy epistle."[5] Luther's hatred for everything smacking of works righteousness

Harold O. J. Brown

led him to a number of oversimplifications and exaggerations, such as the contention of Nicholas von Amsdorf that good works are injurious to salvation, rejected by orthodox Lutheranism in the Formula of Concord.[6]

An Immediate Post-Apostolic Decline?

Ethical transformation and consistent Christian living were such a concern of Christians in the second and third centuries that the Apostolic Fathers of that period are accused of having re-Judaized Paul's Gospel of salvation by faith and replaced it with legalism. Paul's Gospel, about which he expressed concern in Galatians 1, was supposedly adulterated and lost almost immediately. This is a misconception. Would it not have been strange indeed if those closest in time to Jesus and the Apostles had so promptly reverted to Pharisaical legalism? It is important to recognize that the early Christians found no incompatibility between justification by faith on the one hand and and consistent obedience on the other.

The idea that the church almost immediately forgot the true meaning of the Gospel, promoted by Ferdinand Christian Baur (1792-1860), was based on the concept that Christian faith, like all movements of the human spirit, had to follow the principles of the historical dialectic.[7] It is not necessary to describe this trend here, other than to say that if it were correct, it would mean that true Christianity was very short-lived indeed, having come into existence with Paul only to be made obsolete by the resurgence of legalistic moralism during the next generations of disciples. If Baur were right, there would be no such thing as a true continuity of the Christian faith through the ages. Instead of saying, "Plus que ça change, plus que c'est la même chose," we would have to say, "Plus que ça change, plus que ce n'est plus" — the more it changes, the more it is no more.

Speculative theories such as the one that we are discussing foster the erosion of the conviction that there is anything that is identifiably and reliably *Christian* doctrine. Where that erroneous attitude prevails, it is self-evident that we will not have authoritative doctrinal teachings. What may be less self-evident is the fact that because doctrine and ethics *do* go together, if we ever reach the point of really losing ethics, a fatal loss of doctrine will not be far behind. Indeed, this contention is being illustrated by what is going on in much of evangelicalism today. An increasing softness in the realm of ethical standards, especially sexual morals, is being accompanied by a growing tendency to give up "evangelical essentials" in the realm of doctrinal convictions. Among other "fluctuations" we may note vacillation and uncertainty about inerrancy and a tendency towards universal salvation.

We can be sure that Baur's attempt to force the story of the Christian faith into the procrustean bed of Hegel's historical dialectic does not do justice to the fullness of Paul's vision of faith. For Paul faith is not a substitute for good works, but the only motivation actually capable of producing God-pleasing works. Paul excluded neither active obedience nor good works from the life of faith. Although he is *the* great preacher of justification "by faith alone, apart from works of the Law" (Romans 3:28), Paul devotes extensive passages to ethical instruction: "For in Christ Jesus neither circumcision nor uncircumcision means anything, but faith working through love" (Galatians 5:6). Paul spends a fair amount of time telling us what "faith working" implies in several specific areas of ethics. It is true that it is James, not Paul, who warns us that faith without works is dead (James 2:26), but Paul would have said that faith that does no works is not faith at all. Is this so different? I Corinthians offers several explicit examples of Paul's deep concern that the life and practice of Christians conform to their profession of faith: in effect, Paul calls upon Christians to "Trust and obey." Obedience alone would be insufficient, but faith without obedience would not be faith.

The Retreat from Praxis

The interest of the early church in ethics was not contrary to Paul's interest or example. It was typical not only of the second- and third-century church but also of every great epoch of the life of the church until — but unfortunately *not* including — our own. The great revivals of living faith that have shaken the church out of lethargy from time to time in the course of her long history have — until the present century — always been accompanied by energetic efforts towards a reformation of morals. The Cluniac Reform of the tenth century, the rise of the mendicant orders in the thirteenth, the Protestant Reformation, Pietism and the Wesleyan movement — all were accompanied by a significant resurgence of interest in the Christian life, and all produced major treatments of ethics. Our own century is deficient. We look at the highly-publicized moral lapses of a few of our celebrated Christian media personalities, and say, "How could this happen?"

There are many factors that contribute, and certainly the chief among them is the fact that even regenerate men and women have a sin-weakened nature that remains susceptible to temptation. In addition to this deeply *personal* weakness which menaces all who seek to live a godly life, there is a *structural* vulnerability. For a generation evangelical Christians have been forgetting that spiritual renewal without ethical reformation cannot be lasting. It is no more viable than ethical reformation without spiritual renewal. Such ethical reformation necessarily involves the reformulation of ancient ethical principles in contemporary idiom.

It was not until our own century that major movements of spiritual revival have concentrated so exclusively on "soul-winning" to the neglect of the moral reformation of individuals and the transformation of society. Twentieth-century revivalism is the first great revival movement that has failed to generate a true moral reformation.

In the 1950's and 1960's it was possible to assume that when an individual experienced conversion or spiritual renewal, it did not place him in conflict with the ethics of society and of the general culture. Evangelical Protestantism, as both Karl Barth and Francis Schaeffer charged, strongly tends to individualism. Its moral challenge was directed specifically towards the area of personal morality, and simply firmed up the existing professed ideals of bourgeois culture. It has tended to view social problems as the result of individual failings, to be dealt with by individual reform and voluntary assistance. It has always assumed that transformed individuals will transform society. I remember hearing this message quite explicitly at Graham Crusades in which I participated. This attitude was never entirely adequate, because it paid no attention to the intermediate steps and structures necessary to permit personal changes to change society. It has become increasingly inadequate as two things have happened: first, the transformation of social structures has created social problems

275

Harold O. J. Brown

that go beyond the ability of individuals to correct; second, the
transformation of bourgeois culture has put evangelical personal
ethics into conflict with the general culture instead of in alliance
with it. At the end of the twentieth century, we are paying a high
price for this deficiency.

Ethics Social and Political

Must Christians work to change social conditions and to
renew society? May or must Christians work through the political
process to achieve Christian ends even when the political structure is both formally secularistic and practically pluralistic? I
answer, yes, on the grounds that Christ's moral demands reach out
to include society as well as the individual, and that when an
individual has the legal right and responsibility to help society
structure itself, he has the Christian duty to help it to so so in line
with the demands of Christ.

There is no way to deny that the call to follow Christ includes
a call to a distinctive kind of life. The Christian life involves a
personal relationship with Christ, and consequently it must transform the individual into conformity with Christ (Rom. 12:2, I Cor.
11:1, Eph. 5:1, I John 3:2). But it is not the individual alone who
is addressed by the demands of Christ: they flow over naturally
into the community of faith, and — or so I believe — almost as
naturally will have an impact on the surrounding society as well.
Ernst Troeltsch states it well: "The message of Jesus also deals
with the formation of the community based on the hope of the
Kingdom and the preparation for its coming in Jesus himself. . .
His fundamental moral demand is the sanctification of the individual in all his moral activity for the sake of God. . . . The

276

command to love one another is at least bound to influence a small and intimate community."[8] In other words, there is no way for Christians to be a community at all unless their community is shaped by Christ's fundamental demands. Even this limited vision, i.e. the idea that there has to be a practical social ethic for the little Christian community, goes beyond some of the tacit assumptions of individualistic Protestant pietism. Where the Christian community expands and starts to interact on various levels with the general society, the Christian ethic must start influencing society, even if only as a warning voice, as otherwise society inevitably starts to influence it.

As long as the Christian community was small and ostracized, it made no sense for it to try to effect changes in the standards of the pagan culture that surrounded it. With the conversion of the Emperor Constantine, however, that changed. Christian convictions gained acceptance. A succession of Christian emperors wrote many aspects of biblical law into the civil code. To those radicals who hold that any Christian entanglement with the state involves capitulation to the world, this would be highly objectionable. But what is an emperor to do if he is converted to Christ? Abdicate because he is a Christian, or reign as a Christian? Can a senator who is converted do less?

Even before this happened, Christian attitudes began to change general behavior. According to historian William Lecky, from the moment Christianity became a moral force in the ancient world, abortion declined and finally all but disappeared *before* civil legislation was enacted against it.[9]

Christian ethics will change not only the Christian community but society at large. Nevertheless, it is evident that the spread

Harold O. J. Brown

of Christianity did *not* change everything. The institution of slavery endured for centuries. Even though it was gradually abolished in Christian Europe, Christian Europeans kept slaves and fostered slavery in their overseas dominions. Similar examples can be multiplied.[10]

It is self-evident that the Christian doctrine of the Kingdom of God and the Christian love ethic will transform not merely the personal life-style of individual Christians but must also have an effect on the pattern of behavior of the Christian community. What is less self-evident is what should happen when Christianity begins to affect those in power in what was previously secular, non-Christian society. The Emperor Constantine did not significantly change the social policies of the Empire after his conversion, but several of his successors introduced reforms based on Christian principles, notably Justinian I and Leo III. Nothing could be more natural than for an emperor to use his power to legislate according to his best judgment and convictions, to pattern his legislation on his Christian beliefs about justice. Although it is never possible for a ruler, even a complete autocrat, totally to ignore the wishes of the people, the autocrat does not have to balance his own convictions with a host of pluralistic ideas. But what are Christians to do when no one Christian is the *autokrator* with the power to change things, but rather many individual Christians would have to enter the political arena in order to affect the ethics of society? Shall they dare less than Constantine?

The Impasse of Pluralism

In this democracy we are required to set our own legal standards. There is no emperor to whom we could leave the task.

278

Our society is more Christian than anything else, but it is not Christian enough to permit us easily to enact Christian social ethics into law. We confront the impasse of what Johann Millendorfer calls value pluralism (*Wertpluralismus*). If evangelical Christians are to have any impact for the transformation of this society, in which they constitute one of the largest and most highly motivated minorities, but in which their influence is largely felt by default, it will be necessary to kill the sacred cow of pluralism.

Tolerance is an ideal which evangelical Christians can endorse. It requires respect for those who hold differing convictions. "Pluralism" is different. It used to be a descriptive term that merely indicated that many different convictions coexisted within a given social structure: Now it has come to mean value pluralism, namely, that all convictions about values are of equal validity, which says in effect that no convictions about values have any validity. In other words, there is no agreement about the nature of the good life.[11] When Constantine came to power, there was no moral consensus — Christians may have made up only a tenth of the population — but when there is an emperor, he alone constitutes a consensus. In the early days of the American republic, there was no emperor, but there was a moral consensus. Now we are in the situation where there is neither an emperor nor a consensus, and it is likely that we cannot get along indefinitely without both.

From Euphoria to Aporia

The Reagan years, just ended, created a sense of euphoria: "It's morning in America!" The euphoria was shared by evangelicals, who responded to Reagan's optimism even though their analysts — such as the late Francis Schaeffer, and more recently,

Harold O. J. Brown

Charles Colson—kept on warning that the fundamental problems were still growing. After Reagan, it is becoming more and more apparent that instead of euphoria our society is in a condition of *aporia* (bafflement, impasse) — an awareness of incompatible views: there seems to be no practicable way out of our social, economic, and political predicaments. We cannot agree on the solution. We cannot even agree on the diagnosis.

Are we in that situation gloomily predicted by Oswald Spengler in *The Decline of the West?* Are his predictions at the point of coming true? "This, then, is the conclusion of the city's history . . . it sacrifices first the blood and soul of its creators to the needs of its majestic evolution . . . and so, doomed, moves on to final self-destruction."[12] Is this to be the destiny of our "Christian" civilization? Spengler predicted a time in which moral discourse will be impossible, and instead of arguing moral questions, people will debate questions of alcohol and diet. (He predicted this in 1918. In 1989 we have a committed, evangelical Surgeon General who rages about smoking, grumbles about red meat and alcohol, and regularly warns us about cholesterol but preserves a discreet diffidence about his personal "pro-life bias" when it comes to abortion, finding "no evidence" that it is harmful to the mothers who have had the abortion.)[13]

Johann Millendorfer reports a conversation with a futurologist of the Club of Rome, who told of his fears that it will not be possible to change the course of development, because there is no type of human being capable of doing it. He asked: "Is is still possible to hope?" Millendorfer answers with an emphatic "Ja," *provided* that we make the following statement about the type of human that we need: "The type of man that we need in order to change this development must be free of the system-immanent compulsions of society. In other words, fame, power and wealth may not mean very much to him. Instead, this type of human has to assume responsibility for this earth and above all for the brother who lives on it, and generate his own activity from this responsibility. This polarity is found in the redeemed man of the Gospels, now as before, the valid pattern of a fulfilled life. Also, as long as there are real Christians, this world will constantly renew itself. As long as the salt of the earth has not lost its savor, this world will not be ruined."[14] As Millendorfer commented in a lecture in Vienna at Easter last year, "The future will be Christian, or it will not take place."

We need to have such confidence, and to express it. Only Christian, evangelical action on a broad scale can rescue our society from its plunge into self-destruction. But Christian action presupposes Christian ethics, *to will and to do.*

To effect such a rescue, it will be necessary to overcome a century of neglect among evangelicals as well as the massed obstacles of pluralism and secularism in our society as a whole. We must squarely face the phenomenon of a double degeneration, degeneration of Christianity and degeneration of society. Knowing, as Paul says, "the terror of the Lord," we must remind ourselves that for Christ's followers, this "terror" should produce obedience, not the paralysis of fear. We must lose our dread of legalism to the extent that we are willing to make obedience to the law of Christ an altogether natural part of our message.

Our fulfillment of the Great Commission must include "teaching them to observe all things." We must get over the idea that the Law of God and the Word of God are something only for converted Christians of evangelical persuasion: Paul himself advised Timothy that "the Law is not made for a righteous man... but for the ungodly" (I Tim. 1:9). And believing that the Law is good, we must "persuade men." Our task is to proclaim "the whole counsel of God," and a major part of that counsel involves the proclamation of ethical standards for the people, as well as for the church. Whether many will listen, whether many will be persuaded, is *their* problem. Whether we try is *ours*.

[1]Jacques Ellul, *To Will and to Do* (Philadelphia: United Church Press, 1969)

[2]The personal and social ethics of those who repudiate "Lordship salvation" may be exemplary, by a happy inconsistency.

[3]See Robert C. Walton, *Zwingli's Theocracy* (Toronto: University of Toronto Press, 1967) pp. 103-138.

[4]This theme is prominent in the Apostolic Fathers, especially, but not only, I Clement, Barnabas, Polycarp. See H. Dermont McDonald, *The Atonement of the Death of Christ* (Grand Rapids: Baker, 1985), pp. 115-124.

[5]Martin Luther, *Werke*, Weimarer Ausgabe, DB (*Deutsche Bibel*), VI, 10.

[6]*Formula of Concord*, Art. IV, Negative, ii.

[7]This thesis is found throughout F. C. Baur's main works, *Paulus* (1854) and *Das Christentum und die christliche Kirche der ersten drei Jahrhunderte* (1853).

[8]Ernest Troeltsch, *The Social Teachings of the Christian Churches*, tr. Olive Wyon (New York: Harper, 1960) Vol. II, pp. 51, 52, 62.

[9]William E. H. Lecky, *A History of Western Morals* (New York: Braziller, 1955), pp. 20-24.

[10]One curious practice that long survived the establishment of Christianity is that of castration. Jesus takes note of the practice of castrating boys in order to create a class of eunuchs, without explicitly condemning it (Matthew 19:12). The Old Testament forbids eunuchs from serving as priests (Leviticus 21:20), a rule that was taken over by the

Christian church and which prevented the celebrated theologians Origen and Peter Abelard from being ordained as priests. Nevertheless, the practice of castration, so common in the Near East, was practiced in the Byzantine Empire during its entire history without effective opposition by the church.

[11]Christoph Gaspari and Hans (Johann) Millendorfer, *Konturen einer Wende. Strategien für die Zukunft* (Graz, Vienna, Cologne: Styria, 1978) pp. 340-343.

[12]Oswald Spengler, *The Decline of the West*, 2 vol. (New York: Knopf, 1926, 1928), Vol. II, p. 107.

[13]Documentaion can be obtained from the major media almost weekly, e.g., *TIME*, April 25, 1989.

[14]Christoph Gaspari and Hans (Johann) Millendorfer, *Konturen einer Wende. Strategien für die Zukunft* (Graz, Vienna, Cologne: Styria, 1978) pp. 343-344.

RESPONSE TO HAROLD O. J. BROWN

Myron S. Augsburger

"For he himself is our peace, who has made the two one...
to create in himself one new man out of the two ...
to reconcile both of them to God through the cross . . ."

Ephesians 2:14-16

Introduction

Christian ethics is a Christological life-style. While ethics is the science of morality, the guide for right behavior, the underpinning of integrity, Christian ethics finds its full character in the Christ who lived the will of God. Ethics emphasizes the higher expression of humanness, of being human, responsible, free moral agents, of being made in the image of God with the inner resource of a God-given conscience. Ethics, with its various concerns, deals with our relation with others. Therefore ethics, while personal, is not private individualism, morality is never without social dimensions.

Reading the insightful presentation by Dr. Harold O. J. Brown has been a positive experience for me. His emphasis on knowing and doing, on word and deed, on living in obedience to the Word of God is excellent. His paper is a corrective for those who do not see the relation of love and law, of grace and obedience. His call for "orthopraxy" beyond existential experience is greatly needed among us evangelicals; likewise is his call to balance correct doctrine with consistent discipleship as Jesus

Myron S. Augsburger

commissioned us (Matthew 28:19-20). To my thinking he correctly calls for a separation of church and state that emphasizes the role of the church and keeps personal ethics from being hampered and social ethics from being supplanted by the state. His statement that a culture can become pagan while Christians in the culture may be unaware of the seriousness of changes taking place is very penetrating and relevant. I join him in the call for a quality revival that will bring about "the moral reformation of individuals and the transformation of society."

Perhaps between the two of us we can find a stance somewhere between the Reformed and the Anabaptist positions. In part because I stand in the Anabaptist theological position I do raise questions on some aspects of Dr. Brown's presentation. One issue is that our primary calling as Christians is to clarify an ethic for the people of God rather than to "shape the laws of the larger community, of secular society." Christians living by the will of God will qualitatively enrich society.

Another area calling for more clarity is the primacy of God's kingdom. This was basic to the Anabaptist movement, which before Menno had already spread so widely that as Roland Bainton has said, "both Catholics and Lutherans were afraid that all of Europe would become Anabaptist," evidenced by their call for a clear separation of church and state. This was based on not a political but a theological interpretation of the Lordship of Christ, a position held by my colleague as well. This theology in turn calls for an emphasis on reconciliation, love, justice, and peace.

I note the absence of expression of ethical concern over nuclear arms as he lists the two great issues in U.S. since World

War II as consisting in the civil rights movement, and abortion on demand. I also question the references to Emperor Constantine who made church and society (state) to be coterminous, without adequate reference to the resultant "fallen church" or the difference between a Christian state and a "Christian nation." Further, his reference to "value pluralism" and the apparent negation of pluralism seems to make the acceptance of the general pluralism of our "global village" as a setting for evangelistic dialogue something less than acceptable. And finally, more attention should be given to the global network of Christians as our affirmation of the primacy of the body of Christ, affirming as it does the presence of his kingdom, as a realm which is trans-racial, trans-cultural, and trans-national.

A Third Way

My approach to ethics from the Anabaptist perspective, with its high view of Scripture as supreme authority, involving a high Christology which maintains a high view of the community of the redeemed as those who pursue whole-life discipleship, serves to interpret ethics first for the people of God. Separation of church and state is not to be understood as antistructure, but rather freedom in and from societal structures even while we respect them as serving in God's order for creation.

In placing the priority on the Kingdom of God I have frequently described this as a "Third Way," one which recognizes with Paul that there is Greek and Jew but also the people of God as a "Third Way" (I Corinthians 10:32). To contemporize, there is a rightist and a leftist position but also a "Third Way" that is not structured as a similar position but exists as a critique of each that may accept and reject elements of both, depending on an understanding of God's will as discerned by the community of faith.

Biblical Realism

Evangelicals could well work together to achieve a Biblical Realist approach to ethics, especially from a Christological perspective. This would mean that we take the historical Jesus seriously just as we take the historicity of Jesus seriously. Christ expressed the will of God in his total person, in his words, in his deeds, and in his person as the Word Incarnate. The interpretation of ethics Christologically means that we relate ethics to Christ just as we relate salvation to Christ. This calls for identification with Christ in the totality of our lives.

Jesus' emphasis on the two "tablets" of God's will, the first and second commandments, emphasizes one of the higher expressions of social ethics to be found in the Old Testament, "Thou shalt love thy neighbor as thyself" (Leviticus 19:18). He equalized this commandment with the "first" commandment, "Thou shalt love the Lord thy God with all thy heart, with all thy soul, with all thy mind, and with all thy strength." The two are readily held together when we understand the meaning of love as opening one's life intimately to that of another. To love God totally is to open the totality of life to Him, and in so doing we open the totality of our life to what God is doing in the neighbor, friend, or enemy; we don't close anyone out! It is in this sense of openness to God's activity and will for all peoples that we live by the commandment to love the neighbor as one loves himself or herself. This immediately involves us in social ethics.

With Dr. Brown I am calling us to the engagement of ethical practices in family life and sexual morality, community life and the place of worship, the work ethic and stewardship, discipleship and integrity, education and ideals, social order and political accountability, and finally evangelism and justice/peace concerns. The interfacing of the personal and the social is inescapable in each of these areas. We are in no way lone individualists in society but are a part of the social order in which we live as lights to the world, as salt to the earth.

It has been a mistake when we have let the negations of evangelism on the part of liberals in turn drive conservatives to champion a narrow evangelism that neglects the social areas of life and leave it to those engaged in social services to serve without any reference to the gospel. As Carl F. H. Henry has said, "Christianity is always personal but it is never private." Another has said, "We never grow spiritually at the expense of our brother; we only grow spiritually as we take the brother along."

Signs of the Kingdom
In Dr. Brown's fine paper, the concluding section points out the mutual degeneration of society and of Christianity. However, we must reach for something more than a call of obedience to law, even the "law of Christ." From a Christological hermeneutic, the redemptive work of God reflected in the "signs of the Kingdom" manifest in the redeemed community, focuses for us the dynamic of transforming grace. The will of God is actualized only by fellowship with the risen Christ. Jesus himself calls us from law to grace, not only as saving acceptance but as "saved" actions. This moves us from doctrine to practice, to which Dr. Brown calls us as evangelicals.

Myron S. Augsburger

From my perspective, with Christ as the foundation for
ethics, we must achieve a more consistent balance than do those
whose "right to life" emphasis is more for the unborn than for the
born, i.e. the neighbor across national lines; or than those who see
abortion on demand as an ultimate evil but who do not speak to the
nuclear threat as a moral evil. We cannot deal with social ethics
and avoid serious discussion of justice, human rights, peace,
freedom and compassion ministries to those who are poor in this
world. Christians who are leaders in the political or social areas
have the unique opportunity to influence systems to take Christian
insights seriously as they influence policy and practice for the
well-being of society.

Theological Premises
There are several theological positions which we must
recognize as shaping our different convictions on issues:
1. Christology is central for ethics. Not only do we affirm our
faith that Jesus Christ is very Son of God and son of man, we also
identify with him in our lives. In his redemption we relate ethics
to Christology in the same way in which we relate salvation to
Christology. That is, we are saved in relation to Jesus and we
behave our relation to Jesus.
2. Incarnation is God's affirmation that humanness and
sinfulness are not synonymous. Jesus Christ could be truly human
without being sinful. Therefore, it follows that in the new birth, in
regeneration, God is recreating the truly or ideally human as he
recreates us in the image of Christ.
3. Christian ethics is primarily for the redeemed community.
The evangelical church speaks much about our "fallenness," our

sinfulness being a fact which each honest person knows very well. But fallenness is our condition, not our confession! In Christ we are redeemed, that is, liberated from the dominance of sin even while it exists in our lives. Our affirmation is that we are reconciled, brought into right relationship with God "in Christ."

4. Evangelism is a confrontational, life-enriching faith expressed amidst social pluralism. As Dr. Brown says, pluralism is being made into another "ism" like secularism or materialism. However, we can respect the rights of persons to hold any one of many positions in our society and then engage them in a new level of evangelistic dialogue. As our lives express the quality and power of our new life in Christ, we enrich the world around us, elevating their perception and standards by interaction with the higher ethic of the Christian community. A lack of ethical integrity on the part of Christians not only fails God in his expectations of his disciples but fails God in failing to impact the world for a better society.

5. Kingdom values surely involve positive service. As a redeemed community we are a presence of the Kingdom, i.e. a rule of God in society. Seeking first the Kingdom of God and his righteousness (Matthew 6:33) is not a privatistic faith. Paul writes that "God has translated us from the kingdom of darkness into the Kingdom of his dear Son" (Colossians 1:13), and this is a present reality. While we live in the world we are not of the world; we are members of the Kingdom of God.

6. Loving one's neighbor is socially constructive. Such love is not easy; it may be quite costly, but it is lasting in its qualitative enrichment. *Agapè* love, unconditional yet "tough" love, combines personal and social ethics in attitudes and actions of care,

Myron S. Augsburger

correction, and compassion. This neighbor-love stands in direct contradiction to Western individualism.

7. Evangelical faith, shaped by a Biblical Realism, expresses the higher social ethic. Western society, idealizing the ethic of utilitarianism (the greatest happiness for the greatest number of people) must be confronted by the Christian ethic of the will of God for the greater righteousness of all people.

There is no way in which evangelism can be reduced to a privatistic act of commitment, for commitment to Christ engages each disciple in the will of God. On the other hand, there is no way in which the biblical ethic of love for one's neighbor is fulfilled by deeds of kindness alone without sharing the most important thing in life, life in Christ.

Being Christian in the Socio-Political Orders

Our approach to the social and political orders is not one of manipulation, coercion, nor of attempts to control these orders. Rather, we share in the quality of the gospel, respecting the voluntary responses of faith. This approach calls us to respect the freedoms of those who think other than we do about God, be they Muslim, Jewish, Buddhist, Hindu, Animist, or atheist. In our respect for the freedom of others we in turn strengthen possibilities for our own freedom as we call those in authority to seek the freedom and equity of all alike.

The evangelistic approach is to make faith an option for others. It is not trying to control social or political orders but is instead holding them accountable to live up to the highest level of ethics represented in their community of the governed. Being a Christian presence in society, the church is to make that society aware of the relevance of the ethics of Christ, of the Sermon on the Mount, and to call people to take this with utmost seriousness. In so doing, persons will become aware of their own sinfulness and their need of Christ himself and many will be converted. Others who don't experience conversion will still be enriched by their interaction with the Christian ideal; and consequently the social order will be enriched by the people of God serving as "salt to the earth."

Conclusion

Holiness and love are propagated by example, not merely by propositions. Since the Christian life is lived in the social context, it is impossible for one to walk with Christ and not make decisions and perform actions informed by and expressing an intelligent faith. It is unavoidable that Christians deal with issues such as justice, racism, violence, family, education, abortion, alcoholism, drugs, labor and management, compassion for the poor, the right use of power, freedom, peace, art, health, and human rights.

As "God so loved the world that He gave his only begotten Son . . ." so we are to love the world, to seek in every way possible to extend his love into society.

QUESTIONS
FOR DISCUSSION

1. How have differing theological perspectives on such doctrines as law and grace, the kingdom of God, or salvation and evangelism influenced the development and practice of Christian ethics?

2. What influences affecting the practice of Christian ethics appear to be historically unique to our present time? What makes them unique to our day?

3. In what ways must the ethical responsibilities of the Christian differ when applied to the realm of personal conduct, the Christian community, or the pluralistic society? Why?

4. How does appealing to a foundation of Christological interpretation of ethics ("Biblical Realism") demand ethical sensitivity to more issues than are popularly raised?

5. Can a pluralism of values be challenged by the Christian without destroying the political and social freedom of non-Christians?

6. What biblical concerns and principles, if any, are valid considerations for challenging the ethical values and practices promoted by the political and social structures of a society? What methods of making such challenges are warranted and what are unwarranted, wise or unwise? Why?

8

BLACK
EVANGELICAL
BLACK
THEOLOGY

REFLECTIONS ON THE SCOPE AND FUNCTION OF A BLACK EVANGELICAL BLACK THEOLOGY

William H. Bentley with Ruth Lewis Bentley

I. Dynamics and Stages in the Making of a Particular Black Evangelical

Black evangelicals, like their white counterparts, are a many-splendored thing, ranging on the spectrum from Fundamentalists of the right to Evangelicals of the left! In my own experience of passing from Fundamentalism to Evangelicalism, I remember how some of my fondest views were tested at the secular university which opened the door to the initial stage of my experience of academia! I had to submit myself and my church-inculcated beliefs to the rigorous analyses and intellectual acid baths which were the trademarks of modern thought customary at that university.

Thankfully, I had already struck out on my own to acquire sufficient knowledge of the world of modern thought so as to be able to answer questions continually plied by my teen-age Sunday School class. I could not answer them at the time despite my sound working knowledge of the Scriptures, and I would not fake answers. Fortunately, I was often counseled by an understanding Christian couple, who were concerned with the holistic development of all children. They encouraged me not to waste the mind that God had given me. Such advice was quite revolutionary during the late 1940's, at least in the denomination in which I first learned Christ. Most Pentecostals I was acquainted with had little use for what they called "educated fools." I set myself to become educated but not to become a fool in the process. In this way, I could advance myself, and simultaneously give aid to the youth of my people.

I had already begun to search for written materials which could meet my insatiable quest for knowledge. I felt that such knowledge, no matter what its source, could profitably interact with the ultimate truths of Scripture. I thank God that He led me to the kind of materials which Edward John Carnell, Wilbur Smith and Carl Henry were producing at that time. *The Uneasy Conscience of Modern Fundamentalism* [1] especially opened my eyes wide to a kind of intra-Christian warfare that became basic to my growing knowledge of Fundamentalism, with which I identified — even though I was to later understand that Fundamentalists did not consider me and my kind as one of their own! Pentecostals had not yet been elevated to the status of legitimate Fundamentalists! I also gained insight into some of the reasons why Fundamentalists took certain positions on social issues, especially the one concerning Black-white relations. It was the beginning of my struggles to gain understanding of how one could be doctrinally correct and, at the same time, hold backward attitudes toward such an important issue as race in America. I am still trying!

My subsequent educational experiences at the university unsettled me in yet another way. I had difficulty grasping how men and women with whom I had little in common Scripturally were so openly warm, friendly, and accommodating — despite obvious racial differences! My mind was greatly stretched, though not blown, by these antinomies.

Time, learning, and maturation, however, have helped me to understand things much better now. I have come to see, if not to fully understand, how deeply rooted American racial prejudice is, and how myopic many otherwise good people can be to its prevalence! It infests and infects all of us — Fundamentalist, Evangelical, liberal, neo-liberal, secularist, etc. Throughout American secular and church history, it has proven thus far to be inseparable from both secular education and theological theory and practice. I did not escape racism and its deadening effects when studying at Roosevelt University, but I did come to understand many of its subtle, and not so subtle, nuances. I learned there something that would be amply reinforced when I undertook evangelical studies — how much education can conceal even as it reveals. Some of the most scholarly studies on racism in American secular and religious life have been done by the most brilliant men and women around; and yet these same studies have manifested ideas that very clearly evidence racial bigotry.

In this awareness of ubiquitous racial prejudice, I went beyond W. E. B. DuBois, one of my most revered mentors. At this point, it is important for your understanding of where I am coming from on Black evangelicalism for me to give some background on DuBois and the importance of his contribution to the world. DuBois never seemed to have grasped the lessons mentioned above. Throughout his long life span, beginning with his high school studies in Great Barrington, Massachusetts, and continuing through his Harvard doctoral studies, and concluding with post-doctoral studies at the University of Berlin, DuBois ever seemed to be in

William H. Bentley and Ruth Lewis Bentley

pursuit of the rainbow, at the end of which would be found the precious pot of gold — the humanists' ultimate belief that proper education in its broadest sense and the applications thereof to the human situation would bring uncompromised benefits to all mankind. Because of his undying faith in this undeniably worthy ideal, he willingly and selflessly sacrificed himself in the cause of racial justice and human rights. Even though he received a Harvard education (one of the earliest Black American recipients of the coveted Harvard Ph.D.) and studied in world economics at the University of Berlin, under the illustrious A. Schmoeller, no American college or university, with the exception of Wilberforce and Atlanta, would hire him. Though he was a colleague of William James and other Harvard greats, initiator of the famed Harvard Historical Series (with the still-valued *Suppression of the African Slave Trade to America*), the University of Pennsylvania hired him as assistant professor of sociology only long enough for him to complete a study of the Black population of Philadelphia. The study known as *The Philadelphia Negro* broke new ground in the emerging discipline of sociology and was the first example of modern social survey method as applied to the study of an American city. To many it was the first empirical study of its kind at a time when even the prestigious University of Chicago had still not distinguished social work from empirical sociology![2]

For a time, DuBois taught at Atlanta University and from there he issued the little-known "Atlanta Series," a number of monographs which were fairly detailed studies of such basic institutions within the Black American world as the church, businesses, and the family. DuBois' study of the church, called *The Negro Church,* antedated Carter Woodson's book by the same name by at least two decades (and Woodson is rightly called the father of the Black history movement). In this, he further demonstrated his status as a pioneer in sociology.

But DuBois died, in spite of a faith which did not desert him at the end — tired, exhausted by decades of what must have seemed unrewarded dedication to the cause of Black freedom. He was disillusioned by what he considered the falling away from him on the part of his own Black compatriots. He died expatriate, buried in a lonely, undistinguished roadside grave, which my wife, Ruth, accidentally stumbled upon during a visit to Ghana!

With readiness of mind, I confess that few humans have as deeply affected me as this great Afro-American. In numerous ways, he stretched my mind to possibilities that are mind-blowing. From DuBois, I absorbed my love for my people; but I cannot follow him into the path of blind faith in the possibility of a native goodness in man, black, white, Hispanic, Asian, or otherwise that can of itself inevitably do good simply because they have been educated to do so!

Unfortunately, this man's negative experiences with aspects of Black institutional Christianity ill-disposed him to trust in Supernaturalism or God. He had a cultured despiser's disdain for anything resembling an evangelical approach to Christian faith. In my measured opinion, this was a supreme tragedy in the life of this man whose influence on the very conception of Black Studies is, seminally speaking, greater than that of any other man. His work will not die, so long as inquiring Black people live! And though he is dead, his works, as it was said of Caesar, live on. We can only speculate what his life could possibly have been had he come to place his undying trust in Jesus Christ as beginner and finisher of all things!

William H. Bentley and Ruth Lewis Bentley

DuBois wrote at least three autobiographies, one of which is called *Dusk of Dawn*. The subtitle is called "Autobiography of A Concept of Race." It was so entitled because he regarded the span of his life as co-developmental with the emergence of the modern study of race and racism in America. I have chosen to open this essay on a similar autobiographical note — not because I invented Black evangelicalism, nor because of any supposition that I am solely responsible for its development. Black evangelicalism is practically as old as is the appearance of Africans on this continent. Of course it was not as developed at the first as it has come to be; but in a real sense, the maturation of myself as a believing Black Christian has, in some areas, coincided with the growth and development of American Christianity's awareness that the existence and viability of Black evangelicalism is something qualitatively different from that of being a mere clone of white evangelicalism. In some respects, my growth and development has paralleled that of this vital part of the evangelical family.

Again, I do not want to even suggest that I speak for all of Black evangelicalism. As I said before, black, like white, can be a many-splendored thing! Some of my views are simply not acceptable to some other Black leaders. Like the fabled elephant and the blind men, full truth is undoubtedly much greater than any one particular point of view or perspective. "We know in part."

In the twenty-six years I have been a member of the National Black Evangelical Association,[3] I have played a number of parts. In our formative years, when the "big three" were missions, evangelism, and youth ministries, I asked for, and was given, the position of Commissioner of Social Action. For six years, until I was elected National President, I acted to inform, dramatize, and to make our constituency across America aware of major social and theological issues which affect Black life. I stood then, as I have ever continued to stand, on the ground that Black evangelicalism is by virtue of its very "is-ness" not only religiously of a kind with its white counterparts, but also is an undeniable and inseparable component of the entire span of Black American humanity. We laugh, or cry, at the same justice or injustice. We are not spared from being Black in America just because we are Christians. And if we believe that racial identity proceeds from the creative fiat (or otherwise) of Almighty God, then we must pay attention to the fact that before we became Christians, we were born Black! Christ coming into the heart reorients the human person in the experiences and values of the coming kingdom of God that all men might live transformed lives, not change the color of the skin nor abnegate racial heritage — except insofar as a given element in that heritage cannot be made subject to the Lordship of Jesus Christ! I have continued to promulgate that view in my present capacity as Head of the Commission on Theology.

A word needs to be said concerning the format and content of the major portion of this paper. Let me begin by saying what I cannot do because of time and space limitations. I wish that I could give an historical sketch of the genesis and genius of Black evangelicalism, tracing its rise from mainline white denominations to (and through) what Frazier called "the invisible institution"[4] (the Black Church) through the establishment of its first institutional expression in individual African Baptist, Methodist, and Presbyterian groups. Likewise, a discussion of the phenomena of antebellum Black institutional Christianity and how it related to post-bellum rapidity of growth would also be helpful. I cannot explore urban Black Christianity and how Black evangelical Christianity related to the major bodies as I would like. I must limit myself to the scope and function of Black Evangelical Theology as a solution to the ills that face us as a people, and I will offer some suggestions as to where I believe Black evangelicalism must go — if it is to fulfill its God-given potential — and how it can get there. Although oppression is prevalent in other minority contexts, I have chosen to center this essay on the Black group because it is at the ideological extreme of the racial continuum — from white to black.

Documentation will not be exhaustive, but its presence will certainly be evident. For post-World War Black evangelicalism, I lean on some of my own materials, supplemented, where possible, by other available resources. This is to be regarded as an important feature of the essay, for it will make use of some original materials from an era when, so far as I was able to determine, writings of any quality were scarce. During this time, most of what was extant emerged from discussions from the National Black Evangelical Association's Commissions on Social Action and Theology. A bibliography will be offered, briefly annotated in part. The essay is not primarily a polemic, but an irenic Black evangelical affirmation!

II. A Definition of the Scope and Function of a Black Evangelical Black Theology

Black evangelicalism itself, though based upon the same Scriptural mandates as its larger, more explicitly defined sister — white evangelicalism — nevertheless makes use of historical existential data that are qualitatively different from the socio-culturo-political heritage out from which traditional Euro-America emerged.[5] The scope and function of Black American Black evangelicalism, therefore, is at major points to be contrasted with that of its larger, more visible white counterpart.

Historically, Euro-American theology emerged from the interaction and confrontation of Hebrew-based Incarnational theology (or Scripture-based basic teachings with a clearly understood value system that sprang from, and was totally expressive of, the redemptive work of God which has reached attained form in the Incarnate One, Jesus the Christ). The conferred responsibility to proclaim the message caused the disciples to evangelize first at Jerusalem and in ever-widening circles, progressively to the non-Jewish, classical world surrounding them (as set forth in the Book of Acts). In a theological way, therefore, the teachings of Jesus, Paul, John, and the others, confronted the Gentile world head-on, and the logical result for the following centuries was the first attempts at systematic formulation of theology, focussed especially on the world from which developed historically the European family of nations and peoples. Even though the missionary mandate was "to the uttermost parts of the world," special concentration on this European emergent nationalism, virtually transformed a Gospel with originally world-based appeal into a Euro-dominated theology, causing that universal Gospel to become a virtual prisoner to classical-based European culture, values, and norms.

It is worthy of speculation, at least, that had the basic facts of the Gospel been allowed to confront other older non-Christian world cultures and been allowed to indigenize itself within those

William H. Bentley and Ruth Lewis Bentley

cultures and worldviews, as it so thoroughly did in the case of the European (Western) civilizations and cultures, the Eastern world opinion would not so deeply regard Christianity as the white man's religion. After nearly two thousand years, much of it filled with world missions activity of the highest order, Christianity is still overwhelmingly viewed by virtually all non-Western man as essentially a religion for and of the white man. When one reads church and world history, especially that of the most formative eras of the emergence of Christian theology, it is easy to understand why God and His divine providence cannot be entirely to blame for the relative non-spread of the universal Gospel to all parts of the non-Christian world and its imprisonment, for all practical purposes, within the white, Western world.

Although the Gospel did enjoy (within the first four Christian centuries at least) a wide hearing on parts of the African continent, it was as far as is known almost an exclusive hearing on that portion of Africa that was, for almost time immemorial, a part of the Mediterranean world around which much of world civilization moved. Whatever incursions that were possibly made into Saharan, western, and southern Africa, they were soon eclipsed by the emerging world-conquering religion of the Prophet Mohammed! By the time the Moslem conquest had been accomplished, whatever traces of indigenous African Christianity that might have been planted rapidly disappeared. Centuries later, when the white men began to invade that portion of Africa from which the modern African slaves came, there appear to have been no real evidences of the Gospel ever having penetrated those tribes and nations. When western slave enterprise began, therefore, (at least by the fifteenth century), Africans brought with them no discernible traces of a knowledge of the Christ who came and died for all! When, therefore, Christianity was introduced to the African-turned-slave, the identity of the Christ was unknown. To the Christian Gospel, imprisoned within white western culture and civilization, the African was a tabula-rasa! But not necessarily religiously so!

To Africans, the concept of an all-powerful God, even though not directly known and purely worshipped as such, was known, and to some extent, variously believed in. The concept of mediatorship also was known. That, as in other similar religions, is the function of departed ancestors, demi-gods, etc. It seems that man almost instinctively knows that because of his present state, he cannot go directly to the High God except through some form of mediatorship. This, then, the African-made-slave brought with him to the white western world! It undoubtedly facilitated the hearing of the Gospel when it was presented to him. His subsequent understanding and embracing of Jesus, though clearly recognizing the Divinity of Jesus as presented in the Gospel, nevertheless most clearly enabled him to recognize his own sufferings. Truly, the new-world slave especially embraced the full humanity of Theanthropos, the God-man! This special identification of those who were to become Black Americans with the humanity of Jesus, while simultaneously recognizing his kinship with Almighty God, is a key to understanding how, despite the blighting destructive assaults on their humanity, Black creativity could produce among other gifts to the nation, spirituals, blues, gospel songs of their own specific genre, and of course, world-conquering jazz.

William H. Bentley and Ruth Lewis Bentley

As already noted above, the scope of Black evangelicalism is inclusive of latent assumed evangelicalism of the traditional Black institutional church (more explicit especially in the Baptist, Methodist, Presbyterian and Pentecostal groups) — as well as the more clearly defined Black evangelical churches that consciously grew out of the Bible school movement which emerged in the wake of the religious wars called the Fundamentalist controversies of the late twenties and early thirties. This is not to deny the existence of amorphous dissatisfaction with traditionalist Black denominations. Most of the impetus for this conscious Black evangelicalism came from radio broadcasts with their well thought out Bible teachings and their ardent defense of the evangelical fundamentalist faith. Later, as Christian conscience, the Civil Rights Movement and government goadings caused the opening of many Bible schools to Blacks, increasing numbers of Black Christians became involved in the establishment of groups separating themselves very self-consciously from traditional Black denominations. This is essentially the roots and origins of the "Bible Church" movement among Black Christians. To some extent, there is the possibility of unacknowledged evangelicalism among certain members of what was in the late sixties called "The Black Caucus Movement" — so called to explain the positive presence of a significant element of unassimilated Black Christians in the major white denominations. This is a possibility even though they almost totally accepted advanced "higher critical" views of the biblical revelation. It must be remembered that in certain significant cases and until fairly recently, numbers of Blacks were summarily denied entrance into evangelical schools. More than one Black would-be seeker of theological training

310

could truly bemoan the fact that it was easier to go through the eye of Harvard, Chicago, and Yale than it was to enter a certain world-renowned and leading Bible school! A significant number of potential Black evangelicals were lost to the movement simply because the doors of traditional white Bible schools and certain theological seminaries were locked tight against them because of their color!

James Cone's *Black Theology* appeared in 1964. It was concerned with the contextualization of theology that would make it relevant to Black people. Although I had not published by that time, my own embryonic theological reflections, which eventually issued in my specific approach to Black evangelical theology, had rather independently reached a stage similar to Cone's thought even before his book was published. Subsequent books, articles, and learned position papers further developed and expanded ideas and formulations, as Cone and those who followed, added to the growing list of materials expounding the "new" interpretation of an essentially American-based theology. My own critical interactions, though highly sympathetic, nevertheless came face to face with the fact that my evangelical thought and background made me increasingly dissatisfied with certain assumptions and propositions which dealt with the basis of authority in the system. It was, in part, this irresolution that sent me on a more extensive quest for a system with which I could be more theologically compatible. The basic essentials of what I have thus far arrived at are outlined in several parts of this paper.

The function and scope of a Black evangelical approach to a Black theology is to understand, articulate, and expound the

311

nature of a Black-centric Christianity, hampered as little as possible by certain entrapments of traditional white theology, but more specifically reflective of the totality of Black experience, both within and outside of American history and culture. The apparent inability of American Christianity to assimilate the Black religious experience without destroying certain of its basic assumptions and foundations, seems to this author, as well as some others, to call for a theological posture which is designed to deal more adequately with Black humanity and that dignity and viability to which, as creatures of God, it is entitled. This theological posture seeks to maximize the Black American experience to the extent that it can take its legitimate place of equality in America, alongside the dignity of all others!

It is possible, therefore, for Black evangelicals to engage in doing theology which focuses in a special way on the essence of the Afro-American experience. And it is possible to do this without inadvertently or mistakenly making the Black experience normative for that theology. The Black experience is but one source from which such a theology springs. The norm of a theology is not self-generated but comes from the otherness from which comes the drive to create theology. In some theological systems, the theology itself is viewed as virtually sacrosanct and inviolable. Yet even though theology deals with divine things, and in many systems, has a divine subject, it is nevertheless, at bottom, a human endeavor. Even evangelical theology is a human endeavor. It is, in its western form at least, the result of the biblical revelation impacting upon, and being expressed in, western culture. William Frend, in a monumental volume on *The Rise of Christianity—the First Six Centuries*, describes with great clarity the results of the Gospel's invasion of Gentile culture and how it "divinizes" while simultaneously being "humanized" by it. Divine truth, if it is to have its fullest significance, must become incarnated within human experience. Viewed from this perspective, western theological systems are no more normative than is the Gospel incarnated (not imprisoned!) within any other world culture. In a guarded sense, therefore, we should not preach pure theology independent from the Word of God. The Word alone is absolutely normative. It is the Scriptures which are inspired, not the best or worst of theological systems.

This is not said in any way to attempt to escape from the fact or the ubiquitous presence of western theology. After all, Blacks in America are Americans even though that very fact is a major part of our identity problem. Black "is-ness" is always a hyphenated affair. This accursed "two-ness" that DuBois especially and many other discerning commentators wrote or spoke of is, after all, a "two-ness" for which resolution (if there is one) must be finally attained not in Africa, but only in America! In this sense, Black "two-ness" is a perennial problem for finally establishing the content of American identity. America can never become the America that it is possible for it to be until America satisfactorily resolves her Afro-American problem. Certified Black evangelicals cannot retreat from this and are committed by the very dynamics of American reality to follow it to its logical end — whatever that is. As committed believers, we feel that it can be resolved under God, with liberty and justice for all! We need a theology which will enable us as Black Americans to deal with our total experience here. We are not calling for a new Bible, or a new Christ, or a different Almighty God. For all of us who so believe,

313

the God and Father of our Lord Jesus Christ and the biblical revelation given to us through the Holy Spirit are in every way sufficient; but western theology has notoriously failed Black people and virtually all non-European-based people by them as functionally lesser peoples. In so doing, it tends to afford a certain aid and comfort to political, economic, and racial oppression. As the religion of western man, western theology has either preceded him, joined him, or followed him in all missions of world colonialization or conquest. It has singularly been unable to wean western man from his white tribalism or nationalism. There is a real sense in which Christianity (not Christ) is a white man's religion.

Black American theology, evangelical or otherwise, cannot avoid interacting with, impacting and being impacted by western theology (American variety), if for no other reason than the very fact of the "two-ness" of racial identity. To the mind of this writer, there exists no extant system of Black theology which at the present stage of development can fully accomplish this task. It must be done, however, since American theology evinces little tendency to correct its mistakes. The speedy retreat of the country from such high ground as it took in the attempts to correct the errors and mistakes of the past has taken only twenty years to return to business as usual. The resulting devastation has wondrously up-tempoed in the past eight years. Evangelicalism may not follow in the van of retreat, but certainly Black evangelicals must not do so!

III. Black Evangelicalism: Prospects for the Future

First of all, Black evangelicalism must continue to examine and reexamine itself in order to be as certain as possible that it not

only has its ear to the heartbeat of Black America, but that its
perceptions are always informed by the realities of Black life in
America, and that its resultant assessments are judiciously arrived
at in the light of the ultimate standards of the Word of God! This
will necessitate its continually looking backward at where we
have come from in order to better assess current realities and chart
future directions. Surely, it must continue to fashion a theology
which speaks most comprehensively to the totality of the needs of
its people, but it must also run checks on that theology to assure
that it does not run afoul of that Word! Black chauvinism is as
detestable as is white!

At the heart of this theology must be a clear definition of
terms in which salvation, personal and social/institutional, must
never be less than the Scriptural definition of those terms. Blacks
as evangelicals cannot be found guilty of denigrating liberation
down to only human dimensions. After all, salvation has always
meant at least two things in our slave ancestors' existence.
Salvation is the biblical sense of God's deliverance from human
evil through Jesus Christ, and always, never far from consciousness, is also salvation by foot through the underground railroad or
by any means necessary. That is why the slave narratives, such as
have been passed down to us, are so incredibly rich in detailing
exactly what salvation meant to them. If they read with requisite
displeasure Paul's admonitions for slaves to be subject to their
masters, they likewise became equally familiar with the epistle to
Philemon, as well as other equally authoritative biblical statements such as "If you can obtain your freedom, make use of it."
(I Cor. 7:21). No matter what authoritative statements came from
Paul or their masters, slaves were not ignorant of the fact that the

315

ultimate meaning of salvation is total freedom anyway! The essence of the Gospel is liberation. Black evangelicals need to be sure that they do not short-change themselves or anyone else in understanding and proclaiming that divine liberation! In this same connection, it is helpful to understand that although numerous methods were used by slaves over periods of time to effect the human side of liberation, they always subjected to their conscience what they found necessary to do to achieve freedom in the light of what they believed about God, man, and the world. It is far easier to charge John Brown, Nat Turner, Denmark Vesey, and Harriet Tubman with fanaticism than it is to evaluate and searchingly criticize the system of slavery and the violence with which it was enforced. On the walls of the Lincoln Memorial are enshrined the words of "The Great Emancipator" — the undying words that allowed that the Civil War itself may very well be a righteous judgment of the Lord as a consequence of the many years of violence and bloodshed against the slave! Somewhere in the writings of Thomas Jefferson are to be found the words that he trembled when he considered that God was a just God, and that the country would sooner or later have to pay a heavy price for the inhumane system of slavery!

It is true that slavery as a system is no longer with us, but the inescapable aftermath of it continues down to the present day. Reconstruction lasted less than ten years, and it was largely the radical Republicans like Charles Sumner and Thaddeus Stevens rather than the regulars who pushed for and supported it. Black people in America, under slavery or freedom, have seldom benefited from the tender mercies of the Republican Party. Consequently, with consistent regularity, they have voted against it from the early thirties to the present time. It is an expression of extremist frustration, if nothing else! How can one cooperate with the Party that denies you?

The repeal of Reconstruction was the equivalent of the betrayal, as Rayford Logan described it in his book by that name, of the Negro! Restoration of the South to the Old Guard of the South returned Blacks to conditions of peonage and social suppression; and the Ku Klux Klan and lynching became a favorite method of making certain that Blacks got the message of white business as usual.

This is also the period of Jim Crow, which systematically applied ensured the virtual collapse of the Southern agricultural economy and the beginning of the Black "Exoduster Movement" from states like Alabama and Tennessee to Plains states such as Kansas, Nebraska, and Missouri. By the turn of the 20th century, the trickle from the South had increased to a stream which World War I sped up to a swelling tide, which almost immediately increased the Black population of cities like Detroit, Chicago, and New York to populations ranging into the hundreds of thousands. World War II and its aftermaths brought such cities to their present state of overcrowding and consequent urban misery.

Recent changes in the direction of economic plenitude and the resultant population shifts indicate that the post-World War socio-economic situation no longer holds firm. Instead of the urban North, it is now the newly-enriched urban South (and the suburban North) that enjoy the economic expansion. Although numbers of Black Americans have followed the trail back to the South, racial prejudice, class prejudice, and other equally unwelcome concomitants, effectively prevent meaningful numbers of

Black Americans from exercising this option to their advantage. It is more than a joke that in numerous cases the suburbs exist like white doughnut rings strangling the economic growth of center cities from one coast to the other!

The virtual collapse of a viable leadership cadre, coupled with the virtual disappearance of the stable Black family and the decline and near disappearance of a historic Black working class cannot be wished away despite the unprecedented advances achieved by a Black middle class that is undoubtedly far larger and more financially sufficient than at any other time in the nation's history. The perennial plight of the Black underclasses, if it has changed at all, has prolifically increased; and the fact of national employment rates, as the present administration boasts, being higher now than before, cannot gloss over the chilling fact that Black unemployment remains at an all-time high.

Class consciousness among Blacks, as among others, has always existed; but the very success of integration decreased the dependency of Black middle-classes upon the Black masses. Intentional or not, along with the new independence of such middle-classes, went the simultaneous loss of much of the historical Black leadership. This loss of leadership, along with the loss of physical presence in many cases, is a major factor in the collapse of the Black communities. In far too many cases, Black professionals and other members of the Black nouveau riche no longer find it necessary to live among their people; and many of them admit to finding it unnecessary to feel responsible to fill leadership roles. Black role models, no longer present in the community, pass on the view that the best thing one can do for the community is to get out of it. This leads to hopeless despair on the part of many who feel either that the community is not redeemable or that their future is not to be found there. Such hopelessness often is masked by an apparent abandonment to mindless hedonism and self-destructive behavior.

Black evangelicalism, however, need not call, Marxist-like, for a Black classless society! It, like the Gospel, can work together with equal dedication in cooperation with any and all classes; but it must do so with a passion-filled demand for fair play and justice. Civil rights are precious, but God has called men to an even higher calling — human rights! It is the God-endowed right of every man, woman, girl, or boy! When, in a given society, culture, or civilization, civil rights are not based upon full acceptance of the image of God in every one of us, there is something basically and morally wrong with that country which cannot validly be dismissed by applying a liberal dosage of blaming the victim. It would be quite a feat for anyone in this ethnic group, to pull themselves up by non-existent "boot straps," especially when virtually all other immigrant groups in America have had liberal assistance in getting where they are today!

Black evangelicals, and all other fair-minded people, must call attention to the determinative fact that of all groups who share the benefits, Blacks remain the only group brought to this country to make others wealthy rather than themselves. All others, no matter how lowly their American beginnings, came here to better themselves. For them alone, of all American minority groups, they did not leave oppression but were brought into it! No other group has stood in such sharp contrasts, in terms of custom, culture, and physical appearance as have Blacks! Black Americans are the major group whose rights have had, and continually needs to have, special legislation and executive orders perennially drawn up and passed to guarantee us rights that virtually all others enjoy even without citizenship status! Excellent studies have been made to account for the racial antipathy in which Europeans held Africans. When their descendants were brought to the land of the free and the future home of the slave, antipathetic views were so deeply rooted that it has been impossible for most whites, whatever their ethnic background, to break themselves loose from such deeply ingrained attitudes which evolve easily into codes of behavior. Herskovits,[6] DuBois, and others have shown that many Americans operate on the basis of myth when it comes to really knowing the humanity of most Black Americans. Even education, despite an almost superstitious contemporary belief in it as a solver of all problems, ultimately does not shield one from acceptance of such myths as the natural inferiority of Black people. Perhaps a major reason why white extremist groups cannot be destroyed by white people is that they speak for many less vocal people who cannot be brought to entire disagreement with some at least of the extremist views. Perhaps that is also the reason why, despite the many reams of words that are righteously spoken by the "free nations" against racist South Africa, its existence and perpetuation will never be brought to an end by any European nation, or by even Israel itself! South Africa is the logical conclusion for ideas or outlooks of white supremacy — whether they originate or become perpetuated in America, England, Germany, France or Russia. Incidentally, when did anyone recently take a good long look at Australia and her racial exclusivist policies within her own borders? What about its treatment of its own aborigines?

Others may opt out if they wish, but Black evangelicals are under real obligation to raise such questions as these. Black evangelicals must really challenge the American church to examine itself, especially that portion of it that considers itself to be most historically and contemporarily true to the Scriptures. It can properly be argued that seldom in the history of the American church have significant numbers of this group really led the way to social and economic reforms which would have guaranteed Black Americans a more equitable share in the nation's bounty. For those who undeniably have so distinguished themselves in this and related matters, if by some modern miracle they could rise from the grave and speak to us, given the present-day identification of white evangelicalism with the "mid-stream status quo," such leaders might well not be welcome at the very institutions they either founded or with which they were affiliated. Indeed, to many observers, Christian and otherwise, the contemporary American church, whether evangelical or sub-evangelical, has reversed the observation of Paul that "not many mighty, not many noble are called!" Hard questions!

Although Black Americans are the only people of African ancestry who do not have a clearly definable homeland to which they can return or which can provide them with a national frame of reference to which Americans can attribute some measure of respect, they nevertheless occupy a certain posture of prominence such as no other Black group has yet attained. In some cases hated, or at least despised, by other co-members of Black ancestry, at the same time their position within American society causes them to be grudgingly admired. In the 1940's and 50's, freedom movements suddenly filled the pages of world history; but the freedom

William H. Bentley and Ruth Lewis Bentley

struggles of American Blacks began with their introduction into the land that eventually became America. Because they were a racial minority in this land, they were less able to maintain high degrees of Africanism. As it was, skin color and strange customs and habits set them permanently off from the white majority. Self-government, to the extent that dominion status allowed it, was thus more possible in both the African and Caribbean worlds. Yet world leadership in the Black struggle for freedom was sparked here in the United States in a way and on a scale that was the inspiration for oppressed peoples of all colors around the world. The Civil Rights anthem, "We Shall Overcome," is known and understood all around the world; and despite what evangelicals first thought about Martin Luther King, Jr., Sweden admired him and his accomplishments so much that it honored him with one of its highest — the Nobel Prize!

There are, of course, plenty of other Black religious leaders than Black evangelicals. It cannot be gainsaid that a great majority of effort and production in the area of the religious responsibility "to cry aloud and spare not" against modern man's mistreatment of his fellow-man is to be laid at the door of such religious, and other leaders. As is so often the case, Black fundamentalists and, later, evangelicals were so under the spell of white views of their own humanity that they were never free, until now, to see themselves through their own eyes — and even more importantly, through God's eyes!

Black evangelicals as a group owe a debt of undying gratitude to these hearty (and hardy) forerunners. James Cone, Deotis Roberts, and Shelby Rooks[7] did much to begin the process of liberating our minds to this very most important area of our

experience. Gayraud Wilmore, Joseph Washington, John Blassingame, and Franklin Frazier have told the story of Black Radicalism
and Black Religion and how they have mutually influenced each
other to help bring Black Americans to the place of acceptance of
a willingness to contemporarily struggle for full freedom. Stokely
Carmichael and Charles Hamilton taught us about the necessity to
determine to define ourselves as a people. The legacy of American
Negro slavery left us a whole trick bag of self-hate and negative
definitions of ourselves that few of us have cleanly escaped today.

Finally, we owe a debt of gratitude to the great pioneer,
William Edward Burghardt DuBois, whose self-sacrificing labors were detailed earlier. Both he and the dogged Carter G.
Woodson taught us our history and warned as many as would hear
to beware of miseducation! For those who are fortunate enough to
know him and to have read both his essays and poetry, Haki
Madhubuti's deep dedication to the welfare of his people is an
inspiration.

Nevertheless, these have but helped us to recognize the path
of manhood and to strive for it. There remains an unfinished task,
which only we Black evangelicals can do. No matter how valid
and essential the Black experience is, there is nothing in it that can
save us in the fullest sense, a fullness which our slave ancestors
earnestly sought. If we would be truly free, then we must first be
set free by Him who fulfilled that purpose when He came and did
God's will! The evangelical affirmation is that there can be no true
freedom unless the Son sets free! One need not be either obscuran-
tist nor naive to recognize that other lords claim dominion over
man's mind, body, and soul; but the evangelical Christian (there
is intended no denial that Christians of other than evangelical

William H. Bentley and Ruth Lewis Bentley

persuasion may also believe in the ultimacy of the Lordship of Jesus Christ) is as fully persuaded as it is possible for mortal, finite man to be, *that there is salvation in no other.* This saving faith persists in spite of the non-persuasion of others who cannot bring themselves to accept it in the face of very challenging modern alternatives and substantive arguments against the viability of such conviction. Much modern philosophical and so-called theological scholarship and investigation raises the most searching and demanding questions. Indeed, far more questions are raised than are answers given. When answers are in shortest supply, however, the position and affirmation of the evangelical is that given the existence, personality, and nature of the Creator, Maintainer, and Preserver of man and the world, such a God would not leave even modern man adrift ever in the sea of relativity and, worse, tentativity that is the undeniable result of much human thought! Christian experience, though far from infallible, provides a sound basis, grounded on the revealed truths of the Scriptures, that still stand the test and acids of continuing generations of uptempoing modernity. The evangelical is well aware that truth can never be finally decided by counting noses, which is another argument in his arsenal of confidence. Probability might well be the best that unregenerate man can settle for, and as the trusting Christian is a citizen of this world as much as he is of the one to come, it is not altogether possible to escape from the human limitations of such. His trust, however, is in what he had come to know as the Word of God, and he is persuaded that he in whom he trusts is able to, and will, demonstrate his truth when all men will have come to that time in human history when faith will become fulfilled certainty and the thoughts and intents of all hearts will be

Scope and Function of a Black Evangelical Black Theology

revealed. This is the supreme evangelical, and it is fondly hoped that all Christians will come to this position. This is the Black Evangelical affirmation!

[1]Carl F. H. Henry, Jr., *The Uneasy Conscience of Modern Fundamentalism*. Chicago: Wm. B. Eerdmans, 1947.

(Hereafter, books and authors that are mentioned in this paper will not be endnoted unless specific pages are cited. Data on these works may be found in the bibliography.)

[2]The University of Chicago virtually ignored DuBois and his scholarly potential. This author undertook a systematic search through the first ten years of the *American Journal of Sociology*, the University of Chicago's organ, and did not encounter a single article on or by DuBois until about 1911, when a book review of one of his publications was listed. The racial attitudes there towards Blacks were not too far ahead of the prevailing myths widely held. Franklin Frazier was one of their earliest Sociology students, and Carter Woodson earned a Master's degree in history from there. It is difficult to understand why such a leading school did not recognize or at least acknowledge the work of this undeniably competent scholar if race was not a factor. Nathan Hare and other Black scholars press the same point.

[3]The national umbrella group organized in Los Angeles, California, in 1963. Its initial purpose was to form a network of fellowship and joint ministry for Black Christians located in predominantly white organizations. It later came to include being a collective spokesperson in the name of Black evangelical Christians, a status it has enjoyed for over twenty-six continuous years. It was open then, as it is now, to all persons who respect and work for the ideal of reaching primarily the Black Christian agenda.

[4]E. Franklin Frazier, *The Negro Church in America* (N. Y.: Schocken Books, 1966), pp. 16-19.

[5]Historically, Blacks have looked at the Euro-American data as humiliating to their humanity in some respects because only truth from the Euro-American perspective was considered valid. What is African in his make-up was not held in the same regard. This "two-ness" of the American Black is difficult to be accounted for under any other assumption.

325

William H. Bentley and Ruth Lewis Bentley

[6]Melville Herskovits, *The Myth of the Negro Past* (N. Y.: Harper & Row, 1941). (Herskovits notes six Myths that underlie the American attitude toward the Negro. It is a quality of myths that some truth, though not the whole of it, is enshrined in them. White Americans see far more truth in these Myths than Blacks. They included the notions that the Negro slave came from inferior stock which had contributed nothing of value to world history and, hence, was without a past; that he was a "happy darkie," and, therefore, had no present or future sense of reality. In short, he was handicapped by nature and was qualitatively inferior to whites. Education could not alter his inferior state.

[7]References (occasionally annotated) to the works of each of the persons mentioned in this section can be found in the bibliography.

BIBLIOGRAPHY

Because of the brevity of this essay and its highly concentrated form and substance, the following bibliography lists both generalized and specific references. They are suited to enable the reader to search further on his own and to examine the pertinent facts and interpretations of the author, whose views are influenced by a wide variety of sources. Special attention has been made to present works that are both historically genetic and temporally contemporary. References may fit into more than one category.

I. General Works

Brauer, Gerald C., ed. *The Impact of the Church upon Its Culture*. Chicago: Univ. of Chicago Press, 1968.

Bulmer, Martin. *The Chicago School of Sociology*. Chicago: Univ. of Chicago Press, 1984.

Carnell, Edward John. *An Introduction to Christian Apologetics*. Grand Rapids: Wm. B. Eerdmans, 1946.

Fleming, Bruce C. E. *Contextualization of Theology: An Evangelical Assessment*. Pasadena: Wm. Carey Library, 1980.

Frend, W. H. C. *The Rise of Christianity*. Philadelphia: Fortress Press, 1984.

Gertz, Clifford. *The Interpretation of Cultures*. N. Y.: Basic Books, 1973.

Handlin, Oscar. *Truth in History*. Cambridge: Belknap Press of Harvard Univ. Press, 1979.

Henry, Carl F. H. *Remaking the Modern Mind*. Grand Rapids: Wm. B. Eerdmans, 1948.

_____ *The Uneasy Conscience of Modern Fundamentalism*. Grand Rapids: Wm. B. Eerdmans, 1947.

Johnson, Robert K. *The Use of the Bible in Theology: Evangelical Options*. Atlanta: John Knox Press, 1985.

Kraft, Charles H. *Christianity in Culture*. Maryknoll: Orbis Books, 1970.

Kurtz, Lester. *Evaluating Chicago Sociology*. Chicago: Univ. of Chicago Press, 1984.

Loewenberg, Bert James. *American History in American Thought*. N. Y.: Simon & Schuster, 1972.

Marsden, George M. *Fundamentalism and American Culture*. N. Y.: Oxford Univ. Press, 1970.

Smith, Wilbur M. *Therefore Stand*. Boston: W. A. Wilde, 1945.

II. Race and Racism — Genetic and Contemporary

Cell, John W. *The Highest Stage of White Supremacy*. N. Y.: Cambridge Univ. Press, 1982. (Analysis of South Africa and the United States.)

Franklin, John Hope, ed. *Color and Race*. Boston: Beacon Press, 1969. (Contains an interesting discussion of Calvin's theory of the elect as genetic of white racism.)

Frederickson, George M. *White Supremacy: A Comparative Study of American and South African History*. N. Y.: Oxford University Press, 1981.

Gilmore, Anthony, ed. *Revisiting Blassingame's The Slave Community*. Westport: Greenwood Press, 1978. (Scholarly peers respond.)

Jordan, Winthrop. *The White Man's Burden*. N. Y.: Oxford Univ. Press, 1974. (Historical origins of racism in the U. S.)

_____ *White Over Black: American Attitudes Toward the Negro*. Chapel Hill: Univ. of N. C. Press, 1968.

Knowles, Louis, and Prewett, Kenneth, eds. *Institutional Racism in America*. Englewood Cliffs: Prentice-Hall Publ. Co., 1969.

Myrdal, Gunnar, et al., eds. *An American Dilemma*. N. Y.: Harper & Bros., 1944. (In comprehensiveness of survey, still unsurpassed as the Bible of race relations.)

Oakes, James. *The Ruling Race*. N. Y.: Alfred A. Knopf, 1982.

Owens, Leslie. *This Species of Property*. N. Y.: Oxford Univ. Press, 1976.

Poliakiv, Leon. *The Aryan Myth: A History of Racist and Nationalist Ideas in Europe*. N. Y.: Meridian Books Edition, 1977.

Reuter, Edward B. *The American Race Problem*. N. Y.: Thomas M. Crowell, 1970. (Orig. ed. 1927). (Aligned with Chicago school of race relations.)

William H. Bentley and Ruth Lewis Bentley

Van Den Berghe, Pierre. *Race and Racism.* N. Y.: John Wiley, 1967.
Wilson, William Julius. *The Declining Significance of Race.* Chicago: Univ. of Chicago Press, 1978.
Woodward, C. Vann. *American Counterpoint: Slavery and Racism in the North-South Dialogue.* Boston: Little Brown & Co., 1971.

III. Resources on Black Studies

Bennett, Lerone. *The Challenge of Blackness.* Chicago: Johnson Publ. Co., 1972.
Bentley, William H. *The Meaning of History for Black Americans.* Chicago: NBEA/ NBCSC Publs., 1979.
Blackwell, James E. *The Black Community—Unity and Diversity.* N. Y.: Harper & Row, 1975.
Blassingame, John W. *The Slave Community.* N. Y.: Oxford Univ. Press, 1972.
Bogle, Donald. *Toms, Coons, Mulattoes, Mammies, and Bucks.* N. Y.: Viking Press, 1973.
Carlson, Lewis H. and Calhoun, George A. *In Their Place: White America Defines Her Minorities, 1850-1950.* N. Y.: John Wiley, 1972.
Carmichael, Stokely and Hamilton, Charles V. *Black Power: The Politics of Liberation in America.* N. Y.: Vintage Books, 1967.
Cone, James H. *The Spirituals and the Blues.* N. Y.: Seabury Press, 1972.
Cruse, Harold. *Crisis of the Negro Intellectual.* N. Y.: Wm. Morrow, 1967.
Davis, David Brion. *The Problem of Slavery in Western Culture.* Ithaca, N. Y.: Cornell Univ. Press, 1966.
_____ *Slavery and Human Progress.* N. Y.: Oxford Univ. Press, 1984.
Delany, Martin. *The Condition, Elevation, Emigration, and Destiny of the Colored People of the United States.* N. Y.: Arno Press & New York Times, 1965.
Drake, St. Clair and Cayton, Horace R. *Black Metropolis.* N. Y.: Harcourt, Brace & World, 1945.
DuBois, W. E. B. *Atlanta University Publications.* 2 vols. N. Y.: Arno Press and New York Times, 1969. (Orig. ed. 1908)
_____ *The Autobiography of W. E. B. DuBois.* N. Y.: International Publs., 1968
_____ *Dusk of Dawn: Autobiography of A Concept of Race.* N. Y.: Schocken Books, 1968. (Orig. ed. 1940)
_____ *The Philadelphia Negro.* N.Y.: Schocken Books, 1967. (Orig. ed. 1899)
_____ *The Souls of Black Folk.* Greenwich: Fawcett Publs., 1961. (Orig. ed.-1904)
_____ *Suppression of the African Slave Trade to the United States of America.* N. Y: Social Science Press, 1954. (Orig. ed. 1896)
Foner, Philip S. *History of Black Americans. From Africa to Emergence of the Cotton Kingdom.* Westport: Greenwood Press, 1975.

Scope and Function of a Black Evangelical Black Theology

Gatewood, Willard. *Black Americans and the White Man's Burden, 1898-1913*. Urbana: Univ. of Ill. Press, 1975.

Harding, Vincent. *The Other American Revolution*. Atlanta: Institute of the Black World, 1980.

Herskovits, Melville. *The Myth of the Negro Past*. N. Y.: Harper & Bros., 1941.

Hogan, Lloyd. *Principles of Black Political Economy*. London: Routledge & Kegan Paul, 1984.

Huggins, Nathan, Kilson, Martin, and Fox, Daniel, eds. *Key Issues in the Afro-American Experience*. N. Y.: Harcourt, Brace & Jovanovich, 1971.

Irvine, Keith. *The Rise of the Colored Races*. N. Y.: W. W. Norton, 1970.

Kardiner, Abraham and Ovesey, Lionel. *The Mark of Oppression*. Cleveland: World Publ. Co., 1962.

Karenga, Maulana. *Introduction to Black Studies*. Inglewood, CA: Kawaida Publications, 1982.

Levine, Lawrence W. *Black Culture and Black Consciousness*. N. Y.: Oxford Univ. Press, 1977.

Litwack, Leon. *Been in the Storm too Long. The Aftermath of Slavery*. N. Y.: Alfred A. Knopf & Co., 1979.

Madhubuti, Haki. *Enemies: The Clash of Races*. Chicago: Third World Press, 1978.

_____ *Earthquakes and Sun Rise Missions: Poetry & Essays of Black Renewal*. Chicago: Third World Press, 1984.

Manning, Marable. *How Capitalism Underdeveloped Black America*. Boston: Southend Press, 1983.

Miller, Floyd. *The Search for Black Nationality: Black Colonization and Emigration, 1787-1863*. Chicago: Univ. of Ill. Press, 1969.

Murray, Albert. *The Omni-Americans*. N. Y.: Outerbridge & Dientsfrey, 1970.

Robinson, Armistead, Foster, Crain C., and Ogilve, Donald H., eds. *Black Studies in the University*. New Haven: Yale Univ. Press, 1969.

Smith, Jessie C. *Black Academic Libraries and Research Collections*. Westport: Greenwood Press, 1977.

Sterling, Dorothy, ed. *The Trouble They Seen: Black People Tell the Story of Reconstruction*. Garden City: Doubleday & Co., 1976.

Thorpe, Earl. *The Mind of the Negro: An Intellectual History of the Afro-American*. Baton Rouge: Univ. of Louisiana Press, 1961.

Washington, James M. *A Testimony of Hope: The Essential Writings of Martin Luther King*. Jr. San Francisco: Harper & Row, 1986.

Wesley, Charles H. *Neglected History*. Washington, D.C.: Association for the Study of Negro Life and History, 1969.

Williams, Eric. *Capitalism and Slavery*. N. Y.: Capricorn Books, 1966.

William H. Bentley and Ruth Lewis Bentley

Williams, Lorain, ed. *Africa and American Experience.* Washington, D. C.: Howard Univ. Press, 1977.

Woodson, Carter G. *The Mind of the Negro.* Washington, D. C.: American University Press, 1926.

_____ *The Miseducation of the Negro.* Washington, D. C.: Associated Publs., Inc., 1933.

Work, Monroe N. *A Bibliography of the Negro in America and Africa.* N. Y.: Argosy — Antiquarian, Ltd., 1965. (Orig. ed. 1928).

IV. Black Church and Black Religion.

Allen, Richard. *Experience and Gospel Labors of the Rt. Rev. Richard Allen.* Nashville: Abingdon Press, 1960. Reprint edition.

Butler, Alfloyd. *The Africanization of the American Church.* N. Y.: Carlton Press, 1980.

Dickson, Kwesi, and Ellingsworth, Paul, eds. *Biblical Revelation and African Beliefs.* Maryknoll: Orbis Books, 1969.

Drake, St. Clair. *The Redemption of Black Africa and Black Religion.* Chicago: Third World Press, 1970.

DuBois, W. E. B. *The Negro Church.* Atlanta: Atlanta Univ. Publs, 1904.

Frazier, E. Franklin. *The Negro Church in America.* N. Y.: Schocken Books, 1966.

Gaustad, Edwin S., ed. *A Documentary History of Religion in America.* 2 vols. Grand Rapids: Wm. B. Eerdmans, 1982.

George, Carol W. R. *Segregated Sabbaths — Richard Allen.* N. Y.: Oxford Univ. Press, 1973.

Lincoln, C. Eric. *The Black Church Since Frazier.* N. Y.: Schocken Books, 1974.

_____ *Race, Religion and the Continuing American Dilemma.* N. Y.: Hill & Wand, 1984.

_____ , ed. *The Black Experience in Religion.* Garden City: Anchor Press, 1974.

Mays, Benjamin E., and Nicholson, Joseph W. *The Negro's Church.* N. Y.: Institute of Social and Religious Research, 1933.

Mbiti, John. *Introduction to African Religion.* N. Y.: Praeger Publs., 1975.

Paris, Peter J. *The Social Teachings of the Black Churches.* Philadelphia: Fortress Press, 1985.

Raboteau, Albert J. *Slave Religion: The Invisible Institution in the Ante-Bellum South.* N. Y.: Oxford Univ. Press, 1978.

Rooks, C. Shelby. "Towards the Promised Land," *The Black Church,* vol. 2, no. 1,

Sernett, Milton, ed. *Afro-American Religious History- A Documentary Witness.* Durham: Duke Univ. Press, 1985.

_____ *Black Religion and American Evangelicalism.* Meteuchen, N. J.: Scarecrow Press, 1975.

Sobel, Mechal. *Trabelin' On: The Slave Journey to An Afro-Baptist Faith*. Westport: Greenwood Press, 1977.

Synan, Vinson. *The Holiness-Pentecostal Tradition in the United States*. Grand Rapids: Wm. B. Eerdmans, 1971.

Thomas, Latta. *Biblical Faith and the Black American*. Valley Forge: Judson Press, 1976.

Tinney, James, and Short, Stephen, eds. *In the Tradition of William J. Seymour*. Washington, D. C.: Spirit Publications, 1978.

Weatherford, W. D. *American Churches and the Negro*. Boston: Christopher Publ. House, 1957.

Williams, Ethel, and Brown, Clifton. *Afro-American Religious Studies*. Meteuchen, N. J.: Scarecrow Press, 1972. (Valuable bibliographical entries with locations in American universities.)

Woodson, Carter G. *The History of the Negro Church*. Washington, D.C.: Associated Publs., 1921.

V. Black Evangelicalism and Black Theology

Bentley, William H. "Bible Believers in the Black Church," *The Evangelicals*. N. Y.: Abingdon Press, 1967.

_____ "Black Christian Nationalism: An Evangelical Perspective." *Black Books Bulletin*. Vol. 4, No. 1. Chicago: Third World Press, Spring, 1976. (Reprint available from author.)

_____ *The National Black Evangelical Association: Bellwether of A Movement*. Chicago, P. 0. Box 4311, 1988.

_____ *The National Black Evangelical Association: Evolution of A Concert of Ministry*. Chicago: P. 0. Box 4311, 1979.

_____ *The Relevance of A Black Evangelical Black Theology for American Theology*. Chicago: National Black Christian Students Conference (NBCSC) Publications, 1987. (An introduction to a developing Black evangelical Black theology which the author believes speaks more comprehensively and biblically authoritatively to the total situation of Black Christians enmeshed in an American theology that is as white as it is Christian.)

_____ *The Significance of Context in Black Theology*. Chicago: NBCSC, 1980.

_____ *The Six Inaugural Lectures of the William Hiram Bentley Chair of Black Theology*. Sponsored by NBCSC and the Chicago Chapter of NBEA. March, 1987.

Bruce, Calvin E., and Jones, William R., eds. *Black Theology II*. Lewisburg: Bucknell Univ. Press, 1978.

Cleage, Albert B. *The Black Messiah*. N. Y.: Sheed and Ward, 1969. (This book, along with its predecessor, Joseph Washington's Black Religion, sparked the contemporary outbursts of scholarship which eventuated in the academic approach to Black Theology.)

William H. Bentley and Ruth Lewis Bentley

Cone, Cecil W. *The Identity Crisis in Black Theology*. Nashville: AMEC Publishers, 1975. (A brother of the celebrated James. Critiques current Black theology as too designedly Euro-centric.)

Cone, James H. *Black Theology and Black Power*. N. Y.: Seabury Press, 1969. (The book that launched the continuing discussion, though the concept was being explored by internal debate within groups of Black religious scholars as well as in the National Black Caucuses throughout the land.)

_____ *God of the Oppressed*. N. Y.: Seabury Press, 1975. (Comes closest to a formal text on theology. Probably the most thorough presentation toward a theology in the traditional sense. To some, it is Cone's best book to date.)

Dickson, Kwesi. *Theology in Africa*. Maryknoll: Orbis Books, 1984.

Ellis, Carl, Jr. *Beyond Liberation*. Downers Grove, IL: Inter-Varsity Press, 1983. (A young Black evangelical seeks to express the biblical relevancies and beyond.)

Evans, Anthony T. *Biblical Theology and the Black Experience*. Dallas: BEE Publications, 1977. (A searching evaluation of Black experiences and movements which should be confronted by systematic biblical revelation to determine authenticity. One of the two major prongs around which current Black evangelical discussion on Black theology revolves.)

Mays, Benjamin. *The Negro's God As Reflected in His Literature*. N. Y.: Atheneum Press, 1969. Reprint. (A seminal work and predecessor to the WPA-sponsored chronicling of Black autobiographical materials centered in the religious experience of ordinary Black men and women.)

McCray, Walter. Ed. by Ruth Bentley. *Toward A Holistic Liberation of Black People*. Chicago: NBCSC, 1977. (One of the best expositions of a Biblical Christian approach to Black Christian Nationalism by one of the emerging younger Black scholars.)

Mitchell, Henry. *Black Beliefs*. N. Y.: Harper & Row, 1975.

Moyd, Olin P. *Redemption in Black Theology*. Valley Forge: Judson Press, 1979. (Of the James Deotis Roberts genre which comes close to a more traditional evangelical stance.)

Roberts, J. Deotis. *A Black Political Theology*. Philadelphia: Westminster Press, 1974.

_____ *Black Theology Today: Liberation and Contextualization*. N. Y.: Edward Mellen Press, 1972.

_____ *Liberation and Reconciliation: A Black Theology*. Philadelphia: Westminster Press, 1971.

Washington, Joseph, Jr. *Black Religion*. Boston: Beacon Press, 1964. (Famed for its controversial thesis that Black religion is essentially ethico-centric since it has no identifiable creedal basis. Functions to keep all Black Christian theologians alert.)

Scope and Function of a Black Evangelical Black Theology

Wilvliet, Theo. *The Way of the Black Messiah*. Oak Park: Meyer Stone Publishers, 1987. (The hermeneutical challenge of Black theology by a famed Dutch theologian who takes academic Black theology far more seriously than most American white theologicans usually do.)

Wilmore, Gayraud S. *Black Religion and Black Radicalism*. Garden City: Doubleday & Co., 1972. (Shows how inseparable Black religion is from a significant Black social reform movement.)

_____ , and Cone, James H., eds. *Black Theology: A Documentary History, 1966-79*. Maryknoll: Orbis Books, 1979. (The grandest sweep of extant material available at time of publication.)

ADDENDUM

Books by Black evangelical writers have been forthcoming for at least a decade or more. One of the earliest in print was *Shall We Overcome?* by Howard Jones, of the Billy Graham organization. Bobby Harrison, also for a time a member of that organization, followed with his *When God Was Black*. Columbus Salley's (and Ronald Behm's) *Your God Is Too White* and William Pannell's *My Friend the Enemy* were expressions of two of Black Evangelicalism's most astute and articulate spokesmen. Few, however, have had the impact of Tom Skinner's works. Controversial to some, they nevertheless stirred widespread readership. Both *Black and Free* and *How Black Is The Gospel?* still stir debate worldwide.

RESPONSE TO WILLIAM H. AND RUTH LEWIS BENTLEY

H. O. Espinoza

It is no easy task for a Hispanic to respond to brother Bentley's incisive and illuminating paper. For us Hispanics, our historical, cultural and religious pilgrimage to the wonderland of American evangelicalism has followed such a different route! Every ethnic group, including the English, the Germans, the Dutch, and the many other national, cultural and racial groups that have discovered America, including those who today are preaching the Gospel according to Billy Graham, Carl F. H. Henry, J. I. Packer, Kenneth Kantzer et. al., follow different stars, encounter different experiences and are surprised by different consequent realities. Truly, only the grace of God and his sovereign purposes in history hold us together in relative peace!

Historically, my ancestors, the great Aztec, Maya, Inca and other peoples had been on this continent for thousands of years before the southern Europeans arrived in the 15th century. We were here first. We owned and ruled everything, from the North Pole to the South Pole.

But then the Spaniards, the Portugese and the Italians "discovered" us and grabbed the whole continent in the name of their kings and of their popes. Their kings reshaped our race and our culture, and their popes remodeled our religion. The result was the *mestizo* race and culture — a mixture of Latin and Indian bloods, genes, customs and societies, and a syncretistic, myth-laden, idolatrous and oppressive Roman Catholicism — to this day the quasi-official religion of Latin America and the U. S. Hispanics.

The Evangelicals (to us the term means Protestants), did not discover Hispanic Americans until the 19th century. The American and the British Bible Societies, and the Presbyterian, the Methodist and the Baptist churches, were the first evangelical conquistadores. This was, in a very real sense, a second discovery of the New World. The evangelicals arrived with the Bible, a hymn book and the full Gospel. By the "full Gospel" I mean that everywhere they built churches for the salvation and spiritual nurture of the people, schools for their education, and hospitals for their physical needs. And the conquest of Hispanic America by the Bible and by the Evangelical church goes on to this day. May God grant its successful completion very soon!

Today, however, the evangelical church in the U. S. must acknowledge a historical, cultural, social, religious, economical, political and spiritual fact, pivotal to the understanding of the times present and future — the "discovery" of the United States by great masses of unevangelized peoples, and its consequent shattering impact upon the whole of society, including the church. Beginning in the 1970s, millions have come by plane and by ship, walking over bridges, wading rivers, jumping over fences, openly and covertly, legally and illegally.

Among us Hispanics, one of the results of this massive immigration has been not only the staggering increase in numbers but the wide-open opportunity to evangelize our people. Hispanics are coming out of a traditional pagan "Christianity" into a liberating, fulfilling, enriching, Bible-centered, Christ-focused Gospel, in three main socio-cultural evangelical groups:

First, the local congregations made up mainly of recent immigrants who, including the pastor and lay leaders, are monolingual (Spanish-speaking), keep very deep and strong ties to the culture, nationality and identity of the country of origin, and are totally isolated from all cultural, social and political aspects of life in the United States. This first generation U. S. Hispanic is finding an ideal spiritual and cultural home and refuge mainly in independent evangelical Charismatic churches. It is estimated that around 60% of all U. S. Hispanic churches belong in this category and are the fastest growing.

Next we have the second to fifth generation Hispanic who prefers a bilingual-bicultural Evangelical church where life and worship remains for the most part culturally Hispanic, but both English and Spanish are used in varying degrees to the extreme point of inventing new words with, for instance, the root in English and the ending in Spanish. The longer this bilingual-bicultural Hispanic has been in this country, the better educated, more acculturated and more ambitious for success, fame and power he turns out to be. But, for the very same reasons, the more secular, materialistic and indifferent to his spiritual needs and to the Gospel he becomes. Interestingly, though, this is the Hispanic sociological stratum where many Evangelical denominational churches are growing today. Among U. S. Hispanics, the bilingual-bicultural congregation is fast becoming the large, powerful, mainstream, Evangelical church.

And thirdly, and again as a different experience from our African-American brothers and sisters, we rejoice in acknowl-

H. O. Espinoza

edging that the Anglo-American Evangelical churches are winning hundreds of thousands of bilingual and bicultural, and monolingual and monocultural (English only) Hispanics to Christ and to Evangelicalism. Nobody knows how many, but my guess is that the number is beginning to see the one million mark in the distance. This is indeed a key element in the extraordinary historical fact of the discovery of the Gospel of Jesus Christ in and through the Evangelical church, both Hispanic- and Anglo-American, by missions of U. S. Hispanics. The phenomenon includes both the growth of Hispanic-American individuals in Anglo-American churches, and the multiplication of Hispanic congregations within Anglo judicatories and structures.

The very plain fact is that today our Lord is bringing millions of non-Christians to our country, as if he were telling us: "What you have done for world missions and world evangelization is not enough. And since you won't go, I'll bring the lost world to you!" Well, the lost of the world are coming. And they will keep on coming.

We Hispanic evangelicals believe that what some of us call "Mother Church" is, indeed, of all churches — in the words of Dr. Bentley — "the most historically and contemporarily true to the Scriptures."

I dare say, however, that if the Anglo-American evangelical Church recognizes and acknowledges the reality of what God is doing today in the United States, and in the wisdom and power of the Spirit takes decisive and courageous steps at all levels to win millions of true disciples of Jesus among the so-called minority groups, then if this really happens, there is great hope for the future of our country. Otherwise, I dare not guess what will happen. History, however, teaches us some important lessons, for there have been other similar cases.

Let us now consider the title of this session with reference to the ethnic group I represent: The experience of Hispanic evangelical Bible believers.

To begin with, the fact is that for most of us our experience of evangelicalism was fully contained in our encounter with the missionaries sent from the U. S. by the Evangelicals (and again for Hispanics the term Evangelicals means nothing more than Protestants). In my own case. I was born in Monterrey, Mexico, in a hospital built, managed and supported by missionaries. The doctors and nurses were missionaries. Most of my Sunday school teachers throughout my childhood and adolescence were missionaries. My elementary and high schools were missionary schools, and so was the Evangelical seminary in Mexico City where I received my first Th.B.

Farther back, about 125 years ago, my father's father was led to a saving knowledge of Jesus Christ by the first missionary the Presbyterian church ever sent to Latin America, my father also received all his education from evangelical missionaries. For anything wrong with me, please blame the missionaries!

So, for three generations in my family, our experience as Christians — our evangelicalism — has been fully contained in our encounter with the missionaries you sent to us and only with them. We witnessed in each of them the incarnation of Paul's testimony as a missionary: "Our Gospel did not come to you only in words, but also in power, and in the Holy Spirit, and with full conviction, as you well know what kind of persons we were among you because of our love for you." (1 Thessalonians 1:5).

H. O. Espinoza

And making allowance for wide degrees of variation in details and circumstances, this is the Hispanics' experience in meeting evangelicalism — through its ambassadors to the world .

But then we came to the United States and met the great Evangelical Church, the Mother Church the missionaries would tell us about with deep love and longing, and we had a soul-shaking, faith-trying experience. When we met the missionaries we were surprised by love: when we met the church we were surprised by racism, by indifference and by a 19th century Indian-fort mentality. We met a church with a strong commitment to "world missions," but with a crippling definition of "missions" — what we do in other lands, for other people beyond our borders, out there in "the world" — where everybody ought to stay.

And we met a church totally dominated by the Anglo-American secular (not Biblical) concept of power, of money, and of business.

One of the very visible end-results of this experience we have had with the U. S. Evangelical church is that there exists no interaction, fellowship, communion, consultation, or even conversation between Hispanic and Anglo churches even within the same denomination. A few years ago my organization, PROMESA — Hispanic Evangelical Projects and Ministries, and the Latin America Mission, together organized in Miami a few experimental Awareness Seminars. We brought together pastors of Anglo and Hispanic congregations from the same denominations for a couple of days to get acquainted with each other and their pastoral work. It was fascinating to watch their surprise on discovering each other's existence and how much alike, and how different, they are. The sad truth is that the average Anglo Evangelical local church is far more interested, and knows much more about a little church in Timbuktu, than about the Hispanic church across the street.

And so, our experience has left us with an ambivalent attitude: we hold profound and solid evangelical convictions and we love the ideal image we have in our minds of what constitutes a true evangelical; but since our "mother" has slammed the door in our faces so many times, we have concluded that we are not wanted, much less are we loved, and that we might as well build and establish our own Hispanic Evangelicalism.

Maybe one day, when we have enough money according to our mother's standards, and sufficient political power, and when we run our churches by the book according to the Harvard School of Business and the American Management Association, perhaps then mother will then recognize her own children and will speak to us.

But, I don't wish to end in a negative, sour note, because we do love each other and we do need each other.

A few years back PROMESA sponsored, and the Latin American Theological Fellowship organized, a National Conference on Hispanic Evangelical Theology in the United States, a very productive meeting of about 100 U. S. Hispanic theologians. One of the most valuable conclusions, reached in unanimous agreement, was regarding the key areas of opportunity and challenge for U. S. Hispanic evangelicalism. They are:

1. Evangelicalism and discipleship. We are the largest non-Christian racial group in the country. By that we mean that at least 85% of our people have never received Jesus Christ as personal Lord and Savior and are not involved in any kind of church life.

H. O. Espinoza

This is, we believe, a key area of concern for the future of evangelicalism in our land. By all means, and with all means, you and us, must endeavor to win and disciple this major ethnic group.

2. Leadership development. Hispanics are emerging in all fields of human enterprise in the United States. It is urgent and imperative to develop strong, capable Hispanic Evangelical leadership. We are very happy to see the efforts being made by Evangelical denominations and theological institutions to encourage, facilitate, help and provide adjustable academic programs. Dr. Jesus Miranda, President of the Hispanic Association of Theological Education, and one of the foremost Hispanic Evangelical leaders, insists that the future of ethnic Evangelical churches depends entirely on this area of need.

We have taken micro views at our past pilgrimage, our present victories and struggles, and our future promise and challenge. We praise our Father's infinite grace in including us among the redeemed and remain committed, with all our brothers and sisters of all nations, tribes, peoples and languages, to be faithful until our Lord's final victory.

QUESTIONS
FOR DISCUSSION

1. What reflections have contributed to the author's understanding of a need for black theology? How might the black experience make a black theology different from a white theology?

2. What might be different in a black theology when compared to a white theology?

3. How might a black evangelical theology differ from other black theologies?

4. In what ways does the Bible incorporate liberation into the gospel message, and in what ways does it not do so? Should a black theology highlight liberation above other results of evangelism? Why or why not?

5. In what ways might black evangelicalism act as the conscience of the American evangelical church?

9
THE CHURCH

Evangelicals, Ecumenism and the Church

Donald A. Carson

"I will build my church": at one level the declaration is bold and simple; at another it has generated countless complex debates characterized by fine philosophical subtleties and theological niceties. "I will build my church": yet the statement in its biblical context (Matt. 16:13-20 par.) rivals another dominical utterance, "This is my body," for the heritage of heated division it has evoked within the church. "I will build my church": yet millions of men and women who think of themselves as Christians ruefully confess they despise the church even while they insist they worship Christ, while in many parts of the world the recognized and established "church" is being cheerfully abandoned in favor of a mushrooming phenomenon, the "house church" movement.

Both inside and outside the borders of evangelicalism there exists an enormous diversity of opinion regarding the nature of the church, her role in the history of redemption, her boundaries, her governance, and her unity. In the West, the essentially corporate nature of the church, however construed, butts up against our deeply-ingrained devotion to rugged individualism. Meanwhile, at the very moment when large swaths of evangelicals have overcome a defensive fortress mentality, not to mention cultural asceticism and denominational parochialism, the converse dangers are beginning to loom large: acculturation to the surrounding paganism instead of transforming infiltration, devoted attention

347

Donald A. Carson

to the plaudits of what John calls "the world" instead of a single-eyed commitment to please Christ, and a painful loss of confidence in the gospel in favor of fraternal relations with those who disown integral elements of that gospel. There was a time when virtually all evangelicals believed that they proclaimed the true and non-negotiable gospel; in the current environment, not a few evangelicals think they proclaim one form of the gospel. The gain in humility would be attractive were it not for the loss of confidence in the gospel itself.

Discussion of the issues has been hindered as much as it has been helped by recent studies that define one branch or another of evangelicalism in the categories of sociology, psychology and power politics.[1] It is not that such works contain no insights. The problem, rather, is that they ignore the heart of historic evangelicalism: its emphasis on truth, doctrine, Scripture and spiritual vitality, and their outworkings in life, witness and churchmanship. To skirt these issues in any treatment of the defining characteristics and motivations of evangelicalism is to transform the agenda, and thereby subvert evangelicalism, however unwittingly, from within.

No brief paper can claim to redress the balance. What I am setting out to accomplish is much more modest. While acknowledging the enormous diversity that lurks behind the contemporary rubric "evangelicalism" I want to address from a theological perspective those features of evangelical ecclesiology that ought to govern our self-understanding and therefore our relations with others. I shall proceed in three steps, followed by one or two concluding reflections.

Evangelicals, Ecumenism, & the Church

A. The Problem of Evangelical Self-Identity

Two facets of the problem deserve a little probing here:

(1) Who is an "evangelical"?

The term "evangelical" may be approached from several different standpoints.[2] In North America, it functions predominantly to refer to Christians who are loyal to both a material principle and a formal principle. The material principle is the gospel as understood in evangelical protestantism. We insist that salvation is gained exclusively through personal faith in the finished cross-work of Jesus Christ, who is both God and man. His atoning death, planned and brought about by his heavenly Father, expiates our sin, vanquishes Satan, propitiates the Father and inaugurates the promised kingdom. In the ministry, death, resurrection and exaltation of Jesus, God himself is supremely revealed, such that rejection of Jesus, or denials of what the Scriptures tell us about Jesus, constitute nothing less than rejection of God himself. In consequence of his triumphant crosswork, Christ has bequeathed the Holy Spirit, himself God, as the down payment of the final inheritance that will come to Christ's people when he himself returns. The saving and transforming power the Spirit displays in the lives of Christ's people is the product of divine grace, grace alone — grace that is apprehended by faith alone. The knowledge of God these evangelicals enjoy becomes for them an impetus to missionary outreach characterized by urgency and compassion. The *formal* principle is the truth, authority and finality of the Bible.

This summary, or something like it, most self-confessed evangelicals would happily espouse. In this sense, "evangelicalism" is tightly tied to the "evangel" (*to evangelion*), the gospel of Jesus Christ.

349

Donald A. Carson

We must frankly admit that "evangel" and "evangelical" are sometimes used in contexts rather removed from historic "evangelicalism. " To put the matter another way, who defines what this gospel-content, this evangel-content, really is? How many serious churchmen in any tradition would choose to be called *un*-evangelical? That is why this same etymological rootage also accounts for the use of *evangelisch* in German to mean roughly "Protestant," for the use of "evangelical" in the title of the most recently formed Lutheran group in the U.S.A. (even though large swaths of that group are classically "liberal"), and for the appearance of the word in an institutional title such as "Garrett-Evangelical. "

If for our purposes we restrict the word to refer to the evangelical *movement,* historical (as opposed to theological) concerns come into play. "The Evangelical Awakening," known on this side of the Atlantic as "The Great Awakening," rejected high church theology, spiritually bankrupt deism and an orthodoxy of convenience in order to emphasize the truths and vitality I have sketched in. Thus, against high churchmanship, evangelicalism stressed the sufficiency and finality of Scripture (over against a too ready appeal to the voice of tradition), the finality of Christ's atoning death (over against any view that posits an overly sacramentarian theology), and the priesthood of all believers (over against a sacerdotal view of Christian ministry).

In time, however, the impact of the Enlightenment made itself felt at the popular level in the depreciation of the authority of Scripture. Thus, evangelicalism, which had always assumed and sometimes articulated the inerrancy of Scripture,[3] turned to confront this new danger on its flank. In consequence, evangelicalism came to be thought of as a movement characterized by low churchmanship, a high view of Scripture, and evangelistic zeal.

It is quite beyond the scope of this paper to sketch in the complex relationships between fundamentalism and evangelicalism, or to trace the Phoenix-like rise of evangelicalism in this country following WWII. It is enough to point out three factors that bedevil recent attempts to define evangelicalism:

(a) As recently as 1975, an observer as astute as Martin Marty[4] could insist that evangelicals and fundamentalists alike were committed to an inerrancy view of the Bible. This is no longer the case. Many self-styled evangelicals now affirm the "infallibility" of Scripture, understood as referring to Scripture's truthfulness exclusively in matters of "faith and practice." The "faith and practice" formula at the time of the Reformation was meant to be an *inclusive* category, over against the claims of the Roman Catholic Church to have the right to prescribe in these areas. But some modern evangelicals wield the expression in an *exclusive* way, refusing to acknowledge that the Bible is reliable on whatever subject it chooses to speak. In evangelical academic circles, the change in the last decade and a half or two decades is remarkable. This stance has bred some even more startling hermeneutical shifts. For instance, one major evangelical scholar, whose positive contributions have been incalculable, nevertheless recently argued that any passage in the Pauline corpus that seemed to curtail the principle of freedom espoused by the apostle should be ignored by Christian ethicists.[5] Such "evangelicalism" the evangelicals of a bare twenty-five years ago could not possibly have recognized.

351

Donald A. Carson

(b) Many evangelicals in the vanguard of the movement happily apply the label "evangelical" to confessional Lutherans, Presbyterians, Pentecostalists and others (such as Fundamentalists) who do not think of themselves in this category. Mainstream evangelicals who extend the label beyond themselves are not insensitive to the distinctive emphases of these other groups; rather, since the truths and outlook that define the movement are shared by many people from these groups, they mean thereby to establish their own catholicity. Meanwhile, Presbyterians are inclined to see themselves less as a branch of evangelicalism than as a branch of the Reformed tradition; Pentecostalists see themselves less as a branch of evangelicalism than as a branch of the holiness tradition; and Lutherans see themselves as—well, just Lutherans. Although mainline evangelicals are inclined to view Fundamentalists as evangelicals who unwisely permitted themselves to be defined too much in terms of reaction to their perceived opposition, rather than by the Bible, Fundamentalists not infrequently dismiss mainstream evangelicals as compromisers who are only one step away from heretical liberalism. The distinction in perception is reminiscent of the old anonymous ditty:

> He drew a circle and left me out —
> Heretic, outcast, a thing to flout.
> But love and I had the wit to win:
> We drew a circle and took him in.

Thus, unrepentant, I will include Fundamentalists amongst the evangelicals. Casting the net farther back in history, contemporary mainstream evangelicals find an "evangelical spirit"[6] in many groups of the past two millennia, including groups that never thought of themselves as "evangelicals." The inherent ambiguities generate numerous problems in self-definition.

(c) A further pressure on the term arises from the fact that for many evangelicals the expression is almost synonymous with "true Christian." If evangelicalism is unyieldingly tied to the true evangel, if whole-hearted embrace of evangelicalism affirms the truthfulness of the Bible and elementary but profound Christological confessions, not to mention new birth and evangelistic zeal, then we are only a whisker from concluding that non-evangelicals are non-Christians. Suppose, then, someone drops one or two of the historic distinctives of evangelicalism, and calls the hybrid result, say, "liberal evangelicalism" or "[Roman] Catholic evangelicalism." To say such people are *not* evangelicals sounds too much like saying they are not Christians. But if they are Christians in any biblical sense of that word, most evangelicals would want to refer to them as "evangelicals." Thus is born the pressure to apply the term to those who hold positions not traditionally "evangelical." Properly speaking, the question then becomes, How much of historic evangelicalism can be abandoned before it is no longer evangelicalism? Out of this semantic pot-pourri emerge categories like (1) "consistent evangelical" — a category that is meaningful only if "evangelical" refers to a theological position, not to an experience of grace; (2) "liberal evangelical" — a contradiction in terms if "liberal" refers to major matters of doctrine and "evangelical" is historically defined, but a combination that is usually achieved by stripping "evangelical" of most doctrinal content in favor of a fairly sentimental experience of grace; (3) "Catholic evangelical" — which either means one is staunchly

Donald A. Carson

evangelical while trying to remain a member of the Roman
Catholic Church; or, more commonly, that one is trying to marry
evangelical experience with Roman Catholic views of sacrament,
priesthood and liturgy.

The combination of these pressures forces us to think of
evangelicalism as a movement determined by its center, not its
boundary. So understood (as it will be throughout the rest of this
paper), contemporary evangelicalism, consistent and otherwise,
embraces a wide range of people, but not all their theological
opinions.

(2) How deep and diverse is evangelical ecclesiology?

Indeed, we could put the matter more cheekily and ask, "Is
there such a thing as evangelical ecclesiology?"

Two rather different answers are possible. *First*, it must be
frankly admitted that most evangelicals have devoted much less
time to ecclesiology than to, say, bibliology, Bible exposition or
the atonement. There are at least two reasons for this.

(a) It has been argued, persuasively, that most organizations
or societies that focus inordinate attention on their own intrinsic
nature and internal structure are contaminated with too much
introversion and are already sporting signs of decay and death.
Vitality and vibrancy are connected with a mission-focused,
externally-oriented stance that may be self-aware but is not intro-
spective. At its most potent, evangelicalism drums with the
message of Christ crucified; it burns with evangelistic fire, and
deals with questions about grace, sin, apologetics, holiness,
outreach. With but few exceptions, it tends to address ecclesiological concerns only when the pragmatics of evangelical thought
and mission demand some concrete answers. This is not all bad;

indeed, it shares something of the flavor of the earliest decades of the Christian church.[7] Although the modern critical consensus sometimes artificially imposes upon the New Testament documents the rigid model of a movement that develops from charismatic freedom to *Fruhkatholizismus* ("early catholicism"), there is enough validity to the model to mandate sober reflection. Mainline churches may with some justification brand not a few branches of evangelicalism "immature" because of their relatively unreflective ecclesiology; the more vibrant, expanding edge of evangelicalism may perhaps be excused for protesting that its adherents are too busy winning men and women to Christ, too busy building and nurturing the church, to have leisure for an exercise that sometimes appears (again, with some justification) not unlike navel-gazing.

To put the matter in more theological terms, the doctrinal and ethical concerns that tie together the diverse branches of evangelicalism have little to do with ecclesiology *per se*. There are many evangelicals who have written usefully and provocatively on the church, but by and large it is not their evangelicalism that has prompted them to do so. In short, evangelicalism as a movement is much more defined by Christology, soteriology and bibliology than by ecclesiology.

(b) In some sections of evangelicalism the failure to write massive tomes on the church is reflective of a self-conscious reaction against those quarters of Christendom that focus *too much* attention on the church. The ancient formula *credo ecclesiam* ("I believe in the church") is interpreted by the latter as making the church an object of faith; an object of faith because she is the body of Christ, her head; as the body of Christ, the "great mystery" of

Eph. 5:32.[8] It does not take many steps to make this church a mediator, like Christ himself; to assign to this church the deposit of revelation, instead of seeing that deposit lying in the Scriptures; and thus finally to interpret *extra ecclesiam nulla salus* ("outside the church there is no salvation") to mean not that the church is the community of those redeemed by Christ outside of which there is no salvation, but that the church is the community that so mediates salvation that apart from proper connection with her there is no salvation.

Understandably, evangelicals are less than persuaded by this chain of reasoning. To make the church an object of faith because she is the body of Christ is linguistically unwarranted and biblically forbidden. To link the "body of Christ" language with the theme of Christ's headship fails to distinguish two quite different uses of "body" language applied to the church,[9] and to draw a connection with the "great mystery" of Eph. 5:32 is to ignore the paradigm of marriage that is its type. In short, though thoughtful evangelicals are happy to join in the *credo ecclesiam* ("I believe in the church"),[10] this no more makes the church an object of faith than "I believe in the life everlasting" makes the life everlasting an object of faith. *Credo ecclesiam* is the believer's way of affirming that the church, biblically conceived, is the locus of the redeemed, the community of the people of God, the fellowship of those who have savingly drunk from the well-springs of grace and who confess Jesus as Lord.

It appears, then, that evangelical slowness to articulate profound statements on the church springs partly from the fact that its driving impetus lies elsewhere, and partly from the theological suspicion that those who devote too much attention to the church are in danger of diverting attention from Christ himself. Though the suspicion rests on no internal necessity, history provides enough sorry witnesses to warrant some vigilance. But a *second* answer to the question is possible. The problem is not that evangelicals, broadly conceived, have not produced thoughtful ecclesiology, but that they have produced too many ecclesiologies, or ecclesiological studies, ranging from the barely competent to the fairly sophisticated. Old-style dispensationalism so ties ecclesiology to its brand of eschatology that the church becomes a parenthesis in the plan of God. Covenant theology so ties the church to Israel, not only in promise and fulfillment but also in experience of God, that it is hard to see how the church is much more than a racially mixed and non-national Israel, a more knowledgeable version of the old covenant people of God: the olive tree metaphor (Rom. ll) controls the discussion. Evangelical Lutherans continue to wrestle with Lutheran ecclesiology;[11] Reformed theology calls up, say, Bannerman[12] and Berkouwer.[13] Wesleyans have tied their ecclesiology to the holiness movement.[14] The literature is substantial on "the believer's church" tradition that springs from Anabaptist roots, and contemporary Pentecostalists are now raising their own ecclesiological voices.[15] Popular books on the church abound, focusing primarily on practical concerns such as the nature of ministry, the lay/clergy tension, the importance of unity expressed in sacrificial love and the like.[16]

This diversity is more than a diversity of denominational labels. The central visions of the various branches of evangelicalism are, so far as ecclesiology is concerned, substantially different; the understanding of the nature and role of church ordinances/

Donald A. Carson

sacraments is quite different; the church's worship, mission and vitality are all quite differently construed; even the way the canon is put together to undergird the various ecclesiologies may be quite different. A cynic might be forgiven, then, for thinking that there is no such thing as a distinctive evangelical ecclesiology. The evangelical ecclesiologies (note the plural) that exist spring less from the central core of evangelical truth than from the ecclesiastical and spiritual formation each tradition represents *beyond* evangelicalism. The common core, the lowest common denominator, evangelicalism itself, has no integral ecclesiology.

The cynic, I shall argue, is wrong.

B. Toward an Evangelical Ecclesiology

Perhaps I may be forgiven a personal note. In my capacity as Convenor for one of the Study Units of the Theological commission of the World Evangelical Fellowship, I have had occasion to work with evangelicals from around the world on a variety of projects. Two of these focused on the church — the first book dealing with the hermeneutics of the doctrine of the church, and the second with major components to the doctrine itself. Our Study Unit brought together people from Africa, Latin America, North America, Europe, India, Australia and the Far East. They represented highly diverse strands of denominational affiliation: Anglican, Baptist, Brethren, Presbyterian, Free Church, Lutheran, charismatic and others. Papers were assigned, prepared and circulated in advance, so that our meetings devoted most attention to discussing these papers, paragraph by paragraph, in light of our respective understandings of what the Bible says. What at first astonished me, and then pleased me no end, was the very high degree of unanimity we achieved in area after area of Christian thought. A common commitment to the authority of Scripture, enough humility and candor to make each participant teachable, and concentrated time together — these were the ingredients which under God produced books surprisingly unified.[17]

I have therefore become convinced that although we will not agree on every point of ecclesiology, we ought to do more to set forth the points we hold in common. Granted the nature of evangelicalism, these points are likely to be ones that are most tightly tied to our grasp of Christology, soteriology and bibliology. The theses that follow are not meant to be exhaustive; nor are they set out in order of priority; rather, they are representative of the kind of shared ecclesiological perspectives we should be striving for, and to which most of us could agree. Within the strictures of this paper, I can do no more than "prime the pump" at each thesis, even though more than one full-scale book cries out to be written in each instance.

(1) The church is the community of the new covenant. In the sixth century B.C. the prophet Jeremiah, speaking for the LORD, foresees a time when people will no longer repeat the proverb, "The fathers have eaten sour grapes, and the children's teeth are set on edge" (Jer. 31:30). The history of Israel under the Mosaic covenant has been characterized by the outworking of this proverb. The covenantal structure was profoundly racial and tribal. Designated leaders — prophets, priests, king, and occasionally other leaders such as the seventy elders or Bezaleel — were endued with the Spirit, and spoke for God to the people and for the people to God (*cf.* Exod. 20:19). Thus when the leaders sinned, the entire nation was contaminated, and ultimately faced

divine wrath. But the time is coming, Jeremiah says, when this proverb will be abandoned. "Instead," God promises, "everyone will die for his own sin; whoever eats sour grapes — his own teeth will be set on edge" (Jer. 31:30). This could be true only if the entire covenantal structure associated with Moses' name is replaced by another. That is precisely what the LORD promises: he will make "a new covenant with the house of Israel and with the house of Judah" that "will not be like the covenant" he made with their forefathers at the time of the Exodus. The nature of the promised new covenant is carefully recorded: God will put his law in the hearts and on the minds of his people. Instead of having a mediated knowledge of God, "they will all know me, from the least of them to the greatest," and therefore "no longer will a man teach his neighbor, or a man his brother, saying, 'Know the LORD'" (31:31ff.). This does not foresee a time of no teachers; in the context, it foresees a time of no mediators, because the entire covenant community under this new covenant will have a personal knowledge of God, a knowledge characterized by the forgiveness of sin (31:34) and by the law of God written on the heart (31:33). "I will give them singleness of heart and action, so that they will always fear me for their own good and the good of their children after them. I will make an everlasting covenant with them: I will never stop doing good to them, and I will inspire them to fear me, so that they will never turn away from me" (Jer. 32:39-40).

On the night that he was betrayed, Jesus took the cup of wine and said, "This cup is the *new covenant* in my blood, which is poured out for you" (Lk. 22:20), and the church repeats the words to this day. The Epistle to the Hebrews unambiguously applies the words of Jeremiah to the church (Heb. 8, 10). This means that, whatever complex relationships obtain between Israel and the church when the entire canon is considered, in this instance, at least, the connection is typological: the promise of the new covenant, made to the house of Israel and the house of Judah, is applied by the Lord Jesus himself, and by the Epistle to the Hebrews, to the church. Hebrews goes farther yet, and insists that by calling this promised covenant "new" God "has made the first one obsolete; and what is obsolete and aging will soon disappear" (Heb. 8:13). Here and elsewhere in Hebrews, the Christian reader is instructed not to read the Old Testament a-temporally, but with eyes that detect sequence, before and after, the progress of redemptive history (*cf.* Paul's argument in Rom. 4 and Gal. 3). The church, the community of the new covenant promised by Jeremiah and inaugurated by Jesus' blood, learns to read its place in God's sweeping redemptive purposes.

Numerous theological and practical conclusions may be drawn from these biblical connections — though admittedly not all evangelicals would be happy with all of them.[18] The basic truth, that the church is the community of the new covenant, is embraced by virtually all streams of Christianity. The peculiar evangelical contribution to this theme, however, is the staunch insistence that the *nature* of the new covenant not be overlooked: as foreseen in the prophecy of Jeremiah, it is the abrogation of an essentially tribalistic covenantal structure in favor of one that focuses on the immediate knowledge of God by all people under the new covenant, a knowledge of God that turns on the forgiveness of sin and the transformation of the heart and mind. And that brings me to my second thesis:

Donald A. Carson

(2) The church is the community empowered by the Holy Spirit. The Old Testament prophets not only foresaw the new covenant; they understood its motivating power to be the Holy Spirit. As we have already seen, under the constraints of the old covenant the Spirit was poured out on prophets, priests, kings and a select number of other individuals. Moses himself recognized the limitation: when Joshua complained that Eldad and Medad were prophesying in the camp and indignantly demanded that they be silenced, aged Moses replied, "Are you jealous for my sake? I wish that all the Lord's people were prophets and that the Lord would put his Spirit on them!" (Num. 11:27-29). But that, of course, is exactly what the prophets insisted would take place under the new covenant: God would pour out his Spirit on all flesh, on young men and maidens as well as on prophets and priests. This Spirit is the agent that would enable them to follow God's decrees and be careful to keep his laws (*e. g.* Isa. 44:3-5; Ezek. 11:19-20; 36:25-27; Joel 2:28-32).[19]

It came to be understood, then, that the messianic age would be the age of the Spirit. When John the Baptist announced that his successor, the one to whom he was pointing, would not baptize in water but in the Holy Spirit (Mt. 3:11 par.), he was making a messianic proclamation, he was announcing the messianic age. The new birth in water and spirit (John 3:5) is rightly interpreted as an allusion to Ezek. 36:[20] Jesus insists that Nicodemus should have understood what he was talking about, an indictment that gains bite because Nicodemus was "the teacher of Israel" (3:10) and should have followed Jesus' reasoning from the Scriptures. "Water" and "spirit" come together in those Scriptures most tellingly at Ezek. 36: God looks to the times when he will sprinkle "clean water" upon his people so that they will be clean, and "give them a new heart and put a new spirit" in them so that they will have a heart for obedience (36:25-27). Thus all Jesus has added is the "new birth" metaphor itself; its substance had already been foreseen by Ezekiel. What was required, what the new covenant promised, was a personal renewal, a "new birth" if you will, characterized by cleansing and transforming power.

Many New Testament passages converge on the same theme. In the Fourth Gospel, the Spirit, the Paraclete, is sent to all believers in consequence of the Son's glorification via the cross and resurrection. In Paul, the Spirit is the "down payment" or "guarantee" of the promised inheritance of the last day; indeed, "if anyone does not have the Spirit of Christ, he does not belong to Christ" (Rom. 8:9). In short, whatever disagreements evangelicals may entertain about the operations of the Spirit, most would agree that in the New Testament the church is the community empowered by the Spirit, and that this fact controls not a little of the inaugurated eschatology. This drives us to the third thesis:

(3) The church is an eschatological community. The systems of belief that divide evangelicals in the area of eschatology are very substantial, and deserve continued study and reflection. But unless I am misreading Western evangelicalism rather badly, there is growing unanimity on this third thesis. Whatever our understanding of the future displays of God's kingship in Christ, we hold that the culminating, saving reign of God has already dawned in a preliminary fashion. Even within the ministry of Jesus, that saving reign, the kingdom of God, had dawned: "But if I drive out demons by the Spirit of God, then the kingdom of God has come upon you" (Mt. 12:28). God has already "rescued us

from the dominion of darkness and brought us into the kingdom of the Son he loves" (Col. 1:13). We confess that "the kingdom of God is not a matter of eating and drinking, but of righteousness, peace and joy in the Holy Spirit, because anyone who serves Christ in this way is pleasing to God and approved by men" (Rom. 14:17-18).

The texts could easily be multiplied; this thesis is the very stuff of New Testament thought. The church is the exemplification of the running tension between the "already" and the "not yet." Yet it is extremely important to be sure of what should and should not be drawn from this reality. I am not trying to leap from this thesis — that the church is an eschatological community — to full-blown statements of "kingdom ethics," "kingdom theology," "kingdom power" or the like. R. T. France has adequately warned us against such leaps.[21] My point is far simpler, and far more profound. Because the church is an eschatological community, its ties with the new heaven and the new earth are intrinsically more important and more enduring than its ties with this world that is passing away. Christians are citizens of the new Jerusalem; the church is orientated toward the consummation, and joins believers in every generation who cry, "Even so, come, Lord Jesus!" This means, of course, that the church is an eschatological outpost in time; its very identity turns on this reality. That, in turn, entails numerous evangelistic, ethical and social responsibilities. But these responsibilities are based on the eschatological reality, not *vice versa*.

(4) The church is the "gathered" people of God. It is well known that the Greek work *ekklesia* underlies our word "church," and that *ekklesia* in the hellenistic period means "assembly,"

"congregation" or "meeting," even in a pagan context (e. g. Acts 19:32, 39, 41). One of the most striking things about its use in the New Testament is that it occurs in the plural when referring to the various assemblies ("churches") of a region or province (*e. g.* "the churches of Judea," Gal. 1:22), but it is restricted to the singular when referring to assemblies of Christians in any one city. In cities like Jerusalem, Antioch, Ephesus and Rome the Christians multiplied so rapidly that they could not possibly meet in one assembly; and even if they could have found a large enough venue, it was impolitic to meet that way and draw attention to their numbers. But although there were thus many "assemblies" or "congregations" in, say, Colossae or Jerusalem, Paul writes to the *church* at Colossae and goes up to consult with the *church* in Jerusalem, not the "churches" at Colossae and Jerusalem.

These data are well known and have been used to spin off various theories about church government in New Testament times. This exercise in constructing a theory of governance is not without value, though in my judgment less can be securely based on these data than some would have us believe:[22] theories of church government are better based elsewhere, with information from the distribution of *ekklesia* reduced to corroborative status. What is not usually given adequate treatment, however, is how the concept of "church" relates to the concept of "churches" in the New Testament; for the distribution of *ekklesia* in the New Testament documents is but a subset of this larger *theological* question.

Several recent studies have pointed the way forward. The "assembly" or "gathered group" that fundamentally constitutes the church is *theologically* construed in the sort of thinking reflected in Heb. 12:22-24:

365

> But you have come to Mount Zion, to the *heavenly Jerusalem, the city of the living God.* You have come to thousands upon thousands of angels in joyful assembly, *to the church of the firstborn*, whose names are written in heaven. You have come to God, the judge of all men, to the spirits of righteous men made perfect, to Jesus the mediator of a new covenant, and to the sprinkled blood that speaks a better word than the blood of Abel (emphasis mine).

In other words, Christians participate in the heavenly, eschatological, new covenant church (*ekklesia*) of Jesus Christ. O'Brien and others[23] argue convincingly that it is this heavenly, eschatological, new covenant congregation that Paul has in mind when he refers to churches as "the church" (*e. g.* Jesus "is the head of the body, the church" [Col. 1:18]). This means that each local church is not seen primarily as one member parallel to a lot of other member churches, together constituting one body, one church; nor is each local church seen as the body of Christ parallel to other earthly churches that are also the body of Christ — as if Christ had many bodies. Rather, each church is the full manifestation in space and time of the one, true, heavenly, eschatological, new covenant church. Local churches should see themselves as outcroppings of heaven, analogies of "the Jerusalem that is above," indeed colonies of the new Jerusalem, providing on earth a corporate and visible expression of "the glorious freedom of the children of God."[24] That this model is *city*-based — this heavenly church is the church of the new Jerusalem — may go some way to accounting for the peculiar distribution of the singular form of *ekklesia* in the New Testament.

This way of looking at the church is predicated in part on the fact that the church is nothing other than the redeemed people of God,[25] and the people of God have been raised with Christ, hidden in him and seated with him in the heavenly realms (Eph. 2:5, 6; Col. 2:12-13; 3:3). As Lincoln persuasively demonstrates, the notion that the church is *already* seated with Christ in the heavenlies is a kind of spatial equivalent to realized eschatology.[26]

If this theological understanding of the church is basically right, then the ancient contrast between the church visible and the church invisible, a contrast that has nurtured not a little ecclesiology,[27] is either fundamentally mistaken, or at best of marginal importance.[28] Moreover, this stance is fundamentally at variance with the tendency in the Eastern Church to equate church and cosmos.[29] The failure to distinguish adequately between the two breeds a stunning silence in the area of theological ethics, especially in areas of conflict between the radical demands of the Lord Christ and the ostensible autonomy of worldly structures.[30]

(5) The church is a worshiping community. This thesis is no mere truism: the church may virtually be defined as "all those everywhere who call on the name of our Lord Jesus Christ" (1 Cor. 1:2). Worship is currently an "in" subject. Several notable books have appeared claiming to identify some of the distinctive hymns and liturgy of the first century church.[31] Another volume ties true worship to mystery, Holy Communion and the "Canterbury trail."[32] Some popular treatments unwittingly raise profound problems because they evince little reflection on the biblical theology of worship.[33] On the other side of the issue, Prof. Marshall has pointed out that under the new covenant worship terminology derived from the Old Testament (*e. g. latreia/la-*

treuo; "to draw near" language; etc.) is applied to what the Christian or the church is doing or ought to be doing all the time.[34] Christians did *not* think of their corporate meetings as times of worship, but as times of instruction and fellowship. Just as the epistle to the Hebrews finds the fulfillment of the Sabbath in the rest enjoyed by the people of God under the new covenant,[35] so the "drawing near to God" that once depended on rites that could be performed only on set feast days and by prescribed mediators now depends on the finished work of Christ and is thought of as ready access to the divine Presence.

One of the most thoughtful and balanced of writers in this area is D. G. Peterson.[36] He is deeply concerned to develop a biblical theology of worship. Like Marshall and others, he discerns the shift in terminology from the old covenant to the new, and observes how the emphasis on the cultic, the local, the scheduled is transcended in the freedom of our address to God by the mercies of Christ. Nevertheless he argues, on biblical- theological grounds, that this does not mean the church itself, in corporate meeting, does *not* give itself to worship. The worship that must characterize the church's entire life, the worship that virtually defines the church, ought to be supremely evident when the church meets in corporate assembly.

In this framework, the frankly abysmal patterns and experiences of worship that characterize many evangelical churches in the west, both within and without liturgical circles, are fundamentally a reflection of the paucity of our knowledge of God. Our lives as Christians are not stamped with constant worship; small wonder our corporate meetings so frequently reflect the same bankruptcy. Doubtless there are many steps that could be taken to improve the situation; nonetheless, our sorry state of affairs is not amenable to drastic reformation by the simple expedient of adding or subtracting this bit of liturgy or that bit of informality. Reformation in this area turns on deepening our personal and corporate knowledge and experience of God. And that in turn depends on recovering the roots of evangelical spirituality, what Peter Adam calls "the spirituality of the word."[37]

In theory, then, evangelicals are those who claim to know God by faith in Jesus Christ, and worship him in spirit and in truth. We confess, with shame, that in many of our churches neither the knowledge of God nor the worship of God is very deep.

(6) The church is the product of God's gracious self-disclosure in revelation and redemption. The thesis not only affirms God's gracious initiative to a fallen race and insists that the cross was more than exemplary but actually achieved our salvation; but it also reminds us that the church, which has received this authoritative revelation and experienced this gracious redemption, stands permanently under the authority of its head, the Lord Jesus Christ, who is the focal point both of divine revelation and of divine redemption.[38]

Although this thesis cries out for major expansion, the constraints of space and time allow me nothing more than the formulation of two conclusions. First, if this thesis is kept in mind, Christians will remember their place in the scheme of things. We are always debtors to grace, and we are profoundly suspicious of ostensible formulations of the gospel that jeopardize the freedom of that grace. Second, if what we know of God we have learned because of his own kind self-disclosure in revelatory event, in Scripture and supremely in the person of his Son, and if our

Donald A. Carson

knowledge of God at the subjective level has been brought about because of the atoning sacrifice of the Son, whose death redeemed us and gave us access to the throne-room of heaven itself, then we deny our understanding of Scripture and our experience of grace if we do not frankly order our personal lives *and the church,* our corporate life, by the same revelatory word. We believe in one holy, catholic, *apostolic* church. Insofar as God has revealed what the church ought to be, so far also must that revelation shape our categories, goals, structures, discipline, priorities, and destiny. To fail in this regard is to disown the God who has revealed himself to us.

(7) The church is characterized by mission. Once again there are divisions of opinion amongst us as to how best to articulate this mission, how to relate evangelism to the relief of suffering, how to avoid paternalism, and much more.[39] But to sustain an evangelical view of the church entails commitment to mission, to service, to outreach, to evangelism. As the Father has sent the Son, so the Son has sent us (Jn. 20:21). If the church is the body of the redeemed, the redeemed were once themselves "by nature objects of wrath" (Eph. 2:3); and therefore with Paul we count ourselves under obligation to Jews and Gentiles alike (Rom. 1:14), knowing we are but poor beggars telling other poor beggars where there is bread. Because the Bible constrains our view of the human being, we cannot acknowledge as adequate that form of service which seeks to produce converts but does not minister to physical and temporal needs; because our message is "Be reconciled to God" (2 Cor. 5:20) we cannot acknowledge as *bona fide* mission that service which meets temporal needs but which does not seek to win the lost to repentance, new birth and faith. We confess with

shame those instances where we have been doing no more than stealing sheep. But we gladly put up with derogatory remarks about proselytism from those whose syncretism, pluralism or universalism demands that no one is under threat of condemnation (except, perhaps, those who say we all are, apart from the intervention of the grace of God!).

These seven theses do not point the way toward a comprehensive evangelical ecclesiology. They are merely representative of the sweep of truths about the church that bind most of us together. I have either not probed or barely touched sacraments/ ordinances, metaphors such as "the body of Christ, " the traditional "marks of the church" and much more besides. Nevertheless the articulation of these more-or-less common perceptions of the nature of the church has prepared us for the next step.

C. Evangelical Perspectives on Ecumenism

Emerging naturally from evangelical attempts at self-definition (Section A of this paper) and from the rudiments of evangelical ecclesiology (Section B), several important perspectives on ecumenism present themselves.

(1) By definition, the church is made up of regenerate believers. This confession is nothing more than the entailment of the nature of the new covenant, the exemplification of realized eschatology. It is the corollary of understanding the church as the outcropping of the heavenly assembly gathered in the Jerusalem that is above. But this relatively simple point rapidly becomes complex.

First, there are complex issues within the camp. In theory, evangelicalism will not only prove reluctant to label those people

Donald A. Carson

"Christians" who know nothing of the regenerating, transforming, justifying, sanctifying power of God in their lives, but ideally
evangelicalism will also be eager to admit to Christian fellowship
and ecclesiastical unity *all* those who have truly come to know
God. In reality, however, we discover that all sorts of barriers
divide evangelicals from one another. We divide over baptism,
forms of church government, election and predestination, eschatology, degrees of separation, styles of worship and much more.
Although there are many cultural and historically "accidental"
reasons for such divisions, the most fundamental reason lies with
evangelical commitment to its *formal* principle, *viz.* the authority
of Scripture, coupled with mutually contradictory interpretations
of that Scripture.

In other words, our commitment to the gospel of Jesus
Christ, the material principle of evangelicalism, is itself grounded
in the formal principle, the reliability and truthfulness of Scripture; but the latter ensures that what the Bible seems to be saying
about, say, baptism, must also be taken seriously. If then there are
differences of opinion as to what the Bible actually says on this
point, the formal principle of evangelicalism, one of its great,
unifying foci, becomes the basis for considerable division. Historically, those denominations that achieve unity amongst diverse
groups of genuine believers generally achieve this victory by
implying that certain points of biblical revelation are not very
important. If both credo-baptists and paedo-baptists are admitted,
there cannot be a very strongly articulated view of baptism. If both
Calvinists and Arminians are admitted, then although individual
Christians may have strong views as to election, irresistible grace
or the freedom of the will, the church as a whole has invariably

relegated such matters to the status of the *relatively* unimportant. In one sense, that is of course correct. Nevertheless it is easy to understand why in the view of some — especially those who find it difficult to "hierarchialize" their beliefs — the authority of Scripture itself seems to be depreciated.

The second point of complexity concerns the ecclesiology of evangelicals who choose to live and serve in "mixed" churches. Some of these evangelicals deny the rightness of the "believers' church tradition" implicit in the new covenant and the promises of the Spirit. They call to mind the parable of the wheat and the tares — though in fact that parable portrays the kingdom of heaven (Mt. 13:24-30), not the church.[40] Or they point out that empirically all churches eventually attract their own proportion of spurious saints — which is doubtless true, but irrelevant to the nature of the church, since John, for instance, nicely distinguishes between being "with us" and being "of us" (1 Jn. 2:19). Or they remind us of the deplorable state of several of the churches in Rev. 2-3, so deplorable that they are about to inherit wrath, to be uprooted, vomited out, even while still being referred to as "churches" — though the same evidence might suggest to some that if the protracted warnings are carried out, the threatened wrath will effectively "unchurch" the churches in question, while only those Christians who endure to the end will be saved and receive the crown of life, and truly prove to be the church.

Others depend much more on pragmatic arguments. Jonathan Fletcher, who ably serves Christ in the Church of England, points out[41] that in the Thirty-Nine Articles, Article 19 (which defines the church) makes no mention of a *national c*hurch; nor do the formularies. Though he is in the minority, he holds he is more faithful to the church's foundations, *viz.* the Articles and the formularies, than are the majority of the church's leaders. Meanwhile he fears the tendency toward schism displayed by other groups (a variation on the *first* complexity, just discussed), for does not Jesus himself pray for the unity of the church (Jn. 17), and insist that the world will recognize his disciples by their love? In any case he finds the Church of England, in his context, the best boat from which to fish. Analogous arguments are advanced by evangelicals in this country's mainline denominations. The point of protest or even separation is crossed when such a denomination adopts an official stance that many judge unbiblical, and requires its clergy to do the same — *e. g.* the ordination of women. Schism is introduced after all. At the end of the day, the question reduces to what we shall fight over, and why.

My point in these somber reflections is not that all the choices are easy ones, nor that there are no "right" positions, but that evangelical theology, to be consistent with itself, must adopt as a limiting guideline that the church is made up of regenerate believers.

(2) It follows, then, that church discipline must be practiced. Historically, church discipline has sometimes been designated the third mark of the church (immediately following the right preaching of the gospel and the proper administration of the sacraments/ ordinances, the "visible word").[42] Church discipline runs the gamut from gentle, personal encouragement and confrontation to the final sanction, excommunication — a sanction not to be administered hastily or without tears, and only for three kinds of offenses.[43] Church discipline is not only illustrated in Scripture; it is virtually mandated by the nature of the church. And it must be

said, with profound regret, that the failure to exercise firm, compassionate discipline now extends way beyond mainline churches to those that have sprung from the so-called "believers' church tradition." The failure is particularly transparent when local churches boast of "membership" numbers several times larger than the largest of its meetings.

Those of us who have moved between congregations adhering to the "believers' church tradition" and larger ecclesiastical bodies are the first to reflect on the fact that there is often a fair bit of misunderstanding on both sides. Evangelicals who identify with the believers' church tradition sometimes give the impression that evangelicals in the national or mainline denominations do not want to have a pure church, a confessing church. This, demonstrably, in most instances is not true. But many of the latter think of the believers' church movement as sectarian, rigid, exclusivistic; and this, usually, is uncharitable and untrue. Those within mainline denominations usually see the problem as one of strategy and charity: strategy, in that they see themselves to be reclaiming historic denominations, and charity, in that they are temperamentally given to include as Christians those within their denomination's ranks who have not fallen into positive heresy or apostasy. Those within the believers' church tradition are inclined to interpret such thinking as a loss of nerve, an equivocation before the demands of Scripture. In any case, the two positions place themselves at different points along a spectrum, not in diametrically opposite camps.

It would profit little to probe the rights and wrongs of each position here. This much must be said: If the theological reasoning and presupposed biblical underpinnings lightly traced out in this

Donald A. Carson

paper are correct, all of us must come to grips with the mandate
of biblical discipline, and ask how far our own churches approximate to it.

At another level, it is the logic of church discipline that
makes "cooperative evangelism" between evangelicals (broadly
conceived) and others such a troubling point for so many of us. It
is the same logic which makes most of us less than eager to cast
our lot with the WCC.

*(3) From an evangelical perspective, it is not strictly **necessary** to list the sacraments/ordinances as one of the defining
marks of the church, even though the overwhelming majority of us
are happy to do so.* Otherwise we could not conceive of evangelical Salvationists, Quakers and others. This perspective is merely
another way of saying that evangelicals do not elevate sacraments/ordinances to the level of *primary* importance. There are
profound differences amongst us as to what these rites of the
church mean, and how much prominence they should be given;
but there is agreement that the Lord's Table must not be construed
as of rival importance to the completed cross-work of Christ
himself. The reason why, notwithstanding these comments, most
of us are happy to list the sacraments/ordinances as the second
mark of the church is because most of us, appealing to the formal
principle that binds us, understand Scripture to teach that these
rites should be perpetuated in the church. Even so, that does not
mean we place these rites in the same category of things essential
to salvation as, say, the vicarious sacrifice of Christ.

*(4) A Christian who detaches himself or herself from the
church, or a "parachurch" group that is largely independent of
the church, is self-contradictory.* Of course, slippery language

lurks in this sentence. There is a profound sense in which it is impossible for a Christian *not* to be part of the church. The language of self-distancing, however, comes from some Christians who are rugged individualists and from some parachurch groups that speak of the failures of the church which they are seeking to put to rights not by reforming the church but by running competition. But if the thrust of this paper is even approximately right, then such Christians are the church, or, more accurately, they cannot escape being members of this body.

The question then becomes, How as members of the body of Christ, the church, shall I (or we) seek to be related to other Christians? The same formal principle of authority to which they appeal in other areas of doctrine must again prevail. At once all the questions of sacrament/ordinance, church government and accountability, offices/functions within the church, diversity of gifts, and relation between gift and office,[44] surge forward *from the text of Scripture itself.* It will not do for a parachurch organization to duck such questions on the ground that the organization itself is not a church. At the most profound level, the Christians who constitute this parachurch organization inevitably belong to the church. Why then should they not comport themselves in line with what the acknowledged authority, the revealed Scripture, prescribes for the church? The answer has been that although they belong to the church invisible they choose not to belong to the church visible; or, alternatively, they seek a form of "belonging" to a local church, the church visible, that leaves them free to pursue their own ministry. But the distinction between the church visible and the church invisible is, as we have seen, largely artificial. And once that distinction has been all but eliminated, replaced by eschatological and "heavenly dimension" categories, there is less room to hide. The church on earth is the manifestation of the heavenly assembly; and the church on earth, in confessing Jesus as Lord, commits itself to living in obedience to his word. That certainly includes church life, so far as we understand it.

I do not want to be misunderstood. I am not consigning all parachurch groups and disgruntled individualists to the abyss. What I am saying is that the stereotypical position of such groups and individuals is profoundly inconsistent, when measured by biblical norms. It is therefore encouraging to note the number of such parachurch groups that are strenuously seeking not only to establish closer ties with churches, but closer accountability — indeed, *to see themselves and to be seen by others* as arms of the church, extensions of the church.

(5) Evangelicalism's views of Scripture and of the church make sustained cooperation with classic liberalism or with traditional Roman Catholicism extremely problematic. Of course, co-belligerency on some points may be wise and practical — *e. g.* working with Roman Catholics on the abortion issue, or with theological liberals on some genuine issue of social justice[45] or environmental stewardship. But sustained cooperation remains difficult and dangerous.

Consider Roman Catholicism. In their recent "Pastoral Statement for Catholics on Biblical Fundamentalism," the National conference of Catholic Bishops Ad Hoc Committee on Biblical Fundamentalism, while praising the zeal of "fundamentalists" (their use of the category shows they include evangelicals under this rubric), deplored the view that "the Bible alone is sufficient," reduced the authority of Scripture to the position espoused by Vatican II,[46] appealed to "the Spirit-guided tradition of the church and the inspired books," insisted that "the fullness of Christianity" demands "the eucharist and the other six sacraments, the celebration of the word in the liturgical cycle, the veneration of the Blessed Mother and the saints," defended the view that the Pope is "the universal shepherd" in succession from Peter, praised the versions of the Bible "with an imprimatur," and more.

We may be grateful for their candor; the theological chasm between us remains wide. However much we may be grateful for foundational points of agreement — *e. g.* belief in the Trinity, recognition that sin is an offense before God that must be dealt with, concern for the family, opposition to abortion, belief in the resurrection — the points that divide us are not minor. We do not agree with Roman Catholics about the locus of revelation, the definition of the church, the means of grace, the source of contemporary ecclesiastical authority, the significance of Mary, the finality of Christ's cross-work, and more. Though we recognize the immense diversity of contemporary Catholicism, we do not find that official pronouncements since Vatican II have bridged the chasm that remains.

Those forms of so-called "liberalism" that disown the uniqueness of the revelation of God in Jesus Christ, his deity, his vicarious and penal atonement, and the reality of the resurrection do not provide much greater temptation to intimate relations. The recent dialogue between liberal theologian David L. Edwards and John Stott[47] shows that discussions may be worth having; it does not make us sanguine that the fundamental problems of unbelief are about to disappear. The differences of opinion regarding the authority of Scripture, the uniqueness of Christ, the nature of salvation *and therefore the nature of the church* are as wide as ever: indeed, the gap yawns wider.

One of the features of the book by Edwards and Stott is that Edwards chooses the topics for discussion. Because he sets the agenda, only rarely is he forced to face the problems that could be put to him from the evangelical side. In light of the drastic shrinkage that continues to plague virtually all liberal constituencies, it is only proper that we press several questions on them: What locus of authority is there that prevents endless shifts of theological position — positions that are trumpeted to the world as if they are prophecies but seem to us like echoes originating in the world itself, echoes now laced with religious overtones? What is the content of the evangel, and how do you arrive at it? There is neither evangelism nor evangelicalism without the evangel. What, then, is your vision of the church? We say, a little whimsically,

> You say I am not with it;
> My friend, I do not doubt it.
> But when I see what I'm not with
> I'd rather be without it.

Meanwhile, aware as we are of the burning need to demonstrate the love and unity that must be displayed in the lives of those who have closed with Christ, who have been justified by his death and resurrection, and who have by the Spirit already tasted the powers of the age to come, we who call ourselves evangelicals must strive to live out a practical ecumenism of the redeemed. In joint enterprises of evangelism, worship, instruction and service, opportunities abound.

D. Concluding Reflections

Evangelicalism is so diverse that its various branches will hear me in different ways. If we are to examine ourselves with integrity, we ought to pay closest attention to those parts least palatable to our own heritage.

Meanwhile, the secularization of the age (which does not mean that religion affects fewer people but that religion is so emasculated that its influence in human life is largely vitiated) challenges us with the sheer immensity of the hurdles before us. In many parts of American society, ecumenism has become a dead issue, not because it has either triumphed or been defeated, but because it has been outflanked. The great god most widely confessed as Lord in the American "naked, public square" is the great god Pluralism. What need of ecumenism if all "isms" are mere variations of a universal movement toward God? The view most widely despised in many reaches of American society is the one that says it is right and that others are wrong. And no view matters much anyway, except the one that worships Pluralism itself.

This is the time for evangelicalism to understand itself, to resist fragmentation, to return to basics, and to think through its mission in the light of the changeless evangel and the changing patterns of unbelief all around us. And if we love Christ, we will cherish the church, for it is written, "Christ loved the church, and gave himself up for her to make her holy" (Eph. 5:25-26). Our sole confidence is still in him who declared, "I will build my church, and the gates of hell will not overcome it" (Mt. 16:18).

Donald A. Carson

[1]E.g. George Marsden, *Reforming Fundamentalism* (Grand Rapids: Eerdmans, 1987); Nancy Tatom Ammerman, *Bible Believers: Fundamentalists in the Modern World* (New Brunswick: Rutgers, 1987) (I am indebted to Prof. John Woodbridge for this reference); some essays in George Marsden, ed., *Evangelicalism and Modern America* (Grand Rapids: Eerdmans, 1984); James Davison Hunter, *Evangelicalism: The Coming Generation* (Chicago: University Press, 1987). For a careful analysis of the depreciation of theological categories in the definition of the movement, and of the corresponding rise of social science categories, cf. Douglas A. Sweeney, "The Neo-Evangelical Movement, 1941-1960: Toward a More Thorough Historiographical Approach" (M.A. thesis, Trinity Evangelical Divinity School, forthcoming).

[2]For useful taxonomies of the meaning of 'evangelical', cf. amongst many contributions Bruce Shelley, *Evangelicalism in America* (Grand Rapids: Eerdmans, 1967); David F. Wells and John D. Woodbridge, ed., *The Evangelicals: What They Believe, Who They Are, Where They Are Changing* (Nashville: Abingdon, 1975); James Leo Garrett, Jr., "'Evangelicals' and Baptists — Is There a Difference?" in James Leo Garrett, Jr., E. Glenn Hinson and James E. Tull, *Are Southern Baptists "Evangelicals"?* (Macon: Mercer University Press, 1983), especially pp.33-63.

[3]It is quite mistaken to think of "inerrancy" as a modern category adopted by conservatives who are lurching still further to the right: cf. John D. Woodbridge, *Biblical Authority: A Critique of the Rogers/McKim Proposal* (Grand Rapids: Zondervan, 1982).

[4]Martin E. Marty, "Tensions Within Contemporary Evangelicalism: A Critical Appraisal," in David F. Wells and John D. Woodbridge, *The Evangelicals: What They Believe, Who They Are, Where They Are Changing* (Nashville: Abingdon, 1975), 170-188, esp. 173.

[5]F. F. Bruce in an interview with Ward and Laurel Gasque, in *Christianity Today*, forthcoming.

[6]To use the expression of R. V. Pierard, "Evangelicalism," *EDT* 380.

[7]Cf. the central arguments of C. K. Barrett, *Church, Ministry and Sacraments in the New Testament* (Grand Rapids: Eerdmans, 1985), esp. 74-75.

[8]So Andreas Rinkel, writing from the perspective of "The Old Catholic Church" (in R. Newton Flew, ed., *The Nature of the Church* [New York: Harper, 1952] 158), but similar sentiments can be found in Tridentine forms of Roman Catholicism, in some branches of Eastern Orthodoxy, in High Anglicanism and elsewhere.

[9]Cf. Edmund C. Clowney. "The Biblical Theology of the Church," in D. A. Carson, ed., *The Church in the Bible and the World* (Grand Rapids: Baker, 1987) 13-87.

[10]Note the book by David Watson, *I Believe in the Church* (Grand Rapids: Eerdmans, 1979).

[11]Most recently, Eberhard Hahn, *Wo ist die Kirche Jesu Christi? Theologische Beurteilung kirchlicher Trennungen anhand von Fallbeispielen* (Wuppertal: Brockhaus, 1988); *cf.* Martin Heinecken, "Is There a Growing Consensus on a Redefinition of the Church?" *Dialog* 14 (1975) 297-302.

[12]James Bannerman, *The Church of Jesus Christ: A Treatise of the Nature, Powers, Ordinances, Discipline, and Government of the Christian Church* (Edinburgh: T. & T. Clark, 1868).

[13]G. C. Berkouwer, *The Church* (Studies in Dogmatics; trans. James E. Davison; Grand Rapids: Eerdmans, 1976).

[14]Melvin E. Dieter and Daniel N. Berg, ed., *The Church: An Inquiry into Ecclesiology from a Biblical Theological Perspective* (Wesleyan Theological Perspectives IV; Anderson, IN: Warner, 1984).

[15]E.g. John Amstutz, "Beyond Pentecost: A Study of Some Sociological Dimensions of Church Growth from the Book of Acts," in Paul Elbert, ed., *Essays on Apostolic Themes* *Fs.* Howard M. Ervin; Peabody, MA: Hendrickson, 1985) 208-225.

[16]I have in mind the sort of thing exemplified by John Moore and Ken Neff, *A New Testament Blueprint for the Church* (Chicago: Moody, 1985).

[17]D. A. Carson. ed., *Biblical Interpretation and the Church: Text and Context* (Exeter: Paternoster, 1984); *idem*, ed., *The Church in the Bible and the World* (Grand Rapids: Baker, 1986).

[18]For instance, I would argue that although under the Mosaic covenant there is necessarily a distinction between the locus of the covenant community and the locus of the elect/redeemed/remnant, with circumcision being the sign of the former, under the terms of the new covenant the distinction is obliterated. The people of the new covenant have the law written on their hearts, by definition; *i.e.* the locus of the covenant community and the locus of the elect/redeemed/remnant become one. That suggests that baptism, for instance, cannot properly be a sign of the former but not of the latter.

[19]For more extensive probing of the first two theses, *cf.* D. A. Carson, *Showing the Spirit* (Grand Rapids: Baker, 1987), esp. chap.5.

[20]Cf. Linda L. Belleville, "'Born of Water and Spirit': John 3: 5." *Trinity Journal* 1 (1980), 25-41; D. A. Carson, *John* (TNTC; Grand Rapids: Eerdmans, forthcoming) *in loc*.

[21]R. T. France, "The Church and the Kingdom of God: Some Hermeneutical Issues," in D. A. Carson, ed., *Biblical Interpretation and the Church: Text and Context* (Exeter: Paternoster, 1984) 30-44.

[22]For instance, for most of us it is less than obvious that these data can be used to support a theory of presiding bishops who exercise authority over elders. If such a theory were supported by clear statements in the New Testament. the distribution of *ekklesia* might well be taken as corroborative evidence; in the absence of such a theory, we discover that

Donald A. Carson

the same evidence can be made to corroborate one or two other theories of ecclesiastical governance just as well.

[23]Peter T. O'Brien, "The Church as a Heavenly and Eschatological Entity," in D. A. Carson, ed., *Church* 88-119.

[24]Cf. H. Thielicke, *The Evangelical Faith 3: Theology of the Spirit* (tr. and ed. Geoffrey W. Bromiley; Grand Rapids: Eerdmans, 1982) 206-207.

[25]Edmund P. Clowney, *The Doctrine of the Church* (Philadelphia: Presbyterian and Reformed, 1974) 11-24.

[26]Andrew T. Lincoln, *Paradise Now and Not Yet: Studies in the Role of the Heavenly Dimension in Paul's Thought with Special Reference to His Eschatology* (SNTSMS 43; Cambridge: University Press, 1981).

[27]E.g. Bannerman, *Church* 29ff.

[28]O'Brien (" Church") opts for the former; Edmund P. Clowney ("The Biblical Theology of the Church") for the latter.

[29]Eric G. Jay (*The Church: Its Changing Image Through Twenty Centuries* [Atlanta: John Knox, 1977, 1978] 149) rightly summarizes: "The Church is also the image of the cosmos. Like the universe it unites things visible and invisible. . . ."

[30]Thielicke, *Evangelical Theology* 3 218.

[31]E.g. Ralph P. Martin, *Worship in the Early Church* (revised edition; Grand Rapids: Eerdmans, 1975).

[32]Robert E. Webber, *Evangelicals on the Canterbury Trail: Why Evangelicals Are Attracted to the Liturgical Church* (Waco: Word, 1985). *Cf.* his earlier *Worship Old and New* (Grand Rapids: Zondervan, 1982).

[33]E.g. R. Allen and G. Borrer, *Worship: Rediscovering the Missing Jewel* (Portland: Multnomah, 1982).

[34]I. Howard Marshall, "How far did the early Christians *worship* God?" *Churchman* 99 (1985) 216-229. *Cf.* Russell R. Shedd, "Worship in the New Testament Church," in D. A. Carson, ed., *Church* 120- 153.

[35]Evangelicals do not agree on what relationship the Old Testament Sabbath has with Sunday.

[36]D. G. Peterson, "Towards a New Testament Theology of Worship," *RefThRev* 43 (1984) 65-73; *idem*, "Further Reflections on Worship in the NT," *RefThRev* 44 (1985) 34-41; and several studies in preparation. *Cf.* also Jurgen Moltmann, *The Church in the Power of the Spirit: A Contribution to Messianic Ecclesiology* (tr. Margaret Kohl; New York: Harper and Row, 1977) 261-2.

[37]Peter Adam, *Roots of Contemporary Evangelical Spirituality* (Bramcote: Grove Books, 1988).

[38]Robert S. Paul (*The Church in Search of Its Self* [Grand Rapids: Eerdmans, 1972] 284-9) is one of the few who, in attempting a fresh articulation of the theology of the church, begins with revelation.

[39]*Cf.* D. A. Carson. "Church and Mission: Reflections on Contextualization and the Third Horizon," in D. A. Carson, ed., *Church* 213-257.

[40]The distinction between the kingdom and the church is not one of chronology, but of category: the kingdom is primarily the display of God's saving sovereignty, while the church is the people of God.

[41]In *Evangelicals Now* (Jan. 1989) 11.

[42]Bucer emphasized this third mark, while Luther, Melanchthon and Calvin emphasized the first two (though there are certainly adumbrations of the third in Calvin). *Cf.* Paul D. L. Avis, *The Church in the Theology of the Reformers* (Atlanta: John Knox, 1981) 48-50.

[43]Viz. the denial of certain cardinal truths; the impenitent practice of immorality; and divisive lovelessness.

[44]*Cf.* Ronald Y. K. Fung, "Ministry in the New Testament," in D. A. Carson, ed., *Church* 154-212; D. A. Carson, "Church, Authority in," *EDT* 228-231.

[45]Even here one needs considerable wisdom: *cf.* Ernest W. Lefever, *Nairobi to Vancouver: The World Council of Churches and the World, 1975-87* (Washington: Ethics and Policy Center, 1987).

[46]After several re-writings of an originally conservative document, Vatican II finally managed to say, on Scripture, nothing more than that "the books of Scripture must be acknowledged as teaching firmly, faithfully and without error that truth which God wanted put into the sacred writings for the sake of our salvation" (Dogmatic Constitution on Divine Revelation II).

[47]David L. Edwards and John Stott, *Essentials: A Liberal- Evangelical Dialogue* (London: Hodder and Stoughton, 1988).

RESPONSE TO DONALD A. CARSON

Joseph M. Stowell III

Dr. Carson's fine paper offers much to be in harmony with and articulates well the essence of the key issues involved in the scope of the assignment. However, a few key questions arise. What will become of a movement whose name is becoming more symbolic than substantive? Can any articulation of the nature of the church ever be divorced from the marks of the church? Does not a biblical view of the church go beyond functional definition and embrace the priority of a personal commitment to Christ and an obedience to Scripture that produces the character of Christ (Eph. 4:11-14)?

In addition, should there not be a clear and primary emphasis on the place of mutually affirmed and accepted core doctrines as the key issue in the identity of evangelicalism, the nature and responsibility of the church and the standard in ecumenism? Because of what I see as the centrally strategic place of truth, this response will be an extrapolation of Dr. Carson's allusion to the importance of a core belief structure to the three areas addressed — particularly the complex area of ecumenism which alone could have, and perhaps should have, consumed the bulk of our statements.

I beg the liberty, then, to respond in extension of, more than in tension with, Carson's work. I wish to respond by building upon his paper with a specific focus on the strategic nature of a core belief structure.

The thesis of this response is that an unflinching commitment to a core belief structure is the fundamental key to the survival and success of the mission of Christ in us and through us. This could go unstated except for three assumptions that loom large, at least in my perception. Assumption number one is that increasingly the "evangelical movement" is becoming less and less a community marked by clear doctrinal agreement, leaving it as a signature community carrying on in terms of its name rather than its content. Secondly, this response assumes that the church has shied away from its responsibility of the jealous guardianship of its belief base by emphasizing the assertive aspects in its agenda of world evangelization. And, thirdly, that the standards of ecumenism tend to be viewed in terms of accomplishing the mission rather than regard for long-term continuation of doctrinal purity.

In each of these three areas, a core belief structure struggles to hold its rightful place at the strategic center. Both revelation and church history demonstrate the foundational nature of core doctrine. When the church has been buffeted by scandals, immorality and selfish ambition, it has lived to tell the story. However, when the church has abandoned basic biblical positions, it has been set adrift in currents of pluralistic paganism, rarely to find its moorings again. Isn't this the thrust of the warning of Paul as he speaks about the place of "faith and knowledge" in the charter of the church (Eph. 4:11-16)?

In all that Dr. Carson has postulated, must there not be a clearer affirmation of the centrality of our unrepentant rootedness in mutually accepted doctrinal beliefs? I would like to suggest that this clear thread be woven into the tapestry of his statement, lest its primal significance somehow be missed. To do so, this response will deal with the significance of a basic belief structure at the core of evangelicalism, the church and its ecumenical practices.

1. *Evangelicalism, in order to succeed and survive, must establish a core belief structure which both defines and directs evangelicals in the pursuit of their cause.*

In addition to Carson's notations, Hunter's book, *Evangelicalism: The Coming Generation,*[1] documents a broadening belief structure in both lifestyle and doctrine. *Christianity Today* recently included, as an "evangelical scientist", a scholar who has reservations about the historical credibility of the first eleven chapters of Genesis.[2] Congress '88 here in Chicago included leading evangelicals, as well as the Cardinal of the Archdiocese of Chicago. This year's Lausanne II to be held in Manila welcomes selected Roman Catholics as full participants. Whether or not one wishes to attach a value judgment to these developments, it is clear that increasingly the movement is marked more by its name than by its theological core. While I do not wish to oversimplify, over-generalize, or overlook the changes taking place within traditions that were once distinctly separate, I do notice that there is more diversity and a broader constituency under the evangelical umbrella than ever before.

It seems now that acceptability lies not so much in doctrinal homogeneity, but in whether or not we call a person or group "evangelical" and that the liberty to do that revolves around issues apart from a belief structure. "Evangelical" apparently means agreeing with our mission even though not in full agreement with our message. "Evangelical," as Carson points out, calls attention to the new Lutheran denomination (ELCA), which holds little in common with historical evangelicalism. Should the evangelical turf be open to those who may be willing to share our call to world evangelization, even though they may not agree about what constitutes evangelization?

An aggressive mission can hardly be sufficient if it stands alone. Mission without a clear and undiminished commitment to fundamental doctrine is left without power. Of what good is the "great commission" if we do not adhere to the authority of the inerrant Word that holds us accountable? And of what hope is a message without a literal bodily resurrection, and what becomes of impelling grace proclamations if there is with them an admixture of works, sacramental and otherwise? Any movement from core belief structures significantly weakens the fervor and impetus of our mission and, I fear, may plant the seed of the ultimate dismantling of the mission.

Is it not imperative that we anchor our identity in what we affirm to be true? Establishing ourselves as a community marked by a stated belief structure will be a difficult challenge to meet. First, we lack an authoritative "belief statement" that we can look to as a magnet around which we *all* can cluster. Secondly, the increasing complexity and proliferation of hermeneutical styles have seemingly clouded a clear and simple understanding of basic biblical assumptions of the past. Thirdly, fraternalism (whereby I may "sense" a kinship with someone who does not embrace historic evangelical beliefs and yet assume that this feeling of kinship is tantamount to a spiritual oneness) leads us to broader inclusion of some who may not truly qualify. Also, unwillingness to acknowledge that while all evangelicals are Christians, not all Christians are evangelicals, complicates the task. And, fear of being perceived as simplistic, sectarian, or worse yet, separatists, might cause some to have second thoughts.

Yet, without establishing our identity in a common belief system, there is little left except the hollow symbol of a name. Is it not then imperative that at some point soon, a clear *basic* confession be established that will reaffirm the priority of doctrinal assent as step one for the privilege of wearing the name? Such a statement should be basic — not unlike the articulated fundamentals of 1910. It should reflect the Augustinian advice, "In essentials unity, in non-essentials liberty and in all things charity." This core affirmation should be held with unflinching allegiance in a spirit of love and concern for those who differ.

2. With this accomplished, there is then the responsibility to *accept as a church our God-given task to be the guardian over and watchman for our biblical position.* Let me say quickly that the truth does not need the church to guard its intrinsic veracity. Truth is truth. As H. G. Wells is purported to have said, "You can't shoot the truth." Or, in the words of Winston Churchill, "Truth is incontrovertible. Panic may resent it, ignorance may deride it, malice may distort it, but there it is."

Yet, when it comes to the truth, God has given his church the responsibility, not merely of affirming its veracity, but also of safeguarding its place both in the church and in the world. Should we not, with Dr. Carson's permission, add to his section on ecclesiology an eighth point which I would entitle "guardian of the truth"?

Response

Historically, the church has accepted its biblical mandate to defend the apostolic truth structures of Scripture (Acts 20:27-31). Yet now, even from within there are voices present that cast shadows of relativism and pluralism across doctrinal affirmations. There are innuendos that a strong affirmation of truth shackles a broader understanding of the world and truth itself. This threatens to render the church as an army of question marks with no exclamation points as marching orders. The spirit of pluralism makes "Thus saith the Lord" an outdated and unwelcome statement in our pulpits and threatens to leave our doctrinal core as optional rather than obligatory.

Carson's emphasis on discipline as a characteristic of the true church is certainly appropriate. The church was intended to disassociate itself from anyone not holding to key apostolic affirmations which protect the purity of its teachings. In particular, any dilution of the gospel due to legal or sacramental necessities (Gal. 1, Phil. 3) or any distortion of the truth about Christ himself was to be eliminated (III John). It is not insignificant to note that the major departures today have been in these two arenas. The gospel has been reconfigured in liberal, liberation, social and legal terms in mainline churches and traditional Adventism and Roman Catholicism as is noted in Carson's work. Aberrations of the doctrine of Christ mark not only the cults of today, but also Protestant liberal theology. The biblical means for protecting the purity of these elements of truth has been exclusion of and separation from any influence from these sources.

The truth must not be diluted or polluted from within or without, and it cannot be risked for any reason, not even for the advance of missions or for cultural acceptance. This is a principle which is plainly biblical but fraught with some applicational difficulties.

Can we in the application of our stewardship of core truth resist the temptation to compromise in order to be accepted in the view of the larger religious or secular world? Can we bear being misunderstood as we stand for the purity of our core commitments? Can we resist becoming unbalanced and/or falling back into what the previous paper calls a siege mentality that carries one off into a protectionist mode that reduces the world conquest agenda to a weakened position? Can we be biblical separatists without succumbing to the tendency to separate beyond biblical imperatives?

In spite of these challenges, we must not shrink from our ecclesiological responsibility to be gracious and courageous guardians for the purity of the faith once and for all delivered to the saints. And, as such, then we are to be known not by just a name but by this core biblical belief structure which we seek safely to guard and uphold.

3. Establishing our identity in core biblical truth, and safeguarding it, lead us then to face the opportunities and challenges of ecumenism in light of both our doctrinal identity and stewardship. *As a church we must function ecumenically in ways that uphold and do not endanger core belief structures in terms of both proclamation or perception.*

For my part, I will accept Dr. Carson's proposition that old line ecumenism has taken a lethal injection from pluralism and address this response to concerns about the new wave of ecumenism within evangelicalism where the standard for mutual endeavor seems rather unclear.

Response

For some, the standard is set in terms of those who "call him Lord" or who "name the name of Christ" as though basic belief were subordinate to verbal assent. Christ's warning must be sounded here (Matt. 7:21-23).

Equally troubling is the sometime inclusion of those who hold distinctively divergent views of the meaning and/or means of salvation, the deity of Christ and the historical credibility and authority of Scripture. At times, the standard for cooperative endeavors seems to be enthusiasm for our mission. Yet we must also be concerned that those we include may not introduce divergent definitions or motives which are foreign to the mission.

In terms of the centrality of biblical truth and its purity, having standards other than core truth is risky business at best and disobedience at worst. On balance, it is a troubling trend.

For us to say that we will limit partnership to those who hold without qualification our biblical core is a challenge we must face. Unlike mainline liberals and deviant cults, many who are not "doctrinal" evangelicals seem to hold to a large majority of our assumptions. It might seem that we have more in common with them than that which is not common. Yet, isn't the issue qualitative, not quantitative? The challenge is complicated in that many who do not embrace our belief will embrace our mission and even enhance our mission as we seek to reach into their constituencies for Christ. Yet, should not, as I have sought to demonstrate, the mission be preambled by our doctrinal commitments? To subordinate commitment to doctrinal purity to the priority of mission is to undermine the very heart and impetus of mission.

Given the strategic role of mutually affirmed doctrine in our movement and our God-given responsibilities as a church to protect it, both are put at risk in any partnership that threatens practically or perceptually to infringe on that stewardship.

At least two issues rise to the surface here, one of principle and one that is perceptual. If the biblical principle is to disengage from those who hold variant views of the gospel and Christ, then must we not obey? One may object that not all who travel in false systems are adherents to the system. What then of the perceptual dynamic of public association with a "reluctant" representative of that system? Is there not an implied endorsement of that false system even though it may not be verbalized? Do we say by associating with reluctant adherents of false systems that, though there are differences between our system and theirs, they really are insignificant in the light of our mutual mission? Is that what we want to say?

Perhaps we as leaders, activists, or theologically sophisticated can cope with the dichotomy. But can those who fill the pews discern the difference? Do we not foster an undiscerning tendency to pluralism and the associated discounting of the importance of core doctrine among the masses that make up the movement? After all, the forward thrust of the church is not in academe or even in theologians' notebooks, but in the mass of common rather unsophisticated foot soldiers. Do we really want to risk disarming them in terms of their perception of the priority and purity of belief?

If core biblical belief gives rise to our identity and if it is the commodity the church is held responsible to uphold and protect, then it should govern our partnerships in the advance of our mission.

Response

In all of this, there is the danger of becoming captive to the sterility of the cold orthodoxy of a creedal community. Truth is foundational. It is centrally strategic. Yet the mission that forms our aggressive agenda must consume us, not apart from, but in the context of, our doctrinal footings. We must stand unashamedly, bearing the reproach of the cross, the scorn of even the religionists of our day if necessary. Then, having graciously affirmed our ground, we must go forth with all those who agree in kind to do the work of Christ undaunted and undistracted from the task.

[1] Hunter, James Davison, *Evangelicalism: The Coming Generation* (Chicago: The University of Chicago Press, 1987).

[2] Durbin, Jr., Bill, "How It All Began," *Christianity Today* (August 12, 1988).

QUESTIONS
FOR DISCUSSION

1. What problems arise in trying to define who is an evangelical? Can any Protestant, Roman Catholic, or Orthodox be an evangelical? Can a person be a Christian and not be an evangelical?

2. Does evangelical describe people or theology or both? Defend your answer.

3. Why have evangelical Christians not devoted more energy to the study of ecclesiology (the doctrine of the Church)? What are some of the bad effects of this?

4. What are the main differences between the Old Covenant and the New? How do these differences affect biblical ecclesiology?

5. What is the meaning of the assertion that the church "is the exemplification of the running tension between the already and the not yet"? What are the practical implications of this for the church?

6. What steps can be taken to deepen worship in evangelical churches?

7. What governs when and to what extent evangelicals cooperate with nonevangelicals who call themselves Christians?

10

MODERN SCIENCE

EVANGELICALS AND MODERN SCIENCE

Robert C. Newman

As iron sharpens iron, so one man sharpens another.
(Prov 27:17 NIV)

A proverb about individuals—but true, I believe, of Christianity and science as well. Each is a challenge to the other, for better or worse. We evangelicals who train pastors, lead congregations, teach, or do scientific research can help make these challenges work for the betterment of science and Christianity. To see how this is so, let us consider some of the things going on in modern science.

What's Happening in Science

Many do not classify *mathematics* as a science since it studies ideas inside us rather than objects out in nature. Yet there is a strange correlation between mind and universe, between math and science. As Einstein once noted: "The most incomprehensible thing about the universe is that it is so comprehensible."[1]

Strange things have been happening within mathematics, too. The assured results of Euclid's geometry, which stood for over 2000 years, were challenged in the last century. Not, indeed, by claims that Euclid was mistaken; rather that his parallel lines axiom was not the only possibility.[2] Other alternatives, when developed, gave geometries of curved spaces. These turn out to have numerous applications to the real world. So do geometries of many dimensions — whether or not our universe has three, four, eleven or more dimensions itself.[3] Perhaps the universe is a kind of exhibition hall, where God has used all sorts of mathematics somewhere in its construction.

In this century, Kurt Godel proved that logical systems such as arithmetic are incomplete, astounding mathematicians and philosophers alike.[4] If such a system is logically consistent, then it is not fully demonstrable. If it is demonstrable, it cannot be proved consistent. This may be fatal to deductivist hopes that our universe itself is one great self-consistent logical system, with all its features derivable from first principles.

With the advent of computers, mathematics has become more and more experimental (mathematicians would prefer to say "numerical" or "applied"). Not that logical proof has been replaced by trial and error, but electronic calculations allow us to go far beyond anything feasible by hand. And with today's video technology, computers can display objects of higher-dimensional geometry that far surpasses the visualizing ability of our brains.[5] Thus, computers have become an exploratory tool to suggest what theorems may be worth trying to prove. Mathematics, like the sciences, is turning out to be a vast ocean, and we are just getting into its depths.

A century ago, many thought *physics* pretty well complete. The only work left was to determine more decimal places for its basic constants. But the search for these decimals soon shattered this opinion with discoveries leading to relativity and quantum mechanics.

Einstein's theories of relativity, strange as they may be, have been impressively verified.[6] His special theory has an absolute "speed limit" in the universe, approaching which an object's mass increases to infinity, its length goes to zero, and its time comes to a standstill. Measurements of time and space are relative, varying with the motion of the one making the observations.[7] His general theory of relativity restores absolute time to the universe; but locally, time and space are distorted by gravitational fields. In extreme cases, parts of the universe may nearly pinch off from the rest and become "black holes."[8]

Relativity does not extrapolate into ethics, however. The attempt to justify moral relativity from physics is unwarranted. We could equally well argue that an absolute speed limit in the universe implies moral absolutes. Opposition to modern physics by evangelicals for this reason is certainly ill-advised.

Quantum mechanics has been more troubling. It has often been represented as replacing determinism with chance as the basic reality, which certainly disagrees with the biblical worldview. But there are actually several competing interpretations of quantum phenomena,[9] and we need not opt for a random, a-causal universe.

Nevertheless, the phenomena of quantum mechanics are real, and (like relativity) they often seem to mock at common sense. The more accurately we pin down the location of an electron (say), the less definite its motion is. The better we know its motion, the less we know about where it is. In some observations, electrons behave like particles; in others, like waves. What are they, really? The famous double-slit experiment shows that we are not just talking about groups of particles which collectively behave like waves. An individual particle which passes through one slit apparently "knows" whether the other slit is open or closed![10] And when two particles, originally together, move miles apart, one of them somehow "knows" the result of a measurement on the other instantaneously, even though a signal from one to the other cannot travel faster than the speed of light![11] This last feature, however — assuming it stands up under further testing — would seem more of a problem for a mechanistic universe of local interactions than for one controlled by a God who is everywhere present.

Physicists continue to seek one unifying force behind the four basic forces currently known — gravity, electromagnetism, and the strong and weak nuclear interactions. In view of Maxwell's earlier success combining electricity and magnetism, and the recent work of Glashow, Weinberg and Salaam uniting these with the weak interaction, many hope to succeed where Einstein failed.[12] Evangelicals may feel threatened by research of this sort, since we believe God is the unifier of the cosmos. But in fact God has not told us whether he has reserved all unification to himself (so that such searches will prove futile) or whether he has mediated some unity through a created force.

Among the branches of *astronomy*, cosmology is especially interesting to evangelicals. Is the cosmos "all that is, or ever was, or ever will be,"[13] or is it just a part of what exists, and only one act in a greater drama produced and directed by the Creator?

During the so-called Enlightenment, many abandoned the biblical cosmology of an absolute beginning, but in recent years observation and theory have moved back in this direction. The static, eternal universe favored by nineteenth century atheism was replaced in this century by various dynamic models when it became apparent that the stars were running down and the universe expanding.[14] Then the discoveries of the three-degree blackbody radiation and quasars revealed that our universe was hotter and more crowded earlier than it is now, and most investigators abandoned the steady-state cosmology for some form of the big-bang theory.[15] Currently it looks like our universe began absolutely at the big-bang, in contrast to the formerly popular oscillating versions.[16] The main alternative, that the universe is just a three-dimensional bubble in an infinite, eternal universe of unbelievably high temperature and density,[17] has little evidence for it compared with biblical theism.

If the universe began at the big bang, did it just happen or was it created? Evidence that looks like design in the universe has recently been found in the "fine-tuning" which exists between its basic forces. If these forces differed ever so slightly from what they are, life of any chemical sort could not exist. The non-theistic models proposed to explain this seem rather far-fetched.[18]

In *chemistry* (aside from pressing environmental concerns), the main interest for evangelicals has been the chemistry of life. The classic experiment of Miller and Urey in 1952 showed that amino acids could be produced in an atmosphere devoid of oxygen, which seemed reasonable for the early earth. The optimism this generated for life arising spontaneously has since been dampened. There is growing evidence that the early atmosphere contained too much oxygen. Miller-Urey type experiments after 35 years still cannot produce the full set of amino acids found in life. Competing reactions would destroy intermediate molecules needed for synthesis of DNA, RNA and proteins. The simplest system which will reproduce itself is apparently far too complex to form by random processes (without the intervention of an intelligent being) even in a universe as large and old as ours is.[19]

Robert C. Newman

In the past two centuries *geology* has moved from viewing the earth as only a few thousand years to several billion years old. This shift began well before Darwin made evolution scientifically respectable. It was initially based on the discovery of miles-thick geologic formations, which seemed impossible to produce in just a few thousand years, even with the help of Noah's flood.[20] Though this theory was opposed by Kelvin because he calculated that the sun could not be so old, his objections were later overcome by the discovery of radioactivity, which led to both a mechanism for a long-lived sun and a technique for dating geologic formations.[21]

Since then, theologians have split over whether or not the Bible allows for an old earth. Among those who think not, some have rejected the idea that the Bible teaches anything scientific; others have rejected geologic dating.[22] Those who feel the Bible allows an old earth have sought to harmonize the biblical and geological data.[23]

If we take the geologic strata as trustworthy records of an old earth, the fossils reveal an early earth devoid of life. Later on, simple life appears, which remains alone for many millions of years. Then comes the "Cambrian explosion" in which nearly all the animal phyla appear rather suddenly. Later comes the successive appearance of fish, amphibians, reptiles, birds, mammals, and last of all, man.[24] This fossil succession is understood by evolutionists as the natural development of life from simple beginnings. Old-earth creationists see it as evidence for God's successive intervention to create new life forms as the environment is prepared to support each in turn. Young-earth creationists reject the idea that the geologic column is a historical sequence.

Instead, the fossil succession is seen as a result of ecological zoning and the differing ability of various animals to escape the waters of Noah's flood, though both these ideas face severe problems.[25]

The fossils also revealed that plants and animals differed from one region of the earth to another. Darwin's study of such differences among living finches and turtles on the various Galapagos Islands led him to propose his theory of evolution. Such differences also raised questions regarding a universal flood. Did God bring polar bears from the arctic, penguins from the antarctic, kangaroos from Australia and sloths from South America to the ark before the flood (since they appear in the fossil record in these places) and get them back afterward (since they are there now)? Clearly God *could have* miraculously transported them, but nothing like this is mentioned in Genesis. Young-earth creationists have sometimes tried to solve this by postulating a (problematic) rapid continental drift after the flood. Old-earth creationists and theistic evolutionists have often opted for a local or regional flood so that transportation from outside the flood zone would be unnecessary.[26]

Biology has been dominated by an evolutionary paradigm since Darwin's time. There have been ups and downs in its acceptance, and modifications such as the new synthesis and punctuated equilibrium model. Yet some have always rejected it for scientific rather than theological reasons.[27] Among scientific objections, geological investigation has continued to sharpen the gaps between major biological categories in the fossil record rather than making them disappear.[28] Attempts to model mutation and natural selection mathematically have not produced increasing organization.[29] Many biological systems do not look like they can be reached from simpler systems by a sequence of favorable, single mutations.[30] Complex organs like the eye would not form by random mutation in the time available, even though evolutionists assume sight developed several times in the history of life.[31] Nevertheless, the sequence of life-forms in the fossil record, plus a preference in the scientific community (following Hume) for any natural explanation over any supernatural one, means that science will not likely abandon evolution any time soon.[32]

With the rise of microbiology, evidence for the complexity of living things has risen dramatically,[33] putting even more pressure on the claim that life developed by unguided processes. At the same time, similarities of biochemicals across species boundaries have strengthened many in their conviction that all life developed from a single original lifeform.[34]

Before Darwin, arguments for a Designer from organization in living things was a major apologetic for Christianity. But evolution, many feel, destroyed this approach.[35] In recent years, though, the argument has been revived as the complexity of organs and biochemical systems has become more obvious.[36] Mutation and natural selection do not seem to be able to produce such order, yet our own experience shows us that a mind can do so.

Anthropology has often held center stage in the creation-evolution controversy, doubtless because of the clash between definite statements on human origins from Genesis two and various anthropologists. Interpreters of both nature and Scripture have frequently aggravated the situation by unfounded claims,[37] yet a number of troubling facts remain. Numerous fossils seem to be anatomically intermediate between human and ape.[38] The biochemistry of modern man is closer to that of the apes than to the other animals, and (in some cases) is virtually the same for chimp and man.[39] On the other hand, the mental difference between man and ape is vast, even though apes are apparently the most "intelligent" of nonhuman animals.[40] Can unguided evolution really explain the origin of the human mind, or even the origin of animal brains?

With this brief summary, we see that modern science has made a number of discoveries which challenge evangelicals. It has also made others which challenge the "methodological atheism" of the scientific community.

Evangelical Responses to Modern Science

Bible believers have reacted to these challenges in various ways. Three broad approaches have developed to questions regarding the age of the earth and evolution: young-earth creation, old-earth creation, and theistic evolution. Each of these includes some diversity, but can be roughly described as follows.

Young-earth creationists believe the universe, earth and mankind were created just a few thousand years ago. Living things were created more or less instantaneously and have changed very little since then. Scientists are thus fundamentally wrong in believing in an old earth or in evolution. The Genesis account is our basic source of information on origins, and all scientific data are to be interpreted in agreement with the simplest reading of Scripture. Typically, Noah's flood is seen as the source of most geologic strata.[41] A few young-earth creationists reject quantum mechanics and relativity.[42] Some of these, claiming science went astray in the sixteenth century with Copernicus, even reject a sun-centered solar system.[43]

Old-earth creationists, believing that scientists are properly interpreting substantial evidence here, accept a universe and earth some billions of years old.[44] They also believe that mutation and natural selection account for small-scale changes (microevolution) in plant and animal life, thus allowing organisms to adapt in a limited way to changes in climate and environment, but producing no new organs or systems.[45] They part company with evolutionists by noting that the fossil record gives no evidence of gradual transitions between the larger divisions of the biological classification, thus rejecting macroevolution. They interpret the Genesis account and scientific data so as to harmonize, often taking the days of Genesis to be long periods of time.[46] Some hold to a geographically universal flood, others to a regional flood. They see mankind as a special creation of God, some seeing our creation hundreds of thousands of years back, others making it much more recent.[47]

Theistic evolutionists accept the main lines of modern scientific thought on origins, but reject any non-theistic implications.[48] All life is typically viewed as developing from one initial life form, perhaps created by God's intervention, perhaps by his providential guidance.[49] The development of various forms from this original life was also providentially guided. There is some divergence on human origins. Most commonly, a whole population of apes is thought to have evolved into humanity, with no original pair having ever existed.[50] Some, however, believe God breathed into an ape to provide him with a soul, thus producing Adam, the first man. From his side comes Eve, as Genesis 2 says.

In this scheme, there was an original pair, and mankind's fall into sin was a specific historical event.[51]

Unfortunately, then, evangelicals have not found as much common ground as we would like for a unified response to modern science. Yet all can agree that God is Creator, that unguided evolution will not work, that man has a special place of responsibility over God's creation, that the universe really doesn't make sense without God, and that it is crucial for people to recognize this. These are basic and central matters which should not be overlooked in the midst of our intramural disputes.

However, there is no agreement on a detailed alternative model to unguided evolution. Young-earth and old-earth creationists agree that macroevolution is mistaken, and are often united on what its problems are. Old-earth creationists and theistic evolutionists agree that the earth is old, and generally see similar problems with young-earth creationism.

Young-earth creationists and many theistic evolutionists agree that the Bible taken literally does not fit with the modern scientific consensus and generally feel that harmonization is not the right strategy.

We should not be surprised to find such disagreement. After all, evangelicals are not united in a number of areas of biblical interpretation—baptism, church government, eschatology, miraculous gifts today — so why should we expect better agreement when it comes to the interpretation and harmonization of Bible and science? Yet in spite of this we should not give up but should continue to seek solutions in all these areas. In what follows, I give some suggestions as an old-earth creationist for making progress in relating Bible and science.

Robert C. Newman

Science as Exegesis

We are discussing what is commonly called the relation of "Bible and science." In spite of popular use, this pairing of terms is not ideal. Science is basically a method; the Bible basically data. The pair "science and religion" is even worse; religion is such a generic term that almost nothing can be said that is true of all religions. For instance, is atheism a religion? Some better pairs are "Bible and nature" (both data), "theoretical science and theology" (both theorizing from the data), "experimental science and exegesis" (both observing and trying to understand the data). Perhaps religion — like engineering — is application. In any case, consider the parallels between science and exegesis, which seem to be especially fruitful.

From a biblical perspective, it makes sense to view science as the interpretation of God's general (or natural) revelation, just as exegesis is the interpretation of God's special revelation in the Bible. For an evangelical, both nature and Scripture are inerrant sources of information from God. Both have fallible human interpreters. Exegetes (ideally) study the Bible to see what is there, rather than to defend their own theology or denominational tradition. Scientists (also ideally) study nature to see what is there, rather than to defend their own pet theories or the *status quo* in their field. Both disciplines favor a priority of data over theory. Both use beauty, simplicity, cogency, and correspondence with established theories as aids to their own theorizing.

Of course, there are differences. As evangelicals we believe that we have all of the Bible now — a written text of finite length — though we would not claim it contains all there is to know about our infinite God. Nature, on the other hand, though presumably finite, is continually opening up new pages of its text to our view as we build new devices which look further or probe deeper. In addition, the Bible is already given in human languages; nature is not.

If we as evangelicals feel warranted in harmonizing biblical passages which we believe refer to the same historical event, should we not also harmonize the data of nature and Scripture on the origins of the universe, life and ourselves? If we accept Matthew's account that there were two demoniacs whose deliverance caused a herd of pigs to stampede into the Sea of Galilee, though Mark and Luke mention only one demoniac; if we accept Matthew's account of the flight of Mary, Joseph and Jesus into Egypt, though nothing is said about this in Luke; then we should not be surprised that nature may give us information about which Scripture is silent and vice versa.

Many scientists, of course, don't think they are exegeting God's revelation in nature when they do science, but that doesn't mean they aren't. After all, many liberal theologians don't think they are exegeting God's revelation when they interpret the Bible; but if biblical Christianity is true, that is what they are doing all the same. Surely any activity which ignores God is going to be defective in important ways. If science as practiced by secularists has no concern for the universe as a natural revelation, it is up to us as evangelicals trained in science to try to fill this gap.

The Relative Merits of Various Evangelical Options

The three options listed earlier as evangelical responses to modern science seem to differ substantially in how they handle data from nature and Scripture. Young-earth creationists try to

Robert C. Newman

construct the simplest model of origins possible using only the biblical data. The scientific data are then interpreted to conform with this model, whether or not this is a straightforward way to understand them. The idea of creation with apparent age is frequently employed to handle difficulties.

At the other end of the spectrum, theistic evolutionists construct the simplest model of origins from the scientific data, and then interpret the biblical material to conform. For evangelicals this may result in reading Genesis two and three as parabolic or allegorical, and in denying that Genesis one was intended to answer any scientific questions about how God worked.

Old-earth creationists, by contrast, use the data from both nature and Scripture in devising their original models; they seek a construct that does justice to both. Naturally, these models will be more complex than the minimum necessary to fit either set of data alone, but this does not mean we should force a harmonization.

Some evangelicals have noted that science often functions differently in dealing with present-day phenomena than it does when investigating origins. Geisler has distinguished between "origins-science" and "operations-science."[52] From a different perspective, Van Till has suggested a distinction between "formative history," those features of origins which science can investigate, and "ultimate origins," those which transcend science.[53] Both of these suggestions have some merit. Apparently two factors are at work. One is our closeness to the data; the other is the question of immanence vs. transcendence, or providence vs. miracle.

The extent to which we have a "hands-on" relation with particular scientific data forms a continuum. Some phenomena are accessible to the laboratory and repeatable almost at will. Other phenomena cannot be brought into the laboratory. Of these latter, some are beyond our control but repeat at frequent intervals (e.g., periodic phenomena on the sun). Other phenomena repeat at rare intervals beyond our life span (e.g., the life cycle of a star). Some phenomena occur only once in the history of our universe (e.g., the big-bang). Clearly, the reliability of our theorizing decreases as the phenomena are less under our control and less frequently repeated.[54]

God's activity in our world has traditionally been divided into providence and miracle. Evangelicals agree that both occur, though Howard Van Till would apparently like to limit miracle to redemption.[55] Evangelicals disagree on the amount and location of miracle involved — young-earth creationists postulating the most intervention and theistic evolutionists the least.

Theistic evolutionists have sometimes charged young-earth and old-earth creationists with appealing to a "God of the gaps" in postulating divine intervention at one point or another in creation.[56] Granted. Creationists, however, have usually appealed to gaps in the fossil record or in scientific mechanisms as warrant for such suggestions. We should remember, however, that evolutionists, theistic or not, also employ a "god of the gaps" — natural law — which is plugged in even when there seems to be real discontinuity in fossil record or mechanism!

Lastly, a complaint against both young-earth creationists and theistic evolutionists: both resort to fictitious history in their treatment of origins. Young-earth creationists admit using "ap-

Robert C. Newman

pearance of age" to explain scientific phenomena which otherwise suggest an old earth or universe. But since the light from stars, galaxies and quasars tells us something of what was happening on those objects when the light left them, so light from objects more than a few thousand light years away must be, in their view, telling us what would have been happening there if the objects had existed then (which they didn't) — fictitious history. Those theistic evolutionists who deny a real Adam interpret Genesis two and three as parabolic or allegorical — the accounts look historical but they aren't. Again, fictitious history. One sees fictitious history in nature, the other in Scripture. It would be much better, if possible, to handle the data without invoking the concept of fictitious history.

This is not to say that the old-earth creation viewpoint has solved all the problems of relating biblical and scientific data. Further investigation and reflection are certainly needed in this area, and input from young-earth creationists and theistic evolutionists should continue to be helpful.

Conclusions

Evangelicals have been challenged in numerous areas by science. We should not fear that real discoveries will overthrow biblical Christianity, nor should we treat science as an enemy. Instead we should realize that science is in the process of studying general revelation. God will continue to reveal himself to scientists as long as they do not overextend their methodology so as to rule out God or refuse to consider the possibility that he has intervened miraculously into nature.

416

We as evangelicals need to continue working on harmonizing God's revelation in his Word and his world. We should not be satisfied with superficial answers or forced exegesis. We should remember that at any given time, we may not have sufficient information to solve a particular problem or construct a proper harmonization. Therefore, we must carefully scrutinize each new page of general revelation as it comes to light and consider how it may influence our proposed syntheses.

Modern science has also been challenged in numerous areas, not so much by evangelicals as by our God in his general revelation. We as evangelicals need to cooperate with God in helping non-believing scientists (and others) to see these things and to turn to Jesus as their redeemer. We need to be cautious yet faithful in our handling of scientific data, lest we put unnecessary stumbling blocks before others that would hinder their coming to God.[57]

[1]Cited without reference in Carl Sagan, *The Dragons of Eden* (New York: Random House, 1977), 233; a similar statement occurs in Albert Einstein, *Ideas and Opinions* (New York: Crown, 1982), 292: "The eternal mystery of the world is its comprehensibility."

[2]P. LeCorbeiller, "The Curvature of Space," *Scientific American* (November, 1954), 80-86; Rene Taton, ed., *Science in the Nineteenth Century* (New York: Basic Books, 1965), 25-28.

[3]Heinz R. Pagels, *Perfect Symmetry* (New York: Simon and Schuster, 1985), 310-15.

[4]Ernest Nagel and James R. Newman, *Godel's Proof* (New York: University Press, 1958); Douglas R. Hofstadter, *Godel. Escher. Bach* (New York: Basic Books, 1979).

[5]Ivars Peterson, "Twists of Space," *Science News* 132 (October 24, 1987), 264-66.

Robert C. Newman

[6]Clifford M. Will, *Was Einstein Right? Putting General Relativity to the Test* (New York: Basic Books, 1986); Hugh Ross, *Cosmology Confronts the Creator* (Pasadena: Reasons to Believe,1987), 11-13.

[7]A. Shadowitz, *Special Relativity* (Philadelphia: Saunders, 1969); Martin Gardner, *Relativity for the Millions* (New York: Macmillan, 1962).

[8]Ronald S. Adler, "Relativity, Special Theory" in *McGraw-Hill Encyclopedia of Physics* (1983); William J. Kaufmann, III, *Relativity and Cosmology*, 2nd ed. (New York: Harper and Row, 1977).

[9]Paul Davies and J. Brown, eds., *The Ghost in the Atom: A Discussion of the Mysteries of Quantum Physics* (New York: Cambridge, 1986), 31-39; Nick Herbert, *Quantum Reality* (New York: Doubleday, 1985), 16-29, 41-53.

[10]Davies and Brown, *Ghost in the Atom*, 8-11; Herbert, *Quantum Reality*, 65-66.

[11]Herbert, *Quantum Reality*, 211-31; Davies and Brown, *Ghost in the Atom*, 11-19.

[12]Paul Davies, *Superforce: The Search for a Grand Unified Theory of Nature* (New York: Simon and Schuster, 1984).

[13]Carl Sagan, *Cosmos* (New York: Random House, 1980), 4. For evangelical responses, see Robert C. Newman, "A Critique of Carl Sagan's TV Series and Book 'Cosmos'," *IBRI Research Report* 19 (Hatfield, PA: IBRI, 1984); John Wiester, "Carl Sagan's 'Cosmos'," *Christians in Education* 2, nos. 1 and 2 (1985); R. C. Sproul, *Tabletalk* 12, no. 4 (August, 1988); Howard J. Van Till, "Sagan's Cosmos: Science Education or Religious Theatre?" in Howard J. Van Till, Davis A. Young and Clarence Menninga, *Science Held Hostage: What's Wrong with Creation Science And Evolutionism* (Downers Grove, IL: InterVarsity, 1988), 155-68.

[14]Elske V. P. Smith and Kenneth C. Jacobs, *Introductory Astronomy and Astrophysics* (Philadelphia: Saunders, 1973), 509-10.

[15]Robert Jastrow and Malcolm H. Thompson, *Astronomy: Fundamentals and Frontiers*, 3rd ed. (New York: Wiley, 1977), 265-76; Lawrence W. Frederick and Robert H. Baker, *An Introduction to Astronomy*, 9th ed. (New York: Van Nostrand, 1981), 452-57.

[16]Frederick and Baker, *Astronomy*, 457-59; Jastrow and Thompson, *Astronomy*, 276-81; Ross, *Cosomology*, 18-19.

[17]D. E. Thomsen, "Cosmic Cauldron Bubbles Up Universe," *Science News* 121 (1982), 116; M. Mitchell Waldrop, "Bubbles Upon the River of Time," *Science* 215 (1982), 1082-83.

[18]P. C. W. Davies, *Accidental Universe* (Cambridge: University Press, 1982); John D. Barrow and Frank J. Tipler, *The Anthropic Cosmological Principle* (New York: Oxford, 1986); for evangelical treatments, see Ross, *Cosmology*; Alan Hayward, *God Is* (Nashville: Nelson, 1980); Robert C. Newman, "A Designed Universe" (Hatfield, PA: IBRI, 1988);

Evangelicals and Modern Science

John Jefferson Davis, "The Design Argument, Cosmic 'Fine Tuning,' and the Anthropic Principle" (So. Hamilton, MA: Gordon-Conwell, 1986).

[19]Charles B. Thaxton, Walter L. Bradley and Roger L. Olsen, *The Mystery of Life's Origin: Reassessing Current Theories* (New York: Philosophical Library, 1984); Robert Shapiro, *Origins: A Skeptic's Guide to the Creation of Life on Earth* (New York: Summit, 1986); Robert C. Newman, "Self-Replicating Automata and the Origin of Life," *Perspectives on Science and Christian Faith* 40 (1988), 24-31.

[20]Davis A. Young, *Christianity and the Age of the Earth* (Grand Rapids: Zondervan, 1982); Charles Coulston Gillispie, *Genesis and Geology* (New York: Harper and Row, 1959).

[21]Taton, *Science in the Nineteenth Century*, 333; Don L. Eicher, *Geologic Time* (Englewood Cliffs, NJ: Prentice-Hall, 1968), 16-18.

[22]Bruce Vawter, "Creationism: Creative Misuse of the Bible" in *Is God a Creationist?* ed. Roland Mushat Frye (New York: Scribners, 1983), 72-77; Langdon Gilkey, *Maker of Heaven and Earth* (Garden City: Doubleday Anchor, 1965), 25-26; Henry Morris, *Biblical Cosmology and Modern Science* (Grand Rapids: Baker, 1970); Paul M. Steidl, *The Earth the Stars and the Bible* (Phillipsburg, NJ: Presbyterian and Reformed, 1979); John C. Whitcomb, Jr., *The Early Earth* (Grand Rapids: Baker, 1972).

[23]Alan Hayward, *Creation and Evolution: The Facts and the Fallacies* (London: Triangle, 1985); Robert C. Newman and Herman J. Eckelmann, Jr., *Genesis One and the Origin of the Earth*, 2nd ed. (Grand Rapids: Baker, 1981); Pattle P. T. Pun, *Evolution: Nature and Scripture in Conflict?* (Grand Rapids: Zondervan, 1982); Young, *Christianity and the Age of the Earth*.

[24]Steven M. Stanley, *The New Evolutionary Timetable* (New York: Basic Books, 1981).

[25]Henry M. Morris and John C. Whitcomb, Jr., *The Genesis Flood* (Philadelphia: Presbyterian and Reformed, 1961), 270-81. But see Hayward, *Creation and Evolution*, 131-34; Daniel E. Wonderly, *Neglect of Geologic Data* (Hatfield, PA: IBRI, 1987), 59-70.

[26]Frederick A. Filby, *The Flood Reconsidered* (Grand Rapids: Zondervan, 1971).

[27]See W. R. Thompson's introduction to the Everyman ed. of Darwin's *Origin of Species* (New York: Dutton, 1956), reprinted in *Journal of the American Scientific Affiliation* 12 (1960), 2-9; Gordon Rattray Taylor, *The Great Evolution Mystery* (New York: Harper and Row, 1983), 4-12.

[28]George Gaylord Simpson, *Tempo and Mode in Evolution* (New York: Columbia University, 1984 reprint of 1944 ed.), 105-24; Michael Denton, *Evolution. a Theory in Crisis* (Bethesda, MD: Adler and Adler, 1986), ch 8.

[29]M. Kaplan, ed., *Mathematical Challenges to the Neo-Darwinian Interpretation of Evolution* (Philadelphia: Wistar Institute, 1967).

Robert C. Newman

[30]Denton, *Theory in Crisis*, ch 9; Taylor, *Great Evolution Mystery*, 5.

[31]Murray Eden, "The Inadequacy of Neo-Darwinian Evolution as a Scientific Theory" in Kaplan, *Mathematical Challenges*; Michael Pitman, *Adam and Evolution* (London: Rider, 1984), 218.

[32]David Hume, *Concerning Human Understanding*, section X; see Van Till's comments on the methodological atheism of science in *Science Held Hostage*, 133, 135, 139, 143, 147.

[33]Carl Sagan, "Life" in *Encyclopaedia Brittanica* (1970), 13:1083B; Renato Dulbecco, *The Design of Life* (New Haven: Yale, 1987); Maya Pines, *Inside the Cell* (Washington, DC: Dept of Health, Education and Welfare, 1978).

[34]Richard Dawkins, *The Blind Watchmaker* (New York: Norton, 1986), ch 10; Pamela K. Mulligan, "Proteins, Evolution of," *McGraw-Hill Encyclopedia of Science and Technology* (1987), 14:412-17.; Emilie Zuckerandl, "The Evolution of Haemoglobin," *Scientific American* 213 (1965), 1012-20; Francisco J. Alaya, ed. *Molecular Evolution* (Sunderland, MA: Sinauer, 1976). See Denton, *Theory in Crisis,* ch. 12 for a typological perspective.

[35]Bertrand Russell, *Why I Am Not a Christian* (New York: Simon and Schuster, 1957), 9-10; Dawkins, *Blind Watchmaker*, ch 1; Barrow and Tipler, *Anthropic Cosmological Principle*, 83-87.

[36]Denton, *Theory in Crisis*, 26-29, 214-27; Hayward, *Creation and Evolution*, ch 4; Robert Gange, *Origins and Destiny* (Waco, TX: Word, 1986), 33-40, 105-09.

[37]Pitman, *Adam and Evolution*, 91-94; Roger Lewin, *Bones of Contention* (New York: Simon and Schuster, 1987), 54-55, 60-75; Glen J. Kuban, "The Taylor Site 'Man Tracks,'" *Origins Research* 9:1 (1986), 1; Committee for Integrity in Science Education, *Teaching Science in a Climate of Controversy* (Ipswich, MA: American Scientific Affiliation, 1986), 18-21.

[38]W. E. LeGros Clark, *Antecedents of Man* (New York: Harper and Row, 1963); Henri Blocher, *In the Beginning* (Downers Grove, IL: InterVarsity, 1984), 229-30; but see also John Wiester, *The Genesis Connection* (Nashville: Nelson, 1983), 158-90.

[39]Eldon J. Gardner, *Principles of Genetics,* 4th ed. (New York: Wiley, 1972), 305-08. But blood transfusions and organ transplants have not worked well.

[40]Pitman, *Adam and Evolution*, 240-46; Gange, *Origins and Destiny*, 104, 121-36.

[41]Morris and Whitcomb, *Genesis Flood*; Whitcomb, *Early Earth*.

[42]Thomas G. Barnes, *Physics of the Future* (El Cajon, CA: Institute for Creation Research, 1983). See also articles by Barnes, Akridge, Slusher and Bouw in the *Creation Research Society Quarterly*.

[43]W. van der Kamp, "The Heart of the Matter" (Burnaby, BC: the author, 1967). See also the *Bulletin of the Tychonian Society*, 4527 Wetzel Ave., Cleveland, OH 44109.

[44]Davis A. Young, *Creation and the Flood* (Grand Rapids: Baker, 1977); Young, *Christianity and the Age of the Earth*; Daniel E. Wonderly, *God's Time Records in Ancient Sediments* (Flint, MI: Crystal Press, 1977); Wonderly, *Neglect of Geologic Data*; Newman and Eckelmann, *Genesis One*; Hayward, *Creation and Evolution*, chs 5-9.

[45]Except as could plausibly have arisen from random mutations. See, e.g., Pun, *Evolution*, 191-230.

[46]Ibid., 251-71; Newman and Eckelmann, *Genesis One*, 67-88.

[47]Wiester, *Genesis Connection*, 187-90; Robert Brow, "The Late-Date Genesis Man," *Christianity Today* 16 (1972), 1128-1129; William J. Kornfield, "The Early-Date Genesis Man," *Christianity Today*, 17 (1973), 931-34.

[48]F. Donald Eckelmann, "Geology," in *The Encounter Between Christianity and Science*, ed. Richard H. Bube (Grand Rapids: Eerdmans, 1968), 135-70; Walter R. Hearn, "Biological Science," in Ibid., 199-223; Howard J. Van Till, *The Fourth Day* (Grand Rapids: Eerdmans, 1986), 188, 227-31, 264-65.

[49]Richard H. Bube, "Creation (B): Understanding Creation and Evolution," *Journal of the American Scientific Affiliation* 32 (1980), 177.

[50]Richard H. Bube, "Biblical Evolutionism?" *Journal of the American Scientific Affiliation* 23 (1971), 140-44.

[51]David L. Dye, *Faith and the Physical World* (Grand Rapids: Eerdmans, 1966), 136-50; James M. Houston, "The Origin of Man," *Journal of the American Scientific Affiliation* 34 (1982), 1-5.

[52]Norman L. Geisler and J. Kerby Anderson, *Origins Science* (Grand Rapids: Baker, 1987).

[53]Van Till et al, *Science Held Hostage*, 15-25.

[54]Fortunately, marks of frequently repeated phenomena indicating an old earth are abundant in the earth's crust. Large areas of North America are covered by fossil-bearing sedimentary sequences, often with a thickness of several miles. Many of the layer units in these sedimentary columns are rock-types which cannot form rapidly, but require thousands of years to make even 50 feet of thickness. A large percentage of limestones and shales fall into this category. Limestone layers deep in U.S. and Canadian oil fields sometimes include large surfaces showing extensive erosion features, even potholes and steep-walled canyons, which indicate the surface had hardened into rock *before* additional thousands of feet of rock were formed on top of them. These buried surfaces often include fossil sea-shells, which were first securely cemented into the rock surface and then partially worn off by erosion before their final burial took place. Other limestone deposits frequently contain organically formed structures, such as algal mats and coral reefs, which still show the growth patterns of the organisms which produced them, usually with recognizable fossils

Robert C. Newman

of these organisms, some in their normal growth positions, others moved downslope by wave action or sediment flow before final burial took place. See Wonderly, *Neglect of Geologic Data* for abundant documentation of this.

[55]Van Till, *Fourth Day*, 224-27.

[56]Richard H. Bube, "The Failure of the God-of-the-Gaps," in *Horizons of Science*, ed. Carl F. H. Henry (New York: Harper and Row, 1978), 21-35.

[57]My thanks to IBRI colleagues John Bloom, David Bossard, Bob Dunzweiler, Perry Phillips, John Studenroth and Dan Wonderly for helpful discussions.

FIRST RESPONSE
TO ROBERT C. NEWMAN

Pattle P.T. Pun

An Outline

To delineate the theological system of Progressive Creationism, I have developed five theological themes. First, as pointed out by Calvin, God's general revelation through nature (a valid though incomplete avenue of knowing God) complements God's special revelation through Scripture. Secondly, in contrast to Deism's notion of an absentee Creator, the Christian Theism propounded by Calvin sees God both as Creator and as immanent Governor and Preserver, upholding the world by his providential control. Thirdly, a proper methodology in Biblical hermeneutics must be both historical and theological, embracing both testaments. Fourthly, physical death evidently existed before man's Fall, since man's dominion in the created world implies his control of the reproductive pattern of non-human life forms, and the presence of the food chain necessitates the physical death of the things eaten. If God utilized death to maintain life, he could have employed natural selection (among other processes) to bring forth the varieties of life forms in his creation. Fifthly, the creation was good, and it was the Fall which brought about the defective functioning of the food chain and the removal of God's special sustenance which previously kept man immortal. Besides physical death, evil also entered the human race so that mankind and the creation needed to be reconciled to God through the Incarnation and Atonement of Christ.

Pattle P.T. Pun

On examination, current conservative positions on the issues of creation and evolution all have strengths and weaknesses. While "literal" in its interpretation of Genesis, Recent Creationism belittles the vast amount of scientific evidence for natural selection and the antiquity of the earth. It also has deistic implications in maintaining the relative fixity of biological varieties. Though theistic evolutionists have a more holistic outlook regarding God's immanence in nature, their figurative interpretation of the creation account in Genesis denies its historicity and has difficulties in explaining the origin of sin and evil, whether they postulate the conscious rebellion of two uniquely evolving hominids or suggest that a spiritual fall antedated the creation. Finally, while affirming the existential realities of evil and the need for Christ's redemption, theistic evolutionists also drive a wedge between spiritual truths and historical truths of the Bible, contrary to the unity of God's revelation.

If Theistic Evolutionism and Recent Creationism are on the left and the right wing of the evangelical spectrum respectively, Progressive Creationism strives to be in the middle by utilizing the strengths of these positions and avoiding their weaknesses.

A definition of Progressive Creationism:

> "In Genesis one, the pattern is development from vacancy to the finished creation at the end of the sixth day. In manufacturing, the pattern is from raw materials to finished products. In art the pattern is from unformed materials to artistic creation. In life the pattern is from the undifferentiated ovum to the adult. In character the pattern is from random and uncritical behaviour to disciplined and moral behaviour."[1]

Dr. Newman has focused our attention on the apparent conflict between modern science and the evangelical faith. The debate on creation/evolution between theologians and scientists has led to a polarization between those who cherish the literal interpretation of the Scripture at the expense of the validity of scientific explanation and others who accept the evolutionary paradigm without seriously examining its implication for the foundation of the Christian doctrine of original sin. It has been recognized that microevolution is well documented scientifically while macroevolution remains speculative.[2] I now attempt to present a theological system that utilizes the strengths and avoids the weaknesses of these positions in the debate in a perspective known as Progressive Creationism. Dr. Newman's "Old-Earth Creationism" in many ways is similar to this position. I will define Progressive Creationism through the development of five theological themes, given below:

Unity of God's Revelation in Nature and in Scripture

John Calvin's monumental treatise on the *Institutes of the Christian Religion* was based on the two-fold revelation of God: The knowledge of God the Creator and the knowledge of God the Redeemer.[3] For him, God's general revelation through nature and God's special revelation through Scripture are complementary and necessary for men to have a saving knowledge of the Creator and the Redeemer. However, Calvin does not espouse a natural theology that holds that man can come to know God through general revelation apart from special revelation. He stresses the importance of Scripture as a guide and teacher for anyone who would come to God the Creator. But Calvin has definitely de-

425

parted from the medieval mindset which condemns science, and according to which the church views science to be contrary to the Scripture, as exemplified by the Copernican controversy over heliocentricity. Calvin never suggests that we should interpret God's creation from the Scripture alone. He shows great respect for the natural scientists who, by their close observation of nature, can bring us better understanding of God the Creator. In other words, Calvin maintains that general revelation of God through nature is a valid though incomplete avenue of knowing him. Because of man's depravity, he fails to know and worship God the Creator. With the aid of the Holy Spirit, Scripture reveals to man the knowledge of God the Creator more intimately and vividly.

Immanence of God
in His Providential Control over His creation

Calvin also has a holistic view of God's involvement in His creation, whereas popular deism glorifies reason instead of revelation. Calvin has presented to us a worldview that is most consistent with God's revelation.[4] It is based on the assumption that the world and the universe were created by the Creator who sustains them by providence. The creation exists moment by moment only by the direct sustenance of God the Creator. Both the creation and the Creator are part of an external reality rather than an illusion in the mind of man. The deistic implication of Recent Creationism suggests that God's involvement with his creation consists only of miraculous intervention. However, in the context of the Scripture there is no distinction between supernatural or natural if we see his sustaining power in all things. A miracle is an extraordinary event which is accomplished by God as a sign of some purpose of his own. God is equally involved in his providential control in allowing the probabilities determined by natural processes to work for His purposes.

Scripture in General and Genesis in particular:
A Historical-Theological Interpretation

Calvin emphasizes the importance of learning from both the Old Testament and the New Testament in concert. God unfolds more and more concerning himself and his will for humanity in the course of Biblical history. The theological center of the Old Testament as revealed in the New Testament is the testimony of Christ, the Messiah (John 5:39). Therefore, a unifying concept has to be constructed in the context of both the Old and the New Testaments since the two Testaments are mutually interpretive. The methodology in Biblical hermeneutics must be a historical-theological one. Hasel summarizes this method succinctly:

> ...the Biblical theologian ... must claim as his task both to discover and describe what the text meant and also to explicate what it means for today.[5]

The unifying principle throughout the Old Testament seems to be the self-revelation of God through the nation of Israel. The book of Genesis by definition is the book of beginning. It centers on the beginning of the chosen nation of Israel through whom God is to reveal himself to the world. Genesis traces the origin of man's rebellion from God and how God chose Abraham through whom the people of the earth will be blessed. The rest of the book is devoted to the preparation of Israel, tracing her history through the lives of the patriarchs. God's sovereignty in the midst of the rebellion of man is stressed throughout the book.

Pattle P.T. Pun

Natural Selection as One of the Processes
Utilized by God in His Creative Activities

Fred Van Dyke questions the validity of viewing natural selection, which depends on resource scarcity, competition, differential survival and reproduction, as a creative mechanism employed by a benevolent God before the fall of man.[6] Before attempting to address this charge, one has to clarify several factors, discussed below:

1. One has to question the extent to which we can impose human emotion or volition onto the non-human world. When Paul mentions the creation groaning in travail, awaiting its deliverance from the bondage to decay when the sons of God are revealed (Rom.8:19-22), he apparently is using metaphoric language to describe the solidarity of man with the creation. The redemption of the natural world from evil and decay is a corollary of the redemption of the body of man which has been condemned as a result of sin. Paul does not mean to teach that the non-human world has a will of its own which can turn back to God by faith in order to be saved (Eph.2:8). Scientific studies on the volition of animals are inconclusive.

2. Adam and Eve were admonished to multiply and subdue the earth, and have dominion over the animal world before the Fall(Gen. 1:28). This command seems to involve man's control over the reproduction of other creatures and their utilization of the natural resources. Death is probably one of the ways to control population growth. In addition, the word "subdue" seems to mean more than to reign over. It seems to mean "conquer and subject." The same word is used in contexts of conquest in the face of opposition (i.e. Zech. 9:15; Josh. 18:1; II Sam. 8:11 etc.). It seems

428

that some principle was already at work in the earth to which man was introduced in order to conquer it for God. The Bible is silent about the source of this principle. It may have been "Satan" in the form of the serpent which is assumed in Gen.3. However, God's sovereignty seems to have overruled this principle since the creation was *good* (Gen. 1:31).

3. Man is described in one of his original relationships to the rest of creation as being an eater. Other life forms are also introduced as part of a food chain (Gen. 1:29-30,NIV). It seems that there is no compelling reason to justify the claim that animal killing is permitted only after the Fall. Genesis does not provide a theological ground to differentiate between the *nature* of vegetarian and animal life. Biologically, the modern understanding of the cell theory and the genetic basis of life has unified the living world. Moreover, the fossil record of life seems to suggest the presence of carnivorosity long before man's appearance. Therefore, it seems necessary to postulate the existence of physical death in the non-human world to account for the food chain before the human fall.

The understanding of these presuppositions seems to lead to the conclusion that physical death was present in the creation before the Fall. Since God utilized death to maintain life, natural selection, which is based on differential fecundity and mortality, could very possibly be one of the processes God employs to bring forth the varieties in the living world.

Creation was Good:
The Incarnation was Necessitated by the Fall of Man

The creation was good(Gen.1:31). The creation is not the result of the the fall. "The heavens declare the glory of God; the skies declare the work of His hands" (Psalm 19:1), and "His name is majestic in all the world" (Psalm 8:9).

Calvin addresses the problem of the necessity of the Incarnation.[7] God's decrees of the fall and Incarnation run together. Christ would not have had to be incarnated if Adam had not sinned, for Christ was the second Adam (I Cor.15:47; Rom.5:12-21). He was made like man in all respects except sin (Heb.4:15). He was reckoned as a descendant of Adam (Luke 3:38).

God's eternal purpose is to predestine us to be adopted as his sons through Jesus Christ before the creation of the world (Eph.1:4-5). All things were created by the pre-existent Christ and for him. But the necessity of Christ's Incarnation hinges on the fall of man.

As a result of human sin, the ground was cursed (Gen.3:17). The creature is subject to frustration (Rom.8:20). Man's immortality was apparently maintained before the Fall by a special sustenance of God, perhaps through the Tree of Life. As a result of man's sin, God's special sustenance was removed (Gen.3:24). Death and evil entered the human race. Mankind and the creation need to be reconciled to God through the Incarnation and Atonement of Christ (Col.1:20). However, man is to be made a new creation in Christ (II Cor.5:17), not to be restored to his pre-Fall status. Therefore, the Scriptural references such as Is.11:6 and 65:25, which abolish predation, seem to be referring to the millennial kingdom or the new heaven and the new earth and cannot be used to refer to the original creation.

Evaluation of Conservative Positions
on the Issues of Creation and Evolution

1. Fiat Creationism (or Recent Creationism)

This is the most widely published of the creationist viewpoint and has become synonymous with creationism in the popular mind. It emphasizes the "literal" interpretation of Genesis. It was the Creationists who alerted the American public to the dogmatic claim by some scientists that evolution is a fact and who went to court in Arkansas, California, Louisiana, and Texas to require the teaching of Creation science along with evolution in the public schools.[8]

However, the Recent Creationist position has two serious flaws. First, a vast amount of scientific evidence has been amassed to support the theory of natural selection and the antiquity of the earth, which they have denied and ridiculed.[9] Secondly, much creationist writing has "deistic" implications. The stipulation that the varieties we see today in the biological world were present in the initial creation[10] implies that the Creator is no longer involved in his creation in a dynamic way. The creation is seen as having been left to its own devices for the expression of the variability potentially endowed to it at the beginning. This deistic implication is contrary to Heb.1:3, which stipulates that all things are upheld by the word of his power.

2. Theistic Evolutionism

Theistic Evolutionists accept the historicity of the Bible, but some allegorize the Genesis account in order to treat the whole creation account as a "poetic" representation of spiritual truths of

431

the human's dependence on God their Creator and their fall from God's grace by the symbolic act of disobedience. They accept the processes of organic evolution as the ways God used to create humans. They see God's providential hand behind the process of natural selection. Seen in this light, the theistic evolutionists maintain a more holistic theological position concerning God's providence than do the Recent Creationists who have to posit a repetitive divine intervention in cataclysmic proportions.

However, theistic evolutionists have to deal with two theological obstacles:

First are the exegetical problems in the Genesis account of creation. There seem to be eleven historical narratives in the first thirty-seven chapters of Genesis, each delimited by the phrase "these are the names [generations, descendants] of . . . " (Gen. 2:4; 5:1; 6:9; 10:1; 11:10; 11:27; 25:12; 25:19; 36:1; 36:9; 37:2). The contents are linked together to form a roughly chronological account of primieval and patriarchal life.[11] Since few would doubt the historicity of the patriarchs of Israel, it seems unwarranted to assume the creation account as allegorical while the rest of these narratives are historical. The New Testament also regards certain events mentioned in Genesis 1 as actually having transpired (e.g. Mark 10:6, I Cor.11:8,9). Calvin also suggests that the historical account of the six-day creation shows God's goodness towards man in lavishly preparing the world for the habitation of man, the climax of God's creation.[12]

The assumption that Genesis 1 represents a "wide-angle" perspective of God's creative activities and Genesis 2 gives these activities a "close-up" examination may help in our understanding of the creation account. The seemingly conflicting chronological sequences of the creation of plants, animals and man may be resolved by assuming an overlapping[13] of the creative eras in which some of the creative activities may have been contemporaneous or, at least, overlapping. Gen. 2:1-5 may indicate the lack of a farmer to cultivate the field instead of the chronology of the Creation of plants. Gen.2:19 can be interpreted to mean that animals were created *before* Adam so that they can be brought to him for naming. Therefore, the conflicts in the chronology of creation in Genesis 1 and 2 may be more apparent than real.

In addition, the Hebrew word nephesh translated as living soul(Gen.2:7) of man is also used to describe other living creatures in Genesis 1:20,21 and 24. The distinction between man and beast is that man was created in the image of God and other creatures were not. Therefore, in Gen.2:7 we see that man became a living being for the first time just as other creatures. It seems to rule out the interpretation that man is genetically derived from some previously existing living forms.

The second set of problems faced by theistic evolutionsits relates to the origin of sin and evil. George Murphy proposes several solutions to this theological question from a theistic evolutionistic perspective: The first humans, the first to reach reflective consciousness and to be endowed with the image of God, consciously turned away and refused to obey the word of God.[14] This position seems to have scientific and theological obstacles. Scientifically, one has to postulate that a population of pre-existing hominids acquired reflective consciousness and the image of God — for population evolves, not individuals. The mechanisms of natural selection have been shown to be deficient in explaining macroevolution. Alternate theories of neutral mutation and punctuated equilibrium have been postulated.[15] These theories agree that gradual selective process cannot account for macroevolutionary changes. However, the random process they propose to substitute for the gradual natural selection mechanism is difficult to test with controlled experimentation.

As an exception to the evolutionary paradigm, one can postulate that God chose two of the evolving hominids to be Adam and Eve, and endowed them with the image of God. This requires an extraordinary act of God in selecting only two individuals from an evolving population of hominids. To some Progressive Creationists, the extraordinary act that God utilizes to create man from the dust of the earth is as logical if not more consistent. This does not mean that we bring in God for a supernatural event when we cannot see a natural cause. The transcendent God and his extraordinary act of bringing Adam and Eve into existence does not imply "God-of-the-gaps" deism. This stipulation simply stresses the special importance that God attributes to the creation of man. God's providence does not preclude his using extraordinary acts not explainable by known natural means for a special purpose of his own. The act of creation *ex nihilo* itself demands a transcendent God performing an extraordinary act to put together the natural processes in his creation.

Theologically, moreover, natural selection does not explain the efficacy of the Fall which leads to man's death. The Fall was a moral predicament not necessitated by any natural processes. The unity of the human race as derived from a single source and the origin of human death and sin from a single human couple (Rom. 5:12-21) necessitate the incarnation and the redemptive work of Christ. Christ is the second Adam who is to give life to the fallen human race through his obedience and atoning death. He is not the culmination of human evolution.

An alternative to this dilemma is to dispose of the historicity of the "unique" human couple who sinned and were banished from God's blessing and to recognize the existential nature of sin and evil and the need for redemption. This approach seems to compartmentalize reality if pressed to the extreme: that the spiritual realm and the physical realm are independent of each other. The major weakness of the existential emphasis on sin and the fall is the inconsistency of allowing God to act on a personal level through existential encounter while denying God's action in history through creation. This dualistic overtone seems to contradict the unity of God's general revelation through nature and his special revelation through the Scriptures.

Origen propounded a similar view in the early Church. He posited that there was a spiritual fall in which men's souls were also affected.[16] Creation is only a testing ground revealing what has happened in the spiritual realm. Therefore, in essence, creation is the result of the Fall. Man is to be united to Christ and thus to become redeified to the pre-fall state in heaven. This leads to the Manichean implication that the Creation is evil. The necessity of Christ's atoning death is also called into question. Origen's view on creation was anathematized by the early Church. This view is also contrary to the goodness of the creation(Gen. 1).

Conclusion: Progressive Creationism — A Viable Approach
Ramm defines "Progressive Creationism" in terms of development.[17] Progressive Creationism can be briefly defined in our context as follows:

Pattle P.T. Pun

(1) It posits that God is involved in his creation in a dynamic way by shaping the variation of the biological world through the mechanism such as natural selection, thus avoiding the deistic mentality of the "God-of-the-gaps" theory.

(2) It stresses the historicity of Adam and Eve and gives the creation of Adam and Eve special significance since it was an extraordinary act of God that is not explainable by known natural causes.

(3) It focuses on the unity of God's revelation in nature as well as in Scripture and tries to maintain the historical and theological integrity of the creation account.

I submit to you that this is at present the least problematic model in the evangelical response to modern science.

[1]Ramm, B., *The Christian View of Science and Scripture.* (Grand Rapids: Eerdmans, 1954) p. 76.

[2]Pun, P., *Evolution: Nature and Scripture in Conflict?* (Grand Rapids: Zondervan, 1982) 174-230. See also Denton, M., *Evolution, A Theory in Crisis* (Bethesda: Adler and Adler, 1986) and Taylor, G.R., *The Great Evolutionary Mystery* (New York: Harper and Row, 1983).

[3]Calvin, *Institutes of the Christian Religion,* ed. John T. Mcneil, translated and indexed by Ford Lewis Battles (Philadelphia: Westminster, 1960), Vol. I, Book I, Chap. V. p. 53 and Chap. XIV, 180.

[4]Calvin. op. cit. Vol.I, Book I, Chap. XVI, 197-198.

[5]Hasel, G., *Old Testament Theology: Basic Issues in the Current Debate* (Revised and Expanded third edition. Grand Rapids: Eerdmans, 1972) 169-170.

[6]Van Dyke, F. 1986. "Problems of Theistic Evolution," *Journal of the American Scientific Affiliation,* Vol. 38, 11.

[7]Calvin, op. cit. Vol.I, Book II, Chap.XXIV. 471-472.

[8]Kornberg, A. in A. T. Ganesan, Shing Chang and James A. Hoch ed. *Molecular Cloning and Gene Regulation in Bacilli* (New York: Academic Press, 1982) xxi. Also see T. Minnery, November 7, 1980, "Creationists' Tenacity Secures Subtle Change in Science Texts," *Christianity Today*, 64.

[9]Pun, op. cit. 191-230. See also D. Young, *Creation and the Flood* (Grand Rapids: Baker, 1977); and D. Young, *Christianity and the Age of the Earth* (Grand Rapids: Zondervan, 1982).

[10]Moore, J. and H. Slusher, ed., *Biology, A Search for Order in Complexity* (Grand Rapids: Zondervan, 1977) 451-453.

[11]Harrison, R. K., *Introduction to the Old Testament* (Grand Rapids: Eerdmans, 1969) 548-551. See also J. O. Buswell, *Systematic Theology of the Christian Religion*, Vol. I, (Grand Rapids: Zondervan, 1963) 156.

[12]Calvin, op. cit. Vol.I, Book I, Chap.XIV, p. 161. 17. Pun, op. cit. 262-263.

[13]Pun, op. cit., 262-263.

[14]Murphy, G. 1986. "A Theological Argument for Evolution," *Journal of the American Scientific Affiliation*, Vol. 38, p. 19.

[15]Pun, op. cit. 220-224.

[16]Cunliffe-Jones, H., *A History of Christian Doctrine* (Philadelphia: Fortress, 1978) 77-84.

[17]Ramm, B., op.cit. 76.

SECOND RESPONSE TO ROBERT C. NEWMAN

Wayne Frair

Introduction

Currently it is popular to think of science and theology as quite separate theaters of operations. Many suppose science to be the obtaining of knowledge through the senses, whereas theology relies on faith and revelation. A tendency to separate these fields had roots in the early 17th century as the skies and earth were surrendering their secrets to empirical researchers. As studies of nature progressed during three centuries, much of the mystery was removed; and Providence, which had been indispensable, became inessential, then incidental and ultimately, for some, an impediment or interference in their studies of nature. So that today some, for example William Provine at Cornell, have proclaimed boldly that "science and religion are incompatible" and that you "have to check your brains" at the church house door.[1]

However, belief in a supernatural power has been recognized as a distinctively human attribute because such belief is found in all cultures of mankind. In fact the intuitive argument for the existence of God finds evidence in the universality of such a belief. So my understanding of the ideal Christian position is that God is sovereign in all aspects of nature and the creation is an obedient creature.[2]

Christians should have neither a fear nor a veneration of scientists and their methods, but we need to recognize that there are bounds to science. A modern example is genetic engineering.[3] The therapeutic aspects of this (as insulin production) are acceptable to virtually everybody. But tensions tend to arise more when genetic surgery is discussed because of the potential dangers. The answers would lie, as I see it, not in stifling scientific advance, but in appropriate *controls.*

Recently there has been considerable discussion about use of scientific data collected by Germans during the Hitler years when many people became unwilling "specimens" subjected to considerable pain.[4] Even secular humanists who feel that Christians might shackle science by their extra-scientific Biblical revelation recognize for the German situation (and even in "ordinary" living) the necessity for some standards and even ethical judgments.[5] But meaning and morality do not readily emerge from materialistic science. Therefore, because of the basic nature of humanity (selfishness), there is a desperate personal and societal need for what is provided by a person's faith in God and the following of guidelines for living as revealed in the Bible.

The Creation-Evolution Issue

During recent years, the fields of evolutionary studies have shown evidence of considerable turmoil or reevaluation accompanying the explosion of computer technology, use of biochemical procedures, and popularity of newer taxonomic and phylogenetic schemes such as cladism.[6] A major goal of evolutionists is to determine homologies, but understandings of this concept have undergone painstaking revisions. For in many cases similar structures in a variety of organisms are produced by different developmental pathways.[7] The concept of molecular clocks, which temporarily had seemed to open new vistas for understanding origins, has had severe challenges.[8] Iconoclasts have become increasingly active within the evolutionary community,[9] and even the whole evolutionary bulwark is being breached by newly aggressive creationists.

Among the many Christians in various fields of science,[10] there is a broad spectrum of opinions regarding creation and evolution.[11] The main Christian options are young-earth creation, old earth creation, and theistic evolution.[12] It is somewhat difficult to determine actual percentages of Christian professionals in science who would fall into these three categories, but I estimate that well over half and possibly closer to three quarters would belong in the first two categories, namely young-earth creation and old earth creation.

When the issue of origins is being considered, I think it is very important to keep the following distinctions clearly in mind:

I. Primary Causation
  A. Supernaturalism (theism) — God's *choice*
    1. Personal God
    2. Non-personal God
  B. Naturalism (atheism) — universe is self-sustaining, "chance"
II.Secondary Causation
  A. Abrupt Appearance — many kinds, limited changes (sometimes called microevolution)
  B. Macroevolution — one (rarely few) starting organism(s), large changes (adaptive radiation).[13]

Partitioning primary causes from secondary (or dependent) causes can aid our untangling the popular verbiage on these issues (for instance, creation scientist or scientific creationist). Belief that a supernatural God (primary cause) has done the creating unites creationists. But discussions on how it happened (secondary, tertiary, etc., causes) may be held without referring to primary causation. In the 1987 Supreme Court majority decision on the Louisiana creation case, it is clear that in the United States public schools it is acceptable to teach alternate views to macroevolution.[14] This could include the abrupt appearance model[15] (See appendix to chapter, Fig. 1). It is my opinion that competent public school teachers should inform (but not indoctrinate) students regarding what Christian and non-Christian scientists believe.[16] So among evangelicals there do exist differences of opinion regarding the how and when of creation. But the indispensable maxim of all creationists is their tenacious conviction that a supernatural God framed the universe.

Anthropology

The Bible quite clearly places humans in a distinct and elevated position in nature[17] and empirical data confirm this. We have, for example, the capability of exterminating the largest animals ever on earth (blue whales), and we, through cooperative worldwide efforts, have made this planet free from the smallpox viral disease since 1980.

It is true that though many diseases and other aspects of nature (including the weather) are not yet under complete control, we at least have had a very significant influence over most of them. In fact, an ecological imbalance in many cases is challenging us to restore ecosystems.

Physically, humans appear most like the chimpanzee or gorilla or possibly the orangutan,[18] but there are dozens of structural differences between us and these animals.[19] Any normal person readily can distinguish by appearance (phenotype) a human being from one of these apes. However, when chromosomes, genes, and even proteins are compared, the resemblances sometimes have been very close. Reasons for such apparent incongruities have become increasingly clear since the mid-1970's when measurable genetic differences were found not to correlate with gross anatomy. Apparently because of the complexity of developmental processes, when different types of organisms are being compared, genetic or single protein data may not be reliable indicators of phenotypes.[20] It commonly is believed that on the basis of many features, the African chimpanzee and gorilla are more like each other than either is like humans.

There are good reasons for maintaining wholesome doubts about proposed evolutionary intermediates leading to humanity. Currently evolutionists as a rule hold that certain types of extinct *Australopithecus* are the closest hook-up to one line which evolved toward the apes and to another evolving toward humans. But, Oxnard and others are questioning whether a type of *Australopithecus*[21] should be considered intermediate between apes and man.[22] There are questions about the humanity of various fossil forms including Neanderthals.[23] Even though some evangelicals disagree, it is my belief that Biblical Adam dates back no more than a few tens of thousands of years and more likely toward the late rather than early end of this span of years.[24]

Interesting is the fact that in many ways the human body should not be thought of as an advancement beyond apelikeness. In more than twenty important characters people represent immature apes. For example, the growing foot of an ape has toes in line like our foot. But as the ape foot develops, the big toe rotates sidewise where it becomes more thumb-like and useful for grasping.[25]

It is my opinion that the recent mitochondrial Eve hypotheses,[26] though interesting, have done little to unravel human phylogeny. But they have pointed back to a possible source of present humans, and certainly these studies have served to support the Biblical position that all people on earth share a common heritage.[27]

Science Reaching toward Theology

Within publications of many scientists in recent years have been expressions of cravings for something more than and beyond which mechanistic science is capable of delivering. Those expressing these views may be exemplified by a graduate school science colleague of mine who told me one Monday about his weekend dream in which he was standing at the very top of the ladder of his scientific laboratory research. While at this uppermost rung of empirical investigation he looked around and asked the questions, "Is this all there is?" and "Where can I go from here?" From somewhere, which seemed to him deep within the core of his very humanity, came the answer, "Yes, reality consists of more than microscopes and molecules."

It is as former literary atheist Dan Wakefield, who went back to church in 1980, very recently said, "Only a generation ago, we enlightened intellectuals believed science had not only disproved but replaced God; now science is one of the major factors making the idea of God a serious subject again."[28]

In the process of liberating themselves from the imprisonment of mechanistic science, it is the physical scientists who have been leading the way. The celebrated nonChristian astronomer Robert Jastrow represented well this new surge of feeling and faith when he said, "For the scientist who has lived by his faith in the power of reason, the story ends like a bad dream. He has scaled the mountains of ignorance; he is about to conquer the highest peak; as he pulls himself over the final rock, he is greeted by a band of theologians who have been sitting there for centuries."[29]

I echo astrophysicist Robert Newman's feelings that science should not be a game to "explain everything without recourse to the supernatural" but rather "to find out how things really are."[30]

During recent years, as physical scientists have extended their understanding of the basic essence of matter, there has developed what has been termed a "hidden traffic between theological and scientific ideas". Theologian/scientist T.F. Torrance uses the terms "theological science" and "natural science" in discussing the dynamic providential relationship of the supernatural God to his space-time universe.[31]

English astronomer Sir Fred Hoyle and his well-known Ceylonese associate, Chandra Wickramasinghe, have even turned back to William Paley's famous late 18th century design (teleology) watchmaker argument for a creator God, saying that Paley is "still in the tournament with a chance of being the ultimate winner."[32]

Wayne Frair

Even while late 20th century physicists have been expressing sensitivity toward a supernatural dimension, some biologists
have tended to look back toward the materialistic faith of the 19th
century physicist.[33] This has tended toward a degree of polarization within the biological community. On the one hand during the
past quarter of a century there has been an unprecedented welling
up of interest in creation with the inauguration of more than 100
new creationist organizations. Many of these organizations have
professional biologists among the leadership; and not a few of
these biologists are recent converts to Christianity. Some mainline biologists, particularly those embracing obdurate evolutionary and/or atheistic (and even "agnostic") sentiments have felt
threatened. Therefore they have over-reacted against Christianity
and even against theism.

Although a contingent of the scientific community still is
resisting any intrusion of theological thinking, others of their colleagues are beginning to open the door to experience this added
dimension.[34]

Natural science must not be divorced form a proper Christian theological perspective which in its appropriate sense would
possess essential aspects of a medieval (476-1450) and early
Renaissance (1500+) attitude. During those years there was more
of a holistic view of nature in which humans, nature, and God were
part of a grand scenario. There was far more security than for
many "tunnel vision" scientists of the 20th century who have
perceived people as being little more than peculiar puppets
dangling from their chromosomes.[35]

Fortunately, there is evidence now of a thaw in the icy grip
of positivism and reductionism which for decades had held

captive many human minds. We hear quite frequently today of
scientists "finding God." Sometimes such statements evidence
the intuitive grasp of some reality beyond the physical nature of
a star-studded sky or biochemical reactions.[36] This is natural theology.

Just as organisms long have been recognized as more than
the sum of their parts, global ecosystems can be thought of in the
same way. Thus there would be supra-earth processes. The fact
that ideas like this are being discussed today could presage a
movement among scientists away from evolutionary naturalism.

Christian theologians have termed the witnesses to God in
nature the General Revelation of God (See appendix to chapter,
Fig. 2), which in addition to nature would include history and
conscience. I perceive that an important role of the late 20th
century evangelical Christian is to encourage and to capitalize on
these manners of thinking. They represent moves in the right
direction, for they are antecedent stepping stones to the Special
Revelation of God which includes miracles, the Bible (written
Word), and Jesus Christ (incarnate Word). The Christian affirms
on the basis of Biblical revelation that Jesus Christ was the
preexistent supernatural Creator of nature, was on earth completely God and completely human (God incarnate), and that he
died on the cross to make possible "salvation" for all people.

[1]W. Provine, "Scientists, Face It! Science and Religion are Incompatible," *The Scientist* 2(16)(1988)10. For some counter-opinions, see *The Scientist* 2(19)(1988)12; 2(21)(1988)11,12; 2(24)(1988)9,12. Many scientists today are Christians and Bible

Wayne Frair

believers. See for example, E.C. Barrett and D. Fisher, *Scientists Who Believe* (Chicago: Moody Press, 1984). *Literature of the American Scientific Affiliation* (55 Market St., Ipswich, MA 01938) has testimonies and papers written by Christians in science. For some scientists of earlier centuries see: H. Morris, *Men of Science—Men of God*, (Revised ed.; El Cajon, California: Creation Life Publishers, 1988). This book contains brief sections about many scientists, most of whom were active during the 15th-19th centuries.

[2]D.L. Wilcox, *Creation in Time*, Manuscript in preparation.

[3]B. Davis and D.L. Ritter, "How Genetic Engineering Got a Bad Name," *Imprimis* 18(2)(1989)1-5.

[4]A.C. Nixon, "If The Data's Good, Use It — Regardless of The Source," *The Scientist* 2(21)(1988)9,11. F.H. Kasten, "Dissecting The Nazis' Perverse Scientific Practices," *The Scientist* 2(23)(1988)20.

[5]For example, "The Humanist Manifesto II" (in *The Humanist* Sept/Oct 1973) calls for an end of terror and hatred and encourages shared humane values. Unfortunately such writings do not deal realistically with the "sinful" (basically selfish) nature of people.

[6]H. Gee, "Taxonomy Blooded by Cladistic Wars," *Nature* 335 (1988) 585.

[7]V.L. Roth, "The Biological Basis of Homology," in C.J. Humphries, ed. *Ontoqeny and Systematics* (New York: Columbia, 1988)1-26. A good survey of the literature is given here. Within a few years Roth changed her viewpoint in recognizing that homologs do not share developmental pathways. Also see F. Aboitiz, "Homology: A Comparative or a Historical Concept," Acta Biotheoretica 37(1988)27-29; M.Denton, *Evolution: A Theory In Crisis* (Scranton,PA: Harper and Row, 1986) Chapter 7.

[8]See *Journal of Molecular Evolution* 26(1-2)(1987) for a comprehensive review on molecular clocks. Also see R. Lewin, "DNA Clock Conflict Continues," *Science* 241(1988)1756-1759. W-H Li and M. Tanimura, "The Molecular Clock Runs More Slowly in Man than in Apes and Monkeys," *Nature* 326(1987)93-96; C.E. Oxnard, *Fossils, Teeth and Sex: New Perspectives in Human Evolution* (Seattle, Washington: University of Washington Press, 1987); A.R. Templeton, "Phylogenetic Inference from Restriction Endonuclease Cleavage Site Maps with Particular Reference to the Evolution of Humans and the Apes," *Evolution* 37(1983)221-244. See pp.238,242. For gorilla-chimp-human phylogeny the molecular clock hypothesis was rejected at the 1% level. I. Amato, "Tics in the Tocks of Molecular Clocks," *Science News* 131(1987)74-75.

[9]S. Lovtrup, *Darwinism: The Refutation of a Myth* (London: Croom Helm, 1987). This Swedish scientist favors saltation as an evolutionary mechanism. In M. Denton, *Evolution: a Theory in Crisis* (Scranton, Pennsylvania: Harper and Row, 1986) there is a husky attack on macroevolution from many fields. A polyphyletic view has been promoted by C. Schwabe and others. See C. Schwabe and G.W. Warr, "A Polyphyletic View of

Evolution: The Genetic Potential Hypothesis," *Perspectives in Biology and Medicine* 27(3)(1984)465-485.

[10]There are many organizations such as the Institute for Creation Research (P.O. Box 2667, El Cajon, CA 92021) and the Bible-Science Association (2911 East 42nd Street, Minneapolis, MN 55406) which send scientists out as speakers and debaters. The leading creationist research organization is the Creation Research Society (2716 Farrington, Terre Haute, IN 47803).

[11]B. Durbin, Jr., "How It All Began: Why Can't Evangelical Scientists Agree?," *Christianity Today* 32(11)(12 Aug 1988)31-41. For a complete, though concise, survey of evangelical options on creation/evolution see W.H. Johns, "Stategies for Origins," *Ministry* 54(5)(1981)26-28.

[12]R.A. Nisbet, "A Presuppositional Approach to the Four View Model of Biological Origins," *Origins Research* 11(2)(Fall/Winter 1988)1,14-16.

[13]W. Frair and P. Davis, *A Case for Creation* (3rd ed.; Norcross, Georgia: CRS Books, 1983). See also W. Frair, "A Positive Creationist Approach Utilizing Biochemistry" in *Science at the Crossroads: Observation or Speculation. Papers of the 1983 BSA National Creation Conference* (Richfield, Minnesota: Onesimus Publishing, 1985)33-36. W. Frair, "Biochemical Evidence for the Origin and Dispersion of Turtles" in *Proceedings of the 11th Bible-Science Association National Conference* (Cleveland, Ohio, 1985)97-105.

[14]J. Brennan, *Supreme Court of the United States. Opinion No. 85-1513* (19 June 1987)8,9.

[15]A lawyer who argued in the Louisiana case for the defense before the Supreme Court recently has written a book supporting "abrupt appearance." W. Bird, *Origin of the Species Revisited* (2 vols., New York: Philosophical Library, 1989). Also see L.D. Sunderland, *Darwin's Enigma* (Revised ed.; Santee, CA: Master Book Publishers, 1988).

[16]M. Eger, "A Tale of Two Controversies: Dissonance in the Theory and Practice of Rationality," *Zygon: Journal of Religion and Science* 23(3)(1988)291-325. Eger is in physics and philosophy of science at City University of New York. He and Abner Shimony of Boston University agree that creationism could be taught in science classes.

[17]Genesis 1:26-28, 2:7. Only humans triumph over death (I Cor. 15).

[18]A leader in the drive to establish the orangutan (from Borneo and Sumatra) as mankind's closest non-human relative has been Jeffrey H. Schwartz. *The Red Ape: Orangutans and Human Origins* (New York: Houghton Mifflin, 1987) and J.H.S., "The Evolutionary Relationships of Man and Orangutans," *Nature* 308(1984)501-505.

[19]J.W. Rlotz, *Genes, Genesis and Evolution* (St. Louis: Concordia Publishing House, 1970)332-336.

[20]J. Marks, "Evolutionary Epicycles," *Contributions to Geology*, Special Paper 3(1986)339-350.

Wayne Frair

[21]P. Andrews, "Aspects of Hominoid Phylogeny," in C. Patterson, ed. *Molecules and Morphology in Evolution: Conflict or Compromise?* (New York: Cambridge University Press, 1987).

[22]R. Holmquist, M.M. Miyamoto and M. Goodman, "Higher-Primate Phylogeny — Why Can't We Decide?," *Mol. Biol. Evol.* 5(3)(1988)201-216. C.E. Oxnard, *Fossils, Teeth and Sex: New Perspectives on Human Evolution* (Seattle, Washington: University of Washington Press, 1987). Also see S.J. Gould, "A Short Way to Big Ends," *Natural History* 95(1)(1986)18-28. An evaluation of the new "black skull" is found in P. Shipman, "Baffling Limb on the Family Tree," *Discover* 7:86-93. A recent Christian treatment is W. Frair, "Australopithecines: Relationship to Man?," *Creation Research Society Quarterly* 25(1988)151-153.

[23]B. Bower, "Neanderthals Get an Evolutionary Face-Lift," *Science News* 135(15)(1989)229. Others previously have called for a wider than subspecific taxonomic separation of neanderthals and modern *Homo sapiens*. See C. Stringer, "The Dates of Eden," *Nature* 331(1988)565-566 and H. Valladas, J.L. Reyss, J.L. Joron, G. Valladas, O. Bar-Yosef, and B. Vandermeersch, "Thermoluminescence Dating of Mousterian 'Proto-cro-Magnon' Remains from Israel and the Origin of Modern Man," *Nature* 331(1988)614-616.

[24]Genesis 4. See H. Ross, "Will the Real Adam Please Stand Up?," *Facts and Faith* 3(1)(1989)1-2.

[25]S.J. Gould, "The Child as Man's Real Father," *Natural History* 84(5)(1975)18-22. See also S.J. Gould, "Human Babies as Embryos," *Natural History* 85(2)(1976)22-26.

[26]R.L. Cann, M. Stoneking and A.C. Wilson, "Mitochondrial DNA and Human Evolution," *Nature* 325(1987)31-36. Many articles were written after this paper. For example, see J. Wainscoat, "Out of The Garden of Eden," *Nature* 325(1987)13; R.L. Cann, "The Mitochondrial Eve," *The World and I* (Sept 1987)256-263; D. Wallace, "The Search for Adam and Eve," *Newsweek* (11 Jan 1988)46-52.

[27]Acts 17:26

[28]D. Wakefield, "And Now, a Word from Our Creator," *New York Times* 38(Sect. 7 — Book Review)(1989)1,28-29.

[29]R. Jastrow, *God and the Astronomers* (New York: W.W. Norton, 1978)116.

[30]R.C. Newman, "A Critical Examination of Modern Cosmological Theories," *Interdisciplinary Biblical Research Institute Res. RePt.* #15(1982)14. Likewise, an ex-Cambridge professor of mathematical physics now turned anglican priest is "concerned with exploring and submitting to, the way things are." See J. Polkinghorne, *One World: The Interaction of Science and Theology* (Princeton, New Jersey: Princeton University Press, 1986)97.

[31]T.F. Torrance, *Reality and Scientific Theology* (Brookfield, Vermont: Scottish Academic Press, 1985), XXIV.

[32]F. Hoyle and N.C Wickramasinghe, *Evolution from Space: A Theory of Cosmic Creationism* (New York: Simon and Schuster, 1981)97.

[33]R. Augros and G. Stanciu, *The New Biology* (Boston: Shambhala Publications, 1987)226.

[34]The most eminent of French zoologists gives a cautious nod toward metaphysics. See P. P. Grasse, *Evolution of Living Organisms* (New York: Academic Press, 1977)105,246. In a discussion of life , Charles Birch and John B. Cobb, Jr. open doors to thoughts which involve more than just mechanistic aspects of living tissue. See *The Liberation of Life from the Cell to the Community* (New York: Cambridge University Press, 1984). Also, Yale biophysicist Harold Morowitz in his book, *Cosmic Joy and Local Pain: Musings of a Mystic Scientist* (New York: Charles Scribner's Sons, 1987) evidences a reaching out from science toward religion.

[35]A. Koestler, *The Sleepwalkers* (New York: The Macmillan Company, 1959)539. Also see T.M. Sennott, *The Six Days of Creation* (Cambridge: The Ravengate Press, 1984)192,194.

[36]See Ref. 31, pp.83-84.

QUESTIONS
FOR DISCUSSION

1. Which modern scientific theories suggest threatening conclusions to your personal understanding of God's revelation? Why?

2. Should the Christian be concerned about scientific theories arising from general revelation?

3. Should the Christian be as concerned about the handling and interpretation of natural revelatory data as about the handling and interpretation of Scripture? What implications arise as a result of such concern?

4. What theological and theoretical scientific assertions are either confirmed or jeopardized by each of the three popular evangelical responses to modern science?

11
RELIGIOUS LIBERTY

TRIBESPEOPLE, IDIOTS OR CITIZENS?

Evangelicals, Religious Liberty and a Public Philosophy for the Public Square

Os Guinness

"Why did you use the words 'evangelical public philosophy'? They're either completely empty or a contradiction in terms. Today's evangelicals are nothing but partisan and sectarian."

That sharp retort by a Washington journalist expresses one side of public skepticism about an evangelical commitment to any public philosophy, or common vision of the common good. The other side is displayed by many evangelicals and fundamentalists themselves. On the one hand, specific initiatives in public philosophy supported by fellow Christians have been repudiated as "profane, unGodly, anti-Christian and anti-Biblical."[1] On the other, a general obliviousness and suspicion of the subject has been a hallmark of evangelical public engagement in the last decade.

Thus, in an era marked by passionate, public clamor over "me/my/ours," evangelicals in America have often come across as simply one more special interest group in the (ironically nonconservative) Cuisinart mix of interest group politics. Concern for Christian justice has been made to appear as concern for justice for Christians rather than concern for justice for all.

Of course many other groups have acted in the same way and there are powerful reasons for doing so and short term dividends from such a strategy. But this paper stands counter to such arguments. Its position is held by a significant and sizeable number of evangelicals who support a more constructive solution. They argue that (1) for evangelicals the long-term costs of repudiating a public philosophy far outweigh the gains; (2) a deeper analysis of the ideals and interests of both the gospel and the nation underscore the importance of a common vision of the common good; and (3) consideration of this notion is the best way for evangelicals to forge a view of religion and American public life that will at once be faithful, constructive and responsible.

Arguably, no faith community in the United States, apart from the Jewish community, currently has a higher stake than evangelicals in a constructive outcome to recent conflicts over religion and public life. For Jews, their very survival is at stake. For evangelicals, "free exercise" of religion bears directly on their integrity as followers of Christ, their effectiveness as bearers of the gospel and agents of justice around the world, and their responsibility as citizen-participants and heirs of America's earliest faith in the ongoing experiment that is America today. At a time when questions over religion and public life have become a dangerously unresolved issue in American life, and when state repression and sectarian violence around the earth remain a dark feature of a murderous century, evangelicals who close their minds to liberty and justice for all are in danger of becoming as unprincipled as they are unwise.

Along with other American citizens, evangelicals are now directly confronted with a three-fold choice first stated by sup-

Tribespeople, Idiots or Citizens?

porters of democracy in Greece and restated by John Courtney Murray in the early Sixties. The choice is as follows: As the issues of religion and public life continue to arise, will evangelicals respond as "tribespeople," in the sense of those who seek security in a form of tribal solidarity and are intolerant of everything alien to themselves? Or as "idiots," in the original Greek sense of the totally private person who does not subscribe to the public philosophy and is oblivious to the importance of "civility"? Or as citizens, in the sense of those who recognize their membership in a "commonwealth" and who appreciate the knowledge and skills which underlie the public life of a civilized community?[2]

The Achilles Heel of Public Involvement

The evangelical lack of a public philosophy is no eleventh-hour discovery. In 1976, *Newsweek's* "Year of the evangelical," several observers of the national scene examined the newly re-emergent evangelical movement and asked whether it was likely to exert the influence which its history, its numbers and the cultural opportunity might lead one to expect. Would it take advantage of the openings created by important recent restructurings in the worlds of American religion, politics and culture at large? Their answer was an unequivocal "No." Handicapped by lack of any distinctively Christian thinking, evangelical public influence predictably would be either confined to specific, single issues or confused with a myriad of overlapping interests closer to the American flag than the Christian faith.[3]

Thirteen years later, the accuracy of such predictions is all too clear. Failure to articulate and abide by a common vision for the common good has been the Achilles heel of public involve-

459

ment by evangelicals. It is also a central reason why, despite "mainline" Protestantism stumbling in national religious leadership, attention has shifted from talk of an "evangelical moment" to talk of a "Catholic moment." To focus the issue in terms of religion and politics alone: Where evangelicals have shown they have no public philosophy, Catholics—with their strong tradition of natural law and their clear Vatican II stands on religious liberty for all—have proved themselves ready and able to champion the common vision for the common good.

Unquestionably, it would take much more than observations like these to prompt most evangelicals to reconsider their position. Arguments for such a rethink would have to begin with theological principles and move through historical precedents to current political assessments—all beyond the scope of this paper. But if the last decade provides any perverse encouragement, it is that changes are more likely to result from the lessons of practical failure than from high-minded considerations of principle. Yet even there, for example in public opinion surveys, the lesson is plain enough.

How Christians stand in the public eye is obviously not a prime consideration to a community which worships a crucified Saviour. For as Luther said, the world's way of saying "thank you" for the gospel is the cross. But as the tele-evangelists have reminded us, faithfulness may at times be scandalous, but to be scandalous is not itself the mark of faithfulness. Thoughtful evangelicals would therefore do well to ponder the public standing of evangelicalism after more than a decade of high-profile political involvement.

Recent opinion surveys reveal a crucial detail in the picture. On one hand, contrary to impressions of rising extremism and intolerance over religion and public life, the great majority of Americans are actually more tolerant than a generation ago. (A plurality of Americans—45 to 41 percent—believe that there is "less religious tolerance today than there was twenty or thirty years ago," despite the fact that the same surveys demonstrate that there is, in fact, more tolerance than twenty to thirty years ago. This disparity is probably to be explained by the role of activists and, in particular, the impact of new technologies such as direct mail on the inflammation of the issue.[4])

On the other hand, evangelicals can take no comfort from such findings because they are a striking exception to the generally expanding tolerance. (In 1958, 25 percent of Americans would not have voted for a Catholic as President and 28 percent for a Jew. Today these numbers have fallen to 8 and 10 percent. The only numbers that have risen are those who would not vote for "a born-again Baptist," which has risen from 3 percent to 13 percent.[5]) Worse still, a general picture emerges in which recent public involvement by evangelicals is viewed as constitutionally legitimate but intrusive and unwelcome. Among many leadership groups (business leaders, government leaders, academics, priests and rabbis, for instance) evangelicals come out highest as a perceived "threat to democracy." Thirty-four percent of academics rate the evangelicals as a menace to democracy, compared with only 14 percent who see any danger from racists, the Ku Klux Klan and Nazis. [6]

This last statistic is even more startling than it appears. Groups perceived as "alien" and "threatening" are usually the newest and most recently arrived. But evangelicals are the direct spiritual descendants of America's "first faith," and as late as the early twentieth century were thought to be as American as apple pie, almost qualifying to be "the Church of America." Thus the fact that evangelicals should now be seen as "a threat to democracy" while still holding views common to most Americans in the 1950s and still advocated openly in the 1980s by a highly popular President like Ronald Reagan, cannot be excused airily by putting the blame on prejudice and rapid social change. The strongest single explanation is the evangelical repudiation of a public philosophy. Without such a commitment to the common vision of the common good, all public engagement by evangelicals, legitimate, wise and successful or not, is liable to be viewed by others as troubling and even threatening.

Such findings, pondered along with a biblical critique and comparison of specific conflicts such as the furor over *The Last Temptation of Christ* and Salman Rushdie's *Satanic Verses*, should prompt evangelicals to question their manner of political involvement in the last decade. Above all, has it been as faithful to Christ's teaching as intended? Or in the terms of a century ago, has it done "the Lord's work in the Lord's way"? But also, has its analysis of the current situation been accurate? Has it been just, wise and realistic in its proposals? Open to the challenges and concerns of other communities? This paper argues that, too often, the answer is "No," and that nothing would make a greater difference in reversing this conclusion and beginning a constructive contribution to national life than a fresh commitment to public justice by evangelicals

I. A Common Vision for The Common Good

Just before his surprisingly strong showing in the Iowa caucuses in 1988, Pat Robertson ran a two-page ad in the *Des Moines Register*. On one page there was a photograph of John F. Kennedy with the words, "In 1960 the opposition said this man wasn't fit to be president. Why? Because of his religion." On the opposite page was a photograph of Pat Robertson with the counterpoint, "In 1988 the opposition is saying the same thing about this man." The reader was left to draw the obvious conclusion. Robertson's candidacy should no more be disqualified than Kennedy's. But something in the parallel was missing which was to prove fatal to Robertson within a few weeks. Where Kennedy had surmounted his problem by setting out a vision of religion and politics that satisfied his toughest critics (at the Houston Baptist Ministers Association in September 1960), Robertson merely cited the parallel but sidestepped the challenge. He therefore exemplified almost perfectly the wider evangelical lack of a public philosophy. In failing to address the hole in his platform, he made it impossible to expand his core constituency and doomed himself to political disappointment.

Over against such positions, this paper argues, first, that evangelicals are church people before they are a movement and that the church's ideals are best expressed and her interests best served by a principled commitment to public justice; second, that in our time this Christian commitment to public justice is a vital contribution to the much-needed reconstruction of America's public philosophy; third, that the best prospects for reforging the public philosophy today are afforded by a vision of "chartered pluralism;" and lastly, that such a commitment to chartered pluralism offers the evangelical community its best opportunity to prove its integrity and effectiveness in a manner that its numbers, strengths, history and (supremely) its sense of calling requires. The argument is set out in a series of steps.

A comprehensive evangelical statement on religion and public life would require adequate treatment of four main areas: theological foundations, historical review, contemporary analysis and practical policy proposals. Without minimizing the primary significance of the first pair, this paper deliberately focuses on the second, because they are the points where evangelicals are weakest—either because good theology and history never become practical or because bad practical policy lacks good theology and history.

Theology and history will therefore be mostly assumed in this paper because of lack of space, but two reminders should be borne in mind. First, assumption is not avoidance: the theology and history behind the argument are always open to question and scrutiny. Second, the focus on one aspect of policy—the public philosophy—may appear to be an unfortunate narrowing of the issue, but public philosophy is in fact a valuable master theme by which to consider the broader issues of religion and public life today. For the framers, the issue was always stated better as "religion and government" rather than church and state. And today, when it is best approached as "religion and public life in a pluralistic society," the importance of a public philosophy as a master theme quickly becomes obvious.

The first step in the argument is to clarify what is meant by public philosophy, or common vision of the common good. A defining feature of the United States is that, from the very beginning, it has been a nation by intention and by ideas. One of America's greatest achievements and special needs has been to create, out of the mosaic of religious and cultural differences, a common vision for the common good—in the sense of a widely shared, almost universal, agreement on what accords with the common ideals and interests of America and Americans.

Mostly unwritten, often half-conscious, never to be mistaken for unanimity, this common vision has served a vital purpose. It has offset the natural conflict of interests in a pluralistic society, and in particular that impulse toward arbitrariness which is the scourge of totalitarianism and democracy alike. In doing so it has been the binding that maintains unity to balance the richness and pressures of diversity, and transmits a living heritage to balance the dynamism of progress. Most Americans may never have been conscious of any such thing, let alone the term, "public philosophy," but America itself has always been a working model of one, a "public philosophy" in action. For Americans, consensus has always been a matter of compact over common ideals as well as compromise over competing interests.

Defined in this way, the notion of public philosophy needs to be distinguished from two similar but different notions. First, this use of public philosophy is different from the use of the term (quite legitimately) to refer to an individual's personal philosophy of public affairs, and thus to the place of public affairs in his or her worldview. In contrast, public philosophy in this paper refers expressly to public affirmations shared in common with other citizens. A public philosophy should not only be accessible to others in principle; it is unworthy of the name unless it is actually shared in practice—though for evangelicals, it should be added, the theoretical basis for this sharing will not itself be shared by all Americans. It does not rest on some purported "neutral ground," but on an understanding of common history (common, in this case, to all who share in the American experience) and "common grace" (God's gratuitous favor that is common, as the Protestant reformers understood it, to all human beings regardless of their faith or unbelief).

Second, this use of public philosophy is quite different from civil religion. Like civil religion, public philosophy as used here deals with affirmations held in common. But unlike civil religion—which in my view is neither legitimate for Christians nor feasible for anyone today—the public philosophy does not require the common affirmations to be regarded as sacred or semi-sacred in themselves. For most Americans, their commitment to the public philosophy is rooted in their own religious beliefs, but the public affirmations are not themselves religious and it is for this reason that they can be held in common with people of other faiths and no faith.

There have undoubtedly been great changes in this concept over time, most noticeably the softening between the harder-edged notion of Puritan covenant and the rather vague mid-twentieth century notion of consensus. Equally, the very strength of the notion has sometimes created problems, such as the influence of consensus-thinking on the blind eye turned to cultural diversity and on the countenancing of evils, such as the maltreatment of Blacks and Native Americans. These are therefore obvious reasons why the subject has recently fallen into disrepute, why its very mention is challenged in some circles, and why there are sometimes competing proposals among proponents of its recovery.

What is certain, however, is that the weakening or disappearance of the public philosophy has definite consequences too, and from Walter Lippmann's critique of public opinion to the current Volcker Commission on American public service, a deepening stream of analyses have made this connection and redressed the imbalance. What is also certain is that, because people have different and changing values, the common vision for the common good is never static. It is not in the realm of a final answer. Adjustment and readjustment are an ongoing requirement of American democracy. Since no generation declares, lives and preserves this common vision in its entirety, there is a need for reaffirmation and renewal in every generation.

As George Mason wrote in the *Virginia Declaration*, "No free government or the blessings of liberty, can be preserved to any people, but by a firm adherence to justice, moderation, temperance, frugality, and virtue, and by frequent recurrence to fundamental principles." For Americans to become, in Walter Lippmann's words, "a people who inhabit the land with their bodies without possessing it with their souls" would be a sure step toward disaster.[7]

Consensual agreements over the place of religious liberty in public life is only one component of the wider public philosophy— but it is a vital one. Equally, such a consensus is only one of a trio of agencies (the Constitution, the courts, and the consensus) that are all vital to sustaining religious liberty. But because of the personal importance of faiths to individual and to communities of faith in America, and the public importance of both to American national life, a common vision of religious liberty in public life is critical to both citizens and the nation. It directly affects personal liberty, civic vitality and social harmony. Far from lessening the need for a public philosophy today, expanding pluralism increases it. Indeed, for anyone who has reflected on the last generation of conflict over religion and public life, few questions in America are more urgent than a fresh agreement on how we are to deal with each other's deepest differences in the public sphere.

II. The Importance of Religious Liberty

The second step in the argument is to show why the notion of religious liberty remains important to the public philosophy today. For to many Americans, especially among the thought leaders, the question of religion in public life has become unimportant. It is viewed as a non-issue or a nuisance factor—something which should be purely a private issue, which inevitably becomes messy and controversial when it does not stay so, and which should therefore revert to being private as quickly as possible.

A more helpful way of seeing things would be to see that the swirling controversies that surround religion and public life create a sort of sound barrier effect: On one side, the issue appears all passions, problems, prejudices. But break through the barrier, and the issue touches on several of the deepest questions of human life in the modern world. Once these are appreciated, it clearly becomes in the highest interest of the common good to resolve the problems raised rather than ban the topic out of personal disdain or fear.

There are at least five central reasons why, for evangelicals as American citizens, religious liberty remains a vital part of the public philosophy. Expressed as follows, these reasons are also accessible to other Americans:

First, religious liberty, or freedom of conscience, is a precious, fundamental and inalienable human right—the freedom to reach, hold, freely exercise or change our beliefs independent of governmental control. Prior to and existing quite apart from the *Bill of Rights* which protects it, religious liberty is not a second-class right, a constitutional redundancy or a sub-category of free speech. Since it does not finally depend on the discoveries of science, the favors of the state and its officials, and the vagaries of tyrants or majorities, it is a right that may not be submitted to any vote nor encroached upon by the expansion of the bureaucratic state. There is no more searching test of the health of the public philosophy than this non-majoritarian standard: "A society is only as just and free as it is respectful of this right for its smallest minorities and least popular communities."[8] Religious liberty has correctly been called America's "first liberty."

Along with other Americans, evangelicals affirm that unless the public philosophy respects and protects this right for all Americans, the American promise of individual freedom and justice is breached.

Second, the Religious Liberty clauses of the First Amendment are the democratic world's most distinctive answer to one of the entire world's most pressing questions: How do we live with our deepest—that is, our religiously intense—differences?

Some countries in the world exhibit a strong political civility that is directly linked to their weak religious commitments; and others a strong religious commitment directly linked to their weak political civility. Owing to the manner of the First Amendment's ordering of religious liberty and public life, American democracy has afforded the fullest opportunity for strong religious commitment and strong political civility to complement, rather than threaten, each other.

Along with other Americans, evangelicals affirm that unless the public philosophy respects and protects this distinctive American achievement, the American promise of democratic liberty and justice will be betrayed.

Third, the Religious Liberty clauses lie close to the genius of the American experiment. Not simply a guarantee of individual and communal liberty, the First Amendment's ordering of the relationship of religion and public life is the boldest and most successful part of the entire American experiment. Daring in its time, distinctive throughout the world both then and now, it has proved decisive in shaping key aspects of the American story. It is not too much even to say that as the Religious Liberty clauses go, so goes America.

Along with other Americans, evangelicals affirm that unless the public philosophy respects and protects this remarkable American ordering, the civic vitality of the American republic will be sapped.

Fourth, the Religious Liberty clauses are the single, strongest non-theological reason why free speech and the free exercise of religion have been closely related and why religion in general has persisted more strongly in the United States than in any other comparable modern country. In most modern countries, there appears to be an almost ironclad equation: the more modernized the country, the more secularized the country. America, however,

is a striking exception to the trend, being at once the most
modernized country and the most religious of modern countries.

The reason lies in the effect of the American style of
disestablishment. By separating church and state, but not religion
from government or public life, disestablishment does two things:
it undercuts the forces of cultural antipathy built up against the
church by church-state establishments—historically speaking,
established churches have contributed strongly to their own
rejection and to secularization in general. At the same time,
disestablishment throws each faith onto reliance on its own
claimed resources. The overall effect is to release a free and un-
fettered competition of people and beliefs similar to the free
market competition of capitalism.

Along with other Americans, evangelicals affirm that unless
the public philosophy respects and protects this enterprising relationship, both American religious liberty and public discourse
will be handicapped.

Fifth, the interpretation and application of the First Amendment today touches on some of the deepest and most revolutionary developments in contemporary thought. A generation ago it
was common to draw a deep dichotomy between science and
religion, reason and revelation, objectivity and commitment and
so on. Today such dichotomies are impossible. All thinking is
acknowledged to be presuppositional. Value-neutrality in social
affairs is impossible. To demand "neutral discourse" in public
life, as some still do, should now be recognized as a way of
coercing people to speak publicly in someone else's language and
thus never to be true to their own.

471

Along with other Americans, evangelicals affirm that unless the public philosophy respects and protects this new (or restored) understanding, the republican requirement of free democratic debate and responsible participation in democratic life will be thwarted.

It would be possible in each case to spell out the specific Christian ideals and interests behind each point, their specific Christian roots and their precise overlap with those of other faiths. In terms of philosophical roots, for example, all Christians and many Jews go beyond many other Americans by grounding religious liberty ultimately in God's creation. But they can still forge a substantial, overlapping consensus with a far larger number of fellow citizens who ground religious liberty in the *Declaration of Independence* and the assertion of inviolable human liberty.

But most of these specific points can be filled in readily and the immediate purpose is to demonstrate that such reasons are anything but purely sectarian and partisan. In fact, they are widely accessible to, and supported by, most Americans. One conclusion is inescapable: The place of religious liberty in American public life is not merely a religious issue but a national issue. It is not only a private issue, but a public one. Far from simply partisan or sectarian, religious liberty is in the interests of Americans of all faiths and none, and its reaffirmation should be a singular and treasured part of the American public philosophy.

III. The Conflicts and their Context

The third step in the argument is to analyze the factors behind the recurring conflicts over religion and public life, and assess what they mean for religious liberty and public justice in the future.

The conflicts themselves need no elaboration: school prayer and New Age meditation, creation science, secular humanism, textbook tailoring, prayer before high school sporting events, Muslim prayer mats in government offices, Gideon's Bibles in hotel rooms, the Ten Commandments on school walls, blasphemy in films and novels, the Pledge of Allegiance, Mormon polygamy, "Christian Nation" resolutions and so on. For a full generation now the issue of religion and public life has been highly contentious, with an endless series of disputes and the whole subject surrounded by needless ignorance and fruitless controversy, including at the highest levels. Too often, debates have been sharply polarized, controversies dominated by extremes, resolutions sought automatically through litigation, either of the Religious Liberty clauses set against the other one and any common view of a better way lost in the din of irreconcilable differences and insistent demands.

At some point, however, the temptation is to take a quick glance at the contestants, apportion the blame, enlist on one side or another, and treat the whole problem as largely political and capable of a political solution. From that perspective, the problem is one which has been created by an ideological clash (the fundamentalists versus the secularists) that overlaps with a Constitutional clash (the accomodationists versus the separationists) that overlaps with a psychological clash (the "bitter-enders," who insist on commitment regardless of civility, versus the "betrayers," who insist on civility regardless of commitment) which has produced, in turn, two extremist tendencies (the "removers," who would like to eradicate all religion from public life, versus the "re-imposers," who would like to impose their version of a past or future state of affairs on everyone else). All this, of course, is potently reinforced by technological factors such as direct mail and its shameless appeals to fear and anger.

Such analyses may be accurate as far as they go. But they stop before they take into account some of the deepest factors, which means they rule out some of the most effective solutions. Of several additional factors, two are especially important to this argument.

The first is the broader crisis of cultural authority in America. Just before he retired as Secretary of State, Dean Acheson was speaking to a prominent European. "Looking back," he said, "the gravest problem I had to deal with was how to steer in this atomic age, the foreign policy of a world power saddled with the Constitution of a small eighteenth century farmers' republic."[9]

Today, the awareness behind Acheson's remark could be found in many areas outside the field of foreign relations. Indeed, it raises an issue for America that recurs in countless forms: How does the United States currently stand in relation to its origins? As the ongoing bicentennial celebrations of the *Constitution* illustrate again, few other Western nations are so proud of their origins. Yet the question of the present's relationship to the past has been particularly urgent in the 1980s, and in ways which mean the next decade's answers may be decisive for many years to come.

The most obvious expression of this concern is the flood of recent articles, books and commentaries which claim that the United States is experiencing a transformation or restructuring. Some of the more pressing claims about a turning point stand head and shoulders above the rest — that America is experiencing massive social changes in shifting from an industrial to an information society, massive political changes in undergoing another of its regular cycles of party realignments, and massive national and international changes in adjusting to world realities after Vietnam and after the possible demise of the bipolar, superpower world.

Yet none of these shifts rivals the importance of the generation-long crisis of cultural authority through which American society has been going since the early 1960s. Controversies over religion and politics are therefore vital because at stake in the changes, developments and controversies of the last generation are the principles and patterns by which both personal lives and the life of the republic are to be ordered.

American politics, it has been argued, has been characterized by a succession of grand pivotal issues. Between 1775 and 1824, these issues were essentially constitutional, dealing with the institutional arrangements of the new political community. Between 1825 and 1892, they were essentially sectional, involving regional tensions between North and South and Old East and New West. Since then until the 1960s, the pivotal issues were essentially economic and social, centering on the problems of industrial growth and social welfare.

If this is so, the United States is said to be in the fourth great era, and the grand pivotal issue, around which debate and conflict are swirling and a form of culture wars is emerging, is that of cultural authority, which itself can be subdivided into two underlying questions: By what ultimate truths are Americans to shape their private and public lives? And by what understanding are these faiths to relate to each other in the public square?

It has been by ignoring this deeper cultural crisis, the cultural wars it triggers and the two fundamental questions it generates, that many American leaders have tended to treat religion either as a non-issue, a purely private matter with no bearing on the public square, or as a nuisance factor, the bedeviling special interest of certain troublesome sectarian groups. Either way they misread the fact that many of today's deepest national issues have a critical religious component and many of the deepest religious issues have critical national consequences. The importance of religion-and-politics in America today is far more than a "religious issue" or a merely private issue. It is a national issue in the interest of all Americans.

If the impact of the first factor on religious liberty tends to be appreciated more by conservatives than liberals, the reverse is true of the second. The second factor that deepens an assessment of the religion and politics controversies is the recent expansion of pluralism. This is a worldwide phenomenon that links current American tensions to similar trends around the globe. How do we live with each other's deepest differences? That simple question has been transformed by modernity into one of the world's most pressing dilemmas. On a small planet in a pluralistic age the all-too-common response has been bigotry, fanaticism, terrorism and state repression.

Expanding pluralism is no stranger to the American experience. It has always been a major theme in our story, with tolerance generally expanding behind pluralism.

But the last generation has witnessed yet another thrust forward in religious pluralism in two significant ways.

First, American pluralism now goes beyond the predominance of Protestant-Catholic-Jewish and includes sizeable numbers of almost all the world's great religions (Buddhist and Muslim, in particular). Second, it now goes beyond religion altogether to include a growing number of Americans with no religious preference at all (In 1962, as in 1952, secularists—or the so-called "religious nones"—were 2 percent of Americans. Today they are between 10 and 12 percent).[10]

The shock waves caused by this latest explosion can be observed at two different levels in American society. In the first place, the effect of exploding diversity can be seen in the demographic make-up of contemporary American society. The state of California, for example, has America's most diverse as well as its largest population. It now accepts almost one-third of the world's immigration and represents at the close of the century what New York did at the start—the point of entry for millions of new Americans.[11]

California's elementary schools already have a "minority majority" in the first three grades. By 1990, this situation will be reflected in all public school enrollments and soon after the year 2000 in the population as a whole. (The same situation already exists in all of the nation's 25 largest city school systems, and half of the states have public school populations which are more than 25 percent minorities.[12]) The result is a remarkable mix of the diverse cultures of Africa, Asia, Europe and Latin America. It will also be as challenging a project in culture-blending as New York was in nation-building nine decades ago, and Boston was at the birth of the public school movement a century and a half ago.

The effect of the exploding diversity can also be seen in what is a form of cultural breakdown—collapse of the previously accepted understandings of the relationship of religion and public life and the triggering of the culture wars. As a result, a series of bitter, fruitless contentions over religion and politics has erupted, extremes have surfaced, the resort to law court has become almost reflexive, many who decry the problems are equally opposed to solutions to them, and in the ensuing din of charge and counter-charge any sense of common vision for the common good has been drowned.

As always with the trends of modernity, the consequences of increased pluralism are neither unique to America nor uniform anywhere. The disruptive effects can be seen elsewhere in the world, even in totalitarian societies (such as the challenge of the republics to the Soviet Union) and in democratic nations with long traditions of racial and linguistic homogeneity (such as the challenge of new immigrants in Britain).

Nor are the consequences simple. On the one hand, increased pluralism deepens old tensions. Under the challenge of "all those others," many are seemingly pressured to believe more weakly in their own faith, to the point of compromise: the more choice and change, the less commitment and continuity. In reaction, however, others tend to believe more strongly, to the point of contempt for the faith of others.

On the other hand, increased pluralism helps develop new trends. Today's dominant tensions are not so much between distinct religions and denominations. As often as not, they are between the more orthodox and the more contemporary within the same denomination (for example, the recent divisions within the Southern Baptist Convention), or between an alliance of the more orthodox in several religions who oppose the more contemporary in those same groups (for example, the pro-life coalition of conservative Protestants, Catholics, Mormons and so on).

In sum, like it or not, modern pluralism stands squarely as both the child of, and the challenger to, religious liberty—whether because of its presence (given the democratic conditions arising out of the Reformation and the Wars of Religion), its permanence (given the likely continuation of these conditions in the foreseeable future), or its premise (that a single, uniform doctrine of belief can only achieve dominance in a pluralistic society by two means: through persuasion, which is currently unlikely because unfashionable, or through coercion by the oppressive use of state power, which at anytime is both unjust and unfree).

Not surprisingly, these developments and their logic have hit hard the trio of American institutions which have been so instrumental in tempering the forces of faction and self-interest and helping transform American diversity into a source of richness and strength: the Religious Liberty clauses of the First Amendment, the Public School Movement and the American public philosophy. The upshot is that the public schools have generally become the storm center of the controversies, one or other of the twin clauses of the First Amendment have been looked to as the sole arbiter in the partisan conflicts, and (whichever prevails) the common vision for the common good becomes the loser.

Only when the full extent of this damage and the full range of the causes have been taken into account can any prospective solutions be given realistic consideration.

IV. Chartered Pluralism and its Contributions

The fourth step in the argument is to examine the concept of chartered pluralism and its contribution to the current problems. Anyone who appreciates the factors behind the present conflicts is confronted with tough questions. Above all, can there be a resolution to the culture wars and a readjustment to the new pluralism without endangering the logic of religious liberty in public life?

At first sight, the search for a just and commonly acceptable solution to these challenges seems as futile as squaring the circle. The question of the public role of religion in an increasingly pluralistic society appears to be a minefield of controversies, with the resulting ignorance, confusion and reluctance an understandable outcome. Yet if it is correct to trace the problem to forces such as pluralism as much as to ideologies, individuals and groups, then we have more victims than villains over this issue, and the wisest approach is to search together for a solution, not for a scapegoat.

In fact, the present stage of the conflict offers a strategic opportunity. Extreme positions and unwelcome consequences are readily identifiable on many sides, and a new desire for consensus is evident. But where and on what grounds could consensus emerge?

The most constructive way forward is to reforge the public philosophy according to a vision of "chartered pluralism." Chartered pluralism is a vision of religious liberty in public life that, across the deep differences of a pluralistic society, forges a substantive agreement, or freely chosen compact, on three things which are the "3 Rs" of religious liberty in a pluralistic society: rights, responsibilities and respect. The compact affirms, first, that religious liberty, or freedom of conscience, is a fundamental and inalienable right for peoples of all faiths and none; second, that religious liberty is a universal right joined to a universal duty to respect that right for others; and third, that the first principles of religious liberty, combined with the lessons of 200 years of Constitutional experience, require and shape certain practical guidelines by which a robust yet civil discourse may be sustained in a free society that would remain free.

Founded on such a principled pact (spelled out, of course, in far greater depth), the notion of "chartered pluralism" can be seen to give due weight to the first of its two terms. It is therefore properly a form of chartered pluralism, and avoids the respective weaknesses of relativism, interest-group liberalism or any form of mere "process" and "proceduralism."

But at the same time the agreement is strictly limited in both substance and in scope. It does not pretend to include agreement over religious beliefs, political policies, constitutional interpretations or even the philosophical justifications of the three parts of the compact. "Chartered pluralism" is an agreement within disagreements over deep differences that make a difference. It therefore gives due weight to the second of its two terms, and it remains a form of chartered pluralism that avoids the dangers of majoritarianism, civil religion or any form of overreaching consensus that is blind or insensitive to small minorities and unpopular communities.

Three features of this compact at the heart of chartered pluralism need to be highlighted indelibly if the compact is to pass muster under the exacting conditions of expanded pluralism. First, the content of the compact does not grow from shared beliefs, religious or political, because the recent expansion of pluralism means that we are now beyond the point where that is possible. It grows instead from a common commitment to universal rights, rights which are shared by an overlapping consensus of commitment although grounded and justified differently by the different faiths behind them.[13] Second, the achievement of this compact does not come through the process of a general dilution of beliefs, as in the case of civil religion moving from Protestantism to "Judeo-Christian" theism. It comes through the process of a particular concentration of universal rights and mutual responsibilities, within which the deep differences of belief can be negotiated. Third, the fact that religious consensus is now impossible does not mean that moral consensus (for example, "consensual" or "common core" values in public education) is neither important nor attainable. It means, however, that moral consensus must be viewed as a goal, not as a given; something to be achieved through persuasion rather than assumed on the basis of tradition.

Doubtless, further questions are raised by these three points. Do all the different faiths mean the same thing when they affirm common rights? Do all have an adequate philosophical basis for their individual affirmations? Are all such divergences and inadequacies a matter of sheer indifference to the strength and endurance of the compact? Do all Christians have a theological basis that will make them able and willing to affirm such a compact with people of other faiths? Will such a principled pact always be enough in practice, to keep self-interest from breaking out of the harness? The probable answer in each case is "No", which is a reminder of both the fragility of the historical achievement of religious liberty for all and the sobering task we face if we would sustain such freedom today. Indeed, the challenge might appear quixotic were it not for the alternatives.

Expressed differently, chartered pluralism owes much to John Courtney Murray's valuable insistence that the Religious Liberty clauses are "articles of peace" rather than "articles of faith.''[14] But Father Murray's distinction must never be widened into a divorce. For one thing, the articles of peace are principled before they are procedural. They derive from articles of faith and cannot be sustained long without them. Civility is not a rhetoric of niceness or a psychology of social adjustment, but discourse shaped by a principled respect for persons and truth. For another, articles of peace should not be understood as leading to unanimity, but to that unity within which diversity can be transformed into richness and disagreement itself into an achievement that betokens strength.

It should be stressed at once that this proposal for a chartered pluralism is not a futuristic dream or academic exercise. It has taken concrete shape in the recently drafted and published *Williamsburg Charter*. Significantly, the Charter may prove a litmus test of evangelical seriousness over public justice. For while the Charter has received widespread support from American leaders at large and from believers of almost all faiths, including leading evangelicals and the National Association of Evangelicals, other evangelicals have provided its strongest opposition. And repeatedly, it has been their deep-rooted suspicion of the theological rightness of any such common enterprise that has led to their repudiation of affirmations such as the following:

We readily acknowledge our continuing differences. Signing this Charter implies no pretense that we believe the same things or that our differences over policy proposals, legal interpretations and philosophical groundings do not ultimately matter. The truth is not even that what unites us is deeper than what divides us, for differences over belief are the deepest and least negotiated of all.

The Charter sets forth a renewed national compact, in the sense of a solemn mutual agreement between parties, on how we view the place of religion in American life and how we should contend with each other's deepest differences in the public sphere. It is a call to a vision of public life that will allow conflict to lead to consensus, religious commitment to reinforce political civility. In this way, diversity is not a point of weakness but a source of strength.[15]

Understood properly, the concept of chartered pluralism is critical to reforging that aspect of the public philosophy that bears on questions of religion and American public life, especially in the absence of any demonstrable alternative. If it gains acceptance in the three main arenas of conflict—public policy debates, the resort to law and public education—and if it succeeds in addressing their problems constructively, it could well serve as a public philosophy for the public square, truly a charter for America's third century of Constitutional government.

V. Questions and Challenges

The fifth step in the argument is to assess the questions and challenges raised against the concept of chartered pluralism. Such questions, of course, are to be expected. Like a beam of light refracted through glass, any proposal addressing current conflicts is bound to strike the ideals and interests of various faith communities differently. One has only to think of the respective "off stage" concerns of each, such as mainline Protestant concern over declining numbers, Catholic concern over the academic freedom of its Church institutions, Orthodox concern over its Presidential candidate, Jewish concern over Israeli responses to Palestinian intifada and Muslim concern over the Ayatollah Khomeini's death sentence on Salman Rushdie.

It therefore goes without saying that evangelicals have their own concerns. But it is also true that evangelical reactions to the notion of the public philosophy in general and to chartered pluralism in particular are shared by other Americans and may be taken as representative of the concerns of many who are broadly orthodox in faith and conservative in politics.

Evangelicals of one sort or another have raised five principal objections to the notion of chartered pluralism. In each case the objection has a surface plausibility. But deeper examination shows such objection to be quite unfounded. At the same time, the discussion offers a revealing testimony about the public face of evangelicalism in America today.

First, it is objected that chartered pluralism is soft on explicitly Christian statement and therefore essentially a form of secularism. As one critique expressed it, there is "pressure today on Christians to sign statements which seek 'common ground' with unbelievers, and in the process deny Christ and the Bible." Thus, despite the participation of several Christians such as William Bentley Ball, Dean Kelley, Richard John Neuhaus, George Weigel and the present writer in its drafting, the *Williamsburg Charter* was dismissed as "profoundly anti-Christian." "Get it and read it," says the critic, "and you'll see that the faith of the secular humanists is the foundation of this document." [16]

At the root of this objection is a theological deficiency. Obviously, compromise is a peril in all "cognitive bargaining," and individuals will have to decide for themselves whether the charge in this case is sustained. But what emerges plainly in the debate is that no evidence at all exists for such a charge. Instead, such critics share a theological deficiency bearing fateful political consequences. They lack a view of "common grace," or God's gratuitous mercy given, despite sin, to both just and unjust alike. Common grace is a theme which is powerful in the Bible, the Reformers and the Puritans; and evangelicals who are without it are forced theologically to repudiate any notion of a public philosophy. They have no basis for any common enterprise with those who do not share their faith. Having no common grace on which to found a common vision for the common good, their public positions are forced to be all confrontation and no consensus. Commonness, in principle, is considered compromise.

In sum, chartered pluralism is not secularism. Commonness is a gift of God to be enjoyed. Solid ground on which to work for political justice is based on what John Calvin called "seeds of justice" planted in human nature, or "universal impressions of a certain civic fair dealing and order." [17]

Second, it is objected that chartered pluralism is soft on theology and therefore essentially a form of syncretism. (An earlier critique of the *Williamsburg Charter* blasted its drafters and signers as a "hodge-podge of people" and such initiatives as "these Tower of Babel ecumenical committees." [18])

This objection involves a factual error and misunderstanding. Whether or not one views ecumenism and dialogue as worthwhile enterprises, chartered pluralism is quite different. The unity for which it strives is not a unity based on common theological beliefs. The assumption behind chartered pluralism is that, today, expanding pluralism has rendered forlorn any such search for a theologically based unity.

Rather, the unity is based on a common commitment to the rights and responsibilities of religious liberty—across the chasm of religious differences. Of course, given the diversity of theological beliefs supporting these different rights in different ways, unity (as with any human accomplishment in a fallen world) will never be perfect or total. But grounded as it is in common grace, a common vision for the common good can help construct an overlapping consensus that will never be complete yet still deliver a substantial measure of political justice.

In sum, chartered pluralism is not syncretism. Nor need it lead to compromise in any way. It is quite compatible with the most stringent requirements of orthodoxy (whether Christian, Jewish, Mormon, or whatever) as well as those of political civility.

Third, it is objected that chartered pluralism is soft on truth and therefore essentially a form of relativism. This objection has suddenly become widespread among evangelicals, for whom pluralism is now the "P word," a dangerous evil associated automatically with relativism and eschewed as such. Small and innocuous-sounding at first, the objection has enormous consequences for religious liberty in a pluralistic society.

There is unquestionably a link between pluralism and relativism, and books like Allan Bloom's *The Closing of the American Mind* have served us well in drawing attention to it. But to confuse the two is as harmful as to divorce the two, because it muddies the clear thinking necessary to combat the real problem.

Yet pluralism is not in itself relativism. One is a social fact; the other a philosophical conclusion. "All those others" of different faiths just happen to be out there, and no amount of seeing red over relativism will wish them away. But it does not follow philosophically for a second that relativism need be true. Indeed, a stubborn feature of pluralism is the high number of those who unrepentantly believe their faith-commitments to be absolutely true. In the end this is even attested by the fact "that everything is relative has become the last absolute"—the relativist's own absolute.

Christians who confuse pluralism with relativism, and therefore oppose both, need some simple reminders. Was it not in a highly pluralistic setting that the early Church flourished without any compromise of the exclusive loyalty to Christ? And what was the earliest, strongest source of modern pluralism? The Protestant principle, freedom of conscience, which is the greatest generator of choice and dissent in history. And which community of faith was the first to show signs of relativism long before there were many other religions in America, let alone secularists? Protestant evangelicalism in the nineteenth century, though the word used then for the corrosive acid of (predominantly Protestant) pluralism was nothingarianism.

In sum, chartered pluralism is not relativism, and provides every reason to recognize and resist it. As the *Williamsburg Charter* declares, "Pluralism must not be confused with, and is in fact endangered by, philosophical and ethical indifference. Commitment to strong, clear philosophical and ethical ideas need not imply either intolerance or opposition to democratic pluralism. On the contrary, democratic pluralism requires an agreement to be locked in public argument over disagreements of consequences within the bonds of civility." [19]

Fourth, it is objected that chartered pluralism is soft on conflict and therefore essentially a form of pacifism. This objection, often tied in with the first and third objections, is particularly common among political activists. At its heart is the concern that achieving consensus or committing oneself to the rights of others—especially those of one's enemies—is a dangerous and defeatist form of weakness. As, say, with the nuclear freeze proposal, the fear is that recognition of any principled pact with one's opponents is a sure way of "freezing in the imbalance." Or, to change to the sporting metaphor adopted in one conservative memo, "It is comparable to calling the game at the bottom of the fourth with the score: ACLU 10; Evangelicals 1."

At the root of this objection is a misunderstanding of the purpose of chartered pluralism. Contrary to suspicions of milk-toast civility and fear of public nastiness, the goal of chartered pluralism is to strengthen debate, not to stifle it. What we have now is not debate. It is not even a shouting match between two sides. It is only different sides shouting into direct-mail megaphones about their opponents to the supporters on their own side.

Properly understood, chartered pluralism might be described as the equivalent for religion and public life of boxing's "Queensberry rules." Within the "ring and rules" of religious liberty's "3 Rs" (rights, responsibilities, and respect), the Religious Liberty clauses of the First Amendment act as "articles of peace" rather than "articles of faith"— the public setting for a civil but robust form of political engagement in which disagreement becomes an achievement and diversity remains a source of strength.

In sum, chartered pluralism is not pacifism. It provides deep freedom for principled contention between deep differences that make a deep difference.

Fifth, it is objected that chartered pluralism is soft on realism and therefore essentially a form of idealism. Like the fourth objection, this one is well represented at both ends of the political spectrum and even in the middle. In its unreflective form it is so common that it may even be the majority opinion. Its appeal is simple. In an age of macho-style *realpolitik*, all that matters is political and judicial activism. Beat them at the ballot box. Sue them to their knees. First principles are fine as artillery "symbols" in the great *blitzkrieg* of ideas, but to be expected to follow them would be as archaic as a knight's code in the conditions of modern war.

At the root of this objection is a willful ignorance of a simple premise of political freedom: Freedom is ultimately best sustained, not by the legislation of rights, but by the cultivation of roots—those first principles, beliefs and ideals necessary to nourish an ongoing commitment to freedom and law in free societies that would remain free. That is why "We the people" must never be reduced to "We the judges and attorneys."

This point is often forgotten today by liberal and conservative activists alike. But it would have united thinkers as divergent as Edmund Burke and Jean-Jacques Rousseau. It is why James Madison saw that, without first principles, the Constitution is only a "parchment barrier." It is behind Alexis de Tocqueville's assertion that American freedom would depend on American mores, or "habits of the heart," rather than law. It underlies the warnings of contemporary prophets such as Walter Lippmann and

Alexandr Solzhenitsyn. Or, as Justice Antonin Scalia put it simply, speaking of the relationship of freedom, virtue and rights, "In the last analysis, law is second best."[20]

In sum, chartered pluralism is not idealism. In insisting that rights derive from and are sustained only by first principles, it is actually more realistic than its critics. It thus seeks to restore the balance between Constitution, courts, and the ongoing consensus of the citizens that will be vital to the republic.

For anyone who investigates these objections and concludes that the problem is in the eye of the objectors, there is a further twist to the story. Far from proving fatal to the notion of chartered pluralism, an examination of the objections discloses defects in the current evangelical models of public discipleship. Three weaknesses in particular are involved, though only the first two are widely recognized and the third needs to be exposed before it too betrays the requirements of discipleship.

The first deficient model is that of a "privatized" faith. While not the view of earlier American evangelicals or of 18th century English evangelicals, this model was characteristic of most evangelicals just prior to the 1960s because of the influence of dispensationalism. It is perhaps still common among the majority. Weak both theologically and politically, the critical deficiency of privatized faith is its loss of the totality of faith, supremely Christ's lordship over all of life. This problem was ably protested by Carl F. Henry's *The Uneasy Conscience of Fundamentalism*(1947) even before being shown up by events in the 1960s.

The second deficient model is that of a "politicized" faith. This model has been characteristic of a smaller group of evangelicals from the 1960s onward, those who have been actively

Os Guinness

engaged in public life but who have compromised their faith by
failing to be sufficiently critical of the dominant ideology of their
times (whether Left or Right). Weak theologically and counter-
productive politically, the critical deficiency of politicized faith is
its loss of the tension of faith, supremely in the Christian's calling
to be "in" the world, but not "of" it.* This problem was ably
protested by Jacques Ellul's *The Political Illusion* (1967) even
before being shown up by events in the 1980s.

The third deficient model is that of "pillarized" faith. With
the acknowledged failure of the other two models, this one
represents the current temptation of evangelicals. Borrowed from
the Dutch experience, the term "pillarized" refers to a special
dynamic in situations where pluralism and particularism are both
strong. The tendency then is to construct pillars, or concentrated
networks of consistent Christian witness—not only churches, but
Christian organizations of all sorts, such as Christian schools,
Christian businesses, Christian recreation centers, Christian this
and Christian that, Christian everything. Unfairly dismissed as
"Yellow Pages Christianity," this model is actually far stronger
than the others theologically and socially. But there is still a
critical deficiency in this pillarized faith—in a world of publicly
interpenetrating faiths, it relies solely on distinctively Christian
groups and therefore lacks the transforming quality of faith in the
public square. Christians become so secure in their network that
even those who speak a classic Reformed language (including talk
of transformation) end up in what is indistinguishable from a classic Anabaptist lifestyle—set apart from the tough centers of
modern thought and power.

Fashioning a model of public discipleship that combines the missing biblical elements of totality, tension, and transformation will be possible only if the neglected doctrine of vocation is rediscovered. But to those with such a "penetrating" model of public discipleship, chartered pluralism provides a vision of the place of religious liberty in public life that is highly conducive, if challenging, to an enterprising faith. For chartered pluralism is not only a principled pact between faiths, it is also (in terms of action) an invitation to principled participation in public life and (in terms of communication) an invitation to principled persuasion in public discourse.

Once again, constraints of space mean that these statements have to be left at the level of the general. But behind them are detailed reasons and examples. The closer the examination of the objections to chartered pluralism, the more cogent become the reasons for supporting it.

Consequences and Outcomes

The last step in the argument is to set out some of the foreseeable principles and pitfalls that ought to shape prudential judgments as to the best way forward through the controversies.

First, there are three necessary conditions for a constructive solution such as chartered pluralism to be politically successful in achieving justice. Solid concepts and good will are not enough. What is required is intellectual foresight that will anticipate the problem before it becomes full-blown; moral courage that is willing to tackle problems not necessarily considered "problematic" on the current political agenda; and magnanimity that in the present situation will act generously, regardless of its own political position, with regard to the interests of others and especially those of the weaker parties.

Second, there are two unlikely outcomes. These are outcomes which are all but inconceivable and worth stating only because they form the stuff of activist propaganda and counter-propaganda. They are that the conflicts should, on one hand, degenerate into Belfast-style sectarian violence or, on the other hand, result in an Albanian-style repression of religion, especially in the public square. The combined logic of America's historic commitment to religious liberty and the depth of religious diversity today makes these outcomes virtually impossible.

Third, there are two undesirable outcomes, in the sense of two broad possibilities that might occur should there be no effective resolution of the current conflicts over religion and public life. The milder, shorter-term possibility is that there could be a massive popular revulsion against religion in public life. This could take the form of "a-plague-on-both-your-houses" reaction to religious contention and therefore lead, ironically, to a sort of naked public square created, not by secularists or separationists, but by a wrongheaded overreaction to an equally wrongheaded Christian overreaction.

The more drastic, longer-term possibility is that continuing conflict could lead to the emergence of a two nation division in American life, with all conservative forces favorable to religion and all progressive forces hostile. A short time ago, such a possibility would probably have been dismissed summarily. But for anyone who appreciates the effects of two-nation divisions on European countries such as France, the implications of the 1988 presidential campaign are sobering and the cultural fissures are worth monitoring.

Fourth, there are two unfortunate outcomes, in the sense of two broad possibilities that might occur even if chartered pluralism succeeds or if current conflicts simply fade away without apparent damage to national life. The first possibility is that, in the generally civil conditions of pluralism, the way is opened for some faith or worldview that would play the game only to win the game and end the game for others (existing candidates from the secular Left and the religious Right are equally dangerous here).

The second possibility is that, in the same civil conditions of pluralism, civility will itself become so corrupted that, in turn, pluralism is debased into a relativistic indifference to truth and principle. The result would be a slump into apathy, the logic of *laissez-faire* freedom gone to seed. The outcome would be that corruption of the republic from within of which the framers warned.

For some evangelicals, these dangers only confirm the risks of chartered pluralism they feared all along. But mention of the framers is a reminder that the risks are not new. They were built into the experiment from the very start. Such risks are the reason why the experiment is open-ended, and why the task of defending religious liberty is never finished.

As the *Williamsburg Charter* states, "The Founders knew well that the republic they established represented an audacious gamble against long historical odds. This form of government depends upon ultimate beliefs, for otherwise we have no rights to the rights by which it thrives, yet rejects any official formulation of them. The republic will therefore always remain an 'undecided experiment' that stands or falls by the dynamism of its nonestablished faiths." [21]

Os Guinness

A host of further issues requires examination (civil religion, co-belligerence, public communication, public education and so on). But when all is said and done, the final issue for evangelicals must be theological, not political. Are evangelicals going to cling to the trappings of past cultural dominance so that the heirs of the non-conformists, the independents and the separatists become the guardians of the establishment? Or, following the pattern of the incarnation, are evangelicals prepared to lay aside external symbols for a power that is strongest in weakness and clearest in disguise? If American evangelicals today can appreciate and affirm the framers' audacious gamble, and respond to it with a matching daring of faith and dedication to public justice, then their finest hours still lie ahead. Not as tribespeople nor as idiots but as citizens. But if the record of recent years is continued, evangelicals will betray their very character and purpose and bring a chapter to a close that few will long regret.

[1]*The Chalcedon Report*, February, 1989, p. 12.

[2]John Courtney Murray, "The Return to Tribalism," an address to the John A. Ryan Forum, Chicago, Illinois, April 14,1961.

[3]John Schaar, "A Nation of Behavors," *The New York Review of Books*, October 28, 1976, p. 6.

[4]*The Williamsburg Charter Survey on Religion and Public Life*, (Washington, D.C.: The Williamsburg Charter Foundation, 1988).

[5]Ibid.

[6]Ibid.

[7]Walter Lippmann, "The Living Past," (*Today and Tomorrow*, April 13,1943).

[8]*The Williamsburg Charter,* p. 9.

[9]Quoted Erik von Kuenelt-Leddihin, *The Intelligent American's Guide to Europe* (New Rochelle, New York: Arlington House, 1979), p. 407.

[10]*The Williamsburg Charter Survey on Religion and Public Life.*

[11]Harold L. Hodgkinson, *California: The State and its Educational System* (Washington, D.C.: The Institute for Educational Leadership, 1986).

[12]Harold L. Hodgkinson, *All One System: Demographies of Education, Kindergarten Through Graduate School* (Washington, D.C.: The Institute for Educational Leadership, 1985).

[13]See John Rawls, "The Idea of an Overlapping Consensus," (*Oxford Journal of Legal Studies,* Vol. 7, No. 1,1987).

[14]John Courtney Murray, *We Hold These Truths: Catholic Reflections on the American Proposition* (Sheed and Ward, 1960).

[15]*The Williamsburg Charter,* p. 8.

[16] *The Chalcedon Report,* February 1989, p. 12.

[17]See John Calvin, *Calvin's Commentaries: The Epistle of Paul the Apostle to the Romans,* D.W. and T.F. Torrance, eds. (Grand Rapids, MI: Eerdmans, 1976), pp. 48ff; *The Institutes,* (Philadelphia: Westminster Press, 1960), pp. 271ff.

[18]*The Chalcedon Report,* August 1988.

[19]*The Williamsburg Charter,* p. 21.

[20]Justice Antonin Scalia, "Teaching About the Law" (*CLS Quarterly,* Fall 1987, Vol.8,No.4),p.10.

[21]*The Williamsburg Charter,* p. 14.

RESPONSE TO OS GUINNESS

*David Scaer**

The subtitle of Dr. Guinness's paper, "A Common Vision for the Common Good," is so American and patriotic that unless one is willing to forfeit his citizenship, he has no choice but to endorse it wholeheartedly. On the other side of the coin, we might be reluctant to gild the lily. Since the Christian church has flourished here in the United States, we should permit the secularization of society and forgo any alliance of like-minded people. The point is not that we should promote evil in order that good may come out of it (a type of legitimate Pauline argument), but that as churches we should ignore it. Now that is overstating the argument, but the point is made. The God who is revealed in the Gospel is also the God who is working in the world for the benefit of the church. The only really good work of God of which we can be certain in this world is that of the church with its proclamation of the Gospel and administration of the Sacraments. God works behind masks in history; and no one, not even the church, can predict his action or trace his steps.

Chartered pluralism is attractive because it wants to be understood as a reaffirmation of those principles which were operative in the formation of the American Constitution and wants to assure the retention of these principles for posterity. I think that it can be said that ideological pluralism as a basis of so-

David Scaer

ciety was not so much on the minds of the founding fathers as was the idea of a society which already required cooperation. Thus the pluralism of American society came from a sense of self-preservation and self-advancement rather than from an ideal of establishing a pluralistic society. Politics makes strange bed fellows.

Chartered pluralism does not depend on the motives of the founding fathers. Regardless, the end result of allowing divergent opinions is the same. Stated in these terms, we are dealing more with a political manifesto for the nation and not with a religious document, though there are certain fundamental principles which evangelicals are said to have in common with others. It is assumed without argumentation that these principles, which are foundational for American society, evangelicalism, other religions and philosophical interest groups, can be identified and interpreted in the same way. It is also assumed that others are willing to be instructed by evangelicals or at least let them have the lead. Chartered pluralism is an attempt to have the component parts of American society elevate this pluralism to an acknowledged principle enshrined on tablets. It is the evangelical counterpart of canon law.

Guinness's approach is not the first attempt to establish a coalition among opposing or at least differing forces to accomplish a common good. In 1960, the late Professor Ernst Kinder of the University of Muenster told me of a similar plan for uniting Christian denominations under one umbrella, modeled after the (British) Commonwealth of Nations. Each church would be responsible for its own internal governance without any compromise of its own beliefs and procedures. His enthusiasm for the idea may have come from his own personal conflict of being a

500

confessional Lutheran in the Evangelical Church of Westphalia, which had inherited the Prussian Union where Lutherans and Reformed were put on an equal footing. His proposal coincided with the post World War II formation of the Evangelical Church of Germany in which Lutheran, Reformed, and Union, all state related churches, could live side by side. Kinder's proposal for a commonwealth of churches would effectively remove the right of one church to offer a meaningful critique of another and would also effectively render ineffective one church's condemnation of another. I am not so sure that the proper paradigm for Kinder's plan was the United Nations or the Commonwealth, a vestige of the old British Empire which was always in the state of perpetual dying but never quite managed to breathe its last breath. Chartered pluralism, if it is successful, effectively deprives its members of making the critique demanded by the Gospel. If it is unsuccessful, it will be as effective or rather as ineffective as the United Nations and the Commonwealth.

I do not make this analogy to rehearse history but to find a paradigm for the "notion of chartered pluralism." As far as I can determine, it is a clarion call for any number of religious organizations and philosophical interest groups to form a loose association for the expressed purpose of preserving a pluralistic society in which the church can achieve not only its vision for society but its distinctive goals as church. While chartered pluralism is ambitious in mobilizing diverse forces in society for the common good, it is a declaration by evangelicals that their attempt to be the prime force in American society is a failing dream. 1976, the year of the evangelicals, has come and gone and is not likely to return. The best that can be hoped for is an alliance not only with other

David Scaer

Christian religions but nonChristian ones and certain secular forces with men of good will. The goal is now "a common vision for the common good." The bugle call for retreat is sounded. Half a loaf is better than none.

Chartered pluralism is not a completely new idea, but rather a codification of principles which have been part of the American fiber since the founding of the nation. A variety of beliefs have been tolerated since the beginning of the republic and the failure to let one group have its rightful place is seen as potentially threatening to the existence of all other groups. Thus self-survival, a negative goal, exists along with the positive goal of making changes in society, which the groups would recognize as beneficial or at least necessary: "a common vision for a common good." What is new about the chartered pluralism is that it is chartered. It is a type of codicil on the American constitution, detailing certain fundamental principles, which are already accepted practice through a kind of common law. It centers around organizations and groups of people and not simply individuals, as was the case in the framing the *Constitution*. Without denying the religious influences in that document, these came through individuals and not groups. Churches, synagogues, and lodges were not represented, people with diverse backgrounds were. Religious influence was indirect. Chartered pluralism operates with groups. Whether pluralism was, is, or ever will be equivalent to utopia is questionable. An unresolved pluralism in regard to slavery brought the nation to its knees in less than eighty years. On both sides of the issue were men of good will, committed to the same principles of Christ and the Bible as are evangelicals today.

Chartered pluralism works on assumptions which, when carefully examined, may reveal that the unity necessary for concerted action is lacking. Unity may exist more in appearances than in substance. Evangelicals have to ask themselves whether in their attempt to remain or become a leading voice in American society, they are masquerading their principles under other guises. Or have they adopted "the American promise of democratic liberty and justice" as their own? There may be a case of self delusion. While foundational principles may be common to any number of diverse ideologies, they are never so in the same way. Jesus and the Pharisees believed in one God and in the Law, but their understanding of them was so entirely different that any type of chartered pluralism would have been impossible. Where evangelicals come to a common vision with others, they must ask themselves if they have lost the offense of the cross as the totality of their mission or whether it is central at all. Are the foundational principles so general as to be without substantive meaning? Without knowing what the common principles are and how they are to be interpreted, chartered pluralism is first of all without serious content and consequently and eventually inoperative.

Guinness anchors the evangelical participation in chartered pluralism in the concept of common grace, the belief that God's grace works in all people apart from the grace revealed in the redemption of Christ. I am not so sure how this squares with the total depravity of man who is devoted to seeking first his own interests. Man's depravity and self-preservation can serve, as it does for Luther, as a basis of a common ethical movement. Luther's position should have at least an equal billing with Calvin's common grace. Also problematical is that evangelical-

David Scaer

ism seems to assume that its basic principles or at least some of them are identical to, or overlap and parallel, certain principles of American society. Is, for example, the pursuit of "the American promise of democratic liberty and justice" really within the church's task? Taken out of context, it sounds like the manifesto of a mainline denomination, a group which would be, at least in some cases, an unwelcome participant in chartered pluralism. I would feel very uncomfortable in making the American experience the judge of history or norm for others. Without denying the extraordinary success of the church in the American experience, can it be overlooked that the church literally grew by leaps and bounds where it was outlawed and persecuted by a government that used taxes paid by Christians to subsidize pagan cults which stood diametrically opposed to the Christian gospel?

When I first came across the term "chartered pluralism," I had a vision of pilgrims putting their signatures to the *Mayflower Compact* before disembarking in boats on the threatening cold seas around Cape Cod in 1620. Chartered pluralism is another example of Reformed covenant theology, but now extended beyond the church to the respectable groups of people outside the church. Here is a modern revision of the "Half-Way Covenanters." If all people could not be embraced by saving grace, they could at least be embraced by common grace. The concept is intriguing but eventually unsatisfactory. It appeals to me as an American, but not as a Christian. I cannot jump out of my Lutheran skin by becoming a Nestorian so as to live one life in the world and another life in the church. In the world I am completely indiscriminate in my alliances (up to a point) for the improvement

Response

of society and my neighbor in particular, but for the church there are boundaries which can not be crossed.

In the 1520s when the cause of the Reformation was at the point of failure, Philip of Hesse attempted a form of chartered pluralism by bringing together Luther and Zwingli at Marburg in October 1529. This chartered pluralism — and this is what it was — was rejected by Luther simply because there was no agreement on the Lord's Supper. Luther could not join Zwingli against the Catholics for the sake of the Protestant Reformation, but Lutheran and Catholic princes joined together in putting down the Anabaptistic revolt in Muenster simply to preserve a civil society. This showed that cooperation among people of differing beliefs for secular purposes was possible, but it proceeded from a common understanding of society and not from common religious beliefs.

Guinness says that unless the public philosophy respects and protects this remarkable American ordering, the civic vitality of the American republic will be sapped. Few would disagree that a pluralistic society is ultimately beneficial for the church or that the church has a vested interest in societal structures; but I am not sure that this has to be raised to an article of evangelical faith. It would appear that God as the Lord of history is left out of the equation. There is a type of arrogance in the assumption, even if could be proven statistically, that the Holy Spirit makes more or better Christians in a pluralistic society than in others. God's rule over history is ignored or perhaps manipulated in some way. He is moving in history towards his predetermined goals, and by faith we hold that this movement is for the church's benefit. I am uncomfortable with assuming the role of a prophet and claiming that the history of our society and nation is a history of God's work

505

superior to that of any other nation. God worked in the history of ancient Israel, Christ, and the apostles, and has provided an interpretation in the Scriptures. Beyond that I can have no absolute certainty, though I might want to hazard a few opinions. God does work in history and man may learn what God was doing in retrospect, but even then he cannot be absolutely certain. I would feel almost synergistic in manipulating history for the cause of the Gospel.

Consider that the church grew exorbitantly during persecution. Now no one is going to suggest that we arrange for church persecution so that the church can grow more. It would be similar to suggesting that we should sin more so that grace would abound all the more. So we should not put ourselves in God's place to adjust society and history, if by this we believe we are bringing about God's Kingdom. I will work to preserve our form of government, and I support political candidates and parties; but no equation can be made between this work and that of the Gospel. It is God's work, but in a sense totally different from the proclamation of Jesus.

Guinness points to the pluralistic society of the early church as a paradigm for his suggested ordering or reordering of American society. Such pluralism was not created by the church, but was simply a fact of life. The church worked to do away with other ideologies rather than confirming them in such a way that all could become one in Christ. Of course, this abstract goal is never reached, but it will hardly do to suggest that the New Testament situation encourages the church today to promote a pluralistic society.

Wherever the Gospel is preached, it must bring division between believer and unbeliever and between believers themselves. By having religious and secular groups dig beyond the sub-soil of their principles to a foundation common to all, we may give the impression that the offense of the Gospel is no longer at the heart of Christianity.

I am assuming that certain groups for whatever reason will not be accepted within the range of chartered pluralism, unless they toe the line. But who will draw the line and who will be the referees? Evangelicals would be happy to assume these responsibilities, but will the others permit this? Mainline denominations which make it a matter of almost public doctrine that abortion is proper could hardly be seen as making a contribution to "the civic vitality of the American republic." Evangelicals may favor public support of their schools, but would they allow the same for Catholics or secular atheists? Certain abstract principles common to any number of groups may be identified, but there is less certainty about their interpretation by groups associated within chartered pluralism. The principles would then be meaningless and their effective operation impossible.

The Christian even more than the non-Christian is going to do everything in his power to improve society and help the neighbor, especially the one in distress. I see fundamental reasons why this cannot be accomplished through chartered pluralism. Its founding principles are undefinable and its operation unworkable.

QUESTIONS
FOR DISCUSSION

1. How would chartered pluralism promote a more unified Christian voice toward social and political issues?

2. What biblical teaching can be used to justify a Christian in supporting a chartered political pluralism? For example, should a Christian defend the rights of a Muslim or a Jehovah's Witness?

3. Should the concept of chartered pluralism be considered a political concern, approached through political avenues, or considered a theological concern, approached through the creation of new church structures?

4. Is there a limit to a Christian's support of the freedom of others? For example, should the Christian defend the right of Mormons to practice polygamy? Or of homosexuals to practice their freedom? Or of a woman to destroy her unwanted unborn child? Where is the line to be drawn between freedom and just laws?

5. Should the church mute its challenges to a fallen society for the value of pluralism, or is this the only way in which its voice can speak sufficiently clear to be heard at all?

12

AFTERWORD

AFTERWORD
Where Do We Go From Here?

Kenneth S. Kantzer

Where in the world is evangelicalism going today? When we gather together on a Sunday morning for worship, we sing lustily, "Like a mighty army moves the church of God." But in dark moments of the soul as we contemplate the events of our denomination's annual conference, or as we read our morning newspaper, we cry out in anguish, "Nowhere! Absolutely nowhere!"

There are those who are convinced that this latter answer is clearly the right one. Sydney Ahlstrom, widely acknowledged to be the leading historian of the American church in recent years, warned evangelicals that America has come to the end of a 400 year cycle dominated by evangelical Puritanism. And Richard Halverson, chaplain to the Senate and a convinced evangelical, laments, "The [evangelical] church has succeeded in pulling Christians out of the world, out of society, out of community and civic affairs. So often it is a little island of irrelevant piety surrounded by an ocean of need."

The future of evangelicalism, we can safely leave in the hands of God. Our concern at the "Convocation on Evangelical Affirmations" was of a different order. We sought first to determine what we mean by "evangelical". What are its boundaries? Who are in and who are out? Is there any consensus as to what constitutes an evangelical?

513

From a sociological point of view, of course, evangelicalism is no single movement. It is, in fact, a mixture of many movements. Within the broad framework of evangelicalism, each movement wanders along more or less independent of the others. This is not new. At a crucial point in the rise of Protestantism, Luther and Zwingli failed to agree, and each went his own way. Moreover, both distanced themselves from the Anabaptist movements. Since Reformation times, interfaith battles have led the various Protestant denominations to look upon themselves more as threatening rivals than as allies working together to accomplish common goals. Among those who generally are recognized today as evangelicals, we have the Missouri Lutherans, Southern Baptists, dozens of small denominations splintered off from Lutheran, Reformed, or Baptist roots, independents, Fundamentalists, hyper-Fundamentalists, Pentecostals, Pacifists, Puritans within all the mainline liberal churches and "Sojourners" who will not identify with any of the above. Each pursues a more or less independent path, and each in its own right is a "movement".

From his quite different perspective, Carl F. H. Henry defines evangelicalism in theological terms. He seeks to base his definition on biblical teaching and finds the essence of what it means to be evangelical first in the biblical doctrine of salvation by God's grace through faith in the God-man, Jesus Christ, our Lord and Savior. This is the "material" or content principle of evangelicalism as set forth in the Bible. Then he adds a second principle — the "formal" or formative principle of the Bible as the divinely authoritative and completely trustworthy guide for Christian thought and life.

Carl Henry sees the Christ set forth in the Bible in terms of the ancient creeds, Nicene and Chalcedonian. Without according final authority or infallibility to the ancient church or to its credal formulations he, along with all evangelicals, believes these statements correctly define what we mean as to the true humanity and deity of Jesus Christ and protect the church from sub-biblical and sub-evangelical views of Christology. He understands the biblical gospel in terms of salvation secured for sinners by this divine-human Christ and received through faith. This is the good news set forth in the great confessions of the Reformation Period. It forms the very heart of evangelical faith — its content principle.

The second or formative principle of biblical authority he holds to be necessarily tied to its content principle or the good news of the gospel. Biblical authority alone gives the gospel its recognizable shape and consistent form. Believable, defensible and enduring Christianity focuses not on just any gospel, but on the good news according to the Bible. And it is this view of biblical authority that is taught by the Bible about itself and by the divine human Lord and Savior, Jesus Christ. It represents the common doctrine of the church down through the centuries.

Since each of these principles is essential to the other, any attempt to separate them or to deny them or even to weaken their force is just to that extent a departure from genuine evangelical faith. In short, only this particular content principle, structured by this particular formative principle, both joined together inseparably, give us a truly biblical and evangelical faith.

It is evident that we need a term to describe those who adhere to this basic structure of biblical Christianity. However much those who fall within its boundaries may disagree on many other matters of faith and practice, including matters that they consider very important, there has existed, and still exists today, a vast host of those who share "the good news according to the Scriptures". They seek to shape their common core of religious convictions according to the teaching of the New Testament; they adhere to the central truths of Reformation theology in all its major branches; and they continue today in every major denomination as well as in newer bodies that have broken off from them, and in scattered independent groups everywhere, some of which refuse the hand of fellowship, even to other evangelicals who fall outside their own special ingroup.

In order to spell out this common core of evangelical convictions and what it implies for Christian commitment in the light of the issues facing the church today, the National Association of Evangelicals and Trinity Evangelical Divinity School united to call a convocation on evangelical affirmations. They invited a representative group of nearly seven hundred leaders to join them. It seems specially appropriate that this convocation should be sponsored by a group of Christians that call themselves evangelical (the National Association of Evangelicals) and by a seminary that includes the word evangelical as part of its title (Trinity Evangelical Divinity School).

Ten leading evangelical scholars were asked to present papers on issues disturbing the church today, and ten responders were asked to evaluate these papers. At its four day convocation the group of leaders drawn from pastors, administrators representing all major and many minor Protestant denominations, parachurch organizations, and some independents met together in roundtable groups for discussion of the papers. They sought to come to some consensus as to what it means to be an evangelical at the end of the twentieth century. They were asked to answer first the question, "What do we mean by the term evangelical?" and second, "What do contemporary evangelicals stand for?"

It was not easy to gain a consensus regarding these questions. Essentially we were trying to do what Luther and Zwingli had failed to do. The conference consisted of representatives of traditional Lutheran theology, Calvinists loyal to the faith of Calvin and the Reformed churches, representatives of independent churches and parachurch organizations; Baptists, including Independent Baptists, Fundamentalist Baptists, Southern Baptists; and Charismatics. It was like seeking to guide a team of powerful Arabian steeds not to dash off each in its own direction, but to get them to race on the same track.

The result was the evangelical affirmations you see printed in this book. Each roundtable discussion group was led by a chairman with one or more professional theologians as resource persons, and a recorder, who summarized the results of his group and reported them, together with recommendations from every group, to the plenary sessions. Discussion and debate were sharp, sometimes very sharp, and always serious, for the group was discussing matters very dear to their hearts and minds. The original draft presented to the conference at its beginning was completely rewritten. In turn, the rewritten draft went through hundreds of revisions. In one sense, the final draft presented in this book should be considered a rough draft. Yet in the final plenary session these evangelical affirmations were voted on by the participants of the six to seven hundred who had attended the consultation. Only a very small handful refused to approve of the document. Carl Henry counted the negative votes as two. Obviously, these evangelical affirmations do not represent a full confession of faith. Most of the delegates would never have approved it for that purpose. Some do not believe in any short statement of faith. Most of the rest would have disagreed with the statement as inadequate to express what is needed for ordination to the ministry or to serve as a standard for any organized body of believers. That was not the intention of the participants or of the sponsors who called for the consultation. Rather the purpose was to state what doctrinal and ethical convictions mark one off as an evangelical. What are the boundaries of evangelical faith? And what do evangelicals have to say about crucial issues troubling the church today? "Evangelical Affirmations" seeks to be a statement of evangelical identity.

Evangelicals have been divided in the past and they continue to be divided today. Present and entering fully into the discussion at this convocation were dispensationalists and covenant theologians; immersionists, adult immersionists, and paedobaptists; Calvinists and Arminians; perfectionists and Pentecostals; those who supported ordination of women and those who did not; proponents of Episcopal, Presbyterian, and Congregational forms of church government with every variation in between; and many others. But the statement was not approved as a confession of faith adequate to serve a church or a denomination. It was rather intended to say: "What, on biblical grounds, do we recognize to be evangelical? And what are those commitments in today's world that we as evangelicals agree we are or ought to be committed to?"

In recent years especially, evangelicals have received a bad image that we should very much like to overcome. Sometimes this has been a caricature to label evangelicalism as a ridiculous viewpoint. More often, consciously or unconsciously, we have created these impressions by our own actions. We have set forth our convictions sometimes far too stridently and often without carefully nuancing our positions so as to safeguard ourselves against misunderstanding. Because we are opposed to a woman's right to abort her child when she chooses, it has been inferred that we are against women's rights and we are opposed to the personal rights of individuals. Because we are opposed to pornography, we are said to be opposed to free speech and freedom of the press. Because some of us wanted prayers in the public schools and most of us argued that it is right for a town to set up a creche at Christmas time in recognition of the significance of Christ in our culture, and because we want equal rights for Christian students to hold Bible studies and prayer groups as well as photography clubs in public schools, it was assumed that we really want to cram our evangelicalism, by law, down the throats of all Americans. Because we really want Americans to become Christians, some inferred that we really don't believe in separation of church and state and freedom of religion, but would like to return to a New England Puritan theocracy and reinstitute the Salem witch trials. Because some radio evangelists have proclaimed a gospel of "easy-believism," it was assumed that evangelicals think a right theology is all that matters and Christian faith is not concerned about person ethics or social ethics.

None of these conclusions, of course, is valid as a description of evangelical convictions. Evangelicals seek to represent

Jesus Christ as servants — first of all as servants of God and then of the church and of their fellow human beings. It is their earnest desire to promote the gospel according to the Scriptures, for they believe it to be the only hope of a confused world and confused church. But they are committed to winning converts only by persuasion, not by coercion. They support the separation of church and state on the basis of principle, not expediency. They don't want Muslim prayers forced on their children in public schools, and they are equally opposed to forcing Christian prayers on non-Christians who don't want them. They want freedom to worship God according to their own lights, and they are opposed to any attempt to enforce distinctively Christian faith and Christian practices on non-Christians. They want freedom to preach the gospel to others, and they insist that freedom of press, freedom of speech, and freedom of religion should be guaranteed to all.

Evangelicals certainly are committed to sharing their faith with others in the hope of winning others to Christian faith. Not to do so, on evangelical grounds, would represent the crassest form of selfishness and a callous disregard for the good of others. Moreover, evangelicals firmly believe that Scripture gives them clear instruction on this point. Not to share the gospel would be disobedience to the clear command of God. Their appeal to others must be urgent, but it must also call for a voluntary response and never coercion. God does not desire a compulsory response to his love, but a voluntary turning of a free soul to trust in God and to obedience to his will.

The evangelical Christian believes that the gospel brings to him his greatest good — to know God, to receive deliverance from sin and its consequences, to find purpose and meaning for life and to secure power to live lives of obedience to God, usefulness in his Kingdom and service to all humankind. All of this, the evangelical must share if he is to be faithful to his own evangelicalism. We are facing a world that does not really know where it is going. Liberalism has long since lost its power in the church and out of the church. Society itself is ultimately committed to the securing of physical life and health and material prosperity in this world, but the meaning of life as a whole, it does not know.

We even live in a pluralistic church. In part, this is due to the inability of evangelical churches to communicate effectively their convictions to their own children and to their adherents. It is also in part a by-product of the very success of evangelicalism. It is a kind of Constantinian effect: the more successful evangelicals are in evangelism (i.e. sharing the gospel and winning others to Christian faith), the more they bring into the church those who are uninstructed in Christian faith. The failure of evangelicals to hold their own children and to instruct adult converts in biblical faith and practice is undoubtedly the greatest single problem facing the church today. It is certain that this will remain the major problem for the evangelical church for the foreseeable future. In a pluralistic society and, even more, in a pluralistic church, it is evident that this problem can not easily be solved.

Where then do we go from here? We proclaim the gospel and the biblical teaching tied to it. Particularly, we wish to clarify those tension points in society and in our churches addressed by these evangelical affirmations. May God give us the love and the courage to move out and win the hearts and minds of people so that they may hold fast to the gospel and to the Bible that gives it its structure.

It is our earnest hope and prayer that *Evangelical Affirmations* may serve as a study guide for evangelicals — to sharpen our understanding of what we ourselves mean by the term "evangelical," to assist those who wish to identify themselves by this biblical term, and to do so with clear knowledge of what it implies, and what contemporary evangelicals stand for in today's world as we face the end of the twentieth century and a new millennium.

It is our hope, also, that the publication of these *Evangelical Affirmations* will enable evangelicals to present their convictions more clearly in the pluralistic culture in which we bear witness to the gospel and, in doing so, to remove some of the most flagrant, and thoroughly misinformed, charges against evangelicalism. If the world rejects biblical and evangelical Christianity, it is important that it reject it knowing what it really is. Tragically, the world often rejects biblical faith not knowing what it is that it is rejecting.

We are not interested in shaping evangelical Christianity, and certainly not biblical Christianity, into a form that will prove palatable to the sinful hearts and minds of all humans. We are not trying to remove "the offense of the cross". That offense is an inherent part of biblical and evangelical identity. It would be an irresponsible denial of our deepest faith to remove it. Yet we are deeply concerned also to remove false obstacles to the gospel. We do not want anyone to reject a perversion or misunderstanding of the evangelical gospel and, thereby, to be turned away from that which we are convinced is the truth and the truth that makes us truly free from sin and meaninglessness and provides for us ultimate hope and peace.

Where then is the church going? God alone knows. We do not really know whether or not Sydney Ahlstrom is right when he

522

says that we are at the end of four centuries during which evangelicalism has provided leadership in our culture. As we look at government, as we look at the public media, as we look at the universities and intellectual and cultural centers of our society, and alas, sometimes even as we look at the church, we are compelled to admit that he has a point. He may well be right!

On the other hand, as we range our sight around the world and observe the movement of the gospel in black Africa south of the Sahara and in South America, and especially in China, we see some evidence that we may be facing a great revival of evangelical faith around the world. But whether we are pessimistic or optimistic about the success of the evangelical church, it is our task, above all else, to be faithful to the good news, the good news that alone is able to deliver men from the powers of darkness, from sin and discouragement, from hatred and despair, from cruelty and revenge, and to bring men and women and children everywhere into the Kingdom of God's dear Son.

APPENDIX

CONSULTATION ON EVANGELICAL AFFIRMATIONS CONFERENCE PERSONNEL

Sponsors
National Association of Evangelicals
Trinity Evangelical Divinity School

Chairmen
Dr. Carl F. H. Henry, *Co-Chairman*
Dr. Kenneth S. Kantzer, *Co-Chairman*

Executive Committee
Dr. William H. Bentley, *President, United Pentecostal Council, Assemblies of God, Chicago, IL.*
Dr. J. Richard Chase, *President, Wheaton College, Wheaton, IL.*
Dr. Charles Colson, *Chairman of the Board, Prison Fellowship Ministries, Washington, DC.*
Dr. Jerry Falwell, *Founder and Director, "Old-Time Gospel Hour," Lynchburg, VA.*
Dr. Billy Graham, *Founder, Billy Graham Evangelistic Association, Minneapolis, MN.*
Mr. William T. Grieg, Jr., *President, Gospel Light Publications, Ventura, CA.*
Mrs. Rosemary Jensen, *Executive Director, Bible Study Fellowship, San Antonio, TX.*
Dr. Dennis K. Kinlaw, *President, Asbury College, Wilmore, KY.*

Dr. Thomas McDill, *President, Evangelical Free Church of America, Minneapolis, MN.*

Dr. Kenneth M. Meyer, *President, Trinity Evangelical Divinity School, Deerfield, IL.*

Dr. Robert Preus, *President, Concordia Seminary, Fort Wayne, IN.*

Dr. Ray Stedman, *Chairman, Congress on Biblical Exposition, Palo Alto, CA.*

Dr. Jerry Vines, *President, Southern Baptist Convention, Jacksonville, FL.*

Dr. John White, *President, National Association of Evangelicals.*

Dr. Tom Zimmerman, *President Emeritus, Assemblies of God, Springfield, MO.*

Council of Theologians

Dr. Kenneth L. Barker, *Dean of Capital Seminary, Washington, D.C.*

Dr. W. David Beck, *Assistant Vice President for Faculty Development, Liberty Baptist College, Lynchburg, VA.*

Dr. David Alan Black, *Professor of New Testament and Greek, Grace Theological Seminary, West Campus, Long Beach, CA.*

Dr. Darrel Bock, *Associate Professor of New Testament, Dallas Theological Seminary, Dallas, TX.*

Dr. Gerald Borchert, *Dean, Southern Baptist Theological Seminary, Louisville, KY.*

Dr. Jesse L. Boyd III, *Librarian, Trinity Valley School, Fort Worth, TX.*

Dr. Lanier Burns, *Professor and Chairman, Systematic Theology, Dallas Theological Seminary, Dallas, TX.*

Dr. Allan Coppedge, *Professor of Systematic Theology, Asbury Theological Seminary, Wilmore, KY.*

Dr. Robert Culver, *Visiting Professor of Systematic Theology, Winnipeg Theological Seminary.*

Dr. William L. Custer, *Xavier University, Cincinnati, OH.*

Dr. Kenneth A. Daughters, *Dallas Theological Seminary, Mesquite, TX.*

Dr. Bruce A. Demarest, *Professor of Systematic Theology, Denver Conservative Baptist Seminary, Englewood, CO.*

Dr. Wayne A. Detzler, *Meriden, CT.*

Dr. David G. Dunbar, *President, Biblical Theological Seminary, Blooming Glen, PA.*

Dr. Dolores Dunnett, *Principal, Christian Grammar School, Roseville, MN.*

Dr. Walter Dunnett, *Professor of Biblical Studies Northwestern College, St. Paul, MN.*

Dr. Walter A. Elwell, *Dean, Wheaton Graduate School of Theology, Wheaton, IL.*

Dr. Millard Erickson, *Dean, Bethel Seminary, St. Paul, MN.*

Dr. Allan Fisher, *Editor, Academic and Reference Books, Baker Book House, Rockford, MI.*

Dr. Garry L. Friesen, *Vice President and Academic Dean, Multnomah School of the Bible, Portland, OR.*

Dr. George Giacumakis, Jr., *Professor of History, California State University, Fullerton, CA.*

Dr. J. A. Gration, *Wheaton College Graduate School, Wheaton, IL.*

Dr. John O. Grossmann, *Pastor, Grace EFC, Cincinnati, OH.*

Dr. Vernon. C. Grounds, *Denver Theological Seminary, Denver, CO.*

Dr. Wayne Grudem, *Trinity Evangelical Divinity School, Deerfield, IL.*

Dr. Stan Gundry, *Publisher and General Manager, Zondervan Publishing House, Grand Rapids, MI.*

Dr. H. Glynn Hall, *President, Assemblies of God School of Theology, Springfield, MO.*

Dr. Henry W. Hollomon, *Talbot Theological Seminary, La Mirada, CA.*

Dr. Charles L. Holman, *Associate professor of Biblical Interpretation and New Testament, CBN University, Virginia Beach, VA.*

Dr. Jerry Horner, *Dean, College of Theology and Ministry, CBN University, Virginia Beach, VA.*

Dr. R. Kent Hughes, *Senior Pastor, College Church in Wheaton, Wheaton, IL.*

Dr. Donald A. Johns, *Associate Professor of Bible and Theology, Assemblies of God Theological Seminary, Springfield, MO.*

Dr. Alan F. Johnson, *Professor of New Testament and Christian Ethics, Wheaton College, Wheaton, IL.*

Dr. Leslie R. Keylock, *Professor of Bible and Theology, Moody Bible Institute, Elgin, IL.*

Dr. Fred Klooster, *Professor, Calvin Theological Seminary, Grand Rapids, MI.*

Dr. Scott E. McClelland, *Associate Professor of Biblical Studies, The King's College, Briarcliff Manor, NY.*

Dr. Roger R. Nicole, *Gordon-Conwell Theological Seminary, South Hamilton, MA.*

Dr. R. Larry Overstreet, *Professor of Homiletics, Grace Theological Seminary, Winona Lake, IN.*

Dr. Robert D. Pitts, *Professor of Religion and Philosophy, Taylor University, Upland, IN.*

Dr. Stanley E. Porter, *Assistant Professor of Greek, Biola University, La Mirada, CA.*

Dr. Earl D. Radmacher, *President, Western Conservative Baptist Seminary, Portland, OR.*

Dr. Robert L. Saucy, *Professor of Systematic Theology, Talbot Theological Seminary, La Mirada, CA.*

Dr. Kobert N. Schaper, *Professor of Preaching and Practical Theology, Fuller Theological Seminary, Pasadena, CA.*

Dr. Ronald J. Sider, *Professor of Theology and Culture, Eastern Baptist Theological Seminary, Philadelphia, PA.*

Dr. Moises Silva, *Professor of New Testament, Westminster Theological Seminary, Philadelphia, PA.*

Dr. J. J. Stamoolis, *Dean of Graduate Studies, Wheaton College, Wheaton, IL.*

Dr. R. L. Thomas, *Professor of New Testament, The Master's Seminary, Sun Valley, CA.*

Dr. John White, *President, National Association of Evangelicals, Beaver Falls, PA.*

Dr. J. Rodman Williams, *Professor, CBN University, Virginia Beach, VA.*

Dr. Marten H. Woudstra, *Professor of Old Testament Emeritus, Calvin Theological Seminary, Grand Rapids, MI.*

Presenters

Dr. Ruth Lewis Bentley, *Counselling Center, University of Illinois at Chicago, Chicago, IL.*

Dr. William H. Bentley, *National President, United Pentecostal Council of the Assemblies of God, Chicago, IL.*

Dr. Harold O. J. Brown, *Trinity Evangelical Divinity School, Deerfield, IL.*

Dr. Donald A. Carson, *Trinity Evangelical Divinity School, Deerfield, IL.*

Dr. Os Guiness, *Executive Director of Williamsburg Charter Foundation, Washington, DC.*

Dr. Carl F. H. Henry, *Former Editor, Christianity Today, Arlington, IL.*

Dr Kenneth S. Kantzer, *Former Editor, Christianity Today, Deerfield, IL.*

Dr. Robert C. Newman, *Biblical Theological Seminary, Hatfield, PA.*

Dr. James I. Packer, *Regent College, Vancouver, British Columbia, Canada.*

Dr. David Wells, *Gordon-Conwell Theological Seminary, South Hamilton, MA.*

Respondents

Mr. John Ankerberg, *Host & Moderator, "The John Ankerberg Show," Chattanooga, TN.*

Dr. Myron Augsburger, *President, Christian College Coalition, Washington, DC.*

Rev. H. O..Espinoza, *President, PROMESA, San Antonio, TX.*

Dr. Wayne Frair, *The Kings College, Briarcliffe Manor, NY.*

Dr. Nathan Hatch, *Acting Dean, College of Arts and Letters,University of Notre Dame, Notre Dame, IN.*

Dr. Pattle Pun, *Wheaton College, Wheaton, IL.*

Dr. David P. Scaer, *Concordia Seminary, Fort Wayne, IN.*

Dr. Robert Sloan, *Baylor University, Waco, TX.*

Dr. Joseph Stowell, *President, Moody Bible Institute, Chicago, IL.*

Mr. John Weldon, *Senior Researcher,* *"The John Ankerberg Show," Chattanooga, TN.*

Dr. Ralph D. Winter, *General Director, U. S. Center for World Mission, Pasadena, CA.*

Devotional Leaders

Dr. James Leo Garrett, *Southwestern Baptist Seminary, Fort Worth, TX.*

Dr. H. Glynn Hall, *President, Assemblies of God Theological Seminary, Springfield, MO.*

Dr. Roger Nicole, *Gordon-Conwell Theological Seminary, South Hamilton, MA.*

Presiders

Dr. Kenneth L. Barker, *Academic Dean, Capital Bible Seminary, Lanham, MD.*

Dr. J. Richard Chase, *President, Wheaton College, Wheaton, IL.*

Dr. George C. Fuller, *President, Westminster Theological Seminary, Philadelphia, PA.*

Dr. David Dunbar, *President, Biblical Theological Seminary, Hatfield, PA.*

Dr. Dennis F. Kinlaw, *President, Asbury College, Wilmore, KY.*

Dr. Kenneth M. Meyer, *President, Trinity Evangelical Divinity School, Deerfield, IL.*

Dr. Earl Radmacher, *President, Western Conservative Baptist Seminary, Portland, OR.*

Dr. Billy A. Melvin, *Executive director, National Association of Evangelicals, Wheaton, IL.*

Dr. John H. White, *President, National Association of Evangelicals, Beaver Falls, PA.*

Dr. Luder G. Whitlock, Jr., *President, Reformed Theological Seminary, Jackson, MS.*

Roundtable Leaders

Dr. Kenneth L. Barker, *Academic Dean, Capital Bible Seminary, Lanham, MD.*

Dr. David Dunbar, *President, Biblical Theological Seminary, Hatfield, PA.*

Dr. Norman Ericson, *Wheaton College, Wheaton,IL.*

Dr. Timothy George, *Dean of the Divinity School, Samford University, Birminham, AL.*

Dr. Harold Hoehner, *Dallas Theological Seminary, Dallas, TX.*

Dr. Rosemary Jensen, *Bible Study Fellowship, San Antonio, TX.*

Dr. Arthur Johnston, *President, Tyndale Theological Seminary, Holland.*

Dr. Dennis F. Kinlaw, *President, Asbury College, Wilmore, KY.*

Dr. Pat Kissell, *Professor of Nursing, California State University, Fresno, CA.*

Dr. James Kraakevik, *Wheaton College, Wheaton, IL.*

Dr. J. Robertson McQuilkin, *President, Columbia Graduate School of Bible and Missions, Columbia, SC.*

Dr. Steve Clinton, *President, Evangelical Philosophical Association, Internationsl, San Bernadino, CA.*

Dr. Roger Nicole, *Gordon-Conwell Theological Seminary, South Hamilton, MA.*

Dr. Dieumeme Noelliste, *Academic Dean, Carribean Graduate School of Theology, Kingston, Jamaica.*

Dr. H. Wilbert Norton, Jr., *The University of Mississippi, Oxford, MS.*

Dr. Robert D. Pitts, *Taylor University, Upland, IN.*

Dr. Robert Rakestraw, *Bethel Theological Seminary, St. Paul, MN.*

Dr. Luder G. Whitlock, Jr., *President, Reformed Theological Seminary, Jackson, MS.*

Writing Committee

Dr. Kenneth S. Kantzer, *Christianity Today, Deerfield, IL. Chairman.*

Dr. David Dunbar, *Biblical Theological Seminary, Hatfield, PA.*

Dr. Carl F. H. Henry, *Christianity Today, Arlington, VA.*

Dr. Dennis F. Kinlaw, *President, Asbury Coillege, Wilmore, KY.*

Dr. Fred Klooster, *Calvin Theological Seminary, Grand Rapids, MI.*

Dr. David Scaer, *Concordian Theological Seminary, Fort Wayne, IN.*

Dr. John H. White, *President, National Association of Evangelicals, Beaver Falls, PA.*

Dr. J. Rodman Williams, *CBN University, Virginia Beach, VA.*

Dr. John Woodbridge, *Trinity Evangelical Divinity School, Deerfield, IL. Adjunct.*

Affirmations Coordinator

Dr. Richard Allen Bodey, *Trinity Evangelical Divinity School, Deerfield, IL.*